Specters of Revolution

Specters of Revolution

Peasant Guerrillas in the Cold War Mexican Countryside

ALEXANDER AVIÑA

OXFORD
UNIVERSITY PRESS

OXFORD
UNIVERSITY PRESS

Oxford University Press is a department of the University of Oxford.
It furthers the University's objective of excellence in research, scholarship,
and education by publishing worldwide.

Oxford   New York
Auckland   Cape Town   Dar es Salaam   Hong Kong   Karachi
Kuala Lumpur   Madrid   Melbourne   Mexico City   Nairobi
New Delhi   Shanghai   Taipei   Toronto

With offices in
Argentina   Austria   Brazil   Chile   Czech Republic   France   Greece
Guatemala   Hungary   Italy   Japan   Poland   Portugal   Singapore
South Korea   Switzerland   Thailand   Turkey   Ukraine   Vietnam

Oxford is a registered trademark of Oxford University Press
in the UK and certain other countries.

Published in the United States of America by
Oxford University Press
198 Madison Avenue, New York, NY 10016

© Oxford University Press 2014

Excerpts reprinted from Alexander Aviña, "'We Have Returned to Porfirian Times': Neopopulism,
Counterinsurgency, and the Dirty War in Guerrero, Mexico, 1969–1976" from *Populism in Twentieth
Century Mexico: The Presidencies of Lázaro Cárdenas and Luis Echeverría* edited by Amelia Kiddle and
Maria L.O. Muñoz. © 2010 The Arizona Board of Regents. Reprinted by permission of the
University of Arizona Press.

Library of Congress Cataloging-in-Publication Data
Aviña, Alexander.
Specters of revolution : peasant guerrillas in the Cold War Mexican countryside / Alexander Aviña.
pages cm
Includes bibliographical references and index.
ISBN 978–0–19–993657–1 (hardback : acid-free paper)—ISBN 978–0–19–993659–5 (paperback :
acid-free paper)   1. Mexico—Politics and government—1946–1970.   2. Teachers—Political
activity—Mexico—History—20th century.   3. Peasants—Political activity—Mexico—History—20th
century.   4. Guerrillas—Mexico—History—20th century.   5. Insurgency—Mexico—History—20th
century.   6. Asociación Cívica Nacional Revolucionaria (Mexico)—History.   7. Partido de los Pobres
(Mexico)—History.   8. Mexico—Rural conditions.   9. State-sponsored terrorism—Mexico—
History—20th century.   10. Mexico—Rural conditions.   I. Title.
F1235.A84 2014
972.08'2—dc23
2013047265

1 3 5 7 9 8 6 4 2

For my parents
Ana Bertha Godinez Sandoval
Gilberto Aviña Guízar
and, in memoriam,
Pablo Godinez Sandoval
José Inés Torres Sandoval

Here, by the downslope of hills, facing the sunset
and time's muzzle,
near gardens with severed shadows
we do what the prisoners do,
and what the unemployed do:
we nurture hope
                        Mahmoud Darwish, "State of Siege"

CONTENTS

ACKNOWLEDGMENTS

This book contains nearly a decade's worth of invaluable contributions from friends, colleagues, mentors, individuals willing to open their homes and share their stories with a stranger, and family. My first thanks are to those whose stories drive this book. In Guerrero: Fernando Pineda, Tita Radilla, Dr. Andrea Radilla Martínez, Dr. Alejandra Cárdenas, Dr. Arturo Miranda Ramírez, José Bracho, Santos Méndez, Ascensión Rosas Mesino, and Hilario Mesino generously shared their experiences, memories, and hospitality. In Mexico City: José Luis Moreno Borbolla, José Luis Alonzo Vargas, Benjamin Pérez Aragón, Alejandra Avila Sosa, Concepción Solís Morales, and Mario Rechy provided interviews, friendship, and hospitality. Consuelo Solís Morales opened her home to a stranger and generously shared her time and remembrances. An amazing weeklong bus historical "tour" that took us from Mexico City to the Chihuahuan highlands in the spring of 2007 permitted interviews, and lasting friendships, with Miguel Topete, Celia Sánchez, Maricela Balderas Silva, Bertha Lilia Gutiérrez, and Salvador Gaytán Aguirre.

I am deeply grateful to Marjorie Becker for her intellectual and emotional generosity, her unwavering support, and her patience. I was trained as a historian by a talented poet whose preoccupations with language, power, and the complexity of human experience taught me how to think critically about the form and content of academic history. Marjorie's democratic mentorship, based on subtlety and empowerment, gave me the necessary space and time to develop as a historian. I also want to thank other scholars who provided vital support and encouragement. María Elena Martínez encouraged me to think critically beyond the confines of my research topic in order to engage bigger theoretical and historical questions. George Sánchez helped me think about methodological issues while also giving essential career advice for a novice academic historian. Priya Jaikumar challenged me to engage the methodological and epistemological presuppositions of academic history. At different moments, Gladys McCormick,

Veronica Oikión Solano, and Barry Carr generously provided invaluable advice on archival sources and oral history subjects that made this book possible. I am also eternally thankful to Myrna Santiago and Alvaro Ramírez for encouraging me to consider graduate studies during my days as a *fútbol*-obsessed undergraduate student-athlete. Myrna, in particular, provided hours of selfless mentorship and inspired me to become a historian.

Various institutions helped bring this book into fruition. Research and writing were funded by the Haynes Foundation, the University of Southern California Graduate School, the University of Southern California Strategic Theme Initiative, and the Fulbright Mexican Commission (COMEXUS), and by faculty research support from Florida State University (FSU). Support from the Office of the Vice President for Research and the College of Arts at Sciences at FSU also provided important support. I am forever grateful to the Institute for the Recruitment of Teachers (IRT) at Philips Academy and its founder, Kelly Wise, for helping me enter the world of graduate studies and for their radically democratic vision that seeks to diversify teaching faculties throughout the country.

I am grateful to the numerous archivists and librarians who facilitated the research for this book. In particular, I would like to thank the archivists in Galleries One and Two at the Archivo General de la Nación, and the various librarians at the University of Southern California and Florida State University responsible for successfully locating my incessant requests for rare books through interlibrary loans. I am also grateful to José Moreno Borbolla Moreno for generously providing a copy of the digital archive collected and organized by the Centro de Investigaciones Históricas de los Movimientos Armados A.C.

I am especially indebted to Tanalís Padilla, Louise Walker, Adela Cedillo, and Robinson Herrera. Tanalís has steadfastly supported this research project from its inception, providing research and methodological advice while helping me think about the implications of researching a highly politicized historical subject in contemporary Mexico. Louise helped me strive for intellectual precision and clarity of argument, graciously reading draft after draft. Her ruthless and selfless line editing was just what my writing (baroque tendencies and all) needed. Adela's expertise on the history of the Mexican Left helped me to think more critically and analytically on issues of popular protest, political culture, and resistance. Robinson's incisive understanding of theories of violence (and the challenges such theories pose for historians) helped me think about the broader implications of my arguments expressed in this book. I cannot express in words my immense gratitude for all that they did and for all that they taught me. They vastly improved this book. All errors are my own.

Thank you to the amazing friends and colleagues who encouraged sociability and camaraderie within a profession that can be rather solitary. Jerry, Gustavo,

Phuong, Mark, Lalo, Rebecca, Joop, and Ana ensured that graduate studies were characterized by solidarity, friendship, fun, and healthy competition on the basketball court. The Miño-Magni family in Los Angeles spoiled me with delicious Argentine cuisine after long days on campus and lively conversation. In Mexico, Louise and Thom Rath helped me survive my first lonely research stint—as did the warm, caring support of the Amaral family and the friendship of Daniel Rojas. During subsequent research trips to Mexico I was fortunate to befriend María L. O. Muñoz, Tim Wright, Brian Palmer-Rubin, John Kinglemann, Steve Neufeld, and Fernando Calderón. María, especially, supported my work and graciously provided my first publication opportunity. She also provided solidarity watching *fútbol* games at the Coloso de Santa Úrsula. Thank you to you all.

My colleagues at Florida State University have provided a convivial, supportive home. I am especially grateful to Robinson Herrera, Ed Gray, Jen Koslow, Darrin McMahon, Neil Jumonville, Will Hanley, Chuck Upchurch, and Jonathan Grant for their friendship and mentoring. I am grateful for the support and friendship of Vicky Bernal. I am indebted to my colleagues in the Latin@ Faculty Advocacy and Resource group for their inspiring *compañerismo*: Robinson, Delia Poey, Hernán Ramírez, Jennine Capó Crucet, Carlos Bolaños, and José Rodríguez. Thank you also to Mike Uzendoski and Juan Carlos Galeano.

I am especially grateful to my editor, Susan Ferber, for believing in this project and for helping navigate this novice through the labyrinthine process of publication. Thank you to Oxford University Press for bringing the project into fruition. Two anonymous readers provided key, insightful suggestions that greatly improved the book, as did the excellent editing of Michael Durnin

My parents are the first historians I encountered. Arriving in the United States as undocumented migrants from Michoacán during the late 1970s, Ana Godinez and Gilberto Aviña filled our home with stories of Zapata, Hidalgo, and Cárdenas, hoping that such histories would ensure that my siblings and I remain proudly "Mexican" in a sometimes inhospitable foreign land. Their sacrifice, their love, their willingness to work in a country that needs them economically but attacks them politically and culturally, created a nurturing home that encouraged me to become a historian—to tell the stories of people like them. My siblings, Gilberto, Laura, and Itzari, continually remind their (typical) eldest brother of the virtues of irreverence, humor, and laughter. My extended family in Michoacán, particularly the Torres-Godinez family, offered a sanctuary of respite during my research stays in Mexico City and Guerrero. I am deeply grateful for the histories I learned from my late campesino grandfather Pedro Godinez, a Juan Rulfo-like storyteller in his own right.

I could not have finished this project without the patience, love, and support of Ryanne Aviña Banks. Indeed, this book would not have been possible without Ryanne's unpaid labor, most especially with our high-energy toddler son. These pages bear the invisible traces of her love and labor. Her wit and dark humor helped defuse moments of anxiety and self-doubt. And her love helped me look up from the computer screen and scribbled notes to enjoy our family, our lives together. I dedicate this book to my young son Alexander who reminds me of the importance of nurturing hope, even, or perhaps most especially when, we live "near gardens with severed shadows."

LIST OF ABBREVIATIONS

ACG	Asociación Cívica Guerrerense
ACNR	Asociación Cívica Nacional Revolucionaria
AGN	Archivo General de la Nación (México)
ALC	Asociación Local de Cafeticultores
BCA	Brigada Campesina de Ajusticiamiento
CAP	Consejo de Autodefensa del Pueblo
CCI	Central Campesina Independiente
CJM	Confederación de Jovenes Mexicanos
CNC	Confederación Nacional Campesina
COP	Coalición de Organizaciones Populares
DFS	Dirección Federal de Seguridad
DGIPS	Dirección General de Investigaciones Políticas y Sociales
EPR	Ejército Popular Guerrillero
ERPI	Ejército Revolucionario del Pueblo Insurgente
EZLN	Ejército Zapatista de Liberación Nacional
FAR	Fuerzas Armadas Revolucionarias
FECSM	Federación de Estudiantes Campesinos Socialistas de México
FEP	Frente Electoral del Pueblo
FLN	Fuerzas de Liberación Nacional
GPG	Grupo Popular Guerrillero
INMECAFE	Instituto Mexicano de Café
LARSEZ	Liga Agraria Revolucionaria del Sur Emiliano Zapata
LC23S	Liga Comunista 23 de Septiembre
MAR	Movimiento de Acción Revolucionaria
MLN	Movimiento de Liberación Nacional
MRP	Movimiento Revolucionario del Pueblo
OCSS	Organización Campesina de la Sierra Sur
PAN	Partido Acción Nacional

PAOM	Partido Agrario Obrero Morelense
PARM	Partido Auténtico de la Revolución Mexicana
PCM	Partido Comunista Mexicano
PDLP	Partido de los Pobres
POA	Partido Obrero de Acapulco
POCM	Partido Obrero-Campesino Mexicano
POT	Partido Obrero de Tecpan
PPS	Partido Popular Socialista
PRD	Partido Revolucionario Democrático
PRI	Partido Revolucionario Institucional
PROCUP	Partido Revolucionario Obrero Campesino Unión del Pueblo
PSG	Partido Socialista de Guerrero
SDN	Secretaría de Defensa Nacional
UGOCM	Unión General de Obreros y Campesinos de México
UP	Unión del Pueblo
URPC	Unión Regional de Productores de Copra

Specters of Revolution

Introduction: Guerrilla Ghosts in the Mexican Countryside

Perhaps the Mexican military thought a clandestine burial in the middle of the night would erase the memory of Lucio Cabañas and his peasant insurgency. Perhaps they remembered the public adulation received by another slain guerrilla, Genaro Vázquez, during his wake and burial two years prior in February 1972—and the public anger directed at the soldiers present. Memorably one elderly woman verbally abused the soldiers, cursed them, and questioned their manhood. Or the fact that Cabañas and his peasant guerrillas had killed dozens of troops and officers in coastal Guerrero during three years of revolutionary warfare possibly sealed the concealed posthumous fate of the rural schoolteacher-turned-guerrilla. Before dawn on 3 December 1974 soldiers hastily buried Cabañas in an anonymous grave in the municipal cemetery of Atoyac de Álvarez. His family received no notice. Years later the family of a deceased local man built a concrete tomb on top of Cabañas's burial site. The *campesino* guerrilla specter that haunted the Mexican military and the ruling Institutional Revolutionary Party (PRI) for nearly a decade finally seemed to be erased. The memories of an armed struggle fueled conterminously by revolutionary Marxism and long-held rural longings for a world without exploitation, "without that grand theft... the exploitation of the poor by the rich,"[1] appeared buried and forgotten.

Yet specters tend to spontaneously return—at least from the perspective of ruling elites usually caught unaware. On the ground, the state of Guerrero historically seems more like Juan Rulfo's Comala, where the living and the unredeemed dead uneasily coexist.[2] Historical injustices are lived daily in the flesh, especially when they remain unresolved or they tragically repeat themselves. Irresolution and repetition characterize *guerrerense* history.[3] After yet another massacre of unarmed campesinos in June 1995 by state police forces acting upon the orders of the governor, a 100-strong guerrilla force emerged one year later during a commemorative event. Heavily armed men and women sporting baklavas and

1

military fatigues stood watch as one of their own, "Pedro," spoke to the crowd in Spanish and in the indigenous language, Nahuatl. After identifying themselves as the Popular Revolutionary Army (EPR), "Pedro" read a manifesto: "the situation has not changed... repression, persecution, imprisonment, assassinations, massacres, tortures, and disappearances continue as modes of governance of the [Mexican] state, a situation similar to 1967 and 1968 that forced commanders Genaro Vázquez and Lucio Cabañas to take up arms." The speaker concluded with a warning: "we refuse to remain passive and contemplative in the face of injustice."[4] As specters, as memories of failed revolutionary interventions, Vázquez and Cabañas continued to haunt Mexico's rulers two decades after their deaths in the face of continued state terror—and to inspire anew.

In Mexican history rural revolts and revolutions tend to exhibit a distinct spectral quality. Despite tragic military defeats and the deaths of charismatic leaders, the repressed seemingly live on, waiting for revolutionary reenactment within subaltern memories and political registers. Entire corpuses of popular politics gained in moments of revolutionary insurrection become condensed in the metonymic specters of radical figures. Popular revolutionary figures like Emiliano Zapata, Ricardo Flores Magón, Pancho Villa, Rubén Jaramillo, Genaro Vázquez, and Lucio Cabañas transform into ideals that persist and refuse to ignominiously disappear: the ideals of direct action, popular justice, vengeance, solidarity, dignity, the possibility of a more just existence. Such ideals, or utopias, do more than simply survive in clandestine, subterranean fashion. Sometimes they also inspire renewed attempts to "storm heaven," even in times when the mere thought of revolution represents an impossible and anachronistic illusion.[5]

The secret burial of Cabañas vividly captures the counterinsurgent methodology of PRI and military leaders when faced with the incarnation of revolutionary possibility. Kill the guerrillas and secretly bury the bodies to ensure the death of their subversive ideals. They lack understanding that history rarely stays put in a forgotten, disconnected past. The appearance of the EPR in 1996 or the 1994 Chiapan reemergence of Zapata in Mayan deity form testifies to their failure. Past popular insurrections suffered defeat on military battlegrounds but experiences and consciousness gained during those rare moments persist in memory and in language as utopias.[6] Revolutionary attempts draw inspiration from these utopias, from historical examples of popular resistance and, in a way, redeem those past examples through radical action in the present.[7] How and why that occurred in 1960s Guerrero—an example that continues to inspire in contemporary rural Mexico—are two of the questions this book addresses.

The armed struggles led by Vázquez and Cabañas began in the late 1960s in Guerrero, a historical bastion of rural popular resistance and seemingly permanent theater of political violence. *Guerrerense* rural communities have participated in and shaped almost every major political conflict in modern Mexican history. In second decade of the nineteenth century, they prolonged the anti-colonial insurgency against the Spaniards through guerrilla warfare in the desperate years after the execution of independence leaders and priests Miguel Hidalgo and José María Morelos. By the 1860s they had organized a series of regional and interregional, cross-class rebellions that had toppled dictators, fought foreign invaders, and decisively contributed to the military and political defeat of Mexican conservatism. Insurgent rural communities fought to influence the emerging Mexican nation with their own gendered political visions of how to organize society: local patriarchal democracy, low taxes, broad diffusion of federal power, and universal male suffrage.[8] If such visions failed to find space within the national project ruled by Mexican Liberals during the last decades of the nineteenth century, stifled by Liberal politicians and violently repressed by subsequent dictator Porfirio Díaz (1876–1910), they would violently reemerge in 1910.

A classic study of the Mexican revolution (1910–1920) in Guerrero characterized it as a rancher's revolt—a movement organized by a well-to-do rural middle class that benefitted from the economic policies promoted by Díaz but resented his authoritarian political structure.[9] Yet, the revolution in the state proved ideologically complex and fractious. In addition to the ranchers, peasants who adhered to the agrarian program of revolutionary leader Emiliano Zapata in the neighboring state of Morelos fought for land and municipal democracy. Indeed, Guerrero became the only Zapatista-ruled state other than Morelos when Jesús H. Salgado assumed the governorship in 1914. Despite the eventual military defeat of the Zapatistas, their dogged and tenacious decade-long revolutionary struggle forced the inclusion of land redistribution in the 1917 Mexican Constitution. When President Lázaro Cárdenas (1934–40) campaigned in Guerrero promising Mauser rifles to strengthen peasants' defense of land and schools—and subsequently enacted extensive agrarian reform—he seemingly fulfilled and institutionalized the demand for land that partially fueled the 1910 revolution.[10] "No [politician] remembered the agrarian law, no one could enforce respect for the Constitution," a peasant from coastal Guerrero recalled, "until the arrival of Cárdenas who distributed land with such facility."[11] The populist president dramatically impacted a region previously characterized by the reactionary violence exercised by entrenched landed and commercial elites in response to peasant and worker mobilizations inspired by the 1917 Constitution (1920–34).

Popular memories of Cárdenas unsurprisingly minimized the limitations and failures of the president's radical policies and his role in creating a one-party political system tilted toward undemocratic hierarchy. Nonetheless, the "Sphinx of Jiquilpan," along with the 1910 revolution, formed bedrock referents in peasant political cultures as liberatory moments during which Mexican ruling elites manifested the most profound and persistent of rural demands: land and local democracy. The 1930s represented a time when the revolutionary ideals of 1910 finally materialized in the everyday lives of peasants. The postrevolutionary state, it seemed, sided with the laboring masses. As such, the revolution and Cárdenas would haunt the latter's presidential successors after 1940 as political points of comparison. When presidents Manuel Avila Camacho (1940–46) and Miguel Alemán (1946–52) embraced an authoritarian one-party mode of governance and a rapid industrializing economic model with disastrous consequences for the Mexican countryside, peasants protested with Constitution in hand and revolutionary, Cardenista memories in mind.

In Guerrero, the PRI's economic model revealed itself as a form of crony capitalism based on corruption, violence, and the rollback of constitutionally mandated social reforms. Myriad local popular protests in the decades after 1940, from municipal tax strikes and land invasions to work stoppages and statewide civic insurgencies, paralleled similar movements at the national level.[12] They spoke of redeeming a revolution and a constitution betrayed by the PRI. While the governing party reacted in a multitude of ways, usually preferring electoral fraud, targeted assassination, or the use of small concessions and the cooptation of protest leaders, broad and violent repression increasingly became a primary tool of political rule—particularly in the countryside. The 1960s would usher in an era in which Guerrero became a theater of state terror, popular political radicalization, and counterinsurgency.

Peasant guerrillas led by Vázquez and Cabañas emerged from this history. The National Revolutionary Civic Association (ACNR) and the Party of the Poor (PDLP), led by Vázquez and Cabañas, respectively, represented something more than just an armed peasant response to contemporary state terror limited to a backwoods Mexican region. Analyzing their politics, praxis of insurgency, and guerrilla constituency reveals an unexpected constellation of radical traditions crystallized in their insurrectionary movements. Within this guerrilla constellation, Zapatista and Spanish Civil War veterans, along with Mexican university students trained in communist North Korea, provided military advice and training. Subversive messages from revolutionary Cuba, insurgent southeast Asia, and the various US civil rights movements reached the mountains of Guerrero with the help of short-wave and transistor radios. Local oral traditions recounting the exploits of regional agrarian guerrillas during the 1920s, in addition to the Bolivian failures of Che Guevara in 1967, provided strategic lessons in guerrilla warfare. John Womack's *Zapata and the Mexican Revolution* shared shelf space with Karl Marx, Vladimir Lenin, and Soviet socialist realist novels in makeshift guerrilla libraries.[13] High up in the remote mountains of coastal Guerrero a series of local, national, and transnational revolutionary histories converged to comprise the insurgent projects of the ACNR and PDLP.

This book examines how the guerrilla organizations led by Vázquez and Cabañas developed as political options deemed viable and necessary. Starting in the late 1960s, these schoolteachers organized separate armed movements that generally sought the violent overthrow of the PRI regime and the radical, socialist transformation of the Mexican state. Able to attract widespread popular support in their regional areas of operation, namely the coastal communities of Guerrero, these guerrilla organizations represented a serious political-military threat to the postrevolutionary Mexican regime. The PDLP, and the ACNR to a lesser extent, proved successful in obtaining popular support for armed insurgency in part because they emerged as the cumulative armed phase of a longer historical process of grassroots civic activism that targeted *cacique* (political boss) rule in Guerrero.[14] A variety of popular movements that laboriously worked within the political parameters established by the 1917 Constitution preceded the guerrilla insurrectionary attempts. In this process of social struggle repeated state and elite terror—both large-scale massacres and everyday violence—radicalized popular peasant politics and drastically reduced political options for the redress of grievances. In large part, this is a story about the historical formation of popular political radicalization within a context characterized by social-political violence and an exploitative rural economic order.

The immediate history of the guerrilla struggles began in the late 1950s with an effort to remove a particularly violent and corrupt state governor. Peasants, workers, small businesspersons, and state workers created this effort and subsequent popular movements. Despite assassinations, tortures, and massacres, they endured, steadfastly organizing and holding onto the ideals of the 1910 revolution as embodied in the 1917 Constitution and unevenly implemented during the Cardenista 1930s: social justice, equitable economic development, and popular enfranchisement.[15] They held civic marches and protests in 1960; organized opposition political parties at the local and state levels in 1961–2; bravely mobilized independent peasant unions and community-based resource movements in the face of cacique gunmen and state police from 1963 to 1966; and marched to challenge a 1965 state law that criminalized expressions of social dissent. At every turn, these reformist, constitutionally based movements and organizations—embodying a form of "revolutionary citizenship" that acted upon the radical rhetoric of the PRI regime—experienced violence.[16]

ACNR and PDLP guerrilla organizations thus began as popular acts of armed self-defense in reaction to systematic state-elite violence. Revolutionary violence emerged as a response to sustained counterrevolutionary violence. Yet terror alone fails to adequately explain why hundreds joined the guerrilla insurgencies as combatants and even more provided different forms of support. Like other explanatory models of revolution and social movements, whether class struggle or sociological theories based on rational choice and resource mobilization, state

terror as an exclusive explanatory factor potentially retains a mechanical causal-
ity that freezes popular insurgency in a state of negation and inversion. Seen in
this light, insurrectionary action emerges as a constantly reactive, spontaneous
measure against an oppressive government, with the goal of simply "turning the
world upside down" and appropriating preexisting forms of political and economic power—a violent manifestation of the "last shall be first and the first shall
be last."[17] Such an approach fails to appreciate how guerrilla political visions and
definitions of revolution could—and did—radicalize during the course of revolutionary struggle. Rural demands for localized vengeance gradually developed
into revolutionary movements that fought to establish alternative forms of state
power at the national level.

To illustrate the revolutionary politics of imagination displayed by the ACNR
and PDLP this book contextualizes their historical emergence within the immediate "moments of fluidity and rupture" represented by the 1960s, as well as the
longer underground history of popular politics, grievances, and direct action in
rural Guerrero.[18] Such an approach permits an excavation of guerrilla tactics,
radical discourses, and rural constituencies that speak to deeper sources fueling
the insurgencies. Revolutionary violence responded to both a markedly violent
shift in PRI forms of domination and a popularly perceived continuity of social
relations that historically exploited rural communities in Guerrero. The 1960s
witnessed the emergence of popular discourses that linked past and present by
affirming that the PRI, with its repressive ways, had betrayed the radical legacies
of 1910 and Cardenismo. Such betrayal suggested the necessity of revolutionary
redemption in the pursuit of social justice.[19]

Transnational New Left guerilla Marxisms based on direct action, national
liberation, and anti-imperialism also drove the ACNR and PDLP movements.[20]
Both armed organizations forged political ideologies that resembled palimp-
sests, layered by campesino longings forged in the past but still alive and reso-
nant in the present, intimately conversant with "emergent" guerrilla New Left
ideas and practices.[21] Revolutionary theory developed from historical praxis and
experience. Popular political interpretations of social democracy, rooted in the
radical agrarianism of 1910 and Cardenista populism, creatively engaged and
redefined the Marxist-Leninist (sometimes Maoist) armed struggle praxis of
the Latin American guerrilla New Left. Similar to contemporary revolutionary
organizations in Central America, like the Guatemalan Guerrilla Army of the
Poor (EGP), the political cores of the ACNR and PDLP insurgent projects demonstrated an insurrectionary Marxism grounded in local-regional histories and
rural vocabularies, dependent on the active participation of peasant communities.[22] Revolution was conceptualized as a national liberation struggle to free the
country from an oligarchic regime in the service of violent caciques and foreign
capital. "The roots and inspiration of our struggle," a 1968 ACNR communiqué

stated, "exist squarely within national history and national reality; our demands, even when expressed in contemporary terms, are the same as those articulated by Hidalgo, Morelos and Guerrero, Juárez, Zapata, and Villa."[23]

My study is the first to analyze the multiple levels of historical memory and political culture that help elucidate how and why insurgency proved a deliberate choice by guerrillas and their supporters.[24] Most studies on the ACNR and PDLP generally fail to acknowledge the political creativity demonstrated by the guerrillas. A deployed standard set of rigid dichotomies categorizes the identity, ideology, and historical significance of the movements: folkloric rebellions or misguided New Left guerrilla aberrations; inspired by the 1910 revolution or the 1959 Cuban revolution; international Marxism-Leninism or revolutionary nationalism.[25] Works produced by Mexican activists and dissident journalists during the 1970s proved largely descriptive and sympathetic to the guerrillas, offering a counternarrative to government pronouncements that portrayed the ACNR and PDLP as criminal enterprises.[26] Subsequent studies in Mexico and the United States tended to analyze the guerrillas' politics and ideologies while implicitly privileging certain evolutionary models of political mobilization as mature and correct. Authors working from a Marxist tradition tended to emphasize a folkloric peasant aspect to the movements—particularly in regard to the PDLP.[27] One author described the PDLP as politically anarchist, oscillating historically between the figures of Ricardo Flores Magón and the Sergei Nechayev–led Russian Nihilists of the late nineteenth century.[28] A widely circulated work on the PDLP that combined analysis with extensive primary sources evaluated the guerrilla movement as a reactive, "instantaneous vigilantism" with a "hopeless guerrilla" as leader.[29] The first Mexican *testimonio* on the Dirty War translated into English advanced a vision of Cabañas as both a parochial peasant out of place in an urban and industrial Mexico and a relic *caudillo* leader.[30] Recent academic studies on Cold War Guerrero fail to appreciate the dynamic interaction between the multiple political sources that collectively fueled the revolutionary imagination of the guerrilla movements. Instead such studies presuppose circumscribed geographical horizons for campesino politics, presenting a rigid division between ultra-left guerrilla leaders inspired by "international socialism" and an autochthonous peasantry.[31]

Specters of Revolution demonstrates how guerrillas and their campesino supporters could simultaneously embrace and refashion the betrayed projects of the 1910 revolution and socialism on their terms, as they understood them. They interpreted the core of both projects as the recuperation of dignity and the promise of a more just world. Indeed, Guerrero in the 1960s and 1970s affirms recent historiographical insights regarding the creative processes of political interaction that occurred between popular politics and Left ideologies at the local level in Cold War Latin America.[32] The long history of campesino struggles in Guerrero reveals that multiple levels of meaning and historical experience coalesced in terms like socialism, class struggle, and anti-imperialism. To achieve any sort of popular support, guerrillas needed to understand and deploy such meaning and historical experience in their insurrectionary wager to overthrow the PRI regime. The projects of ACNR and PDLP insurgents reflected their simultaneous localized and internationalist roots in Vicente Guerrero and Vladimir Lenin, Rubén Jaramillo and Che Guevara.

Revolutions and revolutionary politics are not only about the social; they are also deeply personal. *Testimonio* literature and recent studies on subaltern political agency evince the key role played by a politics of vengeance, dignity, and pleasure in contouring subaltern participation across a range of political movements and transforming political subjectivity.[33] Present at this level of politics are the individual rage and indignation provoked by reiterated instances of state terror committed against family and community members; the profound transformation of self-understanding propelled by critical engagement with Marxist texts; the joy of joining the guerrillas to momentarily escape a rural patriarchal household; a sense of moral obligation to share revolutionary experiences from 1910 or the Spanish Civil War; and the desire to avenge family members "disappeared" by soldiers or police officers. Such personal politics would prove key to the ACNR and PDLP attracting popular support during the late 1960s.[34]

In coastal Guerrero the politics of rage and vengeance helped unify many communities in their support for the guerrilla insurgencies. When PDLP leader Cabañas spoke in 1973–4 of the "people's patient endurance of bad government, mistreatment by government officials [but not] of massacres," he essentially referred to an existing moral economy of vengeance that violently called for justice and the recovery of communal dignity.[35] (Indeed, the very name of the PDLP's military wing, the Peasant Brigade of *Ajusticiamiento*, refers to the double meaning of "bringing to justice" and "execution" in relation to perceived class enemies.)[36] The task of the ACNR and PDLP was to translate such demands for local vengeance into a broader emancipatory project that directed revolutionary violence against what the ACNR termed the PRI "pro-imperialist oligarchy."[37] In this struggle, as ex-PDLP guerrilla Luis León Mendiola recalled, peasant communities faced a seemingly clear choice: "Are you with the rich or with the Party of the Poor?"[38]

In this task, Vázquez and Cabañas assumed roles as organic intellectuals who emerged as products of a stratum of rural society that directly benefitted from Cardenista populism in the form of land redistribution and political participation. Like their guerrillas and base of popular support, they were not the poorest of the rural poor but came from a campesino class that militantly mobilized after 1917 to implement and protect hard-won social democratic rights enshrined in the Constitution.[39] Born in coastal Guerrero amidst the oft-violent social

polarization of the tumultuous 1930s, Vázquez and Cabañas directly experienced the practice and cost of campesino militancy from an early age. Vázquez
recalled attending campesino assemblies and meetings as a child with his father,
a local campesino leader. Cabañas's family produced famous Zapatista officers
who had waged guerrilla rebellions during the 1920s and prominently participated in the Cardenista agrarian reform of the 1930s—a family that had also lost
various members, including Cabañas's father, at the hands of cacique paramilitaries that practiced terror with impunity.

Both men experienced a different sort of political formation while attending
teacher-training schools. They studied while simultaneously engaged in social
activism at the local and national level during the 1950s and early 1960s. Indeed,
they viewed studying and activism as necessarily fused endeavors. Vázquez and
Cabañas formed part of a broader post-1940 generation of teachers and students
who played a leading role in the disparate popular movements that protested the
PRI's authoritarian suppression of political plurality and its inequitable model of
capitalist development. Rural schoolteachers like Cabañas often led rural communities against local manifestations of the PRI's dual project (for example, cacique land theft, corporate plundering of communal water and forestry resources)
while also participating in national social movements linked to the Mexican
Communist Party (PCM) or the Popular Socialist Party (PPS). Urban schoolteachers, including Vázquez, participated prominently in the widespread labor
strife that characterized Mexico City in the late 1950s and the various democratization struggles that occurred concurrently in provincial regions like Guerrero,
Puebla, and San Luis Potosí. A steadfast defense of social rights enshrined in the
Constitution, in the face of conservative PRI rollback, united such movements.
Years before 1968, traditionally viewed as the beginning of democracy-minded
"new social movements" in Mexico, educators and students valiantly fought to
preserve and make manifest social democratic rights gained through a process of
popular mobilization that had begun in 1910.

Vázquez and Cabañas became organic intellectuals through active participation in popular struggles; their radicalization, in relation to state terror, developed in parallel to the social movements in which they participated. Such
participation, in addition to their upbringing and pedagogical labor in impoverished areas, produced a charismatic "ordinariness" that would characterize
them as guerrilla leaders. Their eclectic political ideologies were grounded in
the everyday experiences of popular protest, organizing dissent, and confronting
regime power.[40] As political polyglots, they demonstrated an ability to speak the
more doctrinaire Marxist dialect of the Latin American guerrilla New Left, while
simultaneously, being well versed in local-regional campesino political lexicons
of revolutionary nationalism and class struggle. Their ability to mediate the two
political languages, and in the process translate local grievances against the PRI

into broader insurgent critiques against capitalism and imperialism using subaltern political grammar, provides another insight into how they gained popular support.

Knowledge and participation allowed Vázquez and Cabañas to ground their revolutionary Marxist ideologies in the quotidian experiences of poor and middling rural guerrerenses. Both men knew that the historical praxis and experience of collective struggle created campesino class-consciousness. Rather than speaking in Marxist tongues to campesinos about a future proletarian industrial utopia of egalitarianism (in evangelical style), both guerrillas learned that unredeemed longings, aspirations, and vengeance could mobilize a robust base of popular support for guerrilla insurgency. The accumulation of recent injustices, along with the unredeemed promises of the Mexican revolution, had created a "spirit of sacrifice" within a rural population that did not take rebellion lightly and that possessed a long memory.[41] That memory formed the political core of both guerrilla movements. They represented themselves as the avengers of a revolution betrayed by the PRI while simultaneously calling for new socialist revolutions to reenact and ensure the redemption of 1910.

Violence

Guerrero guerrillas emerged from a regional society in which violence shaped everyday life for poor and middling guerrerenses living in the countryside or in working-class urban neighborhoods in cities like Acapulco. Violence constituted a social relationship that helped reproduce inequality and domination through two linked manifestations: the subjective violence and terror committed against guerrerenses by identifiable agents (cacique-hired gunslingers or the Mexican army) and the objective or systemic violence provoked by a capitalist modernization program that impoverished the Mexican countryside to subsidize industrialization and large-scale agrobusiness after 1940. Subjective violence involved spectacular instances of overt physical violence that seemingly disturbed the routine of normal everyday life. Objective violence represented the "violence inherent" in that normal everyday life, the more nuanced forms of coercion and discipline that worked toward reproducing normalized but unjust, inequitable relations of political power and economic exploitation.[42] The ACNR and PDLP developed in relation to these manifestations of violence in 1960s Guerrero. In their quest to destroy what the PDLP referred to as the "ruling domination of the rich class and its dictatorship," Guerrero guerrillas viewed revolutionary violence as a means to obtain justice and overthrow the PRI "dictatorship."[43] They fought to end what insurgent Nicaraguan campesinos termed "the time of the rich."[44]

These types of violence form interdependent strands perceived accurately only in relation to one another. Ignoring subjective and objective forms of violence all too easily leads to facile characterizations of ACNR and PDLP guerrillas (or most Cold War guerrilla organizations) as simple bandits and/or instances of Castroist-Guevarist mimicry lacking popular support—characterizations voiced alternately by the PRI and some scholars who later replicated the regime's counterinsurgency discourse and national security heuristics. The explanations advanced in the most widely read works on the Cold War Latin American armed New Left—both the "Cuban Crucible" and "Two Demons" theses—can present their tautological reflections on the metaphysical causes of political radicalization only by disregarding social contexts chronically shaped by violences.[45] In disavowing longer histories of social injustice and political and economic violences in understanding the emergence of guerrillas in Cold War Latin America, such interpretations wage their own academic counterinsurgency. The origins of the armed New Left become obfuscated within a broader scholarly polemic that seeks to place blame on guerrillas forged in the "Cuban Crucible" under the spell of "Guevarismo" for manipulating hapless peasants and provoking state terror.[46]

From the PRI's perspective, the removing of peasant guerrillas from a protracted history of social injustice and violences simultaneously depoliticized them (transforming them into simple criminals or social deviants) and facilitated repressive measures that fundamentally ignored why campesinos turned to revolutionary violence. Counterguerrilla military campaigns became recast, with the help of a largely compliant or coerced national media, as wars against rampant criminality. Guerrillas, as the governor of Guerrero declared in July 1971, simply did not exist.[47] "Depistolization" military programs attacked bandits, cattle rustlers, and narcotics cultivators. Intelligence officers secretly explained popular support for the armed movements as the fanaticism of a few or the result of insurgent coercive actions. Even plausible political allies from leftist political parties like the PCM publicly criticized the violent means used by the Guerrero guerrillas—while recognizing the structural causes that made armed struggle a political option—and their unwillingness to recognize that the "objective conditions" for revolution did not exist.[48] For different political reasons, whether the maintenance of government security or revolutionary orthodoxy, these perspectives collectively failed to recognize the armed movements on their own terms. Indeed, they buried the reasons for insurgency.

This book unearths a marginalized guerrilla political history from below.[49] It reveals the history of undercut social reforms, intensified economic exploitation, and political repression that made possible the golden ages and economic miracles celebrated by the PRI and foreign observers—and radicalized previously reformist social movements. Analyzing the constellation of violence that shaped social life in Guerrero during the 1950s, 60s, and 70s permits an understanding

of why rural guerrilla insurgency emerged as a political alternative. The dangerous choice made by Vázquez, Cabañas, and hundreds more who took up arms
occurred only after they had exhausted other political options in their pursuit of
social justice and electoral democracy while incurring government surveillance,
assassination attempts, and massacres.

Myriad forms of violence thus enabled post-1940 PRI capitalist modernization efforts and strivings for political centralization at the regional level. The
history of popular protest in post-1940 Guerrero, and much of the Mexican countryside, reveals that the economic program advanced by the PRI required a form
of objective violence in its proliferation of economic inequality and poverty in
the rural sector and in its rollback of agrarian gains made during the Cardenista
1930s. After 1938, when cacique gunslingers assassinated twenty-six peasant
leaders in Guerrero, everyday forms of terror and social relations structured by
cacique violence underscored and enabled the economic miracles and political stability hailed by the PRI to domestic and international audiences.[50] The
modern industrial and urban utopia envisioned by the ruling party—based on
the government subsidizing the unrestricted accumulation of capital by private
domestic and international entities—entailed a marked political and socioeconomic reorientation.[51] Achievement of an annual GDP rate that averaged above
6 percent from 1940 to 1970—the so-called "Mexican Miracle"—depended
upon the coercive disciplining of industrial workers and the countryside. The
PRI model of development, as historian Stephen Niblo demonstrates, "[was]
based upon a massive transfer of resources from the poor to the rich and from
the country to the city."[52]

For this exclusionary and inequitable development to operate, the political,
social, and economic rights and reforms for the laboring majority of Mexicans
had to be undermined. In Guerrero, within this decades-long process of undercut-
ting social reforms and constitutional rights, subjective violence—the violence
of caciques—ensured the everyday operation of an objective violence otherwise
known as capitalist modernization. Yet workers, peasants, students, and teachers doggedly resisted and mobilized to defend constitutionally enshrined social
democratic rights after 1940. By the 1960s, such instances of popular protest
had tended to radicalize in the face of escalating violent methods of repression
employed by a PRI regime committed to a logic of governance based on Cold
War anticommunism, national security, and political stability. The increasing
deployment of state terror in 1960s Guerrero as a response to reformist popular
movements produced a regional instance of what Antonio Gramsci referred to
as a "crisis of authority:" the exercise of coercion and force as a primary means
of domination and rule.[53] Counterinsurgency became the logic of governance.

With the development of the ACNR and PDLP by 1967 and 1968, PRI
political leaders ordered a series of unconstitutional military counterinsurgency

campaigns that combined the exercise of extreme violence against guerrilla-supporting communities with economic modernization programs.[54] The PRI's hegemonic need to repossess peasant allegiance during a time of economic crises, middle-class discontent, campesino land invasions, and massive labor mobilizations produced a series of contradictory counterinsurgency campaigns that attempted to win campesino "hearts and minds" while torturing and killing campesino bodies. Rape, disappearances, executions, torture, strategic hamlets, death flights and mass detentions became tools of "pacification" that sought to physically annihilate the guerrilla insurgencies during the 1970s.[55] Military Aravá planes stationed in Acapulco dumped the bodies of suspected guerrillas and supporters into the Pacific Ocean.[56] Hundreds of guerrerenses remain disappeared, last seen at military checkpoints or in clandestine prisons.[57] The tortured, lifeless bodies that appeared on the outskirts of rural communities like Atoyac or the charred corpses that testified to the use of gasoline as a torture instrument were intended to discourage others from questioning or challenging state power.[58] The value of a life, at times, seemed reduced to the communicating of regime messages. One such message articulated to a campesino after several days of torture and incarceration: "behave and go to work."[59]

The thousands of Dirty War victims in Guerrero qualify discussions on the categorization of PRI authoritarianism after 1940.[60] Negotiation and violence (at least the palpable threat of violence) underscored PRI authoritarianism, shaped by local and regional configurations of political and social power.[61] Recent scholarship on the post-1940 era reveals a form of malleable authoritarianism subject to the constant pressure exerted by popular and elite forms of protest expressed through civil disobedience, support of opposition political parties, and even brief instances of "collective bargaining by riot" and armed resistance.[62] Such protest could lead to tangible victories such as the ouster of unpopular governors or the reversal of hated federal policies.[63] It could also provoke the deployment of military units to massacre political dissidents protesting contested presidential election results (as in 1952) or violently attack striking railway workers (1959). Cold War Guerrero, particularly after 1960, demonstrates the extent to which the exercise of violence by the PRI increasingly became an instrument of domination.[64]

Disappeared schoolteachers, tortured campesinos, and razed rural communities thus demand a regionally nuanced redefinition of PRI authoritarian rule. What seemed mild authoritarianism in Mexico City appeared as state terror in the highlands of Sonora, Guerrero, Sinaloa, and Chihuahua, where army units brutally attacked rural communities throughout the 1960s and 1970s. Recognizing such violence helps explain the operation and longevity of PRI rule and does not exclude the more subtle, dynamic relationship between popular protest and regime repression. Indeed, it helps elucidate a tenuous governing framework that differed across regional and local contexts. While Guerrero experienced state terror in the form of counterinsurgency during the 1970s, urban workers and the middle classes enjoyed political and socioeconomic reforms under President Luis Echeverría's "democratic opening" program. South American exiles fleeing military terror found safe haven in Mexico City. Opposition political parties achieved legal recognition in 1977. If Cold War Mexico appeared exceptionally different than a Latin America largely ruled by military dictatorships, coastal Guerrero and other locales reveal a similar, more violent reality.

Voices of Insurgency and Archives of Counterinsurgency

Researching the ACNR and PDLP revolutionary attempts revealed the multiple ways in which repositories of primary sources police or discipline subversive pasts. A number of ex-guerrillas I interviewed, for instance, minimized, glossed over, or refused to discuss important political differences that existed between the guerrilla organizations. This silence makes sense in the context of contemporary Mexican government counterinsurgency strategies that distinguish "good" guerrillas from "bad" in order to encourage leftist factionalism. Other militants refused to discuss the kidnappings of caciques or "revolutionary expropriations" of wealth, lest they incur the vengeful wrath of surviving relatives. Interviews with ex-guerrillas and victims of the Dirty War reveal the contemporaneity of insurgent pasts.

By contrast, the recently released political police and military documents housed at the Mexican National Archives collectively constitute an archive of counterinsurgency.[65] Until recently, declassified political police documents in Gallery One were overseen by a powerful head archivist, a longtime member of the now defunct political police, who controlled access to the sensitive documentary collection. The archive was designed for the counterinsurgent organization of knowledge that facilitated the policing and surveillance of individuals and organizations deemed national security threats. Documents that contain the photographs of captured guerrilla suspects, along with their interrogation transcripts, contain information obtained through torture—and provide evidence that the PRI regime detained such persons prior to their disappearance. Gallery One formed part of the bureaucratic "memory of the state," which facilitated the repressive apparatuses of the PRI to act.[66] Now it acts as centurion for that state memory, controlling access to historical documentation.

Despite such limitations and challenges, the voices of insurgency and archives of counterinsurgency constitute the documentary base of this book.

Principal sources for the histories of the ACNR and PDLP include manifestos, communiqués, pamphlets, and speeches fashioned by the guerrilla participants and supporters; newspaper articles; memos, reports, and evaluations produced by state intelligence agents from the Ministry of the Interior and the Mexican Army to government officials; intramilitary correspondence that detailed counterinsurgency efforts against the peasant insurgents; and oral histories. The texts produced by the guerrilla organizations provide insight into the movements' motivations for armed rebellion and political orientation, their heterogeneous political ideologies, and methods for cultivating peasant support.

Declassified in 2002, documents from the Dirección General de Investigaciones Políticas y Sociales (DGIPS, Department of Social and Political Investigations) and Dirección Federal de Seguridad (DFS, Department of National Security)—as part of the Secretaría de Gobernación (Ministry of the Interior)—and the Secretaría de la Defensa Nacional (SDN, Department of National Defense) reveal the PRI's private transcripts elaborated in response to popular protest and regime criticism.[67] Espionage memos, evaluations, reports on public events, military campaign plans, and daily military telegrams expose attempts to catalog, analyze, and exterminate peasant movements identified as national security threats. While such documents tend to provide deficient analysis of armed movements, they offer the possibility of recovering campesino and insurgent voices, since the reporting agents often reproduced speeches and political pamphlets. Reading such prose of counterinsurgency against the grain may not only highlight the PRI's refusal to view peasant insurgency as political activity on the part of the rural masses, but also provide limited windows to people's lives.[68]

Such popular and government sources offer tantalizing evidence for why everyday guerrerenses decided to take the drastic action of supporting two separate guerrilla insurgencies in Guerrero, which can be heard directly through oral histories. While guerrerenses shape narratives of their past, oral histories reveal cultural meanings and information—slang, jokes, intonation, and rhythms of speech—difficult to reproduce in written form, and they give voice to a population whose historical memories cannot be found in state archives. Like written sources, oral histories can be marked by contradictions, unverified facts, outright deceit, and exaggerations. Yet they elucidate meaning that speaks to the eruption, defeat, and persistence of insurgent peasant yearnings.[69]

This book proceeds chronologically. Chapter 1 traces the history of popular politics and mobilizations in Guerrero from nineteenth-century independence struggles to the Cardenista 1930s, which inspired subsequent peasant politics. Chapter 2 examines the political and socioeconomic situation in the coastal state after 1940, setting the stage for the 1960 civic movement in which tens of thousands of guerrerenses mobilized to depose a nepotistic, heavy-handed governor. Vázquez and Cabañas emerged as key social movement leaders in the struggle against Governor Raúl Caballero. The dramatic resolution to the conflict shadowed future PRI responses to democratic social movements and in Guerrero initiated a gradual process of popular political radicalization. The next two chapters explore the contours of that radicalization as a response to regional cacique and PRI exercises of repression. Chapter 3 outlines the tactical transformation of the 1960 civic movement to oppositional political party for the 1962 state elections within a national framework characterized by the emergence of a revitalized Mexican Left. Focusing on the party's elaboration of a revolutionary nationalist discourse that promised a return to the radical legacies of 1910, the chapter chronicles how the electoral campaign challenged the PRI's one-party authoritarian structure. Chapter 4 narrates the gradual splitting of the Left and the emergence of a radicalized "New Left" during the mid-1960s by following the political paths traveled by Vázquez and Cabañas after the 1962 state elections. After engaging an Old Left reinvigorated by the Cuban revolution and Lázaro Cárdenas's reengagement with national politics, both Vázquez and Cabañas would work to develop New Left guerrilla routes in the face of constant political persecution.

In recounting the politico-military histories of the ACNR and PDLP, Chapters 5 and 6 show how intensified political repression radicalized protest and political demands by the late 1960s. An influx of military forces into the state beginning in 1963 and the criminalization of popular protest in 1965 transformed Guerrero into a counterinsurgent state characterized by the suspension of constitutional rights. In addition to highlighting the guerrillas, these chapters show how military and police forces waged a Dirty War against Guerrero's civilians more broadly. The Conclusion examines the PDLP's failure to create a poor people's state in its inability to overthrow the PRI. Exploring this unfulfilled political community, infused by alternative imaginings of the nation rooted in persistent and unredeemed campesino utopias, contributes to an understanding of how and why Mexican guerrilla groups continue to emerge and embrace armed struggle.

The effects and ravages of the Dirty War continue to haunt Guerrero some forty years later. For many in contemporary Guerrero, the episodes described in this book represent not history but the contours of everyday fears and sadness. The hundreds, perhaps thousands, of guerrerenses tortured and disappeared during the 1970s—and the impunity enjoyed by both military and political officials—continue to haunt the state as unredeemed specters that demand justice. They, along with the ghosts of ACNR and PDLP guerrillas, insist that it is time to tell their stories.

1

Traditions and Legacies of Rebellion

> Guerrillas have always existed in Guerrero. What's new? God gave us
> mountains and guile [*mañas*]. Man gave us poverty and neglect.
> José Natividad Rosales, *¿Quien es Lucio Cabañas?* 1974

Mountains, forming part of the imposing Sierra Madre del Sur, pierce through
the state of Guerrero along an east-west axis. Long considered a seedbed of subversives and armed rebels, and a refuge for fleeing criminals, these mountains
historically form an obstinate obstacle to the productive designs of peasants and
the centralizing efforts of national governments as they occupy at least four-fifths
of the state's surface (Figure 1.1).[1] The sierra contributed to Guerrero's reputation as a frontier region within the Mexican nation despite its relative proximity
to the national capital. Indeed a complete map of the state was not produced
until the mid-twentieth century.[2] Many coastal highland communities did not
enjoy effective roads until the Mexican military built them in the 1970s for counterinsurgency purposes. Such mountainous topography helped shape the state
into distinct cultural and political regions historically prone to an isolation that
generally benefitted a small number of local elites who monopolized economic
activity and prosperity (Figure 1.2). An 1891 newspaper editorial, for instance,
decried the lack of an effective transportation network linking Acapulco to
Mexico City—a network that potentially could disrupt the commercial and
agricultural domination exercised by coastal elites.[3]

Guerrero's rural communities did not wait for the arrival of railways or federal economic development plans to change societies marked by inequality and
exploitation. They organized and mobilized, playing an important role in the
late colonial and postcolonial history of Mexico. Demanding the sanctity of
municipal autonomy and low taxes, while articulating a sophisticated patriarchal
democratic vision that blended notions of economic justice with achieved political rights, peasants confronted a plethora of rulers throughout the nineteenth

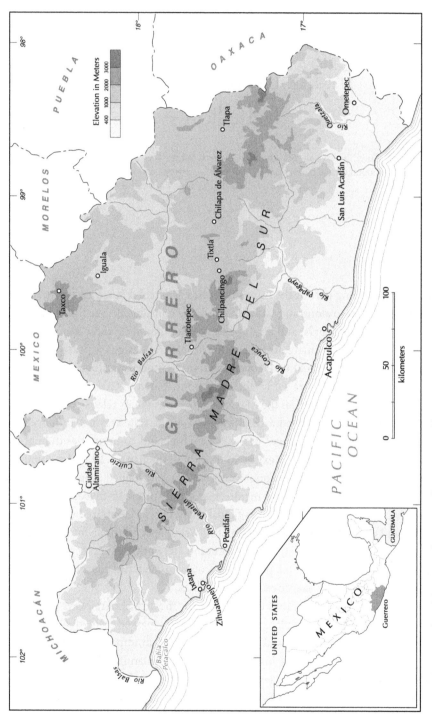

Figure 1.1 Topography of the state of Guerrero (by Peter Krafft)

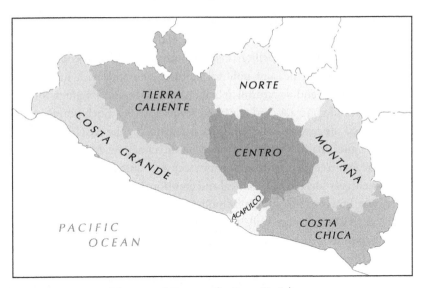

Figure 1.2 Regions of the state of Guerrero (by Peter Kraftt)

century who shared Antonio López de Santa Anna's 1842 judgment that evaluated the political incapacity of Mexico's popular classes: "our people, due to its lack of education, still needs to be led by the hand like a child...the man who leads them needs to be of good intention, a lover of his nation, and truly a Republican."[4] Such themes found full expression in the indictments voiced by Conservative Lucas Alamán in 1830 that described contemporary guerrerense peasant rebellions as apolitical "barbarism" that attempted to "ruin all property... [and] cause a desolation a hundred times more terrible than that of the 1810s."[5]

Such elite repudiation of subaltern politics should not be surprising; indeed, it shaped, with few exceptions, elite intellectual and political cultures throughout Latin America during the nineteenth century and beyond. Nonetheless, Mexican elites necessarily engaged with and confronted the political visions and practices of the rural masses, since revolutions emanating from the countryside dramatically and consistently impacted political developments in the country. From the 1810 independence struggles to the revolution of 1910 and beyond, community-based peasant movements able to articulate local grievances as meaningful analyses of broader national ills and forge cross-class regional insurgencies shaped Mexican state formation. Within such struggles and revolutions to define Mexico as a nation-state, the active and constant participation of rural guerrerenses proved decisive.

Two centuries of peasant resistance and rebellion in Guerrero shaped the guerrilla insurgencies led by Vázquez and Cabañas that broke out during the late 1960s. Contextualizing the ACNR and PDLP within a longer history of peasant politics and mobilization disrupts counterinsurgent narratives that posit the guerrillas as apolitical bandits or outside communist agitators who duped hapless rural folk into suicidal rebellion. Instead, both guerrilla insurgencies emerge as processes rooted in peasant political cultures saturated with utopias: the memories of failed and successful rebellions, unredeemed longings for land tenure and local democracy, and martyred revolutionaries. Such utopias subsequently shaped the revolutionary projects articulated by the ACNR and PDLP, grounding a guerrilla Marxism predicated on direct action. ACNR and PDLP guerrillas recognized that historical grievances and unredeemed, unforgotten visions potentially formed the political and emotional core of collective action.

There was, however, no essentialist model of peasant politics and action based on static, unchanged, or even millennial revolutionary visions. A demand for the respect of community lands voiced in 1843 possesses a meaning different from similar petitions articulated in 1960. That persistent peasant demand for land tenure expressed in 1960 reveals one reason why it remained meaningful after more than a century, a popular revolution, and agrarian reform: the persistence and adaptability of rural structures of domination in Guerrero. If domination advances a historical vision characterized by continuity, even permanence, then peasant insurrections in postcolonial Guerrero represent those rare moments that produce constellations of revolutionary change and alternatives.[6] Those moments, even in defeat, leave behind subversive traces.

This chapter examines five such historical moments: the long process of independence beginning in 1810; peasant efforts to influence the political character of the postcolonial Mexican state from 1821 to 1848; the 1854 Ayutla revolution; the dictatorship of Porfirio Díaz at the close of the nineteenth century; and the 1910 Mexican revolution. Together they provide an opportunity to demarcate the elementary aspects or forms of peasant utopias as expressed through insurgency and how such utopias continued to inform subsequent peasant mobilizations.[7] When the ACNR and PDLP attempted to organize new revolutions during the late 1960s, they encountered rural peoples and communities that carried their rebellious histories with them.[8]

Revolution of 1810

Mexican independence arrived at an endpoint in 1821 starkly different from those initial moments in September 1810 when priest Miguel Hidalgo organized an indigenous peasant insurrection in modern-day Guanajuato state. While the anticolonial revolution began as an autonomist movement seeking greater political participation and influence within the Spanish colonial system, the achievement of independence in 1821 with the negotiated Plan of Iguala reflected more than ten years of intense political transformation and innovation among all of Mexico's social classes, in cities and throughout the countryside. The military tenacity of peasant insurgents who refused to admit defeat after the deaths of Hidalgo and his successor, José María Morelos, forced key concessions in the Plan of Iguala, namely, expanding citizenship to include all men and maintaining the recently revived 1812 Cádiz Constitution (with special emphasis on the creation of municipalities). Such concessions reveal two of the pillars of insurgent peasant political cultures that developed in the course of anticolonial struggle: municipal patriarchal democracy and political-juridical equality for all adult males.[9] As themes that motivated peasant political action throughout the nineteenth century, 1810 represented their foundational moment. As a crucial arena for widespread insurgent activity from 1808 to 1821, the region now known as Guerrero spawned a politics, popular republicanism, and an organizational form, intervillage rural coalitions able to forge alliances with local and regional elites, that shaped the formation of Mexico as a nation-state throughout the nineteenth century.[10]

Following the capture and execution of Hidalgo by royalist forces in 1811, Morelos assumed the mantle of insurgent leadership and presided over a radical political shift in the revolutionary imaginary of the rebel forces. Morelos moved from describing the revolution as the protection of the "captive" Ferdinand VII's rule in late 1811 to proclaiming at the opening of the Anáhuac Congress in September 1813 that "sovereignty resides essentially in the people…when [sovereignty is] transmitted to Monarchs that are absent, dead, or captive, such sovereignty flows back to the people…who are free to reform their political institutions whenever it suits them."[11] The radicalism (and novelty) of the switch from royalist to anticolonial republican politics resided in the practice of popular sovereignty legitimizing, indeed encompassed within, a form of representative and independent government.

By the time Ferdinand VII returned to the throne in March 1814, abolishing the Cortes and the 1812 Cádiz Constitution some two months later, insurgents led by Morelos had already experienced the political effects unleashed by the Anáhuac Congress in Chilpancingo.[12] At this central Guerrero town Morelos presented his famous "Sentiments of the Nation," an anticolonial document in which the rebel leader stated that sovereignty arose from the "people"—a gendered, caste-less definition of a masculine body politic—and not the king.[13] Crucially for mulatto and indigenous peasant rebels, the insurgent priest and the Anáhuac Congress also declared the abolishment of slavery, the termination of tribute demands, the end of *repartimiento* and excise taxes, and the confiscation of Spanish wealth for national interest. Morelos advocated, without overlooking the strategic aim of gaining popular allegiance, the rectification of the very problems that had formed the cornerstones of rebellious peasant political cultures during the late colonial era.[14] By eliminating slavery and caste distinctions, Morelos essentially challenged the premises of Spanish colonial hegemony that used "cultural difference as a signifier of racial inferiority and the use of the notion of racial inferiority as a legitimate claim to rule."[15] The action of declaring independence (on 6 November 1813) thus required demolishing a colonial social order based on a "sexual economy" that regulated access to the wombs of Spanish and Creole women, and racialized caste distinctions and corresponding rights, privileges, and duties.[16]

If the Anáhuac Congress signaled a political rupture between metropole and colony, the elaboration of a constitution for the liberated insurgent zone in the hot-lands of Michoacán in late 1814 cemented the idea of popular sovereignty and republican governance in the revolutionary imaginary of peasant insurgents. The Apatzingán Constitution of 22 October 1814 marked the elaboration of an alternative republican polity, rooted in both Enlightenment principles and Spanish legal and political traditions, which transformed colony into nation and colonial subjects into citizens-in-formation.[17] While the constitution drew heavily from "Sentiments" and the work of the Anáhuac Congress, it introduced a plural executive office and a powerful legislature in light of Morelos's military disasters in Michoacán in late 1813. Both documents and their widely publicized and distributed ideals marked the transformation of rural political cultures from royalist to republican in the insurgent zones. Liberal nationalism and popular sovereignty thus underscored the transition of colonial subjects formerly defined by racial categories into "American" republican citizens.[18]

Peasants concretely demonstrated such political cultural transformations in their contact and participation with the liberated zones that collectively constituted an ephemeral, fragmented "insurgent state." Within most of Guerrero and Oaxaca and swaths of Michoacán, Veracruz, and Puebla, insurgents forged a weak state that in the course of five years (1810–15) and amidst violent royalist counterinsurgency efforts organized elections, formed a congress, and created a constitution. Villages comprised the basic social unit of the rebel government, facilitating the collection of taxes crucial to the maintenance of the state and regular army. They also retained varying degrees of autonomy that shaped the organization of elections at the local level in ways that did not always follow the constitutionally mandated precept of universal male suffrage.[19] Such ceding of power by the state to local communities ensured continued popular support for the insurgency. Morelos's organizing of a village-based militia system to supplement his army further guaranteed that sovereignty truly emanated from the armed "people" to the representative rebel state.[20] It also proved quite useful in organizing guerrilla warfare campaigns in the years after royalist forces captured the insurgent priest in 1815. As the incipient insurgent state withered away under sustained attacks by royalist armies, peasant communities in Guerrero supported small guerrilla forces led by Vicente Guerrero, Isidro Montes de Oca, and Juan Álvarez until independence in 1821.[21]

After independence the municipality would assume a key place within peasant political cultures. The 1812 Cádiz Constitution had permitted the establishment of municipalities in villages that contained 1000 or more "souls"—a requirement followed in 1812 and again in 1820 when Spanish liberals forced King Ferdinand to reinstate the Constitution. In Guerrero alone, seventy-one municipalities emerged in the eight months prior to the Plan of Iguala. Within a short time, the municipality became what historian Peter Guardino termed "the symbolic center of rural political life" and the vehicle through which Guerrero (and Mexican) peasants engaged the Mexican state-in-formation throughout the rest of the nineteenth century.[22] Defense of the municipality would come to signify the vigilant protection of local democracy and male citizenship rights against possible state encroachments—a possibility turned reality in the decades that followed Independence.

Popular Federalism, 1821–1848

Conflict and ephemeral compromises characterized efforts to forge a new nation in the forty years after Mexican independence. Elites clashed over the proper source of state sovereignty in the emerging federalist and centralist political factions from the late 1820s to the 1840s. Would Mexico comprise a centralized national entity that restricted political access to social elites, limited suffrage, and practically erased the political importance of municipalities? Or would the former Spanish colony operate on the federalist premises of mass male political participation, a powerful legislature and weak executive, and political power spread to the state and local levels? Following the abdication of Agustín Iturbide as constitutional monarch of Mexico in March 1823 and the ratification of the 1824 Constitution by provincial and Mexico City elites, such questions established the parameters of political debate and political coalitions in the nascent nation.[23]

Peasant participation as voters and/or combatants, proved decisive to both military and political outcomes as they forcefully inserted their political visions into the national halls of elite politics. Demands such as municipal democracy, low taxes, a federalist distribution of state power, and universal male suffrage grounded the rural political imaginaries of peasants in the everyday terrains of struggle and produced a "popular federalism" that underscored the Ayutla revolution of 1854 led by independence hero Juan Álvarez.[24] Fundamentally, this subaltern political register challenged democratic promises rarely put into practice by elites and articulated alternative peasant definitions of citizenship and nationalism.[25]

Recalling the moment when Guadalupe Victoria took office as Mexico's first president in 1824, conservative intellectual Lucas Alamán wrote in his memoirs that the former insurgent "found himself in the most prosperous of circumstances; the republic enjoyed calm; the parties had been controlled; and there was an expectation of a happy future."[26] In the Guerrero countryside, Alamán's recollection proved largely accurate, as most insurgents had turned their attention to municipal politics. For regions such as the Costa Grande and Tierra Caliente—bastions of the independence insurgencies—the era of 1820–35 proved auspicious for peasants as mass suffrage laws stipulated by the 1824 Constitution allowed them to "control municipalities and defend their resources and limited the power of appointed officials whose colonial counterparts had exploited peasant resources."[27] Such participation essentially reproduced at the local level political battles over the dimensions and substance of the nascent Mexican state. Questions over municipal control, who paid taxes, and who voted replicated national issues of sovereignty, political power, and citizenship. As centralists began their counterrevolution in the late 1820s, peasant communities in Guerrero mobilized and forged village coalitions, armed protest, and regional insurrection to protect their local definitions of federalism based on municipal autonomy and lower taxes.

Anti-Spanish sentiment formed an additional facet of peasant cultures in Guerrero. The predominance of Spanish merchants and landholders within Guerrero's economy (and Mexico's), as well as the political activities of certain Spaniards within the centralist camp, helped crystallize anti-Spanish Mexican nationalism. Mulatto militias from the Costa Grande assaulted and killed several Spanish merchants in 1827 and 1828, calling for the strict application of a December 1827 Federal Expulsion Law aimed at Spaniards. The Tierra Caliente indigenous village of San Miguel Totolapan sparked a region-wide rebellion in 1829 that sought to expel non-Indian residents they identified as Spanish *chaquetas*, a term used during the 1810 revolution to derogatively describe Spanish troops.[28]

Rumors of internal plots that sought to return Mexico to Spanish rule further intensified anti-Spanish sentiment, Mexican nationalism, and popular mobilization. Rumors became insurgencies in 1828 when peasant guerrillas led by Antonio López de Santa Anna and Juan Álvarez successfully installed Vicente Guerrero as president. Utilizing the figure of the Spaniard to symbolize "absolutism" and foreign "tyranny," while simultaneously evoking the Spanish connections of Mexico City elites, the 1828 Revolution of La Acordada managed to forge regional coalitions between provincial elites and indigenous, mestizo, and mulatto peasants for national designs. The radical, yet conflicted, definition of grassroots democracy advocated by Guerrero and his political allies converged with local interpretations of federalism espoused by the peasant insurgents that carried the Afro-Mexican independence hero to power. The stage was set for more than two decades of federalist-centralist strife.[29]

The centralist counterrevolution successfully culminated in the 1836 adoption of centralism as the nation's constitutional system—though not without instances of peasant rebellion in the Costa Grande led by Álvarez.[30] Centralist regimes severely curtailed regional and local political autonomy by removing state governors and state legislatures, replacing them with state-appointed departmental governors. Most municipalities vanished as the centralists increased their population requirements, while suffrage was limited to persons with an annual income over 100 pesos. Personal taxes also dramatically increased. Economic and political privilege defined an exclusionary political system that recalled the colonial political system and operated on elite apocalyptic visions of race and caste war.[31] This centralist system, wrote federalist intellectual José María Luis Mora in March 1837, "monopolized political power, elections, property of all types, education and economic development... based on keeping the masses in a state of ignorance and degradation... they will not love it."[32]

Mora's prediction proved prophetic as a series of indigenous peasant revolts broke out in the 1840s in Guerrero and other parts of the Mexican nation. Fueled primarily by land disputes, head taxes, and a wholesale exclusion from the centralist political system, indigenous peasants from the Central region community of Chilapa initiated an armed rebellion in 1842 that rapidly included the participation of dozens of villages from the Tierra Caliente region in the west to La Montaña region that bordered Oaxaca. While decades-long land disputes initially provoked the Chilapa uprising, the application of a national income tax in 1841 and its replacement with a head tax in 1842 united peasant villages and increased the insurgency's ranks by the thousands. In an area rich in linguistic and ethnic diversity, the peasant insurgents managed to forge an intervillage coalition that temporarily bridged potential ethnic divisions and also included some small landholders from the Chilapa region.[33] Regional elites like Álvarez who had previously organized similar insurgencies found themselves collaborating, at least halfheartedly, with the centralist government led by Santa Anna to suppress a rebellion that soon spread into parts of Morelos, Oaxaca, and Michoacán.[34]

What did the rebels want? In October 1843, the rebel leaders issued a manifesto that called for the reorganization of local power structures, demanding community autonomy and local democracy in deciding land and tax issues. Later that year, the villagers of Xonacatlán issued a revealing addendum:

> due to the promises that were made in the year 10 [1810], we do not want our earned right made in the form of coins but with the lands that we presented and demanded to this date, and that all types of taxes that

oppress our communities be moderated...and that the republic and
not personal caprice rule. Death to the despotic general Santa Anna and
to his miserable slaves.[35]

Through their proclamation Xonacatlán's villagers attempted to present their
legitimate political demands to a broader public, in part in an effort to respond
to Mexico City–based denigrations of the movement as barbaric and in part,
crucially, to entice potential allies.

The proclamation provides insight into the postindependence peasant definitions of local political power and the sort of national government they desired.
This vision of the state, falling largely along federalist lines, called for a form
of local patriarchal democracy enacted through municipal politics and universal male suffrage. Insurgent peasants also wanted a state willing to rectify the
objects of their complaints against encroaching large landholders (increasingly
involved in commercial agriculture) and maintain fair levels of taxation.[36] Such
demands facilitated the forging of a cross-class, intervillage movement intent on
participating in, and drastically shaping, national politics. Peasant communities
that took up arms to combat centralist regimes during the 1840s contributed to
the latter's downfall and would form the popular backbone of the 1854 Ayutla
revolution.[37]

The Ayutla Revolution of 1854

The creation of Guerrero as a federal entity in 1849 was motivated by widespread peasant mobilizations. While some scholars argue that the formation
of Guerrero only consolidated the developing political and economic power of
local and regional caciques, the state also legitimized and institutionalized some
of the demands articulated by peasant communities since the 1820s and subsequently during centralist rule.[38] Operating under a restored federalist system, the
laws of the new political entity reduced taxes to 1820s levels, cautiously increased
the number of new municipalities, installed universal male suffrage without prerequisites, and expanded the definition of citizenship to include male agricultural laborers. Additionally, the state's constitution sanctioned the right of the
populace to take action against individuals who committed treason against the
state or federal government.[39] In effect, this provision both legalized the right to
rebel against "treasonous" government officials and legitimized earlier instances
of peasant rebellions that posited their acts as patriotic duties enacted against
despotic governors.[40] The new state and its accompanying federalist constitution
seemingly represented a popular victory after a decade of peasant resistance to
centralist regimes.

Neither the disastrous culmination to the defensive war against the United States in 1848 nor the military ascendancy of regional federalist leaders during the anti-American resistance managed to completely remove influential centralist figures, or even Santa Anna, from the political scene. By 1852 Santa Anna had returned from exile to rule the country and reimpose a political order that rejected the representative electoral system and sought to undermine political power at the local and state levels by removing elected town councils and municipal governments. He called for an authoritarian central government that monopolized political power and fiscal collection for a privileged few. The very presence of Alamán as government minister evoked memories of royalist traitors and the centralist clique that had assassinated Vicente Guerrero during the early 1830s.[41] Peasant insurgency, unsurprisingly by this point, began in Guerrero in March 1854 when Álvarez issued the Plan of Ayutla.

As a document that called for the removal of a "despotic" ruler and not for a radically new social order, the Plan of Ayutla nevertheless emphasized themes that resonated with the politics of popular federalism, in particular the rejection of monarchically inspired "Orders, treatments, and privileges openly opposed to Republican equality," conceptually linked to exterior threats to "the independence and liberty of the nation."[42] The document sought to arouse popular support for the fight against Santa Anna and to establish a provisional political framework in the immediate aftermath of the insurgent victory over conservative forces. Ideological content seemingly missing from the plan emerges in the speeches that Álvarez gave throughout Guerrero and Morelos and in other published documents.[43] Álvarez reminded his peasant guerrillas that Santa Anna, with his "instinctual despotic tendencies," had joined "the party of parricide" that had fatally betrayed Vicente Guerrero. To the inhabitants of Cuernavaca in October 1854, the guerrilla leader invoked the "imperfect" 1824 Constitution that proved unable to unite the nation, yet nonetheless displayed gradual and potential signs of improvement "when calmly discussed and sanctioned by the legitimate representatives of the nation"—a process interrupted by centralist intrigue. Accusing Santa Anna and his "parricide faction" of "undermining...the columns erected by patriotism in support of democratic institutions," Álvarez listed the violation of popular federalist principles: the undermining of community and municipal political power, persecution of the judicial and legislative branches, attempts to "enslave" citizens under a monarchy, and the pillaging of public funds. The fight against despotism, he concluded, constituted the patriotic duty of all Mexican citizens.[44]

Coalitions negotiated between insurgent rural communities and provincial elites like Álvarez ensured a final military victory over Santa Anna by August 1855.[45] In their articulation through armed struggle of a political vision that included local and state autonomy, universal male suffrage, and low taxes,

Guerrero's peasant guerrillas helped consolidate the national emergence of popular federalism after decades of regional elaboration.[46]

Porfirian Prelude, 1876–1910

Throughout the first half of the nineteenth century, Guerrero's peasant communities forged regional political cultures predicated on local patriarchal democracy and the practice of male universal citizenship. Everyday forms of state making that involved arduous intracommunity conflict resolution and electoral participation, in addition to armed resistance organized along intervillage and cross-class lines, culminated in the 1854 Ayutla revolution, ending two decades of centralist rule. As such, popular politics contributed in setting the national stage for the Liberal-Conservative conflict and French invasion that ensued shortly after the promulgation of the 1857 Constitution. In a context characterized by intense "high" political strife, civil war, and foreign invasion, popular federalism became an integral component within an emergent popular liberalism that developed as peasants engaged reform laws and ideological designs pronounced by the Liberal faction led by Benito Juárez. Lacking the unity its descriptive label suggests, popular liberalism connotes multiple political meanings discussed at the communal level in places like Guerrero's Tierra Caliente, highland Puebla, and central Morelos—places with a strong popular federalist tradition that not coincidentally later formed part of the peasant vanguard of the 1910 revolution.

In Guerrero, defense of the municipality and voting rights for all males regardless of ethnic and social origin continued to form the backbone of peasant politics during the 1855–76 period. Newly enacted Liberal land laws fused questions of local autonomy with local definitions of communal land tenure, while peasant military participation against insurgent Conservatives and French troops facilitated the articulation of peasant visions of nation and citizenship. Such visions tended to link more inclusive definitions of citizenship based not on property ownership or ethnic or social origin but on civic and patriotic duty in the face of external threats. Defense of the nation in dire times entitled peasants to political and economic rights within a democratic and patriarchal social order. While little research exists for Guerrero in this time period, the region's earlier protracted engagement with popular federalism and the important military role played by guerrerense rural communities in resisting the French invasion suggests a similar process.[47] Local and rural definitions of liberalism, conceptually welded to patriotism and underscored by "democratic patriarchy," thus produced radical "alternative nationalisms" that stood in stark contrast to the fractious political imaginary of elite Liberal politicians and intellectuals.[48]

The unwillingness of Liberal ruling elites to incorporate the increasingly radical peasant interpretations of liberalism ensured the failure of their hegemonic political project by 1869.[49] That same year the alienation of communal lands, decreed by liberal laws, sparked peasant rebellions in seven states.[50] Porfirio Díaz, military officer and war hero, emerged amid the political instability in 1876 with his antireelection Plan de Tuxtepec and promises of restoring local and state autonomy. Such promises soon proved ephemeral as the Oaxacan general consolidated political power during the following decade. His "return" to the presidency in 1884 initiated three decades of authoritarian rule characterized by the (momentary) defeat of local government and the centralization of political power in the hands of a few within the federal government.[51]

Political prefects and land tenure represented the main peasant grievances during the *Porfiriato*. Operating at the district and municipal levels, prefects and subprefects brought despotism to the everyday lives of peasants.[52] In charge of police duties and the ever-rare redistribution of land and collection of taxes, and possessing the legal right to suspend members of *ayuntamientos* (community councils), prefects entered local political arenas fashioned by decades of rebellion generally provoked by outside infringements on local autonomy.[53] During the so-called *Pax Porfiriana*, the state of Guerrero experienced repeated instances of civic protest and rural violence directed at the prefect and the duties assigned to that institution by federal law. By 1890, the killings of four prefects and numerous assassination attempts moved Díaz to repeatedly advise state governor Francisco Arce—a three-term governor from Jalisco—to exercise strict control over local officials and to remove some of the more notorious personages. Díaz received numerous letters from peasant communities that described prefects as feared and hated officials. One such letter from Acatepec in La Montaña region dated April 1892 claimed that the prefect Felipe León "maintained the community in a state of slavery with all the services he demands ... [and] forced us to work without food."[54] This town, like many in La Montaña region, suffered the arbitrary rule of corrupt prefects who oversaw the dismantling of communal lands, privatization of "unused" public lands by middling and large landowners, and the collection of high taxes.

The issue of land tenure also provoked constant and localized peasant unrest. Yet the rise of haciendas, aided by the 1857 Constitution and Lerdo Law, assumed a different form in Guerrero, in contrast to sugar-cane dominated Morelos or regions where railroad construction dispossessed peasant communities of their lands. While the state witnessed the doubling of large haciendas from fifty-one to 100 in the course of thirty years (1871–1901), a different form of land tenure, the *rancho* or small landholding unit, grew during the same period.[55] Aided by Liberal land laws and Porfirian economic policies, ranchos mushroomed in the Tierra Caliente and Norte regions of the state and their owners formed a newly emergent urban and rural middle class that would play a crucial role in the 1910 revolution. Haciendas dominated the coastal regions. Prominent cattle grazers from five families remained in conflict with neighboring indigenous communities in the Costa Chica, while Acapulco-based Spanish merchants set up an expansive commercial monopoly that controlled agriculture in the Costa Grande. In the decades prior to the revolution, both rancho and hacienda combined to create a system of rural domination characterized by sharecroppers forced to pay exorbitant land rents with their harvested goods.[56]

By the turn of the century, a different societal group largely created and fostered during the *Porfiriato* organized a foreshadowing rebellion. A group of young intellectuals, village merchants, lawyers, schoolteachers, small and middling ranchero landowners, and students attempted to overthrow an unpopular governor imposed by Díaz via fraudulent electoral means in 1900.[57] After a hotly contested election and much-disputed electoral result, incumbent governor Antonio Mercenario emerged victorious over guerrerense politician and landowner Rafael del Castillo Calderón. Popular discontent soon forced Mercenario's resignation but Díaz appointed yet another outsider, Agustín Mora, as interim governor until the rescheduled elections set for 1901. While Mora's attempts to obtain popular support foundered, a reenergized and growing Castillo Calderón campaign began to face intensified harassment and persecution carried out by regime officials. When the opposition candidate suffered physical attacks, he and a group of supporters left Chilpancingo for the nearby town of Mochitlán. Only days before the elections on 8 April, partisans in the Costa Grande town of Atoyac distributed a manifesto that "demanded the right of the people to vote freely in the coming elections"; in other words, they wanted no reelection but a definition of democracy strictly limited to voting rights.[58]

Díaz sent Colonel Victoriano Huerta to suppress the rebellion. Honing counterinsurgency skills that would make him infamous some years later in Morelos and Yucatán, Huerta brutally ended the disorganized and ill-equipped uprising in Mochitlán. The colonel summarily executed a number of rebels and deported others.[59] Yet, the military victory for the Díaz regime failed to resolve the underlying factors that provoked the 1901 uprising. While the ranchero social group that supported Castillo Calderón continued to work for "free elections" and "no reelection," dispossessed indigenous peasant communities in the Tierra Caliente envisioned the end of haciendas and the return of lands owned since colonial times. Mestizo and mulatto sharecroppers and landless peasants in the Costa Grande harbored an intense nationalist hatred for their Spanish commercial overlords. Many had not forgotten that the Plan of Iguala granted citizenship rights to the former colonizers or that a law passed by the Mexican Congress in December 1828 decreed the expulsion of Spaniards from the country. In sum, the state of Guerrero harbored a heterogeneous collection of political registers and demands by the early 1900s.

Many Revolutions, 1910–1940

Guerrero experienced the development of a revolution driven primarily by the despotism of political prefects and demands for the recuperation of local democracy. These two general demands, largely shared by the emergent middle-class rancheros and peasant communities, offered the possibility of forming multiclass alliances—that long-honed tactic used by rural guerrerenses throughout the struggles of the nineteenth century. Yet, other class-specific demands lurked beneath the surface. Peasant definitions of patriarchal municipal democracy and citizenship (the foundations of popular liberalism) clashed with the ambitions of an emergent local-regional cacique network focused on no reelection; peasant demands for the return of expropriated lands or the redistribution of hacienda lands conflicted with ranchero belief in the sanctity of private property.[60] For Zapatista insurgents in the Tierra Caliente, the recuperation of communal land signified justice; for rancheros like Ambrosio Figueroa, such popular actions represented criminality and banditry committed by "the ignorant class of the People [Pueblo]."[61] With such dramatic differences, initial ephemeral alliances joined under the 1910 anti-Díaz banner of Francisco Madero, or the momentary 1913 movement against the usurper Victoriano Huerta, evaporated.

During the military phase of the Mexican revolution (1910–20), three political currents generally defined the struggle in Guerrero. Largely divided along regional lines, these included: the dominant rancheros from northern Guerrero led by the Figueroa brothers and supporters of Francisco Madero and Venustiano Carranza; a militarily weaker yet peasant-supported Zapatismo in the Tierra Caliente region captained by small landowner Jesús H. Salgado; and, in the Costa Grande, a protean, inconsistent current led by rural schoolteacher Silvestre Mariscal. Exceptions existed in each region, such as the Zapatista Cabañas brothers from the Costa Grande and the small contingencies of Zapatistas in the ranchero-dominated north near the city of Taxco. After the fall of Díaz and his successor Madero's hesitancy to institute land reform in November 1911, Zapata proclaimed the radical peasant Plan of Ayala decrying the Maderista betrayal. Demands for the redistribution of lands and patriarchal local democracy based upon peasant guerrilla militias were soon echoed in the Tierra Caliente.[62] For a few days prior to the announcement of the Plan of Ayala, Salgado had proclaimed his own peasant program: "we went to the battlefield to destroy an odious cacique system that trampled the law and insulted the rights of citizens... the dispossessed have yet to officially retrieve their lands even though it was promised in [Madero's] Plan de San Luis." He also condemned "odious taxes" and promised all soldiers a parcel of land "the same as other classes; all of us in equality and true fraternity." A peasant revolution in the southern state had begun: "We go to the conquest of our rights in full possession of our liberties, without asking anyone for them... to forcibly overthrow enemies of the People now constituted as the bad government."[63]

Insurgent actions revealed specific grievances and utopian glimpses. Prior to the falling out with Madero in 1911, Salgado's forces executed a number of hated political prefects in the Tierra Caliente region. When entering the city of Coyuca de Catalán in April 1911 in search of an unpopular prefect to kill, guerrillas immediately entered the unguarded municipal archives, seized land tenure and tax documents and burned them in the street.[64] By the time Madero-aligned peasant insurgents captured the cities of Iguala and Chilpancingo in 1911, they had established a specific political ritual grounded in recent history: the burning of archives, assaults on merchant houses and large businesses, the raiding of granaries, and the pillaging of government offices for weapons and ammunition. The attacks on municipal archives represented a complete physical disavowal of the Porfirian era by destroying the bureaucratic papers that documented the dispossession of peasant lands, the jailing of debtors, and the military conscription of regime dissenters.[65] Peasant revolutionaries across insurgent factions practiced similar rituals, often beyond the control of their leaders.

The culmination of Zapatista radicalism in Guerrero occurred in March 1914 when forces led by Salgado and Zapata captured the capital city of Chilpancingo. For a brief and unprecedented period, a Zapatista occupied the governor's chair and attempted to radically reorganize guerrerense society along popular peasant lines. Named provisional governor by the Zapatista revolutionary junta, Salgado and three captains implemented a series of radical reforms throughout most of the state: the suspension of land rent payments; the authorization for landless peasants to cultivate unused federal lands and hacienda grazing properties; the expropriation of hacienda lands from those opposed to the revolution; the abolition of political prefects; public education for all children; and the removal of mayors (alcaldes) appointed during Huerta's tenure.[66] Calling for municipal elections in November 1914, Salgado decreed that locally and democratically elected (most likely only by males) municipal authorities possessed the power to choose commissaries, chiefs of police, and other officials so as to prevent "the participation of individuals who collaborated with past regimes... and could lead the people down the path of tyranny and injustice."[67] Such radical changes, some actualized though the exigencies of war prevented large-scale implementation, represented the popular demands and necessities that nourished the Zapatista movement in Guerrero with vitality and creativity. For a brief fleeting moment, most of the state experienced a sort of popular power: potentially (though not explicitly) anticapitalist, simultaneously nostalgic and revolutionary, and difficult to categorize along orthodox political lines.[68] If the Carranza forces in 1915 managed to overthrow the Zapatista government, the eventual victors of the revolution failed to erase its subversive memory. Indeed, peasant intransigence and bellicosity forced the victors to implement municipal autonomy and agrarian reform in the 1917 Constitution. Memories of popular power remained alive throughout the countryside in spite of military defeat.

These memories nourished a series of popular movements that attempted to implement the potentially radical social clauses of the 1917 Constitution—municipal democracy and agrarian reform—in the Costa Grande region during the 1920s (Figure 1.3). While military Zapatismo largely failed to enter the region during the 1910s, Zapatista officers Pablo, Pedro, and Tiburcio Cabañas managed to introduce radical political ideals to the municipality of Atoyac de Álvarez. Peasant communities in Atoyac tended to conceptualize Zapatismo as social justice and "a [broader] struggle of all the poor."[69] As an elderly woman from Atoyac named Carmen Téllez recalled, "[General] Pablo Cabañas did not mess with Madero, Carranza, or [Alvaro] Obregón…he only wanted that the lands of the sierra not belong to the rich of Atoyac."[70] Nearby in Acapulco, an exiled union organizer arrived in 1919 to enter the fight against wealthy Spanish commercial interests that controlled the Costa Grande. Eventually dubbed the "Lenin of Guerrero," Juan Escudero played a vital role in coastal attempts during the 1920s to realize hard-fought constitutional rights in the everyday lives of peasants and workers. The arena for such struggles, at least initially and in contrast to the preceding decade, was a constitutional one. Intractable regional power-holders and their privately financed paramilitary units ensured that it turned violent.

The "Lenin of Guerrero" founded the Worker's Party of Acapulco (POA) in 1919 with the idea of capturing municipal power through electoral means. Guided by the anarcho-syndicalist ideas of Ricardo Flores Magón and marked by his experiences with the Wobblies in California and the House of the World Worker in Mexico City, Escudero combined leftist radicalism with reformist tactics. He organized agrarian committees, unions, and cooperatives along with the POA, refusing to conceptualize the political and the economic as separate spheres of existence. The POA elaborated a working program based on the 1917 Constitution that called for just wages for workers; the defense of human rights; honest public servants; active electoral participation; the eight-hour work day; public education; redistribution of land; the organizing of health campaigns; and the construction of a road between Mexico City and Acapulco.[71] Escudero sought to implement the program in 1920 after being elected as city mayor by a broad multiclass coalition of rural and urban workers, small merchants, low-level government bureaucrats, public workers, and small landholders.[72]

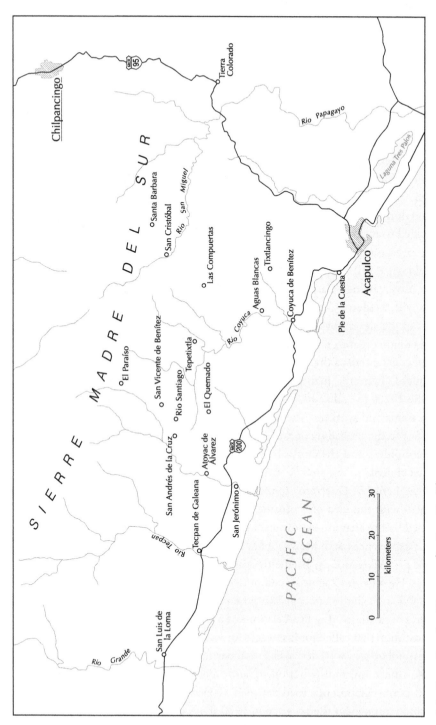

Figure 1.3 Costa Grande of Guerrero (by Peter Krafft)

Under the banner of "good government and police," the POA ruled for three years and attempted to radically reorganize city life under constitutional auspices. POA activists like Maria de la O helped organize working-class women and neighborhoods and distributed the party newspaper, *Regeneración*. By 1922, the POA had spread north throughout the Costa Grande, organizing party "branches" and winning municipal elections in Tecpan de Galeana, Coyuca de Benítez, Atoyac de Álvarez, and La Unión. POA agrarian militants like Valente de la Cruz and the Vidales brothers organized committees of landless peasants that petitioned the federal government for land and encouraged the development of regional agricultural infrastructure. As municipal president of Tecpan, Amadeo Vidales permitted landless campesinos to cultivate federal lands illegally used by large-scale livestock ranchers.[73]

Popular attempts to democratize regional politics and economic production based on the constitution elicited violent responses from regional caciques, oligarchs (particularly the main Spanish merchant houses) allied with large landowners and sympathetic military officers. Under the cover of national civil war in December 1923 during the Adolfo de la Huerta rebellion, soldiers executed Escudero and his two brothers.[74] POA militants who fought to suppress the revolt and defend President Álvaro Obregón also faced assassination attempts at the hands of privately financed cacique forces. Months before, in July 1923, POA municipal officials and peasant leaders organized a self-defense guerrilla force of two hundred men in Atoyac after police killed a popular peasant leader, Manuel Téllez. Famed local agrarian activists and revolutionary veterans like Pedro Cabañas, Silvestre Castro, and Feliciano Radilla joined the guerrilla movement as popular politics radicalized in the face of sustained elite-sponsored violence.[75] Paramilitaries and national revolts taught Costa Grande peasants that only the rifle guaranteed constitutionally mandated municipal electoral results and agrarian reform.

That lesson contributed to another Costa Grande peasant guerrilla uprising in 1926 that lasted for three years. Facing an antiagrarian reform state governor who falsely charged POA politicians and local peasant leaders with treason (and continued paramilitary violence), Amadeo Vidales organized the Liberatory Movement of Economic Re-integration for Mexico in May 1926. The name of the movement signaled its origin: the failure of progressive reform movements like the POA to profoundly restructure political and socioeconomic relations of domination in the Costa Grande during the 1920s. As a small merchant and radical politician, Vidales directly experienced the hegemony exercised by Spanish and other foreign commercial interests in the region. Thus, his Plan de Veladero manifesto seemingly exhibited anti-imperialist tones of national liberation, calling for the expulsion of Spaniards from Mexico and the redistribution of their "goods" to municipal governments for the financing of local industry.

Far from advocating a radical redistribution of the means of production to the rural masses, the Plan de Veladero mirrored some of the economic protectionist stances present in the developmental plan elaborated by President Plutarco Calles.[76] The radicalism of the program is apparent when compared with the system of domination that existed in the Costa Grande.

Proclaiming adherence to the 1917 Constitution, Vidales posited Spaniards as the target of a regional insurgency that sought to complement Mexico's political independence with economic emancipation: "we have lifted our rebellious banner with weapons in hand to protest the unjust Spanish dominion over what is ours."[77] Attempts to forcibly expel Spaniards began with the failure of 300 Vidalistas to capture Acapulco. Federal military units forced the insurgents to adopt guerrilla warfare. With experienced guerrilla experts like Pedro and Pablo Cabañas in their ranks and broad popular support throughout the region, the Vidales-led rebels survived for three years. While the Mexico City press ridiculed the group as anachronistic for articulating demands expressed 100 years earlier, Costa Grande landless and sharecropping peasants knew that local domination exhibited a Spaniard form. The ensuing military counterinsurgency campaign—burning of villages, rape, extrajudicial assassinations, and torture—was waged against the region for supporting the rebels. One military officer, Colonel Miguel Henríquez Guzmán, used a brutal tactic that remained etched into popular memory: cutting off the hair braids of peasant women suspected of collaborating with the guerrillas.[78] Yet, military violence failed to fully quell the rebellion. As campesino leader Valente de la Cruz wrote in 1925:

> the rich, gold-laden misters will finish off current agrarian leaders, just like they did with previous ones...yet the seed of liberation has been planted in the popular consciousness of contemporary youth that refused to tolerate Porfirian despotism and did not fear the rigors of war...spring season will bear the fruit of that seed with vigorous and urgent action.[79]

Subversive politics reemerged in the populist "spring" of the 1930s during the presidential administration of Mexican revolution veteran Lázaro Cárdenas.

The idea of the "revolution" forcefully endured in Guerrero as Cardenismo left a profound imprint on the political imaginary of Costa Grande rural communities. When President Cárdenas (1934–40) promised weapons to peasants while on the campaign trail near Acapulco in 1934, he spoke to an audience that had lived through fourteen years of low-intensity warfare as it struggled to redeem the agrarian and democratic ideals of the Mexican revolution. The region had already witnessed the flowering of radical political parties and agrarian unions after 1920, their subsequent radicalization when confronted by cacique violence, and the adoption of guerrilla warfare as a self-defense tactic. By initiating an agrarian reform program (*ejidos* [collective landholding], credit, irrigation, and infrastructure) that unfolded unevenly and haphazardly in the face of violent cacique resistance, Cárdenas fortified popular rural demands by providing them with institutional legitimacy.[80] Moreover, the general legitimized prior cycles of armed peasant struggles by positing them as valid defenses of the Mexican revolution. With the redistribution of land, Cárdenas seemed to demonstrate that the postrevolutionary state could fulfill revolutionary promises. As a *cafeticultor* (coffee producer) from the Atoyac area reminisced, "no [politician] remembered the agrarian law, no one could enforce respect for the Constitution, until the arrival of Cárdenas, who with such facility distributed land... and fulfilled his campaign promises (of 1934) to change the living conditions of the campesino class of Atoyac."[81] With all its limitations and undemocratic undercurrents, Cardenista agrarian reform finally achieved what local peasant organizations fought for during the 1920s: the economic and political displacement of Spanish and national commercial and large landholding caciques.[82]

Cárdenas and *Cardenismo* thus became key cultural referents in regional peasant political cultures of the Costa Grande. Many rural communities embraced agrarian reform based on the ejido model and organized to obtain other promises articulated by Cárdenas: agricultural technology, credit, infrastructural development, schools, and hospitals.[83] Coffee-producing peasants in Atoyac like Rosendo Radilla[84] believed such promises indicated that, as Cárdenas declared in 1934, "progress would be socialized [and] campesinos would constitute the principal beneficiaries of economic development."[85] Rhetoric turned into reality for twenty-one rural communities in 1939 when government pronouncements decreed the redistribution of coffee-producing lands and processing mills to the region's campesinos. Decades later these twenty-one cafeticultor communities, highly organized and boasting an armed self-defense militia, would shelter the ACNR and form the logistical core of the guerrilla PDLP's campesino base of support.[86]

Cárdenas's tenure was subsequently remembered as a time when the postrevolutionary state embodied the driving utopias and promises unleashed by the 1910 Mexican revolution because it collaborated with campesinos in their favor. Ensuing presidential administrations would face popular criticisms fundamentally based on comparisons with the constantly reimagined Cardenista utopia.[87] Despite the rollback of populist policies like agrarian reform after 1940, revolutionary hopes and demands remained active in the countryside. As sociologist Andrea Radilla Martínez wrote in her seminal study on Atoyac's coffee-producing peasants, "hope and the desire to fight or resist largely emanated from [peasant] experiences with Cardenismo... there are still some alive who met him or others know him from stories told in the furrows, during the cleaning of coffee trees, in ejidal assemblies, over cups of coffee...his picture adorns [humble rural dwellings] alongside Zapata."[88] Alongside the national portraits of Zapata and Cárdenas, local portraits of Salgado, Escudero, de la Cruz, de la O, Vidales, and Radilla populated the walls of Guerrero's peasantry. Folksongs immortalized them. Clandestine memories lingered—as did calls for revolutionary redemption.

Why the perceived need for redemption after Cárdenas? The presidential administrations of Manuel Avila Camacho and Miguel Alemán Valdés (1940–52) enacted a sustained rollback of key social reforms. Modifications to Article 27 of the Constitution that practically ended land redistribution (1942–3), the end of socialist education, and changes to the federal labor law that restricted worker rights in 1943 in the name of national unity undermined hard-earned popular rights gained in previous decades. Alemán's zealous embrace of rapid industrialization repositioned the Mexican countryside as subsidizer of capitalist modernization.[89] This change in course by the postrevolutionary state, as perceived by the workers and peasants, provoked a series of disconnected, yet thematically related, popular movements from 1940 to 1952 that collectively worked within the legal arena and based their diverse demands on the 1917 Constitution: land, schools, labor rights, credit, infrastructural development, and municipal autonomy. This historical period, bookended by a 1941 massacre of workers in front of the presidential residence and a massacre of protesting Henriquista supporters in Mexico City during the summer of 1952, witnessed a struggle over the "real project of the Mexican Revolution" in the post-1940 era.[90]

Robust Histories

Thinking back to the early days of the PDLP insurgency in the late 1960s, Lucio Cabañas recalled the difficulties in recruiting campesinos for armed struggle. Attempts to enlist peasants enraged by continuous state repression in a revolutionary guerrilla war against the PRI regime initially failed. When Cabañas spoke of guerrilla warfare, they responded with: "hey *Profe* [teacher], which General will come to our aid? What is the date of the uprising? Just tell us when and we'll be there." Atoyac peasants, the PDLP leader later realized, actively waited for a Zapata or Vidales to organize a recruitment effort, proclaim one of the innumerable Plans that crowd Mexican history, and announce a fixed date for revolution.[91] In traveling throughout the Atoyac mountains visiting remote peasant communities and conversing with their inhabitants, Cabañas realized that he was traversing a region with a rich political culture of rebellion and where peasant communities embraced their historical trajectory of resistance and struggle. In seeking guerrilla converts, the schoolteacher-turned-PDLP leader glimpsed a different mode of peasant resistance, one that dated back to the nineteenth-century insurgent exploits of federalist and liberal peasants, reinforced by the 1910 revolution, and consolidated during the agrarian wars of the 1920s and 30s. In sum, he learned that peasant historical experiences in mass mobilization and insurrection are rarely, if ever, forgotten.

Yet this long history of peasant politics and insurgency proved bittersweet. Guerrerense peasant participation in the processes of Mexican state formation beginning in the early nineteenth century was paralleled by the development of a regional cacique social formation that sought to monopolize political and economic power in the hands of a few. While the 1910 revolution and Cardenista land reform managed to uproot the regime of caciques fostered during the Porfiriato, aspiring new caciques consolidated their place in the postrevolutionary order. The institutionalization of some peasant demands under the 1917 Constitution and during Cárdenas's presidency produced a hegemonic governing framework yet failed to guarantee the fulfillment of such demands in practice and on the ground in Guerrero. During the 1940s and 1950s these rural demands reemerged in a series of union and civic struggles that subsequently questioned and exposed the postrevolutionary regime eight years before the infamous 1968 student massacre in Mexico City. The civic insurgency that engulfed Guerrero in 1960 tested the willingness, indeed the ability, of the "Revolution turned into Government" to renegotiate the postrevolutionary hegemonic framework.

A Lesson in Civic Insurgency

> In the same way that a canto exists in the imagination of the poet before
> it does on the printed page, the arrival of a new social organization
> exists in consciousnesses and wills.
>
> Antonio Gramsci, "One Year of History," 1918

In the midst of a postwar economic "miracle" and an intensifying global cold war, tens of thousands of guerrerenses organized to topple an autocratic state governor. A movement that began in 1959 with a single goal, involving a vast cross-section of Guerrero's civil society, developed through civil disobedience a radically, albeit patriarchal, democratic vision that promised a profound social restructuring. This heterogeneous democratic vision was intended to displace a society fundamentally structured by *caciquismo,* or boss politics. Such a vision extended democratic struggles beyond state-sanctioned political institutions ("the vote") into economic, social, and cultural realms and took the social democratic promises of the Mexican Constitution seriously. The bearers of that democratic vision doggedly requested, through mass mobilization, the actual application of constitutional rights—rights borne from a popular revolution that socialized democracy in Mexico. Some of the movement's demands, such as municipal and local autonomy and lower taxes, had gone unredeemed for decades. Organizational forms, too, resurrected memories of the electoral battles waged by the Acapulco Workers Party (POA) during the early 1920s or the tax strikes waged by Costa Grande communities in 1945. Thus, the 1960 civic movement, and the ensuing electoral and union struggles it inspired, formed part of a long trajectory of popular political participation filled with memories, failures, and silences.

The new quality of the movement resided in its recuperation and redefinition of gendered political subjectivities that provided lived meanings to such abstract terms as "citizenship" and "democracy."[1] Citizenship became an everyday active practice defined from below, by citizens who organized and mobilized, in the words of protestors, "against a bad [state] government"[2] that "exploited, stole from, molested, and assassinated *el pueblo* [the people]."³ Democracy, too, developed into everyday practice for the civic insurgents. In the course of creative, statewide civil disobedience campaigns, they demanded to exercise some level of democratic control over their lives: over their labor, their municipal governments, the taxes they paid, and the role of their federal government. Within the fractious political imaginary of the *cívicos* (the nickname of the 1960 movement participants), the active expression of dissidence—expressed within constitutional and legal limits—represented a civic duty in the face of a governor who they believed had treacherously violated the postulates of the Mexican revolution.

Social heterogeneity marked the 1960 civic movement. Urban middle-class professionals, teachers, and low-ranking government bureaucrats demanded access to political channels restricted by a postrevolutionary state that tolerated regional boss politics. Campesinos viewed political participation as the gateway to inclusion in the PRI's restrictive economic modernization program that posited the countryside as exploited subsidizer of urban and industrial development. Women sought to end their treatment as eternally sacrificing souls of the nation responsible for maintaining it afloat and innately moral "political housekeepers" with limited civic rights.⁴ Facing a dual fight against structural forces that pillaged the countryside and a "modernizing patriarchy" that rendered reproductive labor both invisible and indispensable to national development, campesina women assumed the multiple burdens of organizing, working, and familial care-giving to actively participate.⁵ In the course of struggle, they and the rest of the participants in the civic movement acted to redeem their constitutional rights and, in the process, became citizens.

Such popular activism radically altered Guerrero's political topography and created new political forms that posed a reformist challenge to the ruling PRI regime. How would the regime respond to the social democratic challenge? Would it side with a popular movement that originated autonomously from the PRI party structure, attempt to co-opt movement leaders, or continue to buttress the stubborn authoritarianism of local-regional boss politics? To answer such questions, this chapter delineates the sociopolitical history of the 1960 civic movement. Spearheaded by the Guerrerense Civic Association (ACG) and its young leader, Genaro Vázquez, the civic movement comprised one of several regional democratization movements that prefigured the more famous 1968 Mexico City student protests. These civic movements formed part of a broader set of social struggles that signaled increasing popular dissatisfaction by the late 1950s with the PRI's program of capitalist modernization and one-party political rule. In 1960 Guerrero thus emerged on the frontline of popular struggles that called for constitutionally based reform through civic action and mobilization, rather than state patronage.

A new generation emerged as movement leaders. Teachers and students trained in Mexico City at the National Teachers Training School (Normal nacional) received instruction from progressive Spanish Republican exiles and actively participated in a series of student and union movements during the 1950s.[6] Many students with guerrerense origins, like Genaro Vázquez, would return to their home state for the 1960 civic insurgency. In central Guerrero, the Rural Teachers Training School "Raúl Isidro Burgos" (better known as Ayotzinapa) provided an additional key source of movement leaders and activists (Figure 2.1). As linchpins of Lázaro Cárdenas' socialist education policies of the 1930s, *normales rurales* like Ayotzinapa continued to cultivate the ideals of social justice and community engagement after the PRI's post-1940 rightist shift. Students like Lucio Cabañas at Ayotzinapa would develop a politicized student-teacher identity that fused rural education with protecting and practicing the radical principles of 1910 and Cardenismo in the campesino communities they served.[7] "We were born [politically] in Ayotzinapa," Cabañas would later recall.[8]

As students and teachers, this new generation of leaders witnessed at the local level the socioeconomic inequality produced by the PRI's capital-friendly economic policies. They also directly experienced the violent wrath of the

Figure 2.1 Political mural in contemporary Ayotzinapa that includes Genaro Vázquez and Lucio Cabañas. Picture courtesy of Tanalís Padilla.

ruling regime when questioning its undemocratic methods and policies of rule. The story of Vázquez, beginning with his vanguard role in the cívico movement, provides a microcosmic yet lucid picture of how violent PRI responses to civic-popular movements inspired by the constitution and 1910 radicalized scores of social activists and everyday citizens for decades to come.

"...He Thinks Like Zapata, Like Villa..."

In the attempt to convince her father to accept Genaro Vázquez as her choice for husband, Consuelo Solís used the latter's radical politics—and notions of heroic masculinity—as bargaining chips. "He thinks like Zapata, like Villa, like you," she remembers telling her skeptical, hard-working father from the state of Hidalgo. "Well I admire the *cabrón* and his ideas," he responded, "but not to be your husband!"[9] By the time he relented and the marriage took place in 1959, Vázquez was already an experienced political leader. Born to a campesino family in the Costa Chica town of San Luis Acatlán on 10 June 1931, Vázquez described himself as the son of a campesino leader.[10] As a child, he remembered attending *ejidatario* assemblies and meetings with this father. With some help from state officials, he obtained primary and secondary education in Mexico City at the Francisco I. Madero and Rafael Dondé schools. After finishing preparatory studies at San Ildefonso, he entered the National Teachers Training School and obtained his teaching credential as an urban schoolteacher in 1956. At the Normal Nacional, Vázquez began a two-decade-long career as a charismatic, popular political activist and leader. According to his wife, Consuelo, he led a student movement within the National Teachers Training School that demanded more scholarships, improved dining facilities, and the removal of an unpopular school rector.[11] Vázquez and his wife later participated in the 1958 strike and takeover of the Secretariat of Public Education building led by the Revolutionary Teacher's Movement (MRM).[12] His work as a schoolteacher and involvement in Mexico City–centered political movements did not prevent him from knowing the political situation in his native state. As he recalled during a 1970 interview: "in the course of my studies and during the exercise of my profession I never lost contact with guerrerenses...they would come talk to me about their problems and they designated me as their representative before the Agrarian Department."[13]

During the formative years of his political ideology, methodology, and praxis, Vázquez continually displayed remarkable political pragmatism and nonsectarian thinking. Within a sectarian and dogmatic institutional Left that spent hours debating the proper road to socialism, the benefits of an alliance with the so-called "national-democratic bourgeoisie," and expelling "heretical" members—while often caught unprepared by the autonomous and democratic demands of 1950s popular movements—the schoolteacher's political acumen stood out. He was "antiparty,"[14] believing that political parties like the Mexican Communist Party (PCM) were unable to truly represent and lead Mexican workers. Such ideas coincided with those of José Revueltas, one of the "heretical" Marxists, when the radical writer criticized the PCM for failing to lead a "headless proletariat" during the massive worker mobilizations of the late 1950s.[15] Praxis, coalition building, and the sharing of common goals mattered more to Vázquez than party affiliation or ideological orthodoxy. Before the emerging popularity of Antonio Gramsci's writings in Latin America during the late 1960s and early 70s, the man who "thought like Zapata, like Villa" busily engaged in a multifronted "war of position." Vázquez helped forge an interclass "historical bloc" that would challenge one particularly despotic state governor in 1960.[16]

Prologue to 1960

During the twenty years that preceded the 1960 civic movement, PRI leaders and international observers celebrated economic miracles in the form of 6.5 percent annual GDP growth and political stability, while the Mexican countryside lived a different reality. As an overwhelmingly rural state, Guerrero intimately experienced the effects of an inequitable economic project dependent on the rural sector to subsidize rapid industrialization and feed burgeoning cities. Campesinos obtained artificially suppressed prices for their agricultural products to enable low prices and low wages for urban workers. The de facto end of agrarian reform (despite momentary revivals during the López Mateos and Echeverría presidencies) led to the reconcentration of land in places like the Costa Grande and created a reserve army of workers who moved into urban centers in search of work.[17]

Agrarian state policy focused primarily on the financing and the creation of vast capitalist agricultural zones. Furnished by state-funded infrastructural projects such as irrigation, such large-scale zones produced crops destined for export. In regions where campesinos held onto their ejidos, they often faced the incursions of state-owned and foreign corporations on communally owned forest and water resources. Rural women maintained rural societies alive, subsidizing the developmental program with unpaid household labor: cleaning, caring for children and sometimes family elders, and cooking. Many campesinas also worked outside of the home to supplement household income.[18] In sum, economic inequality became the hallmark of the so-called Mexican Miracle.

In Guerrero the Second World War produced significant changes, particularly in the Costa Grande region. Wartime demands spurred coastal peasants to shift from the crops they traditionally grew to ones with greater export potential, like copra (dried coconut meat) and coffee.[19] Regional caciques also changed their agricultural focus but not their methods: usurer credit, the cornering of harvests, and the monopolizing of industrial processing plants necessary for copra and coffee production.[20] Having lost land and political power during the Cárdenas years, this reconstituted agrarian bourgeoisie emerged to monopolize local and regional markets, credit, and transportation networks. In the absence of significant federal support for small rural producers, this group controlled the regional economy through a web of intermediaries that purchased crops, provided credit at exorbitant rates, and formed part of the local political class. By "purchasing, processing, and selling" the products of *copreros* (copra campesinos) and cafeticultores, this reconfigured "commercial bourgeoisie" managed to control the regional economy without necessarily owning large swaths of land.[21] This structure of domination, which included the systematic use of paramilitary gunslingers who terrorized nonconforming ejidatarios, shaped the character and demands of campesino movements that emerged during the early 1950s.[22] Such movements, instances of independent rural union organizing and mass strikes led by cafeticultores and copreros, would later link their struggles for economic justice with broader national issues involving political democracy—culminating with their prominent participation in the popular democratic movement that shook the state in 1960.

"The Cruel Reality that Reigns in the Suffering State of Guerrero"

The military man who emerged as governor of Guerrero in 1957 possessed a troubled and bloody past. A day after the July 1952 presidential elections in Mexico City, hundreds of supporters of the recently defeated presidential candidate General Miguel Henríquez Guzmán gathered to protest what they considered the fraudulent election of PRI candidate Adolfo Ruiz Cortines. Defying government proclamations not to organize public protests, the defiant Henriquistas gathered at the Alameda Central. Stationed nearby, a military unit under the leadership of General Raúl Caballero Aburto watched the protestors. Born in 1902 in the Costa Chica region of Guerrero and a veteran of the Mexican revolution, General Caballero had recently completed a series of military courses at Fort Knox. Facing the peaceful congregation of civilian Henriquistas on 7 July 1952, he participated in their violent, forcible removal from the Alameda Central.[23] Hundreds of protestors suffered severe beatings. According to some eyewitnesses, the brutal actions left hundreds dead.[24] Five hundred Henriquistas languished in prisons. As the repression against Henriquista supporters spread from Mexico City to provincial regions, General Caballero gained sympathy and support from the newly elected Ruiz Cortines. The president would not forget the general's endeavors—which perhaps explains why he anointed Caballero as the governor of Guerrero for the term of 1957–63.[25]

Like his counterpart in Chihuahua, the old Villista General Práxedes Giner Durán,[26] General Caballero confused the state, in the words of one 1960 civic leader, "with the barracks he previously commanded in his attempts to dominate civil society with an iron fist."[27] Away from the state some thirty years and possessing the support of only a few Costa Chica caciques, General Caballero entered a volatile "high" political culture as an outsider. Intricately defined by unwritten laws, patronage, *compadrazgo* and cacique networks, and familial ties, it included an uneasy coexistence of competing wealthy families that seemingly turned the state into a series of fiefdoms. Assuming a tenuous office (only three of his predecessors had managed to complete their gubernatorial terms in the prior forty years), the general perceived a dual threat to his rule. The first came from passed-over gubernatorial candidates that formed part of Guerrero's cacique power network and possessed affiliations with political figures at the national level. The most important federal player, Donato Miranda Fonseca, worked with President Adolfo López Mateos (1958–64) as the latter's secretary of the cabinet. A native of Guerrero, Miranda Fonseca forged links to important socioeconomic interests in Acapulco during his tenures as federal deputy and mayor.[28] Second, the general inherited a state characterized by recent waves of independent rural union activism and mass strikes during the 1950s that potentially threatened cacique interests in the Costa Grande.

The general wasted no time in making up for his lack of cacique or popular bases of support. As way to ensure loyalty within his own administration—and to maximize the profitability of his position as governor—Caballero packed the state government with compadres, brothers, nephews, nieces, uncles, aunts, and distant relatives serving as attorney general, treasurer, tax collector, customs officer of Acapulco, and chief of Acapulco's urban police, among other positions.[29] Throughout his gubernatorial tenure, he managed to impose his candidates for municipal presidencies around the state—in general, bad political choices, according to undercover DFS agents.[30] For example, citizens from the Costa Grande municipalities of San Jerónimo and Coyuca de Benítez sent telegrams to the ACG Mexico City office in 31 December 1959 and 6 January 1960, respectively, citing the unconstitutional imposition of Caballeristas in their municipal governments. In the case of Coyuca de Benítez, telegram writers accused the caballerista municipal president of being a murderer.[31] Such accusations voiced against the imposed Coyuca de Benítez municipal government proved accurate as the local ACG leader, Dr. Galdino Guinto, later survived an assassination attempt at the hands of Aurelio Avila Hernández, secretary of the municipal council who "received instructions directly from the state governor who had ordered the destruction of that [ACG] committee."[32]

Nepotism and the constant violation of municipal autonomy reflected the broader programs of political centralization and fiscal modernization advocated by General Caballero from the start of his gubernatorial term. In reorganizing and "modernizing" the state's tax-collecting apparatus under the Ministry of Treasury and State Economy, the general's new tax policies targeted the state's lower and middling classes while leaving untouched Acapulco-based transnational corporations, forestry companies, and national capitalist interests. During May and July, two new taxes emerged by decree: the first charged Acapulco residents from specific neighborhoods with "urbanization" fees, and the second elevated existing taxes on alcoholic beverages. Caballero established a State Office of Alcohol and put his nephew Armando Caballero in charge. The nephew and his father, Enrique Caballero Aburto, subsequently established a monopoly on mezcal production. Additional taxes on coffee, copra, real estate, grocery stores, urban services, goods sold in small businesses, and foodstuffs (with the exception of maize and beans) eroded the possibility of the governor developing any sort of legitimacy among the state's laboring and middling classes.[33]

The increased taxes burdened Guerrero's poor and middling campesinos. Caballero, at least rhetorically, took office promising to modernize the countryside with a reorganized fiscal system that taxed agricultural products and, subsequently, deposited such funds in bank accounts owned by campesino cooperatives and unions. Such promises helped the governor attain the valuable support of PRI-affiliated coprero unions (Regional Union of Copra Producers, URPC) early in his tenure. Copreros believed that collected taxes on copra production would infuse capital in their newly created organization—the Mercantile Union of Coco Producers and its Derivatives (UMPC)—that sought producer control over the entire commercialization process. For a brief period in 1957–8, the Local Association of Cafeticultores (ALC) viewed the increased taxes on its coffee products in a similar light. With the help of URPC members and assessors, the ALC organized the Mercantile Union of Coffee Producers in 1958 to obtain the vast majority of funds gained from the coffee taxes. Designed to displace traditional agro-bourgeois commercial networks, such "autonomous" campesino cooperatives seemed to confirm the neo-Cardenista populist slogans pronounced on a national level by newly elected President Adolfo López Mateos.[34]

The honeymoon between Caballero and the countryside proved fleeting. Closer contact and affiliation with the PRI and local politicians corrupted the earlier autonomous and economic democratic impetus of the URPC and ALC. By mid- to late 1959, the divide between rank-and-file campesino militants and union leadership dramatically widened as the latter forged ties to the PRI and even secured political positions at the state and municipal levels. Revenue obtained from the copra and coffee taxes failed to reach union members, most likely embezzled by the Caballerista government or by union leaders. Caballero installed ALC leader Raúl Galeana in 1959 as the municipal president of Atoyac, while local caciques like Candelario Rios negotiated alliances with URPC leadership. As rank-and-file campesinos experienced increased taxes levied by Caballero and saw any potential benefits absorbed by corrupt leaders, the Costa Grande region joined the cities of Acapulco, Chilpancingo, and Iguala as the cauldrons of discontent that would produce robust bastions of ACG support in 1960.[35]

Dissidence, as the discontented realized from the beginning of the general's tenure, exacted a heavy, sometimes fatal price. At times working one's land or just living day to day sufficed to provoke state-sponsored violence. After one month in office, Caballero announced a statewide "depistolization" campaign, similar to one he had led some years earlier in Veracruz, for public safety and anticrime purposes. Implemented by a newly consolidated police apparatus that put five police bodies under the direct control of the governor, the depistolization program soon turned into a campaign of extortion, repression, extrajudicial killings, and suppression of public protest. By January 1959, according to a telegram sent by one courageous newspaper director from Acapulco to Minister of the Interior Gustavo Díaz Ordaz, more than 1000 guerrerenses had died at the hands of state police forces.[36] Locations such as the Melendez Pit on the Taxco-Iguala road or the "Trozadura" near Atoyac, became infamous as execution grounds and impromptu burial sites.[37] Specific officers like Francisco "La Guitarra [the Guitar]" Bravo Delgado and Tibe Paco inspired tremendous fear among the citizenry.[38] According to Dr. Pablo Sandoval Cruz, a leader in the 1960 movement, the consolidated police forces constituted no more than "official" smokescreens for paid gunmen who served at the behest of the governor and his nepotistic regime. An internal analysis produced by the DFS soon after Caballero's fall from power in early 1961 listed the use of such "criminal groups" and their acts of "assassinations, theft, and plunder" as a crucial factor in the "development of the Guerrero situation."[39]

As the same DFS report explained, the use of violent criminals masquerading as state and municipal police officers allowed the general and his family to take over and maintain vital economic sectors. The analysis argued that "in controlling all of the economic sectors of the port [Acapulco] and the entire Costa Grande, an economically rich sector, [he] used Francisco Bravo Delgado (a) 'La Guitarra' as a medium of repression and terrorism to maintain control… [Bravo Delgado] was always protected by Enrique Caballero Aburto [the governor's brother and head of the Acapulco tax collection office]."[40] Campesinos who lived on the coastal outskirts of Acapulco experienced firsthand the "mediums" of violent repression used by the governor's brother. In 1957, a campesino community living alongside the Acapulco–Puerto Marqués coastal road was violently expelled because a "brother of the governor wanted to divide that zone's land holdings." They watched as gunmen burned down their small cabins. The same occurred to a group of campesinos from Cumbres de Llanos Largo, a hamlet located on the southern part of the Acapulco bay. Tuncingo, a neighboring community, suffered a more savage fate: some of their residents were "machine-gunned" because their communities obstructed the development of lucrative private beaches and wealthy residential zones to the south of the Acapulco beaches.[41]

Such instances of repression committed by state police forces occurred throughout the state during Caballero's tenure and affected most sectors of civil society. Rural hamlets, such as those coffee-producing communities in the mountains above Atoyac, suffered the assassinations of ejidatarios who refused to cede their lands. Elected municipal presidents who refused to leave their public posts to Caballero supporters faced torture, assassination attempts, and, at times, death. Such was the case with Angel Betancourt, municipal president of Cutzamala de Pinzón. He was shot to death on 19 January 1958 and posthumously hung from his genitals by his killers.[42] Elected officials were not the only ones at risk. State university students who demanded qualified professors, professional courses, adequate installations, increased state funding, and institutional autonomy clashed with a Caballero-formed group of violent athletic thugs dubbed the "Pentathlon." People jailed for alleged crimes faced the possibility of police lynching, either hanged at La Trozadura or thrown into the deep pit of the Pozo Meléndez. Progressive activists and independent-minded PRI militants experienced vigilance, harassment, and the threat of Article 145 of the Mexican Constitution: the crime of social "dissolution" and sedition that, according to ACG militant Antonio Sotelo, became "in vogue" during Caballero's term.[43]

The general's method of ruling "through the medium of terror," as a group of Atoyac coffee producers argued, helped forge the popular movement that would eventually end his violent reign.[44] Repression, taxes, and the flagrant use of public funds and property for personal enrichment produced a widespread civic insurgency.[45] Expressed differently by a participant of the 1960 movement:

> the 1960 movement was a protest movement against bad government…yet above all, it was a movement that still believed in a system of government borne from a popular revolution. It was an entire people that demanded a change in the system of government in favor of another more democratic one; it was the hope for a new dawn.[46]

Like previous popular struggles in Guerrero, the 1960 civic movement initially rallied under the banner of "Death to Bad Government." General Caballero had become the dramatic personification of bad government, responsible for the "cruel reality that reigns in the suffering state of Guerrero."[47]

The Formation of the ACG

Popular discontent with the policies of General Caballero started almost immediately after he took office in mid-1957. In response to the governor's nepotistic and violent rule, different sectors within guerrerense civil society coalesced into an effective oppositional movement united by common goals. The ACG stepped into this turbulent political situation. Working within an umbrella organization dubbed the Coalition of Popular Organizations (COP), the ACG directed a statewide, multiclass, democratic movement for two years that initially sought only one demand: the removal of General Caballero from gubernatorial power. Yet, in the process of democratic struggle, the ACG developed and posited an alternative interpretation of the "Mexican revolution."

When the ACG was founded remains unclear. DFS agents traced the origins of the group to the city of Iguala in 1958 when townsfolk organized the "Igualteco Civic Association" in order to demand more public funds from the state government. By mid-1959, the DFS had begun producing frequent and detailed reports on the ACG, providing information regarding meetings, plans, and members, thus suggesting that they identified the group as a potential threat early on.[48] Former members tend to cite 1959 as the founding year of the organization. Antonio Sotelo Pérez, a native of the Costa Grande community of San Luis San Pedro, recalled that guerrerenses who lived and worked in Mexico City began to meet in early 1959 to discuss their state's problems. Another participant, Blas Vergara, cited the formation of the ACG in 1959 as the continuation of the 1958 Mexico City teachers strike led by Othón Salazar and the MRM, which involved the participation of Vázquez and other future ACG members.[49]

Whatever the original founding date, it seems clear that by the end of 1959, the organization had received on a consistent basis multiple complaints and calls for help from several guerrerense communities that faced the imposition of municipal authorities chosen by the general. As several journalists began to publicize the dark side of the Caballero governorship, the ACG initiated a series of organizational networks that brought together campesino unions, teachers, local chambers of commerce, dissident municipal governments, university students, normalista students, small business groups, and urban labor unions (taxi drivers, electricians, vendors, etc.).[50] Using his experience as representative of campesinos before the national Agrarian Department, Vázquez cultivated the support of four independent peasant unions made up of copreros, cafeticultores, and palm and sesame campesinos. As president of the PRI-affiliated

Confederation of Mexican Youth (CJM), Vergara introduced the support of national student organizations, including the Federation of Socialist Campesino Students of Mexico (FECSM).[51]

From its inception, class and political heterogeneity characterized the membership of the ACG. Disaffected PRI members, such as the ACG's first president Professor Dario López Carmona, schoolteachers, housewives, doctors, lawyers, Acapulco-based independent journalists, entire town and city *barrios*, and small-scale ranchers joined students, dissident politicians, and union members. Individual leftist militants from the PCM and Mexican Worker-Peasant Party (POCM) and the Vicente Lombardo Toledano-led Popular Socialist Party (PPS) also joined.[52] With López Carmona and Vázquez elected as ACG president and vice-president, respectively, in September 1959, the organization's main political divides visibly emerged in its leadership. A predominantly Tierra Caliente regional bloc led by López Carmona largely opposed a direct action civic campaign directed against Caballero, instead preferring the collection of inculpatory evidence and its presentation before the Federal Senate and President López Mateos. Throughout the anti-Caballero campaign of 1960, this group continually challenged the participation of non-PRI activists as leaders within the ACG (particularly PPS members) in order to prevent "outside manipulation... [from] conducting habitual oppositional work."[53]

In contrast, a Vázquez bloc comprising campesinos and urban poor advocated a more radical posture that included notions of social justice and direct action; the mass mobilization of campesinos (at times armed in self-defense), workers, and students; the organizing of protests and strikes statewide; and a frontal civic challenge to the Caballero regime. Despite differences and internal conflicts—including the constant accusation that Vázquez was a PPS infiltrator—the goal of removing the general from the governor's palace initially worked to provide cohesion and unity.[54] Following the elections of López Carmona and Vázquez, the ACG organized teams "to travel throughout Guerrero, [and] form municipal Cívico committees in charge of collecting evidence, grievances, and news in order to present them to the people and the federal government."[55]

The ACG first targeted the Costa Grande for proselytizing. In October 1959, Vázquez, Sotelo, and the rest of the leadership council arrived in Acapulco and forged a crucial working relationship with the PPS-led Acapulco Civic Association—a political relationship that in 1960 would bear fruit when Caballero took on the progressive municipal president of Acapulco, Jorge Joseph Piedra. Traveling north along the Pacific coast, the cívicos arrived in Coyuca de Benítez, a bastion of coprero activism that had played an important role in the massive 1952 URPC copra strike. Upon the arrival of the ACG, the opinions voiced by locals at a town-hall meeting revealed a restive impatience with PRI authoritarianism and cacique domination[56] as they experienced it during the course of the URPC coprero movement:

> We don't want the ACG to become part of the PRI in the manner of the URPC or the ALC, or to have anything to do with the CNC. We will join the ACG if they can guarantee us that their struggle is truly independent and autonomous from all of the organizations or political parties that always play an embarrassing role as lackeys of the government.

According to the testimony of Antonio Sotelo, local ACG militant Dr. Guinto spoke to assuage their fears. A visibly moved and emotional Vázquez followed:

> Our civic organization, constituted on 10 September 1959 in Mexico City, has the obligatory mission of struggling shoulder to shoulder with the popular masses of workers and campesinos in order to reclaim our constitutional rights, infringed upon by the current governor. We cívicos struggle independently of all organizations manipulated by the bourgeoisie. We will not rest until achieving the disappearance of gubernatorial power in Guerrero.[57]

On 22 October 1959, Coyuca de Benítez formed the first municipal Cívico Committee.

Continuing northward, the ACG formed more local committees in the municipal capitals of Atoyac, San Jerónimo, and Tecpan de Galeana. Drawing on the rich history of campesino activism in the Atoyac region, the ACG formed a committee comprised exclusively of non-Priísta cafeticultor and coprero activists and created subcommittees that reached out to the surrounding mountain hamlets and communities. San Jerónimo, a region that witnessed the creation of the Union of Authentic Copreros of Guerrero to combat the corrupt URPC, proved "to be one of the most combative [ACG committees] during the most critical moments of the anti-Caballero movement."[58] By late 1959 and early 1960 similar committees formed in Iguala and throughout the regions of the Costa Chica, Tierra Caliente, and Norte. The Ayotzinapa normal—a bastion of communism and progressive politics in Guerrero since its inception during the 1930s—forged a strong working relationship with the cívico committee in nearby Tixtla and brought student leader Lucio Cabañas into the struggle.[59] Cabañas remembered: "During the times of Caballero Aburto we organized the people. We went to many little communities and organized meetings wherever we went." The relationship forged in struggle between normalista students and campesino communities proved so strong "that no campesino shot or threw rocks at students who stole onions, carrots, or radishes."[60]

This movement, "this legal struggle with democratic tints that radicalized as the problems went unresolved via legal channels," rapidly spread as Caballero continued to increase taxes on urban homes, "lucrative professions," alcoholic beverages, and livestock slaughter and purchase.[61] Despite an awareness of the tenuousness of his rule, as he revealed during a newspaper interview as early as February 1959, the general also continued the infamous depistolization campaign.[62] A notorious executor of that campaign, Francisco "La Guitarra" Bravo Delgado, provided the ACG with the opportunity to realize its first public act.

In February 1960, Bravo murdered Luis Lara in Zihuatanejo for refusing to sell a small plot of land he worked in town. Lara was not the first ACG member to suffer a violent death. In early February 1960 "unconditional supporters of Caballero" ran the car of Acapulco cívico committee leader Napoleon Lacunza off the road after weeks of death threats.[63] Yet, Lara's murder at the hands of the infamous "La Guitarra" brought the ACG onto the public stage. A respected and humble young man, his murder produced popular outrage. Local residents sent a flood of protests to public officials at all three government levels. "La Guitarra" provided his own interpretation of events in an interview given to an Acapulco newspaper five days after the murder on 22 February 1960: "I killed Luis Lara in self-defense. I attempted to fulfill an arrest order signed by the governor... in order to resolve the invasion of land plots belonging to Jorge Olvera Toro."[64] At the time working in Mexico City, the leadership council of the ACG set out to the port city at the invitation of local sympathizers. A massive number of citizens met the ACG leaders in front of a home owned by Lara's family and proceeded to organize a demonstration, aided by some youths who took over a local radio station and invited listeners to join. Receiving word that "La Guitarra" had obtained orders to arrest the leadership council, the cívicos left Zihuatanejo, avoiding both the nefarious gunman and an ambush organized by the state police.[65]

From that moment on ACG leaders López Carmona, Vázquez, Sotelo Pérez, Blas Vergara, and others traveled throughout the state in fear of Caballero's hit-men and police forces. Prior to the assassination of Lara on 5 February 1960, López Carmona had received a death threat from another infamous Caballero gunman (and relative), Edmundo Miranda Añorve, who promised the ACG president "a visit to his home."[66] In addition to the possibility of violence, the ACG faced constant red-baiting that emanated from the governor's place. Caballero deployed the image of communism to describe and discredit the political efforts of the ACG, facilitated by a national and international Cold War context in which any sort of dissidence became linked to a host of "subversive" images. In the words used by Caballero and his supporters: "the [ACG] agitation is supported by the bearded ones of Fidel Castro," "the agitation headed by leftists... follows a plan hatched against [Mexican] institutions and constitutional precepts by a party that is not precisely Mexican: the party of [Valentín Campa, Demetrio Vallejo, and Othón Salazar]," and "the agitators are impostors and traitors of your country [*patria*]."[67] Caballero publicly ridiculed the ACG, labeling its members "civi-locos" and "persons of low moral stature," while also linking the cívicos to local delinquents and criminal elements.[68] Alternating between descriptions of bearded communist insurgents and petty criminals, this public discourse of counterinsurgency attempted to subsume the legitimate origins of and political messages espoused by the ACG.

Yet, the increasingly public efforts of the ACG, in the form of highly organized, statewide rallies and demonstrations, subverted the general's best efforts. While reading his "Third Government Report" on 1 April 1960, with Luis Echeverría in attendance representing President López Mateos, along with other prominent Congress members, the ACG matched Caballero's speech by organizing large protests in the key cities of every state region. ACG leaders responded to the general's accusation by asserting "that the people of Guerrero are one hundred percent *lopezmateísta* and, as such, General Caballero lies when he attempts to portray us as enemy agitators of the regime."[69] With the constant articulation of one clear and coherent message—the disappearance of gubernatorial powers—the ACG began to forge a systematic opposition with a common goal capable of uniting a broad cross-section of guerrerense civil society. Caballero's use of newspapers to disqualify the ACG as "civi-locos," the dropping of anti-ACG propaganda leaflets from airplanes, and the organizing of paid progovernor rallies increasingly failed to stymie the development of the organization into a mass social movement.[70] Left with few options, Governor Caballero responded with targeted repression and violence.

Such options, ironically, only expanded the ACG struggle, by adding new demands while shedding light on the most repressive aspects of the general's rule. An intransigent Caballero had arrest warrants for ACG leaders issued on 23 April 1960 in the city of Iguala. The following day, after a high-profile public rally in the city of Arcelia that included the participation of ACG leaders, state police stopped the taxi in which Vázquez, López Carmona, Sotelo Pérez, and Olimpo Aura Pineda (copresident of the Mexico City committee) were traveling to Iguala. According to Sotelo Pérez, the state police arrested both the president and vice-president of the organization, threw them into a police truck, and stopped on the outskirts of Iguala to enact a mock execution. Having followed the police truck to ensure his comrades reached the city's municipal jail, Sotelo recalled that such an act—including the actual firing of carbines—served to "plant the seeds of terror" in both activists.[71] Upon reaching the municipal jail, Vázquez and López Carmona were "accused of committing harm, airing threats, and for criminal association [*asociación delictuosa*]." Sotelo Pérez and Aura Pineda immediately left for Mexico City to publicize their detainment, resulting in the sending of a telegram to President López Mateos's office and the presentation of a protection order before the district judge of Acapulco to "protect them from solitary confinement, bad treatment, and whatever else puts their lives in danger."[72] Vázquez and López Carmona would remain in jail for nearly a month.

Until the detainment of ACG leaders, organized university students from the State College in Chilpancingo had largely remained outside of the ACG social movement. Yet the decree pronounced on 30 March 1960 that transformed the institution into a state university radically altered the dynamic between university students and Governor Caballero. For the decree raised expectations among the student body, leading them to believe that the new university would enjoy institutional autonomy, increased funding, and qualified administrative officials and teachers. Instead, as a professor and militant of the 1960 movement recalled, "in practice, the State College [and not the university] continued to exist."[73] Students demanded the resignation of college director Alfonso Ramírez Altamirano, citing his authoritarian leadership, mismanagement of the institution's budget, and lack of a university degree as major factors. The students experienced firsthand the nepotism that characterized Caballero's term as the college director, a Costa Chica compatriot of the general, ignored their demands. In April a law student was severely beaten by the state police chief, Captain Pedro Ampudia; after being beaten and jailed, the aggrieved student, Teodoro Vega, was informed that it was a case of mistaken identity. On 20 April 1960 university students marched through the streets of Chilpancingo demanding the removal of Ampudia from his post for "being a traitor of the mother country for stupidly trampling on the Mexican Constitution."[74] Days after the 24 April detainment of Vázquez and López Carmona, students from both the State College and Ayotzinapa joined ACG demonstrations for the release of its leaders and the removal of Caballero—culminating in a massive 12 June demonstration in Chilpancingo.[75]

Such developments defied the evaluations produced by the DFS as early as 2 May 1960. An unknown intelligence officer cited the parallel development of the ACG and university student movements while emphasizing the distance and disconnectedness of the two. Arguing for the ACG's inability to raise "an anti-Caballero consciousness among the general population," the officer gave the example of the unwillingness of university students to join the movement. The DFS agent confidently stated "the people in general...have been cool toward the protests organized by Dario López," failing to recognize how Caballero-inspired repression and violence could (and did) unite both movements.[76] A common origin of grievances and the articulation of a revolutionary nationalist discourse that portrayed Caballero as a betrayer of the Mexican revolution and Constitution facilitated the ACG-student alliance. Soon joined by a trade organization that represented small businesses, the buttressed alliance organized a 12 June demonstration in the state's capital city.[77]

Building on such momentum and increasing popular support, over 100 ACG militants from throughout Guerrero traveled to Mexico City four days later to seek an audience with the president. As speakers Vázquez and Vergara railed about the "anarchic, violent situation" created by Caballero and his gunmen in front of the National Palace, ACG members carried signs showing the group's patriotism and respect for López Mateos. Received by a political functionary of the president, Vázquez—de facto leader of the ACG after López Carmona's refusal to return to Guerrero after his release from prison—presented their case: "the [ACG] is against the government and authorities of the state of Guerrero due to the crimes and arbitrary acts that have been recently committed."[78]

Following the Chilpancingo and Mexico City demonstrations, the general intensified his anti-ACG counterinsurgency prose through progovernment newspapers and by attending an audience with President López Mateos on 22 June. Dismissing the accusations launched against his administration and listing his public works projects, he characterized ACG activists as disaffected PRI militants frustrated by their inability to obtain governmental posts. Moreover, the general argued, the campaign remained localized primarily in Mexico City because in Guerrero "exists absolute calm."[79]

The ACG waited a week to respond. Sending a long, detailed report to President López Mateos that listed "a series of irregularities provoked [by the regime] headed by General Raúl Caballero Aburto," the civic organization expanded its original singular goal of removing the general from power to include demands "1. That those criminals who have murdered campesinos and other guerrerenses be punished [and] 2. That the Law of Responsibilities be strictly and completely applied, without exception, to all public officials that embezzled state public funds."[80] Describing Caballero's "degeneration" of the state's political system and continual violation of individual rights as the "repression of our aspirations and citizen behaviors" situated the ACG within a group of regional movements that sought the redemption of the Constitution and revolution through civic activism based on constitutional rights. Moreover, they used popular historical interpretations to justify their demands and activism. Appealing to President López Mateos using a paternalistic discourse that exalted his patriotism and presidential power, the document justified federal intervention on the grounds that "suffering" Guerrero "has always constituted a firm bulwark of our democratic institutions."[81] As such, the ACG and other contemporary popular protest movements in Mexico City, San Luis Potosí, Puebla, Sonora, Chihuahua, and Morelos tested the self-proclaimed revolutionary status of the "revolution turned government" and its willingness to negotiate.

Acapulco

One additional developing situation, involving the general and an intransigent but popular municipal president, contributed to the brewing social crisis by mid-1960. Since the colonial days of the Manila Galleon, Acapulco had been the de facto capital, in commercial and political terms, of Guerrero. The port city was historically monopolized commercially by foreigners (namely Spanish) immersed in global markets, and its legacy had survived intact through Mexican Independence and the revolution of 1910. As late as 1926, armed popular movements had demanded the reapplication of an 1828 federal law that oversaw the expulsion of Spaniards from Mexican soil, and, according to the Vidales peasant guerrillas, a redistribution of potential wealth and economic opportunities to the inhabitants of the city and the surrounding Costa Grande. The so-called "stabilizing modernization" that had characterized post-1940 Mexico sought not to undermine the port's legacy, but to transform Acapulco into a tourist destination capable of attracting national and international tourist and commercial capital. The presidential administrations of Avila Camacho and Alemán had promoted an inequitable process of urbanization involving the expropriation of surrounding campesino ejidal lands for the development of beaches and resorts, particularly that carried out by Mexican, Canadian, and American corporations. Rural migrants from neighboring Costa Grande and Costa Chica fulfilled the need for cheap labor, as the city's population increased more than 600 percent over the course of twenty-three years (1950–73).[82]

By the time Jorge Joseph began his term as the city's municipal president in January 1960 (popularly elected yet also directly appointed by President López Mateos), he faced a drastically class-stratified city, with its tax collecting departments under the control of Caballero's relatives and a large number of migrants arriving every day. A longtime PRI militant with important political anti-Caballero connections at the national level, the municipal president also exhibited a strong independent streak. Perhaps his childhood days in the port city, spent delivering radical newspapers and political pamphlets produced by Juan Escudero and the Workers Party of Acapulco (POA), had left an indelible imprint in his political consciousness.[83] Perhaps Escudero's radical efforts in 1921 to 1923 to morally cleanse the city had contributed to Joseph's own early campaigns to shut down various profitable bars, brothels, and other vice centers owned by Caballero relatives and associates. The general owned the most important and "elegant" brothel, the "Quinta Evangelina." In addition to provoking Caballero's ire, the closure of such businesses drastically reduced tax revenues brought into the municipal treasury. As Joseph's popularity increased both in Acapulco and throughout the state, Caballero plotted the municipal president's downfall. The decision by Joseph in July 1960 to permit the occupation of the

Ejido de Santa Cruz by 4000 landless heads of families and the return of lands expropriated in 1948 to their original campesino owners in El Marqués proved to be the final straw.[84]

As the Joseph-Caballero conflict increased during the summer, the municipal president faced the impending bankruptcy of the Acapulco municipality. Enrique Caballero Aburto, the governor's brother and head of the tax collection office of Acapulco, contributed to the deteriorating situation, according to a DFS report, by "depleting the municipality's revenues and ensuring that it receives only small payment amounts, though [Enrique's] office publicly denies such charges as lies."[85] Unable to pay teacher salaries by September, Joseph also blamed the nonpayment of taxes on hotels with low occupancy. A month later, the municipal president resigned after facing economic, political, and social attacks, the last in the form of popular demonstrations led by the self-proclaimed and enigmatic "King Lopitos" (Alfredo López Cisneros, head of a pro-Caballero neighborhood association).[86]

Pro-Caballero newspapers stated that Joseph had requested a leave of absence, days after he had stated that he had left in fear for his life, singling out "La Guitarra" and several police organizations as threats. Joseph also revealed that the governor had bribed two *regidores* (municipal council members) and had threatened the other four with death if they did not vote to remove the municipal president. After producing a list of thirty-seven people murdered by Caballero's police forces, Joseph met with ACG leaders—including Vázquez—on 19 October at his Mexico City residence.[87] In addition to discussing ways to further organize and systematize the popular anti-Caballero movement led by the ACG, the group now led by Vázquez suggested the possibility of a statewide tax strike. To the surprise of those attending, the ACG president suggested a forcible takeover of the Government Palace in Chilpancingo.[88]

Direct Action

By late October, the state of Guerrero had witnessed three disparate social movements cohere into a systematic offensive against the government of General Caballero. Joseph's ouster from power in Acapulco—the most important municipality in the state—provided concrete evidence of one of the general's violations of municipal autonomy. On a practical level, the incident permitted the civic organization to enlist the port city's various unions and popular organizations from which Joseph had enjoyed constant support. Almost simultaneously, the incipient university student–ACG alliance blossomed into an outright alliance when students raised the red and black strike flag on 21 October. Provoked by the threats of expulsion announced by the pro-Caballero rector Ramírez Altamirano, students belonging to the Federation of University Students (FEU) took over sections of the university campus and demanded the rector's resignation. A day after the announcement, one national newspaper described the composition of the strike in Chilpancingo: "the University of [Guerrero], the Normal Rural of Ayotzinapa, a number of high schools, and twenty-two middle schools tumultuously launched the strike, dangerously complicating the situation of an already battered governor."[89] Further stoking the student opposition, the rector proclaimed the automatic expulsion of all striking students. Following suit, the general reissued arrest warrants for Vázquez and López Carmona, while his allied municipal president of Tixtla issued warrants for two prominent student leaders (and ACG members) at Ayotzinapa, Lucio Cabañas and Inocencio Castro.[90]

Internally, the ACG—with newly incorporated allies— continued to debate the use of civil disobedience tactics to further weaken the Caballero regime. Discussions of a statewide tax strike and other union-based strikes also included the sending of delegations to Mexico City to meet with the president and congress. Yet, such internal debates revealed the ideological differences that characterized the ACG from its inception. Vázquez's insistence on the use of direct, pacific civic action as a pressure tactic that complemented legal procedures contrasted with the fears of bloodshed expressed by López Carmona. Such divisions provided the ACG with a disjointed but generally unified effort, with Vázquez in Chilpancingo organizing mass demonstrations and López Carmona in Mexico City collecting evidence to present before the federal congress. As both leaders prepared to carry out their tasks, the governing general in Guerrero unequivocally chose the path of violent repression in his attempt to smother the burgeoning social movement.[91]

Almost immediately after declaring their strike, university students faced the aggressions of a rival student "shock" group financed by Caballero. The "Pentathlon" attacked striking students on 22 October while the latter explained their movement to the residents of the San Antonio neighborhood in Chilpancingo. Women residents of San Antonio saved the students by stoning the aggressors and later participated in the student movement by forming a "small popular guard." That same day, municipal police under the orders of Caballero murdered campesino Sebastian Salgado Aparicio in the Tierra Caliente town of Teloloapan.[92] Such instances followed the strategy of targeted, localized violence exercised by the governor from the beginning of his tenure. Yet, the ACG's decision to make Chilpancingo its base of operations in late October, in addition to the ongoing student strike, forced a change in repressive tactics and led to the arrival of the national army.

Vázquez decided against his previous idea of taking over the state capitol of Chilpancingo, yet remained intent upon directly confronting the Caballero regime. In a strategy that aimed to physically manifest the popular support gleaned by the ACG over the course of a year, a thirty-person contingent of ACG and Frente Zapatista (a Zapatista veterans group) militants marched to the center of the city on 29 October, cordoned off the state capitol, and carried out a sit-in strike (*parada cívica*).[93] Standing on an improvised platform, Vázquez decisively announced to the crowd that "from this moment on, the entrance of Caballero Aburto into this government building is strictly prohibited." Strategically located in the center of the state capital, the permanent civic sit-in allowed the diffusion of ACG messages to a wide audience. ACG member Antonio Sotelo Pérez recalled that women on their way to the city market and bus drivers dropping off customers stopped to hear "denunciations of the bad government." Bus drivers and passengers, in particular, helped spread the word to other parts of the state.[94] In the throes of a civic insurgency, the city remained off-limits to the besieged general. Acting on the orders of Caballero, army soldiers and state police officers (led by Caballero's nephew) moved in on 31 October to forcibly dislodge the civic sit-in under a hail of bayonet strikes and blows. They also arrested Vázquez and Salvador Sámano, head of the Frente Zapatista.[95]

The day of 31 October marked the first of a series of confrontations between the ACG and various repressive state apparatuses that only increased popular support and sympathy for the civic organization and completely isolated the general. While Vázquez and Sámano remained imprisoned (and were receiving death threats), the ACG relocated the civic sit-in to a nearby plaza in front of the student-held university campus that displayed a large black and red flag.[96] Repeated instances of police and army violence helped fuse the student and civic movements. On the same day of Vázquez's detention, student leader Jesus Araujo declared at a demonstration attended by 10,000 that they had "decided to join the permanent popular struggle" and demand the resignation of Caballero.[97] In the coming days, campesinos, Chilpancingo small businesses, municipal governments from throughout the state, and the Chilpancingo city council joined the civic movement, culminating in a 6 November demonstration attended by more than 5000 persons, a quarter of the city's population. Though the act ended with the intervention of the army—and almost thirty wounded protestors—the violence catalyzed the formation of the Coalition of Popular Organizations (COP) and a city-wide general strike the next day. No longer alone in the struggle against Caballero, the ACG helped forge a broad alliance that included over thirty unions, associations, municipal governments, state bureaucracies, and chambers of commerce.[98] The COP laid siege to a deteriorating regime through a tax strike and the organizing of mass demonstrations while collectively demanding the resignation of Caballero,

Throughout the month of November the cities of Acapulco, Iguala, and Chilpancingo experienced demonstrations and daily "lightning political meetings." In an attempt to garner popular support and national attention, the ACG sent numerous petitions and letters to Mexico City addressed to President López Mateos and Congress.[99] The Cámara de Diputados (analogous to the House of Representatives) and Senate initially refused to discuss a detailed COP petition that listed the constitutional violations and crimes perpetrated by the Caballero regime presented before them on 9–10 November—the same day the ACG published a COP list of demands in a national newspaper.[100] Three guerrerense *diputados* (representatives) promised at a 12 November demonstration in Chilpancingo—one that included 6500–10,000 participants—to introduce the matter before their chamber "because of the obligation to listen to the will of the people... and to provide a just solution for the people." Disputing recent red-baiting accusations aired by Caballero, Diputado Enrique Salgado Sámano justified the necessity of taking the case to the Cámara "now that this movement is not communist but spontaneous, from the people."[101] While the return of the diputados to Mexico City produced minimal impact in the game of musical chairs played by the unwilling Senate, the COP planned a grand march on the fiftieth anniversary of the Mexican revolution.[102]

More than 20,000 guerrerenses silently marched in the streets of Chilpancingo on the anniversary of the 1910 revolution, demonstrating an acute frustration with the federal government's unwillingness to act. They reaffirmed that "our struggle was framed within state and federal laws, especially within that marked by the state constitution of Guerrero."[103] Walking through the city streets dressed in black and under the watchful eyes of soldiers and their bayoneted rifles, they carried signs that proclaimed the death of the revolution and pledged support to their "savior" President López Mateos. When they had reached the end of their march in the plaza in front of the main university building, they sang the national anthem and hung the national flag alongside the red and black strike banner. Speakers demanded the resignation of Caballero, the "Judas" of the revolution, they presented analyses of the present condition of the revolution and decried the "shameful" performance of their state congressmen. In his speech, Professor Domingo Adame Vega best encapsulated the emergent civic consciousness demonstrated by the COP and cívicos: "What took place some fifty years ago is happening today in Guerrero. Back then the people [pueblo] saved itself through the use of arms, while today that struggle is conducted with the weapons of law." Caballero may have corrupted the revolution, but the cívicos sought its urgent redemption.[104]

Caballero, forced to seek refuge in the Costa Chica after the cívico takeover of Chilpancingo, responded with more violence. On 25 November battalion troops dislodged COP and ACG members from the Alameda Granados Maldonado, leaving a large number of wounded and cutting off the striking university students from the Chilpancingo community. Soldiers detained more than 200 protestors and laid siege to the university, blocking water, food, and electricity from the students inside. For the next month, soldiers essentially instituted a state of emergency within Chilpancingo, restricting access to certain areas. As Caballero organized a luxurious wedding for his daughter, campesino groups from Atoyac headed by ejido leader Luis Cabañas offered Vázquez the services of 1600 armed campesinos to send the federal government "a message."[105]

By the last day of December, COP leader Sandoval Cruz recalled, some twenty-two or twenty-three ayuntamientos participated in the social movement. In places like Taxco, community members took over the municipal government and reorganized the police forces. Regular demonstrations were held every day in the cities of Atoyac, Acapulco, Iguala, Tlapa, and Tixtla.[106] By the end of 1960 Caballero ruled in name only.

The Political Imaginary of the ACG

In one year, the ACG and COP had successfully forged—through difficult daily discussions, negotiations, and activism—a series of multiclass and interlocal alliances that constituted a regional hegemonic bloc and achieved the resignation of General Caballero. Their vision, voiced contemporaneously though disparately throughout Mexico, involved "a return to what they considered as the original trajectory of the Mexican Revolution, defined as Cardenista populism, that in Guerrero they considered blocked by the governor."[107] Similarly expressed by protestors in 1960 Chilpancingo, "[we are] against the [politics] that govern our state because it is contrary to all programs of social justice, because it represents the regression of the Mexican Revolution and without it there will be no popular progress."[108] The idea that associated betrayal of the revolution and Constitution with the general's performance as governor united an ideologically and socially heterogeneous social movement. Restoration, indeed redemption, of both the revolution and Constitution through civic praxis provided the movement with a cohesion based on both social solidarity and historical purpose.

Such restorative motives lead some leftist scholars to emphasize the lack of radicalism in the ACG/COP political platforms, labeling the organizations as misguidedly reformist tricked by the "democratic humbug"[109] of the Mexican Constitution.[110] Yet such evaluations tend to minimize the importance of historical context and process while misunderstanding popular politics. In a country where the ruling party had sought to co-opt and appropriate popular organizations (or physically eliminate dissident ones), the autonomous and independent origin of the ACG represented a radical gesture. Moreover, the organization's popular interpretation of the Constitution that encouraged the actual physical manifestation of hard-earned political, social, and economic constitutional rights further challenged PRI rule. Civil dissent in the form of demonstrations, nonpayment of state taxes, and general strikes intended not to undermine the Mexican state but rather reenlist its help (as during the days of Cárdenas, cívicos commented) in the struggle against an unconstitutional governor. In the process, cívicos forced the state to concretely match its revolutionary nationalist rhetoric. A diverse group of students, campesinos, housewives, professors, small business owners, shopkeepers, Zapatista veterans, government workers, municipal governments, disaffected priístas, communist and socialist militants, and even a small number of right-wing Sinarquistas prevented an effective red-baiting of the movement. Contrary to General Caballero's media proclamations regarding cívico "communism," ACG and COP members continually reaffirmed their commitment to President López Mateos and worked within the legal precepts of the Constitution. In sum, the ACG and COP represented guerrerense civil society.

While struggling against high taxes, violations of municipal autonomy, nepotism, and state repression, cívicos became citizens through the active engagement and practice of their constitutional rights. To paraphrase anthropologist Armando Bartra, a citizen is made, not born.[111] For all of their political innovations, the ACG and COP faced severe limitations. The ideologically heterogeneous make-up of the ACG, for instance, tended to produce intense internal wrangling over appropriate tactics, the participation of leftist militants from the PCM and PP, and the incorporation of economic demands into its program. Intelligence records provide a glimpse into the last two tumultuous months of the 1960 social movement, characterized by a power struggle between López Carmona and Vázquez.[112]

The gendered definition of citizenship practiced and expressed by the ACG and COP represented a key shortcoming. As male guerrerenses became citizens in the process of struggle against the Caballero regime, the implicitly masculine nature at the core of citizenship and the exclusion of women changed little.[113] According to historian Jocelyn Olcott the granting of full suffrage rights to Mexican women in 1953 had failed to displace an assumed "male political subject," particularly when a "chivalrous" president granted such rights.[114] Guerrero proved no different. In a male-dominated 1960 social movement—with demands tied to the removal of the state governor—issues of women's labor, sexuality, and reproductive potential (and who controlled them) remained silenced, as did the class-specific contours of such issues. Overthrowing Caballero, not the radical transformation of gender roles, remained the primary concern of the ACG and COP.

Yet, silence did not mean passivity. The political crisis that developed in Guerrero also provided opportunity for the transgression of traditional gender roles and a redefinition of what physical spaces constituted sites of political action. Women who participated in the social movement by fulfilling "helpmeet" roles (providing food for the civic sit-in and student strike or harvesting crops in place of a campesino cívico husband) transformed food-vending stalls and kitchens into terrains of political exchange and solidarity; the act of cooking became subversive political action against Caballero in solidarity with the ACG. Those who stood guard at barricades, formed self-defense units, and physically confronted soldiers in Chilpancingo exhibited a militant political dynamic largely incongruent with dictates emanating from ACG leadership. As such, the fusion of women's everyday unremunerated labor with acts of open resistance momentarily disrupted the gendered political dichotomies of personal-political, public-private, masculine-feminine. Brief glimpses of alternative visions and social relationships that challenged gender norms emerged in the course of the anti-Caballero struggle.

Campesinas like Gregoria Nario remembered that campesina housewives actively and publicly participated in Atoyac's ACG protests with their small children alongside them.[115] Others like Consuelo Solís Morales subsidized their husbands' anti-Caballero activities by continuing to care for their children and maintain households. By December 1960 Solís Morales cared for two infant children—the youngest born prematurely due to stress caused by economic hardship and political persecution suffered by the Vázquez-Solís family.[116] Mercedes de Carreto and teacher Julita Escobar formed part of the COP's five-person leadership council. Escobar and Altagracia Alarcón Sánchez signed onto the anti-Caballero movement as municipal councilwomen from Chilpancingo and Chilapa, respectively. Anita de Brilanti joined the movement as coleader of Taxco's Silversmiths Union, while Virginia Hernández and Sara Reyes helped lead the Union of Small Merchants of Tixtla. In Acapulco, the Union of Revolutionary Guerrerense Women led ACG lightning meetings and distributed COP literature.[117] Government workers also participated. In December 1960, women telephone operators in Chilpancingo organized themselves and joined the COP. They listened in on phone conversations between government authorities and provided valuable intelligence to ACG and COP leaders. Caballero's assistant attorney general complained, "they could not have any confidential phone conversations without their proceedings getting reported back to the subversive leaders."[118] Photographs taken in Chilpancingo reveal the pervasive and active public presence of women during demonstrations and daily political meetings.

Two photographs in particular epitomize the actions of cívicas—and their radical transgressions of cultural and political patriarchy—during the last months of the general's governorship. The first shows a middle-aged woman named Clementina Oliveros walking in front of a group of soldiers with General Julio Morales Guerrero. Angrily gazing back at the soldiers, Oliveros flashes a "discourteous" hand sign to the noticeably offended general. The second photograph places Chela Natarén at the scene of the massacre that ended the rule of Caballero in Guerrero. In the words of her friend Virginia Juárez:

> around three o'clock the church bells rang; I was in the house. The bells were only used in case of emergencies and people were to gather and organize when they rang. On Guerrero Street [Chilpancingo] the people had gathered; there was much firewood and we were told not to let the soldiers pass. We linked arms with one another, intertwined, in a manner that they could not pass... but the soldiers fell upon us and we defended ourselves with pieces of firewood and rocks. All of the sudden I saw myself in the middle of the street alone, a few meters from my friend Chela Natarén. They told us that they were fake bullets, but they were not.

That photograph, taken on 30 December 1960, shows a solitary Natarén charging a group of advancing soldiers, apparently covering the retreat of her fellow protestors.[119]

A Massacre

Like the rest of his electrician comrades, Enrique Ramírez participated in the anti-Caballero movement. On the afternoon of 30 December 1960, the electrician looked for the military officer in charge to ask permission to hang a banner from a lamppost. Unable to find the officer, Ramírez decided to climb the post and hang the banner that read "Death to Bad Government." A soldier stationed nearby responded by shooting him. As Ramírez lay dying on the Chilpancingo street, eyewitnesses spread the word and used church bells to call COP and ACG members into action. Soon thousands of enraged protestors faced off with soldiers from the 24th Infantry Battalion under the command of General Julio Morales Guerrero. They fired three volleys into the civilian crowd. Lasting no more than fifteen minutes, the military attack against the civilian protestors left at least twenty-three dead (including two soldiers) and forty wounded. Fifty-five detainees were tortured in clandestine and makeshift prisons. Before dawn the next day soldiers stormed the university building, physically assaulted the striking students, and dragged them off to the municipal jail. The permanent civic sit-in ended in bloodshed.[120]

Vázquez received word of the massacre while organizing in Huitzuco. He quickly asked Luis Cabañas for an important meeting. The prominent campesino leader from Atoyac reminded Vázquez of his previous offer to organize 1600 campesinos into a guerrilla force. Many people in the sierras of the

Costa Grande, Cabañas continued, possessed hunting rifles and proved willing to "grab the bull by the horns." According to Sotelo Pérez, present at that meeting, Vázquez responded:

> If the federal government does not order the disappearance of gubernatorial powers in Guerrero, we cívicos need to raise the consciousness of the pueblo in order to prepare it for a possible future confrontation with the State through a war of national liberation. If the government of Caballero Aburto does fall, then the cívico groups will not disintegrate but strengthen themselves in order to keep the [social] movement alive.[121]

Five days after the massacre the Senate voted to remove Caballero from power. The general, who once told a writer that he was a "disciplined soldier" and "would go wherever I am ordered to," soon left the country for military attaché positions in Central America.[122]

"1960 Produced Great Lessons for the People"

The ouster of General Caballero seemingly confirmed Guerrero's reputation as "'ungovernable,'" the political graveyard for aspiring governors unable to balance pressures from caciques and *agrarista* campesinos. It formed part of an older historical script, identified by historian Paul Gillingham as a "ritualized...mechanics of overthrowing governors," that characterizes guerrerense political history since the 1850s.[123] Yet the 1960 civic movement also demonstrated novel political and social features. Cívicos confronted a despotic state governor through the multiclass, statewide organizing of civil disobedience and mass mobilization to reclaim violently repressed constitutional rights. They exploited cleavages within the upper echelons of the PRI regime and strategically exposed gaps between "official" revolutionary nationalist discourse and practice to force the ruling party into deposing one of their own. Cívicos successfully deposed a loyal PRI military man who had cut his teeth during the revolution with the victorious Constitutionalist side and had dutifully followed orders in the 1952 repression of Henriquistas.

Thus, the 1960 civic movement exhibited both new organizational tactics and old popular demands. The autonomous origin of the ACG beyond PRI party structures and the emergence of schoolteachers as movement leaders formed part of a recent national trend characterized by independent popular mobilizations that upheld the 1917 Constitution as their banner. Politically formed within educational institutions that seriously engaged and sustained alive the radical legacies of the 1910 revolution and Cardenismo, teachers like Julita Escobar Adame and Genaro Vázquez played key roles as organizers, leaders, and intellectuals. Old demands—municipal autonomy and economic democracy—mingled with new urban middle class demands for the protection of small businesses from unjust taxes. Other gender-specific longings, such as the extension of democracy into households or making women's labor public went politically unrecognized but were actively present. An almost religious devotion to the legitimacy of the revolution and Constitution—combined with the skillful deployment of official PRI discourse—united the civic movement's variegated demands and participants.

Neither the Chilpancingo massacre nor the designation of guerrerense Supreme Court Justice Arturo Martínez Adame as interim governor on 4 January 1961 managed to suppress the democratic impulse unleashed by the ACG and COP. While "Death to Bad Government, Death to Caballero" had served as a unifying rallying call for over a year, the yearning for a meaningful democracy in which active citizen participation ensured the application of constitutional rule had formed an implicitly subversive subtext. After the massacre and Caballero's ouster, the civic social movement took more direct action to institutionalize the democratic gains of 1960. Such action involved the taking over of municipal governments by ACG and COP members and organizing directly elected ayuntamientos. During the two-year interim tenure of Martínez Adame, ACG and COP ayuntamientos ruled twenty-three of seventy-five of the state's municipalities.[124] Citizenship continued to signify active mobilization in defense and application of constitutional rights.

The next two years would prove crucial for the popular masses of Guerrero. The 1960 social movement tested the PRI regime's willingness to live up to its discursive revolutionary nationalism. Yet the ensuing popular ayuntamientos and the ACG's preparations to enter the 1962 state elections as an opposition political party challenged the democratic foundations of PRI rule. How would the regime handle an independent social movement turned political party that critiqued PRI successes and failures as a ruling party and questioned its self-proclaimed status as sole legitimate "heir" to the 1910 revolution? According to Consuelo Solís Morales, 1960 "produced great lessons for the people... and great hope."[125] The social movement produced more. It created new popular democratic forms that redefined power relations between the ruled and the rulers and demonstrated that victory for "the people" was possible. A year of history had closed, but the history of democratic struggle in Guerrero continued.

3

A Moment of True Democracy

Enough with all of the Caballero Aburtos...we want a government of
the people, for the people.

Genaro Vázquez, 2 December 1962

"Death to Bad Government" represented one of the powerful rallying phrases
of the sustained mass popular mobilizations organized by the ACG in 1960.
By forcing the ouster of Governor Caballero Aburto, ACG militants had managed to temporarily kill bad government and the general's political career.
What the ACG and COP needed to do was sustain the series of fragile civil
society alliances fundamentally based on a collective disdain for Caballero
Aburto and effect lasting political reforms. Deeper, historical longings lurked
beneath the 1960 social movement. For Atoyac cafeticultor José Tellez,
the social justice achievements of the Cuban revolution that he gleaned in 1960
from Radio Rebelde short-wave radio transmissions and student leaders like
Cabañas evinced "a hope that things could change for us, we were tired of so
much exploitation at the hands of *acaparadores* [local loan sharks and market
corerers] and the bank. We were tired of the abuses and assassinations carried
out by regimes such as Caballero Aburto."[1]

That hope for the end of economic exploitation and for enduring democratic
reforms propelled the ACG's transformation from social movement to opposition political party in early 1962. The active, engaged citizenry that had formed
the 1960 anti-Caballero social movement and organized a short-lived experiment of popular municipal rule in 1961 refused to cede their hard-earned democratic initiative and return to the paternalistic politics of the PRI regime. In
the course of social mobilization participating guerrerenses developed a civic
identity that included political and economic dimensions, linking demands for
social justice to political democracy. Rooted in the progressive social reforms
contained in the Mexican Constitution, they sought the reorientation of "an
economy designed for export production, corrupt public officials, and a new
group of latifundistas [landed elite]" toward one that fundamentally prioritized

infrastructural and capital support for the exploited ejido sector in the country-side.[2] To do this, the ACG stipulated, required "saving" the 1910 revolution from "opportunists" and "the new rich" that comprised a "corrupt" PRI.[3]

Such popular attempts to save the Mexican revolution using a constitutional-legal framework implicitly (and increasingly explicitly) asserted that the PRI regime had failed as the "institutionalized revolution." Increasing social inequality and polarization, along with the intensifying of one-party polit-ical rule, challenged the regime's self-portrayal as the democratic and progressive embodiment of the Mexican revolution. High-ranking PRI and military officials responded by directing several civilian massacres, unofficially suspending con-stitutional rights, and closing legal channels for the expression and redress of popular discontent. Guerrero proved no exception. The region formed part of the vanguard of regional popular protest movements that emerged to contest PRI political and economic policies, challenge enduring cacique boss rule at the local-regional levels, and demand fundamental reform. If during the 1940s and early 1950s such protest movements reinforced an emerging and develop-ing postrevolutionary state,[4] by the 1960s they critically interrogated that state's ideological and political justifications for rule. In other words, they demanded that the PRI practice its revolutionary, democratic preaching.

For articulating such demands, popular movements in Guerrero were subjected to increasing levels of state violence—despite playing by constitutional, legal rules. Like the 1960 anti-Caballero movement, the ACG's attempt to win the governor-ship and municipal offices resulted in another massacre and subsequent state terror campaign. As part of the ACG leadership, Vázquez and Cabañas directly experi-enced this linked history of reformist popular mobilization and violent regime responses. Moving within national and regional political milieus marked by a briefly revitalized and resurgent Mexican Left in 1961, both ACG leaders returned to the state in 1962 intent on defeating the regional PRI. The resulting widespread elec-toral fraud, harassment, and violence would force both men to seek solutions using Old Left political tactics. Facing a regime that punished legal forms of pacific dissent with real and/or threatened violence, they would eventually forge an alternative, guerrilla New Left political option with popular support. In that story of popular political radicalization shaped by repeated instances of state terror that crushed "a moment of true democracy," the 1962 state elections form a crucial chapter.[5]

Direct Democracy in 1961

What the federal agents classified as "anarchy" and the "loss of the principle of authority" in the aftermath of the 1960 Chilpancingo massacre, for guerrerenses comprised a sort of democratic spring.[6] Longtime professor and leftist militant Martín Tavira Urióstegui recalled the era as "perhaps the only occasion during which direct democracy functioned in guerrerense lands."[7] In addition to the end of Caballero's gubernatorial term, the release of jailed ACG and COP activists and the popular occupation of more than half of the state's municipal governments seemingly revealed the fruition of democracy at the state and local levels. Yet, the democratic spring proved ephemeral, internally conflicted, and severely limited. While Caballero supporters suffered violent backlashes in ACG bastions like Atoyac and Iguala, cívico leaders faced assassination threats and attempts. For instance, an urban police sublieutenant shot and killed a prominent cívico in an Iguala bar just days after the Chilpancingo massacre.[8] The COP gradually disintegrated as some participating groups, such as the Union of State Employees and the Federation of University Students, reaffirmed their intrinsic links to the PRI party structure while the new interim gubernatorial administration of Arturo Martínez Adame co-opted important COP leaders.[9]

In contrast, ACG members who followed their organization's autonomous stance looked to the capture of municipal governments as a means to consolidate the democratizing impulse forged during the anti-Caballero struggle. Such attempts began prior to the Federal Senate's vote to remove Caballero from the governorship. On 2 January 1961, days after the Chilpancingo massacre, Cabañas helped lead a failed attempt to oust the municipal president of Atoyac, Raúl Galeana Ruiz, for his allegiance to the governor.[10] This singular focus on taking over municipalities largely replaced the type of political work and organizing with campesino, civil, and syndical organizations that characterized ACG efforts during the 1960 social movement. Such abandonment led to a neglect of the broad reformist demands postulated in November 1960 in the sole pursuit of municipal power and divided the ACG (and an increasingly irrelevant COP) at the very moment it required political cohesion to build upon its victory over Caballero.[11] Facing an appointed interim governor pressured by the federal government to undermine the cívico municipalities, the ACG failed to organize an effective defense. Over the course of little more than a year, it eventually succumbed to corruption and internal wrangling over political posts. Democratic experiments in direct popular rule at the municipal level thus disintegrated.

Internally, the ACG also experienced intense political strife previously subsumed by the group's negotiated stance against Caballero. With the Senate's removal of the general from power, the ACG's unifying platform disintegrated and the question of how to proceed divided the leadership council. For López Carmona and other disaffected priístas, the *raison d'être* of the ACG vanished with the Senate's vote to oust the general. To continue its social activism without giving the interim governor a chance, it believed, only produced the "permanent conservation of upheaval."[12] A simple transfer of gubernatorial power from one PRI-designated governor to another proved insufficient for Vázquez and his more radical supporters. Improving the lives of impoverished guerrerenses fundamentally required much more, as they stipulated in a pamphlet dated 10 January 1961: "the fundamental and integral restructuring of ejidos; the economic fortification of municipalities; the disappearance of latifundios; the liquidation of cacicazgos; the abolition of state unemployment and the authentic democratization of all popular organizations."[13] In other words, Vázquez and his radical cadres called for the profound socioeconomic restructuring of everyday guerrerense life—a call that echoed progressive facets of the Mexican Constitution, demanded actual implementation, and signaled nationwide contemporary problems in the Mexican countryside.

The internal division involved competing visions of the PRI regime and its relationship with what journalist Mario Ezcurdia once termed "the principles of the Mexican Revolution," as codified within the 1917 Constitution.[14] The López Carmona faction conceptualized that relationship as organic and firmly legitimate. Refusing to consider the antidemocratic Caballero regime as typical of the PRI's ruling methodology at the national level, the group conceived the praxis of the 1960 social movement in a manner that resembled the colonial-era relationship between loyal (but rebellious) New Spain subjects and the Spanish king. Such popular protest questioned not the legitimacy of the ruling party, but the actions of a few "bad" local functionaries who deserved the reprimands issued by the PRI leadership.[15] The restoration of fair governance marked the political endpoint of the López Carmona faction.

Throughout the anti-Caballero movement, López Carmona resisted the incorporation of activists belonging to leftist political parties—whom he labeled as "habitual protestors"[16]—and continually recast the origins of the ACG as strictly nationalist and priísta. In the weeks leading up to the Chilpancingo massacre, the Mexico City–based ACG president attempted to expel Vázquez and other radical ACG members for supposedly collaborating with PPS members and "harming the popular movement of Guerrero even more than they already have with their [recent] actions."[17] Those recent actions—the statewide tax strike, the permanent civic strike in Chilpancingo, and massive demonstrations—that finally captured the attention of the federal government and national press, frightened López Carmona. Such actions, he and his supporters realized, pointed to a radicalization of the social movement (and its demands) that would not end with the removal of Caballero from power. Given an additional impetus by the Chilpancingo massacre, the ACG entered what government intelligence agents called "a new combative phase" that achieved the election of Vázquez as president and the abandonment of lopezcarmonista politics during the first days of January 1961.[18]

By "new combative phase," the DFS agents referred to the takeover and reorganization of municipal councils and presidencies by the Vázquez-led ACG in the immediate aftermath of the Chilpancingo massacre. In contrast to the lopez-carmonista approach that assumed federal intervention in the face of gubernatorial despotism, the more direct Vazquista methodology tested the willingness of the PRI regime to fulfill its radical rhetoric and revolutionary myths. For the newly elected ACG leader, such tactics represented a prolongation of the 1960 social movement by continuing to instill constitutionally protected civic rights. Vázquez justified such praxis by citing the Mexican Constitution and the progressive legacies of the 1910 revolution (grassroots democracy and municipal autonomy) as the sources of inspiration for the movement. The pre-1961 demand for the removal of Caballero and the post-1961 ACG occupation of municipal governments both signaled the citizens' popular desire to exercise some level of democratic impact on their state's political life. They wanted to politically express themselves beyond the rigid confines of the PRI's theater of electoral spectacle by designating their own local and state authorities. Restoring municipal autonomy after three years of Caballero-imposed officials marked not only an important political victory but also an attempt to institutionalize the democratic effervescence unleashed by the anti-Caballero movement at the municipal level. "Maintaining the spirit of [democratic] struggle," COP leader and PCM militant Dr. Pablo Sandoval Cruz recalled, and raising awareness "that the people needed a space of [political] power through [popularly elected] ayuntamientos" constituted the primary challenge for the ACG from 1961 to 1962.[19]

Such democratic attempts produced mixed results throughout 1961. By the end of the year, few municipal governments remained in the hands of ACG militants and those that survived faced internal and external threats. Yet, the anti-Caballero social movement and the experiment in popular municipal rule drastically shaped Guerrero's sociopolitical topography. Local-regional caciques and PRI leaders faced an active and heterogeneous body politic formed by citizens willing to act in the defense of constitutional rights. During the course of the struggle, democracy in Guerrero acquired social and economic qualities inseparable from its political, usually strictly electoral, definition. Guerrerenses who participated in the 1960 social movement and in the recuperation of popular municipal autonomy decided they wanted to exert control over the conditions of their everyday lives: to expand democracy to the workplace, varying levels of government, voting booths, independent labor unions, and schools, but not necessarily to homes or gender relations.

A stark contrast to the PRI definition of democracy, the guerrerense civic version signaled a need to renegotiate the governing structure formed in the decades that followed the 1910 revolution. More than five years before the

1968 Mexico City student movement, regional civic insurgencies in Guerrero (and similar ones in San Luis Potosí, Morelos, and Puebla) challenged the PRI regime's ability to rule hegemonically, that is, their ability to respond to popular dissidence with nuance and negotiation rather than with violence and terror. Such early 1960s movements, in particular the 1962 Guerrero state elections, foreshadowed the decline of official party revolutionary myths, a beginning of national crises, and the gradual emergence of radicalized New Lefts.

That Old-time Mexican Left

The year 1960 brought Vázquez back to his native state and transformed him into a regional leader with national reach. The formative years he had spent in Mexico City during the 1950s as a student aspiring to become a teacher and lawyer, as an activist struggling for union democracy within the 1958 MRM strikes, and as a representative of Guerrero campesino groups before the national Agrarian Department had provided him vital organizational experience and entry into Mexico's variegated leftist world. He had also learned that constitutional rights required organized popular action to ensure their application—a lesson in full display throughout the 1960 anti-Caballero movement. Yet, soon after his election as president of a newly restructured ACG, Vázquez faced a moment of political uncertainty. In the midst of anticaballerista harassment, popular municipal rule, and the disintegration of the COP, the ACG leader emerged as a sort of municipal coordinator of thirteen popularly elected ayuntamientos. The ACG organized statewide assemblies that collected grievances, created programs that offered solutions to immediate socioeconomic problems, and presented them to a disinterested interim governor.[20] Demands for land, credit, roads, potable water, electrification, schools, medical clinics, and jobs—long-held yet unredeemed promises from the federal government—fell upon deaf ears.[21] In Atoyac, such government apathy led to popular action. Cabañas joined Vázquez and other ACG leaders in a series of land invasions that used "Viva Zapata!" as their battle standard and cast local class warfare as a struggle between the "huarachudos [the sandal-wearers] and the privileged."[22] A decade later that same struggle would reemerge as a guerrilla revolution of the poor.

Yet, for Vázquez such actions suffered from the absence of organization, the absence of a unifying political program, and the absence of political direction. Taking over municipal governments and recuperating stolen land represented important popular conquests. The crucial questions for the ACG leader were how to maintain and reproduce those victories. In other words, how could the lower and middling classes of Guerrero carve out a space of direct democratic power within the state political system in order to exert some level of control over their everyday lives? In search of answers, and facing increased persecution at the hands of a reconsolidated state government, Vázquez returned to the place that had shaped his activist consciousness. Reaching Mexico City in March 1961, he discovered a city of political vibrancy, activity, and division. His travels through the labyrinthine Mexican Left reveal the beginning of complex political fissures neatly encapsulated by Old versus New and an enthusiastically resurgent Cardenista approach to redeeming the Mexican revolution.

What did this acronym-rich leftist world look like in early 1961 after a decade of PRI anticommunist attacks and purges? Two small communist parties with minimal union presence, the PCM and the POCM, and a broadly defined leftist PPS directed by authoritarian Vicente Lombardo Toledano integrated the institutional Old Left. A number of expelled PCM members gathered around José Revueltas to form the Leninist Sparticist League (LLE).[23] Affiliated independent unions like the General Union of Workers and Peasants (UGOCM) and, to a lesser extent, the recently formed Revolutionary Teachers Movement (MRM) led by Othón Salazar served as mass organizations. The former capably mobilized thousands of land-invading campesinos in northern Mexico during the late 1950s (usually against the dictates of PPS leadership), while the latter included a large number of PCM teacher-militants without coming under the party's direct control. In the countryside, socialist campesino students at twenty-nine normales rurales formed an extensive, militant national network still animated by the radical legacies of 1910 and Cardenismo. By 1960, the communist parties had begun a process already initiated during the mid-1950s in Mexico City by striking university students and nonsectarian leftist intellectual forums: a disavowal of the 1910 revolution as the eventual conduit leading to the establishment of socialism and the call for a "new democratic revolution for national liberation."[24] If as vanguard institutions the PCM, POCM, and PPS never delineated the specifics for fomenting a new revolution, individual militants from those parties would subsequently play key roles in the formulation of revolutionary New Lefts throughout the 1960s. The PPS, in particular, was a seedbed for future New Left intellectuals and the first modern guerrilla movement in Cold War Mexico integrated by rural schoolteachers, students, and campesinos: the Popular Guerrilla Group (GPG) led by Arturo Gámiz.[25]

Vázquez entered this diverse leftist world still experiencing the repercussions of the 1958–9 railroad workers' strikes and the Cuban revolution. The former provoked serious internal discussion following the dubious performance of the PCM (and other leftist parties) and President López Mateos's violent response in his use of the army to suppress the strikes in 1959.[26] As a union strike that began by positing wage hike demands and ended in a 100,000-plus national mobilization that sought union democratization and autonomy, the results of the railroad workers' strikes stimulated debates regarding the political role of the PCM (and the PPS to a lesser extent). Unable to shed the "labor unity" fetishism of the 1940s and trapped within a historical teleology obsessed with discovering a section of the national bourgeoisie capable of carrying through a national-democratic revolution, the PCM, according to critics like José Revueltas, failed to act as a revolutionary vanguard party.[27] Worse yet, the party's infamous dogmatism—"a struggle between those that simply recite Marxism versus those who attempt to comprehend and realize [Marxism]"—contributed to the elaboration of rigid theory that failed to reconcile "with the particularities of the Mexican environment."[28] Such misunderstanding led not only to a mishandling of the railroad workers' strike, but also to flawed analyses of other contemporary social movements such as the land invasions that rocked northern Mexico from 1958 to 1962 and the civic insurgencies in Guerrero and San Luis Potosí. Despite adopting a "new democratic revolution for national liberation" thesis at the 1960 Thirteenth Congress that signaled a rupture with previously held Browderist and popular front dogma, the PCM continually failed to realize that power and politics were not the exclusive domains of the party and/or state.[29] The "new revolution" would arrive from elsewhere.

Domestically, the railroad workers' strikes exposed the inability of the PCM to make the "new revolution," painfully exposing the party's theoretical misperceptions and practical unpreparedness. On a continental level, the 1959 Cuban revolution fulfilled a similar revelatory function in relation to Latin American Communist parties.[30] For a generation of young leftists who had witnessed the violent suppression of brief democratic springs by authoritarian states during the early 1950s, and their communist parties' continual toeing of a nonconfrontational muscovite line that stressed electoral participation,[31] the revolution led by Fidel Castro seemingly provided a new path for radical social transformation; a "new" tactic of rural guerrilla warfare; a "new" revolutionary protagonist in the form of the peasantry; a "new" battleground in the countryside; and a "new," urgent recasting of the Marxist dialectic that believed armed insurrection created the "objective and subjective conditions favorable to revolution."[32] Revolution appeared as a tantalizing, realizable goal in contrast to communist parties' postwar efforts to achieve equitable economic development and social democratization in alliance with the ever-illusory nationalist-democratic bourgeoisies in the face of state repression. Latin America's various New Lefts thus emerged from a historical context characterized by violently frustrated social democratic aspirations, repressive authoritarian regimes, emergent countercultural practices,[33] and a Caribbean revolution that "infused the oppressed of Latin America with the hope and confidence for a better future."[34]

Geographical context, of course, shaped the impact, meanings, and popular reception of the Cuban revolution. In that sense, there were many Cuban revolutions. The utopian and radical messages gleaned from Radio Rebelde by aspiring teachers crowded round a shortwave radio in Ayotzinapa, Guerrero, or by university students in Morelia, Michoacán, dramatically contrasted with the counterinsurgent lessons gleaned by US military specialists at Panama's School of the Americas.[35] In Mexico the island revolution, at least initially prior to Castro's definition of the revolution as Marxist-Leninist, provided a unifying impulse under the banner of internationalism, nonalignment, anti-imperialism, and revolutionary redemption. Moved by the prospect of agrarian reform in Cuba and the revolution's anti-imperial implications (seen, for instance, in the nationalization of key industries), former president Lázaro Cárdenas convened the Conference for National Sovereignty, Emancipation, and Peace in March 1961 in Mexico City.[36] For several days sixteen Latin American delegations, a number of national leftist and progressive organizations, and representatives from the Soviet Union, China, and several African countries discussed US imperialism, proposed enacting agrarian reform programs and strengthening labor unions, called for the nationalization of natural resources, and denounced Third World poverty. Tagged as "subversive" and "antipatriotic" by the mainstream Mexican press, this conference produced a final document that stressed the importance of defending the Cuban revolution and demonstrating solidarity with the rebellious island.[37] "Cuba," Cárdenas would declare after the Bay of Pigs fiasco, "is not alone."[38]

The conference fleetingly unified the broader Mexican Left—PCM, PPS, POCM, progressive activists, Cardenistas, excommunicated and/or "heretical" Marxists, and independent socialists. Cuba's revolution transformed the achievements and principles of the Mexican revolution "into objects of social reflection and ideological contention."[39] Agrarian reform and the nationalization of industries in Cuba both invited comparison with early twentieth-century Mexico and prompted domestic debates on the progress of the Mexican revolution after decades of "institutionalization." Such debate forced President López Mateos to famously declare in July 1960 that his government "was extreme left within the Constitution."[40] For Mexican leftists like Cárdenas, still beholden and faithful to the progressive discourses of the 1910 revolution, Cuban achievements exposed Mexican failures. In contrast to the PCM's call for an ambiguous "new revolution" in the aftermath of the 1958–9 national strikes, Cárdenas exhorted the need for self-criticism and introspection in order to put the revolution back on track.[41] In sum, the former president called for redemption. The Conference for National Sovereignty, Emancipation, and Peace, limited and circumscribed as it was by a media blackout, produced the blueprint for how to achieve that elusive redemption of the Mexican revolution. Five months later, during the first days of August 1961, the Movement of National Liberation (MLN) emerged under the tutelage and leadership of Cárdenas.

Having reached Mexico City in March 1961, Vázquez participated in Cárdenas-led attempts to rectify and save the revolution. As representatives of the ACG, both he and Blas Vergara attended the Conference for National Sovereignty, Emancipation, and Peace.[42] At the conference Vázquez discovered that what was rotten in Guerrero was rotten in Mexico, much of Latin America, and the rest of the Third World. Final conference resolutions that stated political independence was impossible without economic emancipation resembled the definition of democracy forged in the course of the anti-Caballero struggle in 1960 Guerrero. The call for anti-imperialist struggle and the positing of a revolutionary Cuban exemplar resonated with guerrerense experiences of popular struggle during the 1950s against multinational corporations based in Acapulco. Ideas of US imperialism embedded in the specific guerrerense and Mexican contexts and the centrality of anti-imperialism as the path to national self-determination would later comprise key components of the ACG and ACNR political imaginaries. In 1961, particularly after the failed Bay of Pigs invasion that April, such ideas saturated the leftist political contexts inhabited by Vázquez.[43] Anti-imperialism, represented most immediately by the Cuban revolution, capably unified a fractured and disarrayed Mexican Left.

The civic leader spent the rest of 1961 between Mexico City and Guerrero. As Cárdenas, intellectuals from the Círculo de Estudios Mexicanos (CEM), PPS, PCM, and PRI militants worked to found the MLN that summer, Vázquez participated in several ACG protests.[44] Now permanently in the sights of government intelligence agencies, he traveled to Chilpancingo in June to help organize a counterdemonstration scheduled for the ACG bastion of Iguala. With the help of other leftist militants, the cívicos sought to counteract a PRI "political rally that stressed unity with the President of the Republic and the Mexican Revolution." Vázquez "stayed in Chilpancingo all day and during the night continued to roam the University... accompanied by a lone schoolteacher," the DFS memo concluded.[45] Upset with the interim's governor "lenient" treatment of ACG members in the aftermath of the Chilpancingo massacre, the DFS actively tracked the man they labeled a "communist agitator" as he traveled to and from Mexico City and Guerrero.[46]

During his travels throughout 1961, Vázquez prominently displayed the political lessons he had learned as a student and young teacher participating in the teacher union struggles of the late 1950s and as a cívico leader in 1960 Guerrero: the value of nonsectarian political positions and the importance of forging political coalitions under key unifying demands. Such lessons most likely attracted him to the MLN. While sources disagree over his presence at the August 1961 founding of the organization (indeed, MLN documents do not list Vázquez or the ACG), the MLN's unification of progressive groups under the banner of anti-imperialism, defense of national sovereignty, democratization of the nation, and redemption of the Mexican revolution—not to mention the weighty figure of Cárdenas—proved alluring and hopeful. Despite its seemingly subversive name, considering an international context marked by radical national liberation movements, the MLN represented "an agglutinating organism" composed of various social movements and political interests, largely integrated by middle-class leftist urbanites and with a limited presence in the countryside.[47] The MLN couched its constitutionally based demands within the discourse of revolutionary nationalism and called for their actual application. To achieve national liberation they postulated the following: the proactive participation of the state in economic areas to ensure a more equitable model of capital accumulation; agrarian reform accompanied by serious modifications to constitutional Article 27 and the Agrarian code; the right of workers and peasants to form independent and democratic labor unions; the release of political prisoners and derogation of Article 145; the implementation of laws that strictly regulated foreign investment; and the passing of laws that ensured the participation of opposition political parties in all elections.[48]

The profound influence of previous popular movements is evident in the political program of the MLN. Populated by participants in the Jaramillista uprisings, the labor strikes of the late 1940s, General Miguel Henríquez's 1952 presidential campaign, and the massive student, teacher, telegraph, electrical, and railroad workers movements of 1956–60, the MLN drew from the political imaginaries of movements that legally challenged the PRI regime over the "true" nature and purpose of the Mexican revolution.[49] Instances of state repression had not yet fully exhausted the widely held belief among the majority of progressives and leftists that the postrevolutionary state and the 1917 Constitution still represented the vehicle by which to achieve a more just and equitable society. In extolling the Cuban example, Cárdenas emphasized the inadequacy of armed struggle in Mexico "to improve the living situation of our people" in the days that followed the Conference for National Sovereignty, Emancipation, and Peace. At the MLN founding conference, the former president reaffirmed that "[the MLN] is a licit organization, that does not undermine the principles established in the Constitution. It will be an organization that will contribute to the realization of the postulates of the Mexican Revolution, consecrated in our political Constitution."[50] In other words, Mexico, unlike revolutionary Cuba, already possessed a revolution structurally capable of improving the lot of Mexico's impoverished masses. Mexico required not armed struggle but political will and legal popular mobilizations with the aim of pressuring the PRI regime.

Cárdenas's reemergence and the foundation of the MLN confirmed for Vázquez the legitimacy of the 1960 anti-Caballero movement in relation to the movement's motives, demands, and civil disobedience tactics. As a constitutionally based movement that sought the removal from the governorship of a corrupt, alleged "betrayer" of the Mexican revolution and Constitution, the 1960 civic insurgency paralleled the MLN in their respective desires to reorient the "institutionalized revolution." The political paths of Vázquez and Cárdenas thus intersected. In November 1961, the former president helped create a National Union of Land Solicitors (UNST), designed to aid campesinos through the bureaucratic labyrinths of federal agrarian offices, and appointed Vázquez as secretary general.[51] The ACG now possessed a stable organizational and political link to Guerrero and national landless and smallholding campesinos. Upon his return to Guerrero at the end of 1961, ready to organize "a fabulous reception" for Cárdenas in Iguala, the ACG leader briefly stopped in the state of Morelos. At a moment of personal political clarity and confidence, Vázquez met with Rubén Jaramillo, a man who possessed extensive experience in dealing with the PRI regime.[52] For two decades, Jaramillo had used strikes, guerrilla warfare, the formation of an oppositional political party, and land invasions to force the regime to live up to its revolutionary rhetoric. For two decades he had faced state terror and repression. While the two men failed to "arrange coordinated political actions," the brutal assassination of Jaramillo, his wife, and three sons by the Mexican army six months later was to profoundly affect Vázquez and a generation of future guerrillas.[53]

In contrast to Vázquez's travels within the upper echelons of the Mexican Left, Cabañas moved primarily within national student networks characterized by rural social activism, elastic leftist ideologies, and community engagement. A speaker at an April 1961 gathering of rural socialist students in Michoacán best summarized the political philosophy and praxis of these student-activists: "At the present hour organized students should possess the following thinking: WORK, STUDY, and ORGANIZE to rescue our Revolution and unite it with other American attempts to establish democracy, peace, and progress."[54] The speaker also identified the Cuban revolution as a motivating factor for students and the Mexican Left. Like the MLN, progressive and leftist student organizations linked anti-imperialism and solidarity with Cuba to domestic efforts to "rescue" the Mexican revolution. Such efforts occurred within a legalistic constitutional framework that placed public pressure on the López Mateos presidency to withstand US diplomatic pressure to isolate Cuba and to "defend the [social and political] conquests achieved by the Mexican people."[55] Within such networks, student identity required an active social component that combined demands for educational reforms with broader social problems that extended beyond the classroom. For students studying in normales rurales this component practically became a duty. As sons and daughters of campesinos, rural normalista students "studied for the peasantry" and searched for radical solutions to resolve the everyday issues faced by peasants.[56] As historian Tanalís Padilla notes, schools like Ayotzinapa constituted spaces of political radicalism where the legacies of 1910 and the socialist education policies of the Cárdenas 1930s remained alive and practiced.[57]

After the 1960 anti-Caballero movement, Cabañas divided his time between studies at Ayotzinapa, political organizing in Atoyac (at times for the MLN), and travels throughout the country as leader of various Guerrero student organizations.[58] By October 1961 he had been elected as the Secretary General of the Federation of Socialist Campesino Students of Mexico (FECSM), a national organization that connected students across twenty-nine normales rurales. A fellow rural schoolteacher trainee and subsequent guerrilla comrade described Cabañas's presidential tenure at FECSM as "two of the best years ever experienced by the normales."[59] As part of his leadership duties, the guerrerense student traveled widely and began establishing organizational and personal links throughout the country. Certain links, like befriending fellow leftist student activists in Chihuahua (Arturo Gámiz), Durango (Miguel Quiñónez), Michoacán (José Luis Martínez Pérez) and Veracruz, proved crucial in later years when Cabañas fled to the Atoyac mountains with insurrectionary designs.[60] Normalista students from Michoacán like Modesto Trujillo and Luis León Mendiola would later join Cabañas's guerrilla project. The PCM also provided the aspiring rural schoolteacher with a national network and experience in community organizing. Cabañas joined the youth wing of the Communist Party (JCM) some time in 1959.[61]

By the end of 1961, Cabañas had traveled widely within a national rural student network animated by US aggressions against the Cuban revolution and was gradually radicalized by both increasing domestic levels of repression and political polarization provoked by an emergent anticommunist movement. DFS agents tracked his movements on various trips to Mexico City, Tamaulipas, and throughout Guerrero and kept tabs on his interactions with Puebla students after a university reform movement ended with violent right-wing attacks and state violence.[62] From the national capital, the student leader collected grievances and complaints from specific normales that ranged from demands for the destitution of unqualified school authorities to broader structural issues related to rural public education.[63] Cabañas also participated in national student congresses. At the congress of the National Federation of Technical Students in Tamaulipas he publicly discussed "student conflicts with the Right and the clergy, and declared that rural students are socialists."[64] Subsequent congresses in Atoyac and Iguala, in December 1961 and February 1962, respectively, revealed the shared political goals of progressive student organizations, the MLN, and an ACG reorganizing itself as a political party. They wanted to "save" the Mexican revolution, banish regional political-economic boss rule, resist an "imperialism that destroys national sovereignty," and prevent the undemocratic imposition of so-called elected PRI officials.[65] The attempt to implement these goals in Guerrero began in the early months of 1962.

The Guerrero State Elections of 1962

Vázquez returned to his home state at the end of 1961 to discover a coastal Guerrero both decimated by natural disasters and increasingly militarized. Hurricane Tara had wreaked havoc in the Costa Grande in November, flooding agricultural lands and creating "a precarious economic situation."[66] Earlier in September a peasant uprising had rallied under the banner of "justice for the poor," led by dissident general and revolutionary veteran Celestino Gasca, and had erupted throughout various Mexican regions, including the Costa Grande municipality of La Unión.[67] While the Mexican military quickly and violently repressed the rebels in La Unión, it expanded its counterinsurgency operations to target nonviolent dissidents belonging to the ACG and leftist political parties. From the simulated execution of ACG leader Antonio Sotelo Pérez in San Luis San Pedro to the incarceration of nearly 100 persons, the short-lived Gasca rebellion provided an excuse to target and silence opposition to regional PRI governments.[68] In San Luis Potosí, a state that experienced a civic insurgency analogous to the ACG anti-Caballero movement in 1959–60, state agents arrested civic leader Dr. Salvador Nava and accused him of belonging to the Gasca rebellion. DFS internal memos asserted that in a context where "popular opinion in the relation to the PRI is that the Party has not fulfilled in satisfactory fashion its obligations [to the citizenry]," the arrest of Nava and supporters "should be handled by the Authorities with an iron fist to prevent Navismo from recuperating strength."[69] The iron fist would increasingly become the PRI regime's option of choice in dealing with social dissidents.

In the midst of militarization and targeted repression, Vázquez sought to refashion the ACG into an oppositional political party aimed at achieving political power via electoral means. The year-long counteroffensive waged against the popular municipal governments by the PRI and the handpicked interim governor Martínez Adame highlighted the insufficiency and fragility of the ACG's previous strategy in the aftermath of the 1960 anti-Caballero movement. Moreover, rumors about the PRI's gubernatorial candidate for the upcoming state elections threatened popular gains made since 1960. Dr. Raymundo Abarca Alarcón, an obscure military doctor from Iguala, enjoyed the complete support of the state's traditional caciques—the same brokers of political and economic power angered previously by General Caballero Aburto and his decision to support PRI-allied agricultural unions prior to his removal. With the 1962 elections, caciques from throughout the state saw an opportunity to close ranks and reinstall a particularly undemocratic form of ruling. They possessed a powerful ally, the man who designated Abarca Alarcón as the PRI candidate: Donato Miranda

Fonseca, power broker from Chilapa (Centro region), secretary to President López Mateos, and aspiring contender for the presidency.[70]

ACG leaders and members approached the 1962 state elections both optimistic of the democratic possibilities and wary of possible state retribution. Guerrero's recent history provided dramatic examples of both possible outcomes. Vázquez most vividly represented the seemingly irreconcilable duality that would characterize the ACG's historical trajectory as opposition political party. While his participation with the MLN evidenced a willingness to work within the confines of the postrevolutionary state and a belief in Cardenista revolutionary nationalism, his experience with the 1960 Chilpancingo massacre had given him pause as to the democratic capacity of the PRI regime. His late 1961 meetings with two emblematic political figures further highlight the tension. In mid-December, he helped organize a public reception in Iguala for Cárdenas, whom Vázquez described as the "noble exponent of the true Mexican Revolution."[71] That same month, the ACG president also met with Morelos peasant leader Jaramillo. Considering his personal history (as Zapatista fighter, sugar cooperative leader, recurring guerrilla chieftain, gubernatorial candidate, PCM member, and land invasion organizer), Jaramillo may have warned Vázquez not to trust the Janus-faced PRI regime.[72] An ACG editorial published in an Acapulco newspaper perhaps best captures the uneasy tension: "We do not discard the possibility that we will now suffer reprisals but as ACG members we are prepared to demonstrate that, with the Mexican Constitution in hand, we work within the Law."[73]

The attempt to institutionalize the popular democratic power unleashed in 1960 beyond the restrictive political confines of the PRI began in February 1962. During two separate meetings in coastal Atoyac and the Tierra Caliente city of Tlapehuala, the ACG agreed to enter the upcoming state election and contend for a variety of municipal and delegation posts.[74] The governorship, too, emerged as an electoral target. Drawing from their bastions of support in the Costa Grande and Tierra Caliente, the reconstituted ACG began to exhibit a markedly class character expressed within a rural cultural idiom that pitted the rich against the poor. While still advocating a popular-front strategy parallel to the MLN, the group included members from regions that had experienced turmoil, class polarization, and radicalization during the post-1960 era of popular municipal rule. ACG militants from Atoyac, for instance, participated in land invasions during 1961 that included the participation of both Vázquez and Cabañas. The participation of the PPS and Frente Zapatista—an organization comprising Zapatista veterans of the 1910 revolution—also demonstrated a leftward shift in political demands, if not in their decision to participate in the electoral process. One particular Frente Zapatista activist, its leader José María Suárez Tellez, possessed a long personal history of agrarian and radical struggles in and out of the labyrinthine PRI structure.[75]

Vázquez publicly expressed the intentions of the ACG in early March by stating, in the words of a DFS agent, "that his organization from now on demands the definitive purging of the PRI's caudillo methods and invites the pueblo to freely express their demands in an upcoming ACG congress in Iguala." Subsequent declarations reported in the state press announced that the upcoming Iguala congress "would demonstrate to the PRI that the ACG was the true representative of the people and thus the voice of the masses."[76] Such statements marked a profound political shift in the discourse of the ACG. Political and socioeconomic criticisms—first seen in the latter stages of the 1960 social movement—had moved beyond personal figures (such as General Caballero) to become systemic critiques. Thus, for the duration of the 1962 elections, the ACG placed the PRI on trial for, in its words, "betraying" the Mexican revolution and Constitution. A vast "movement of the masses, a social movement throughout the state of Guerrero" would serve as critical jury.[77]

The ACG publicly presented its critique and proposed solutions at a March 11 rally in the historic city of Iguala. Aided by university student and agrarian leaders, Vázquez unveiled a twenty-two-point program that meshed a refashioned Cardenismo with local legacies of struggle that involved issues of grass-roots patriarchal democracy and campesino control over agricultural production. Exhibiting recent ideological influences on ACG leaders, the program reads like a local-regional version of the MLN's national program, minus the calls for anti-imperialist struggle. Like the MLN program, the ACG electoral platform stipulated demands already enshrined within the Mexican Constitution, yet largely ignored or distorted by government officials, and called for their actual application. Redemption, not revolution, thus comprised the subtext of the lengthy program. Working within a constitutional framework, the ACG forcefully identified the symptoms of a malady that threatened to consume the Mexican revolution as a contested political project and ideal.[78]

In contrast to the MLN program, the ACG platform managed to link national problems with local grievances.[79] In the realm of agriculture, demands for the industrialization and cooperativization of agricultural production, and the breakup of large landholdings, signaled the chronic difficulties faced by small and middling copra and coffee producers in coastal Guerrero. Such demands harkened back to campesino efforts during the 1950s to organize independent rural unions and control their crops' multistage production process as an attempt to circumvent the economic hegemony of the regional commercial bourgeoisie. In calling for land redistribution and campesino control over production, the ACG both highlighted the failings of state-led agrarian reform since the late 1930s and, like the Jaramillistas in Morelos, prefigured the massive campesino mobilizations that shook Mexico during the 1970s—campesinos moved by "issues of production, self-management, autonomy, and democracy."[80] Such demands demonstrated a rural willingness and desire to redefine a PRI-led capitalist modernization program that used the countryside as an exploited subsidizer of urban development and industrialization. They wanted what Cárdenas had promised long ago during his presidential campaign: "Mexican agriculture will be modernized [along collective lines]. This modernization will also achieve a more just and equal nation. Campesinos will be the principal beneficiaries of economic development, with an increased standard of living."[81]

Despite the subsequent exclusionary modernization programs enacted by Cárdenas's successors, such promises and hope endured in the Guerrero countryside.[82] Intertwined notions of citizenship and local democracy similarly persisted. With the 1960 anti-Caballero movement freshly in the background, a movement that had witnessed Guerrero men and women alternately inhabiting and refashioning citizenship throughout the course of social struggle, the 1962 ACG program called for "the democratization of the political system of the Ejido, the Municipality, the District, the State, and the Nation."[83] As presented by the ACG, democracy was redefined from an amorphous theory limited to the high chambers of national government to a practiced form of governance meaningful in the everyday lives of Guerrero's communities—a form of governance that refused to recognize barriers between the political, the social, and the economic realms. Indeed, citing the ejido as the first social level targeted for democratization evidenced the inseparability of political participation and economic production.[84]

Yet, starting with the ejido simultaneously signals the radicalism of the ACG proposition and its conservative preservation of a patriarchal rural order. Ejido-based agrarian reform enacted during the 1930s and thereafter had depended upon the maintenance of patriarchal campesino households structured by a sexual division of labor that assigned peasant women to unrecognized, unpaid domestic labor—labor that crucially subsidized and made possible an exploited Mexican countryside after 1940. The contours of democracy and citizenship for women with the ACG project thus proved ambiguous. Despite the widespread, fundamental role of women within the movement, the ACG did not seek to radically undermine traditional gender roles. Nationally, women's mobilizations and struggles over decades had succeeded in obtaining the right to vote in national elections in 1953 without disrupting the gendered codes of citizenship that upheld male authority and tended to view women as auxiliary political helpmeets.[85] The ACG failed to overcome such democratic shortcomings. Nonetheless, women played crucial roles in the 1962 electoral campaign. The role of caregiver often gave way to that of political organizer or local ACG leader. During the 1962 elections, for instance, Iguala would become a "politicized community," an ACG bastion, only because "young and old women…actively and passionately participated" in the struggle.[86] As supporters and voters of an opposition political party, their transgression proved more subversive than that of their male counterparts in the eyes of the PRI regime.[87] They risked becoming Malinches, that particularly Mexican gendered synonym for treason.

Treason. Communists. Poor sandal-wearers. Insane. Such pejorative labels graced the pages of local and regional newspapers as the ACG began a whistle-stop campaign tour throughout Guerrero after presenting its program in Iguala. From March 1962 until its state congress in August, Vázquez, Cabañas, and the ACG leadership organized a series of public demonstrations and protests to save the Mexican revolution and Constitution by voting the corrupted PRI out of state and local offices. As expressed in an ACG leaflet: "in the upcoming Guerrero elections, citizens will elect hombres completely committed to popular interests. We will never again permit the betrayal of our people's heroic struggle. We repudiate electoral fraud and will end the imposition of outside party officials."[88] At meetings that drew anywhere between hundreds and thousands of participants (numbers depend on the reporting source, either DFS agents or ACG militants), ACG orators lambasted the PRI as corrupt, expressed support for revolutionary Cuba, and presented the twenty-two-point program—all the while affirming their commitment to the electoral process and President López Mateos who publicly guaranteed safety for the ACG.[89] By May, DFS agents described the ACG as a "very strong organization" responsible for "the most significant outbreaks of agitation in the state."[90]

Viewing the opposition party through the lens of a global Cold War that tended to equate all dissidence with the spreading specter of communism, government agents who followed ACG leaders focused on public expressions of support for Cuba, socialism, and communism.[91] For instance, at a July gathering in Acapulco, a DFS agent translated the criticisms voiced by MLN leader Braulio Maldonado against large landowners, North American capitalism, and the Catholic Church as "a clear provocation to perturb social order against governmental systems."[92] For the PRI regime, dissidence signified communism and, hence, subversion. Such state-centered, national-security-oriented perspectives generally led to a disavowal of historical and structural factors that influenced the ACG's emergence. Rather, DFS analysts claimed the opposition party represented only the "instrument" of PPS socialists and "renowned" communists.[93] US consulate officials later repeated that claim, positing the ACG as a municipal-level political manifestation of the "communist inspired" MLN.[94]

During the summer months of 1962 the ACG vividly displayed the social capital it had gained as a leading anti-Caballero organization two years earlier. Various unions, municipal presidents, ejidal commissaries, and other local officials joined the campaign as the ACG prepared for the election.[95] The party proposed candidates for the position of *regidor* in seventy municipalities and for *diputado* in all of Guerrero's electoral districts.[96] At its second statewide congress in Chilpancingo on 1 August 1962, the ACG elected its candidate for governor, José María Tellez Suárez, after vociferous internal debate. Upon accepting the nomination, Tellez Suárez remarked, "they called ACG members crazy when we organized against Caballero Aburto and yet the movement succeeded in defeating him. [Despite the typical PRI electoral fraud tactics] justice will take us to victory."[97] To begin the official gubernatorial campaign, the ACG chose a small, yet symbolic town near Iguala. At Ixcateopan, the supposed burial place of the last Aztec emperor Cuauhtémoc,[98] Vázquez extolled the virtues of Tellez Suárez while accusing ex-president Aleman of betraying the Mexican revolution by allying himself with bankers, the "political clergy, and Yankee imperialism." A similar theme of betrayal and redemption marked the subsequent speech given by ACG Tierra Caliente leader Blas Vergara as he called for campesino unity to prevent "the Revolution from falling into the hands of opportunists." Cabañas, a prominent national student leader and head of the ACG's Youth Action committee, followed by decrying the exercising of PRI violence against a rural teachers training school in Chiapas.[99] Alluding to the nationalist symbolism of Cuauhtémoc's alleged grave, Suárez Tellez provided the conclusion: "We prefer to sink into the shadows of not-being rather than ignominiously lose our inalienable right to elect our governing officials."[100]

Vázquez and Cabañas collaborated closely from the August congress until the elections that took place on 2 December 1962 as they, Suárez Tellez, and the ACG traveled the state eliciting popular support.[101] Significantly, the campaign assumed an explicitly gendered and regionally specific class tone as the ACG posited itself as the party of the "humble people" struggling against a PRI constituted by "the perfumed class" and supported "by uptight wealthy ladies."[102] In Iguala and the surrounding communities, Vázquez organized study circles in which ACG militants, many of them schoolteachers, read and explained texts like *The ABC of Socialism* to the party's rural supporters. As a participant, Concepción Solís Morales remembered the goal of the study circles: "[To teach campesino communities] that the poor were not born poor because God willed it…they were born poor because they formed part of an exploited peasant class…there was a better, more just way to live."[103] In September ACG leaders defined that better, more just way in front of an Iguala rally. The party organized and struggled "for a true democracy that highlights and resolves the economic problems of the humble people and the implementation of true social justice."[104]

In late October at another Iguala assembly, Suárez Tellez delineated the contours of class struggle embedded in the elections: "the struggle now is not between me and Dr. Abarca but rather between the poor and the rich." On election day, the ACG gubernatorial candidate told the people of Teloloapan that "he was the candidate of the people, that is to say, of the poor, of the campesinos and all workers in general that are tired of suffering hunger and misery caused by bad government officials who only seek to enrich themselves."[105] Such criticisms tended to exclude the national president, López Mateos. Vázquez and Suárez Tellez resorted to the proven formula of representing the president as tricked and betrayed by his corrupt underlings while assuring ACG supporters that López Mateos guaranteed a fair and free election. Such reassurances and the overwhelming level of popular support displayed throughout the campaign generated significant confidence within ACG ranks. Just weeks before the election, Vázquez told an Iguala newspaper, "We know we will win the elections because the people are with us. From the 25th [of November] we will not leave Chilpancingo until six years later." Even on the night of the elections, the ACG president predicted an overwhelming victory.[106]

A time-tested PRI strategy of electoral fraud allegedly impeded an ACG victory. PRI officials controlled polling booths throughout the state and frequently manipulated votes cast (changing ACG to PRI votes) in municipalities considered bastions of opposition political influence. ACG militant Antonio Sotelo Pérez recalled how military and state police units often accompanied voting officials, harassing and intimidating voters. Votes mysteriously cast by the deceased and newborns repeatedly sided with the PRI in the Costa Grande municipality of Tecpan de Galeana.[107] An ACG pamphlet distributed a couple of weeks after election day described additional PRI tactics: the use of hired gunslingers to discourage campesinos from voting, the noncounting of votes cast for the ACG, and the payment of 15 pesos by caciques to campesinos to vote for the PRI.[108] Such tactics failed to stop the ACG's political proselytizing. Despite the unfavorable results, the party continued to organize and hold public rallies after election day to peacefully challenge the electoral fraud. A number of municipalities that refused to recognize the 2 December results as legitimate remained in local government buildings, preventing the transfer of political power to PRI officials.[109]

State repression began in earnest after the disputed election results, marking a shift in regime tactics used against the ACG. Previous attacks against the opposition party during the campaign had been largely limited to PRI-sponsored yellow (and red-baiting) journalism, constant vigilance by government spies, and harassment. Acapulco did witness a brief shoot-out in late October when ACG member Paula Aviles called the supporters of PRI candidates Abarca Alarcon and Ricardo Morlet Sutter (for municipal president) "homosexuals."[110] Immediately after the results were announced, regime security forces began to target ACG leadership and detain scores of party militants. On 5 December two militants claimed the state police officers "kidnapped them," eventually jailing them in Chilpancingo.[111] Days later the state justice department issued an arrest warrant for Vázquez and others. DFS agents described the motive behind the arrest warrants as "the voicing of criticism against the PRI, Dr. Raymundo [sic]

Abarca Alarcon, and Donato Miranda Fonseca."[112] Regime tolerance for critical political organizing and public criticism had ended.

As the ACG struggled to reorganize and marshal protests amid state persecution, military and state police units mobilized throughout the state to occupy municipal palaces, detain protestors, and encircle dissident communities in the Costa Grande and Tierra Caliente. The military thwarted attempts to capture municipal palaces in strongholds of support such as Tecpan de Galeana, Acapulco, and Iguala. Throughout the last week of December, Vázquez and Iguala ACG leader Israel Salmerón dispatched telegrams to President López Mateos urgently protesting the military occupation of municipal palaces as constitutional violations that "sowed terror" and pitted "the army versus the people" at the behest of local caciques.[113] Vázquez questioned such acts, including the continued persecution of ACG members by state police officers, as unnecessary since "the [ACG] has always acted within the Law." At a protest in Iguala on 30 December, the ACG president reasserted the organization's legality: "the ACG will continue the struggle as always respecting the laws and the words of the President of the Republic."[114]

"The People Do Not Forget"

Unlike the legalistic focus and constitutional adherence of the ACG, the PRI regime viewed the opposition political party through the lens of national security and political stability. Popular protest would not dictate the resolution of the conflict as it had done at the end of 1960. On 30 December 1962 state police officers and soldiers opened fire on a large ACG crowd in Iguala led by Vázquez that had organized a "permanent sit-in" in front of the municipal palace. As the crowd commemorated the 1960 Chilpancingo massacre and organized to prevent the newly "elected" PRI candidates from assuming their posts in the municipal palace, shots rang out, killing seven and injuring twenty-three.[115] After years of state persecution and harassment, some ACG members, including Vázquez, carried firearms for protection and responded with gunfire. One police officer died, shot down either by his fellow officers or by ACG gunfire. Though Vázquez managed to escape, government officials subsequently charged him with the death of the police officer *in absentia*. The ACG president would spend the next several years constantly on the move to avoid state and federal law enforcement officials.

Both internal DFS investigations and the outgoing governor blamed the ACG for provoking the attack. DFS accounts claimed that the gunfire began when state police attempted to frisk ACG members carrying weapons. Refusing to be frisked, the ACG members allegedly opened fire first and the police responded in kind.[116] Such an improbable scenario flew in the face of three years of peaceful and legal ACG political activity. While at least 156 ACG members sat in jails, some wounded by gunshots (at least one died in custody),[117] Governor Adame Martínez misleadingly announced in his final gubernatorial report that "a group of agitators, with the sole purpose of disturbing public order, attempted to take over the municipal palace of Iguala...provoking and attacking the police who repelled the aggression."[118] A memorandum produced by the US Embassy characterized the massacre "as a communist inspired attack against the local authority." Concerned with the increasing political strength of the "communist controlled MLN" at the national level from an American perspective, its author argued that the "Iguala incident"

> has, however, been favorable to our interests here, as it is a clear indica-
> tion that the government, using the combined strength of the Army,
> the Attorney General's office, and state and municipal authorities,
> is prepared to engage in a carefully planned operation to thwart the
> Cardenistas and the MLN.[119]

Such analysis presciently anticipated the type of counterdissidence and counterinsurgency campaigns organized by the PRI in Guerrero for the next fifteen years and, intermittently, for the next three decades. Soldiers left their barracks to confront so-called "agitators" and patrol the state in early 1963 and they have yet to return.[120]

In contrast to official versions, rural communities and working-class neighborhoods throughout Guerrero remembered the Iguala massacre as yet another violent act perpetrated by a governing regime that refused to abide by its own democratic and constitutional rules. An ACG pamphlet distributed in late January 1963 protested post-massacre repressive tactics enacted against its militants, including widespread torture, illegal detentions, and warrantless searches of residences. The pamphlet also warned of a certain amorphous—yet very real—level of popular political radicalization: "The People do not forget, nor will it allow itself to be humiliated."[121] To prevent more massacres and humiliation, Vázquez and Cabañas would traverse the well-worn paths of the Mexican Old Left in search of new political routes that promised justice and revolutionary redemption.

4

Retreading Old Paths, Forging New Routes

> All we asked the government for was justice. We did so through peti-
> tions. Nothing provided resolution. On the contrary, the government
> threw the *federales* at us to finish us off.
>
> "Ignacio," ACNR campesino guerrilla, July 1971

Just days before he died in early 1972, Vázquez responded to leftist newspaper editorials that criticized his use of violence as a means of inducing social
change: "the violence has been imposed upon us by the executioners that govern and pillage our people, that murder our people when they protest or defend
themselves. They are the ones that have made violence into a 'magic formula' [of
revolution]."[1] Soon thereafter, from the mountains of Atoyac, the guerrilla group
led by Cabañas explained its motivations for ambushing an army patrol: "the
federal army has committed various illegal acts, crimes... in particular against
campesinos... characterized by a great number of dead, disappeared, kidnapped,
tortured, and illegally detained persons. We will respond with an eye for an eye
and a tooth for a tooth!"[2] For both Vázquez and Cabañas, violence and direct
confrontation with the PRI regime represented the only viable path for social
change by the early 1970s. Yet, how did they reach such a conclusion? How did
two activist schoolteachers, who had based their prior political participation on
the legitimate authority of the Mexican Constitution and the progressive legacies of the 1910 revolution, transform into rural guerrilla leaders waging socialist
insurrections on the PRI regime?

Prior to organizing guerrilla insurgencies, Vázquez and Cabañas had traveled
the political paths of the Mexican Old Left. Throughout the early to mid-1960s,
both figured prominently in electoral efforts and the formation of opposition
political parties, independent unions, and popular front groups as the means
through which to achieve a more just and equitable social order. They participated in the revival of Cardenismo with the MLN, the organizing of the

Independent Campesino Central (CCI) as a counterweight to PRI-aligned peasant unions, and the People's Electoral Front (FEP) that ran as a broadly defined leftist umbrella group for the 1964 national elections. Yet beginning with the 1962 state elections and the bloody aftermath of the Iguala massacre, both teachers would increasingly experience the intransigence of a regime that increasingly focused less on cooptation as a form of defusing popular discontent and more on violent repression in Guerrero. In Iguala and with the statewide militarization that followed, the PRI demonstrated a will to prevent a repeat of the 1960 anti-Caballero movement in which the participating masses dictated the terms of resolution, namely, the removal of Governor Caballero from power. State violence and the criminalization of dissidence characterized social life in the state after 1962.

Facing a regime that repeatedly punished legal forms of pacific dissent and protest with violence, Vázquez, Cabañas, and hundreds of others became guerrillas determined to organize new revolutions, overthrow the PRI regime, and implement their own conceptions of socialist states. In the face of systematic state repression they forged an alternative, armed New Left political option— one both poignant and imaginative—that combined creative readings of Marxist theories with revolutionary practice.[3] The erasure of legal channels of protest and state terror stimulated popular radicalization. Contemporary expressions of political radicalism—primarily the Cuban revolution, the emergence of anticolonial national liberation movements, and the Sino-Soviet split—certainly influenced the content of the armed New Left revolutionary imaginaries of Vázquez, Cabañas, and their guerrilla fighters—as did local-regional historical legacies and experiences of armed struggle.[4] But it was state terror that shaped the material form such imaginaries would take and, insurgent guerrerenses believed, reduced the possibilities of overthrowing an authoritarian government to the use of guerrilla warfare. Equally important, such terror radicalized their initially reformist political demands into socialist projects rooted in local-regional subaltern political cultures while expressing universal revolutionary messages. After 1962, Guerrero showcases the manner in which the repeated repression of popular movements working within constitutional channels by the PRI regime gradually shaped the future ACNR's and PDLP's willingness to act in insurrectionary fashion. Political violence necessitated the search for new methods.

Political Travels through the Old Left, 1963–1966

After the Iguala massacre, Vázquez escaped Guerrero with the help of MLN militants directly connected to former Baja California governor and MLN leader Braulio Maldonado. While the persecuted leader took refuge in the vast capitalist agricultural fields of Sinaloa and Sonora picking cotton and tomatoes, ACG members and supporters experienced what the ACG newspaper *30–30* described as terror. Students, poor and middling campesinos and campesinas, housewives, small businesspersons, teachers, and dissident municipal officials whose participation had made the ACG possible for more than two years now faced illegal imprisonment, the ransacking of homes, state indictments on trumped-up charges, and torture. In Mexico City, state agents maintained permanent vigilance on Consuelo Solís Morales and her four young children.[5] Military units concentrated on the ACG strongholds in the Costa Grande municipalities of Tecpan de Galeana, Atoyac, and San Jéronimo employed scorched earth tactics. The violence also spread southward into Vázquez's home region of the Costa Chica. By mid-1963 an article titled "Terror in Guerrero" appeared in the independent leftist journal *Política*:

> During the months of March and April, hundreds of soldiers, in armored vehicles, have dedicated themselves to destroying communities. Among others… Santa Lucía in Tecpan de Galeana… Contepec de los Costales, San Luis Acatlán, La Barra and others in the Costa Chica. Over 400 homes in the last three cited communities were destroyed by military vehicles and set ablaze by soldiers, leaving in misery more than 2,000 families. The military "victory" was sealed by the detainment of dozens of campesinos, with beatings and mistreatment for the victims—including women and children—for the "crime" of having participated in the political opposition.[6]

The article continued by delineating some of the specific techniques of terror utilized by the rampaging soldiers:

> murder and torture were the modalities favored by the military, practiced on, among others, José Hernández and Juan Barrientos, campesinos from the Costa Grande… one local leader of coffee producers nicknamed "Tobacco" from El Ticuí, municipality of Atoyac de Alvarez, was viciously tortured this past March: they cut off his testicles and tongue to make him confess that he "hid weapons" and he was finally killed by splitting his body in half. The crime was committed by soldiers under the command of Colonel Olvera Fragoso. Such is the "duty" fulfilled by 20,000 soldiers deployed in Guerrero.[7]

One of the Costa Grande communities, Santa Lucía, provides an example of how political persecution and economic exploitation were combined during the

terror campaigns of 1963. The ejido was one of fourteen that leased their wood-
lands to a logging company, Maderas Papanoa, during the 1940s. Federal law
dictated reciprocity between the logging company and ejidos: employment, just
wages, and a percentage of earnings marked for the eijdos. In theory, company
and ejidos enjoyed an equal business partnership. Yet, the reality on the ground
was different. Melchor Ortega, a powerful right-wing businessman and personal
friend of ex-president Miguel Alemán, controlled Maderas Papanoa and intimi-
dated the participating ejidos when they opted to cancel the logging contract in
late 1962.[8] According to a protest letter sent by the ejidal commissary of Santa
Lucía to the Secretariat of National Defense in November 1963, Ortega used his
influence with the head of the Acapulco military zone to send in army troops.
On 23 September, twenty-five soldiers entered the ejido and began ransacking
homes, brutalizing campesinos, and stealing money. They simulated the execution of five campesinos by hanging them near their homes until some fainted.
Taking three of the tortured campesinos with them, the soldiers moved on to
the neighboring ejido of Las Humedades for a repeat performance. Reaching
the city of Petatlán, the soldiers turned over the detained campesinos to judicial
authorities, accusing them of homicide.[9] Due to Ortega's maneuverings, according to one Santa Lucía resident, "the presence of military soldiers was transformed into something common and ordinary."[10]

Santa Lucía serves as a microcosm for rural Guerrero after the 1962 state elections. The defeat of political opposition and dissidence through force permitted
caciques like Ortega (with their allies in the governor's palace) to reassert their
power and enlist the aid of a deployed military force that reached an estimated
20,000 by the end of 1963. Like other persecuted activists, Vázquez, tagged with
an arrest warrant, lived in semiclandestine fashion separated from his family and
dodged state agents while continuing to partake in oppositional political work.
Using his network of MLN contacts, the ACG leader traveled throughout the
country searching for new political direction. In early January 1963, Vázquez
secretly entered Mexico City to participate in the founding of the CCI, an independent peasant organization that claimed to represent 100,000 campesinos on
a national scale and worked to pressure the federal government to implement
agrarian reform. Like the MLN, the CCI included a variety of political and ideological currents, forging links with the PCM and independent leftists. Later in
April, Vázquez participated in the creation of the Electoral People's Front (FEP),
a PCM-dominated electoral party that would run a socialist candidate in the
1964 presidential elections.

Yet, these supposedly new political routes kept returning a frustrated Vázquez
to what sociologist Francisco Gómezjara described as the "round universe of
Stalinist reformism" and intraleftist sectarian divisions—culminating with the
FEP conducting another electoral experiment that the fugitive schoolteacher

knew would most likely fail.[11] He also knew from personal experiences that state violence potentially could accompany impending electoral defeat. The Costa Chica community of El Pacífico represented one more example of what could happen to regime dissidents. Provoked by accusations that the community's residents belonged to the FEP, soldiers and state police forces attacked the small community in late July 1963. During ten hours of horrific violence they raped women, executed seven campesinos, and ultimately set the town ablaze before retreating.[12] In the face of such state violence, Vázquez concluded that the search for new political pathways required a gradual break from an institutional Old Left that continued to work within a legal framework while eternally waiting for the objective conditions of revolution to develop.

State repression and individual persecution pushed the ACG leader to flirt with the heretical margins of Mexican Marxism.[13] This was not a first for Vázquez. During the 1962 electoral campaign he had obtained support and advice from expelled PCM dissidents and had begun to read classic Marxist texts.[14] By March 1963, his friendship with Cárdenas and the ex-president's intercession afforded Vázquez some legal protection, which enabled him to continue political organizing. Subsequently he and a group of guerrerense teachers, most of whom had studied at Vázquez's alma mater, the Normal nacional, and had participated in ACG movements, organized a Marxist reading group they dubbed "Melchor Ocampo." The members of the reading group would later form the leadership core of the guerrilla ACNR.[15] Coming into contact with PCM "heretics," ranging from José Revueltas–inspired Sparticist cells (LLE) to the "pro-China" Bolshevik Communist Party (PCB), Vázquez and the ACG leadership intensely studied and engaged a critical, revolutionary Marxism-Leninism that also included Maoist strands. They reencountered the radical Third Period of the Comintern when revolution appeared imminent, tangible, and necessary.[16] Such study and engagement profoundly changed the ACG in terms of political doctrine and organizing structure.[17] They presented their "New Route" months later in the ACG bastion of Iguala in October 1963.

The ACG "New Route" represented a New Left gauntlet fashioned by the experiences of 1960 and 1962 and enhanced by the Mexico City political travels of the ACG leadership. A reflective document that evaluated the national context and recent political experiences, the "New Route" unmasked the PRI regime as an antidemocratic ruling institution aided by so-called opposition parties and dependent upon a "Cardenismo...that misleads campesino and student sectors with its pseudo-leftist positions as mediated by the MLN." The ACG thus clearly announced its break with the Cardenista experiment of the early 1960s despite past alliances between the Guerrero group and the MLN, not to mention the personal friendship between Vázquez and Cárdenas. On a broader level, the break with the MLN symbolized a break with the institutional Mexican Old

Left. Criticisms of the PPS as a petit bourgeois party and the PCM as an "opportunistic, misnamed" nonparty unwilling to "openly struggle in the streets for the reforms included in its program" further cemented the rupture. Singling out the CCI as a failed communist creation, the ACG leadership accused the PCM of "complementing the [PRI] measures of control and mediation for campesinos, [thus] providing fresh impetus to the official and discredited CNC."[18] The theoretical influence of Mexican Sparticism and Revueltas in such vibrant critiques complemented the local-regional political experiences of Vázquez and the ACG.

A theme of unmasking and revelation permeates the "New Route" document. Having exposed the PRI and its slavish oppositional parties, the authors move on to questions of political demands. The violence of 1960 and 1962 taught the surviving ACG members that "the electoral path does not solve [working class and campesino] problems and the secret, universal vote is a bourgeois trick." Rather, they promote the necessity of

> a popular revolution that does not signify the changing of persons in charge of the bourgeois government; rather, it means a radical political and economic regime change; the installation of a popular and democratic government based on the direct participation of workers, poor campesinos, revolutionary intellectuals and sectors of the bourgeoisie that agree with our demands; that represents the first stage of socialism; these objectives are not attained with an electoral strategy. Voting cannot end class struggle and ensure the destruction of a bourgeois State that exploits us.[19]

The "New Route" concludes with an urgent call for revolutionary praxis with traces of young Marx, Luxemburg, Liebknecht, Lenin, and Guevara: "revolutionaries struggle...to destroy bourgeois society. Revolutionary ideals are not meant for simple exhibition but for putting them into practice."[20]

The principal author of the document, Vázquez, left unanswered the question of how to enact revolutionary praxis. Furthermore, contradictions riddle the political visions and criticisms put forward in the "New Route" manifesto. For instance, the call for a "popular revolution" and the enactment of a "democratic and popular government" closely resembles the political lexicon of the MLN's founding documents and the PCM's call for a "new democratic revolution for national liberation" adopted at the Thirteenth Congress in 1960. At the time the "New Route" was presented, moreover, Vázquez still belonged to the MLN and continued to work with the noncommunist faction of the CCI after that organization split in 1964. Thus, the "New Route" should be read as a declaration still in the process of development when Vázquez presented it to the ACG leadership in October 1963, and an example of the contradictory, at times uneven, process of political radicalization. In other words, declaring a new route did not signify the immediate embrace of armed revolution. Though his break with the PCM proved final, Vázquez continued to work with dissidents and leftists of all stripes. All the while, the ACG slowly transformed into the nucleus of a future revolutionary vanguard party, dubbed "30th of December" to commemorate the Iguala massacre.[21]

Cabañas's search for a new route diverged from Vázquez's, proving more localized, prolonged, and communist. As a descendant of agrarian revolutionaries and guerrillas, Cabañas came of age likely hearing about the insurgent experiences of Zapata, the Vidales brothers, de la Cruz, and Cárdenas from great-uncles who fought in the Zapatista army and alongside the Costa Grande guerrillas of the 1920s. In contrast to Vázquez, Cabañas did not leave Guerrero for his education. Forged in the student-teacher tradition of leftist struggle at the Ayotzinapa normal rural, historic cradle of Guerrero communism,[22] he joined the communist Left as a student via the Youth wing (JCM) of the PCM during the late 1950s and went on to become a rural schoolteacher and campesino organizer. [23] An organization infamous for its political rigidity, sectarianism, and constant internal purges, the PCM nonetheless produced important cadres like Cabañas, who joined "mostly out of moral compulsion—an applied ethic of right and wrong in political and daily behaviour—to which personal interest and enhancement must be subordinate."[24] While the "red priests" of the PCM leadership debated Marxist orthodoxy and organized communist versions of the Congregation for the Doctrine of the Faith, rank-and-file militants politically organized rural women, workers, and peasants at the local-regional levels in pursuit of social democratic rights.[25] They risked everyday cacique and state violence in the struggle to obtain social justice. Expelled PCM members would lead some of the key movements—worker, campesino, student, and guerrilla— in the post-1940 era.[26]

As a JCM member, Cabañas organized fellow students in Ayotzinapa and the surrounding peasant communities to support the broader 1960 movement led by the ACG and COP.[27] Following his subsequent participation in the 1962 ACG electoral campaign, he completed his studies at Ayotzinapa and received the title of rural schoolteacher—a title that enabled him to join the Revolutionary Teacher's Movement (MRM) led by communist Othón Salazar.[28] Following a brief stint teaching in the Costa Grande community of El Camarón, Cabañas obtained a permanent teaching post in the mountain town of Mexcaltepec (near Atoyac) and immediately immersed himself in a local community struggle against a logging company.[29] He helped local officials draft petitions that demanded the logging company fulfill its legally mandated reciprocal obligations (profit sharing, paved roads, potable water, telephones, and electricity). When the company failed to respond, community residents blockaded roads into the surrounding forests and sawmills and organized "self-defense" brigades. Such direct actions forced the company to begin fulfilling its contractual responsibilities, though state officials punished Cabañas by transferring him to a school in Atoyac for his "subversive" participation. Mexcaltepec did not forget the schoolteacher's efforts. In addition to coffee-producing ejidos, Costa Grande mountain communities like Mexcaltepec that organized resistance and radicalized during their struggles to protect forests against logging companies throughout the 1960s would form a stronghold of campesino support for the PDLP in the 1970s.[30]

By mid-1964, the charismatic schoolteacher had distanced himself from the ACG permanently, joined the PCM, and assumed the PCM-assigned duty of organizing Costa Grande campesinos for the communist faction of the CCI and rural schoolteachers for the MRM.[31] Continually embroiled in local community struggles and movements, Cabañas embodied the archetypal post-1940 rural schoolteacher as local organic intellectual. In contrast to their pre-1940 counterparts, portrayed as beholden to the demands of an expanding state and inspiring campesino resistance, rural schoolteachers after 1940 tended to serve as spokespeople for local grievances against the state.[32] Trained at rural institutions largely characterized by political radicalism and catering to the sons and daughters of campesinos, schoolteachers often grew up and labored in conditions of poverty and misery similar to those of their students. At schools like Ayotzinapa, the boundaries between studies and politics, classrooms walls and the surrounding impoverished communities, proved practically non-existent. Local conditions of poverty, economic injustice, and exploitation colored interpretations of global events. Felix Bautista, a longtime comrade of Cabañas, recalled that they listened to Radio Rebelde and received radical literature from China and Russia at school during the late 1950s and early 1960s.[33]

Unlike the empty rhetoric of the PRI, the demands for democracy and agrarian reform voiced at rural institutions like Ayotzinapa exhibited an immediate urgency. Cabañas remarked that he honed his political abilities as a student at Ayotzinapa during the 1960 anti-Caballero movement: "They say that Lucio went to the mountains and discovered how to organize the people. But we, from the time of Caballero Aburto, have organized the people. As students we studied in order to help campesinos. We were born in Ayotzinapa."[34] Activism and pedagogy thus tended to merge as the responsibility of the rural schoolteacher. Practical exigencies faced by a peasant population in Guerrero with high rates of illiteracy reinforced the local standing of teachers. Both Cabañas and Vázquez often helped campesinos elaborate and present petitions to governmental officials. In northern Mexico, normales rurales like El Mexe (Hidalgo), Salaices (Chihuahua), and Saucillo (Chihuahua) produced male and female rural schoolteachers who organized land invasions and local anticacique resistance.[35] Historian Tanalís Padilla's assessment of the role played by schoolteachers in the earlier Jaramillista movement strongly resonates with the Guerrero case: "As these educators became the first to encounter the contradictions of spreading the government's doctrine of progress and modernization, they often went from agents of state consolidation to village leaders who articulated community grievances against the state itself."[36]

As a student activist and national president of FECSM from 1961 to 1963, Cabañas had access to a national network of potentially like-minded rural students and schoolteachers.[37] As FECSM president, Cabañas traveled throughout the country in 1963 and constantly petitioned the Ministry of Education (SEP) to increase the number of scholarships for rural students. DFS agents who tailed him claimed that "he rarely attends classes and dedicates himself to constant travels" while using Mexico City as a sort of base.[38] Like many rural teachers, Cabañas concurrently belonged to the PCM and the MRM, national organizations that encouraged the creation and consolidation of local political networks. During 1964 Cabañas and a group of comrade teachers, labeled "a throng of communists" by local caciques,[39] traveled throughout the Costa Grande organizing local MRM chapters and attracting teachers in an attempt to displace the PRI-allied official teacher's union (SNTE).[40] Simultaneously, the tireless teacher-activist worked with the CCI, recruiting campesinos and organizing peasant congresses that denounced the price manipulation of coffee and copra by cacique middlemen, the lack of credit available to small and middling ejidatarios, and the continued forestry conflicts with rapacious logging companies.[41]

Through his activism, Cabañas forged local, regional, and national networks that involved the participation of normalista students, rural schoolteachers, campesinos, communist militants, the families of schoolchildren, local governing authorities sympathetic to popular demands, and entire rural communities—networks that proved crucial when Cabañas later escaped state persecution and forged a clandestine guerrilla army. In 1964–5, the schoolteacher continued to follow the PCM path fundamentally based on acts of civic dissidence and the organizing of campesinos and teachers. Periodically leaving the Costa Grande, he traveled to Tlapa in February 1965 to organize the First Indigenous Campesino Congress of La Montaña under the auspices of the CCI-communist faction and joined by MRM leader Salazar. During the gathering, Cabañas delivered scathing criticisms that, along with his constant participation in local agrarian struggles, angered state officials and caciques. He blamed various "Judas presidents" for betraying the revolution and called for "the humble classes, so often the victims of injustice and forced to live in misery, to organize a general strike."[42] Similar gatherings held throughout 1965, characterized by vociferous criticisms of state and federal governments, led local caciques to petition the SEP to transfer both "communist agitators," Cabañas and fellow PCM teacher Serafín Núñez, out of Guerrero.[43]

Exiled to the northern state of Durango, the teachers reached their new post in Tuitán, where they immediately helped organize the Women's Union of Tuitán. From December 1965 to July 1966, Cabañas and Serafín created headaches for local caciques as they and the Women's Union organized a 50–60 km march on foot to the capital city of Durango demanding food for the women's children and jobs for their husbands.[44] By the time the MRM managed to secure the teachers' return to Guerrero in mid-1966, Cabañas had participated in the Congress of the Durango Federation of Workers and Campesinos and supported a multiclass civic movement calling for the creation of a local steel industry.[45] Evidencing his commitment to nonviolent forms of political activism, Cabañas rebuffed the efforts of Gámiz's GPG guerrilla survivors to enlist his help in reconstituting the guerrilla movement in Chihuahua.[46] Prior to his return to Atoyac in August 1966, he enrolled in a PCM political preparation course in Mexico City, where he met Raúl Ramos Zavala—future urban guerrilla leader and Marxist theoretician.[47] While in the capital, he also took a Nahuatl language course at the Bellas Artes Palace. When Cabañas finally reached Atoyac, he found the municipal capital embroiled in a school conflict with undertones of class struggle.[48]

Unlike Cabañas, Vázquez necessarily led a semiclandestine political life from 1963 to 1966 to avoid arrest. Immediately after proposing the "New Route" for the ACG in October 1963, the persecuted civic leader worked as director of economic planning for the newly constituted and CCI-allied Revolutionary Agrarian League of the South "Emiliano Zapata" (LARSEZ)—a series of united independent rural unions that demanded land redistribution and social justice for campesinos.[49] Teachers trained at the Normal nacional who belonged to the "Melchor Ocampo" reading group led the different unions that collectively constituted LARSEZ. Throughout 1963 and 1964, the ACG collaborated with groups like the CCI and the MLN, helping to organize Costa Grande campesinos and anti-Abarca Alarcón demonstrations. Yet, privately Vázquez and ACG cadres worked to transform the organization from an opposition electoral party into a potential revolutionary vanguard party.

By August 1964, the ACG had circulated a founding manifesto of sorts that unequivocally identified the rural "capitalist cacique" as the embodiment of the PRI's economic modernizing efforts in the countryside that required repression and sustained an exploitative social order. To combat the PRI and its "capitalist caciques," the ACG called for the creation of "clandestine committees of struggle," with three to seven members, engaged "in the labor of propaganda, agitation, organization, and direction of the People, working in clandestine fashion to ensure the continuity of popular struggle." The manifesto outlined a "Seven-Point Program" that called for: the removal of Governor Abarca Alarcón; radical agrarian reform; political freedom, union autonomy, and the creation of a government led by the "popular classes"; "scientific" management of the national economy; the expropriation of mines owned by "North American" capitalists; the rescue of Guerrero's "forestry riches" from "rapacious" lumber companies (and cacique Melchor Ortega) that violated campesino usage rights; and the organizing of literary campaigns and fomenting "cultural development" for the masses.[50] Rooted in the local experiences of Guerrero, the Seven-Point Program provided a national "New Route" for all of rural Mexico.

The manifesto, and its call for the People "to respond to each state repressive action in kind," prompted a government investigation into whether "communist guerrilla cells" existed in Guerrero.[51] Such fear, along with the continued activist defiance of ACG-allied groups like LARSEZ, prompted the PRI regime and Governor Abarca Alarcón to violently repress these groups, "justified" by a decree he passed in May 1965 that practically suspended constitutional guarantees in the state. Any idea, plan, or program that was considered to destabilize the public order would result in jail and monetary fines. Any idea, program, or plan that challenged the PRI would result in violence and persecution.[52] Vázquez became "the most dangerous agitator of the state," in the eyes of the ruling regime, persecuted throughout 1965–6. ACG militants risked assassination at the hands of state police forces.[53] In the face of such violence, a series of cívico-allied groups led by a cadre of ACG leaders created the People's Council of Self-Defense (CAP) in April 1966 to help facilitate coordinated defensive measures against state repression. Adopting the Seven-Point Program, the CAP mobilized weekly demonstrations that protested "the political and economic repressive situation created by the bad government of Abarca Alarcón" and the murder of CAP militants like Pedro Cortés in San Luis Acatlán.[54] In late July, CAP mobilized once again in Iguala after a confrontation between activists and state police forces. Police invaded the home of prominent ACG militant and CAP leader Elpidio Ocampo, and shot and killed his son Delfino.[55] Ocampo would later join the guerrilla ACNR.

By November, the CAP added the release of Vázquez from prison to its demands. In front of the Mexico City MLN headquarters in 1966, state police agents operating beyond their area of jurisdiction detained and kidnapped the ACG leader, who had evaded arrest for three years. Guerrero judicial authorities charged Vázquez with crimes dating back to the 1960 and 1962 massacres: homicide, defamation of public officials, criminal association, and resisting arrest. In truth, he was arrested for challenging local-regional caciques and PRI officials.[56]

The Massacres of 1967

While Vázquez languished in a prison cell, Cabañas found himself embroiled in another local community struggle. In 1967 he joined an Atoyac movement organized by the poor campesino families of schoolchildren to oust an unpopular school rector. Beginning in April, a coalition of schoolteachers, families, civic activists, and campesinos initiated protests to demand the removal of the school rector, perceived as corrupt and arbitrary, and the reinstatement of a popular teacher who had been accused of imparting communist ideas.[57] Cabañas explained the specific demands of the movement in a 1969 PDLP communiqué distributed throughout Atoyac: "free public education; that no quotas should be charged on the parents of schoolchildren, and that school authorities not demand that impoverished students wear daily school uniforms."[58] The liberation of political prisoners, including Vázquez, and the removal of Governor Abarca Alarcón soon joined the list of original demands as the movement radicalized in the face of intransigent local and state governments. A pamphlet distributed by the movement on 30 April described how "the rich mock the poor, stealing their harvests by paying low prices."[59] Slogans began appearing on city walls calling for "Death to the Bad Government of Abarca Alarcón."[60] The movement to remove the school rector evolved into a larger critique of campesino afflictions.

By mid-May, the local oligarchy had demanded the personal intervention of the governor and initiated a campaign of threats. In response, Cabañas proclaimed at a 17 May assembly, "if they kill or injure any one of us, then we will finish off all of the rich townspeople."[61] State judicial and educational officials— including two platoons of armed police and seventeen state police officers— arrived that same day but did not remove protestors, who had taken over the Plaza Cívica. As Cabañas presented a speech the next morning, state police officers attempted to take the microphone away from the schoolteacher. A scuffle ensued, and police officers fired into the crowd of protestors who were trying to protect Cabañas. Seven deaths—five protestors and two state police officers— and dozens of injured were the casualties of an operation targeting one protest leader. Army soldiers stationed in Atoyac intervened to end the massacre.[62] With the help of various women, the charismatic schoolteacher escaped into the neighboring mountain range. Days later the State Attorney General charged Cabañas with several crimes, including "the diffusion of ideas that altered order and public peace" and homicide.[63] According to state officials, Cabañas had provoked the massacre.[64]

Popular rage throughout the Costa Grande had not dissipated when another civilian massacre occurred in Acapulco. A thousand campesino copreros from the Regional Union of Copra Producers of Guerrero (URPC), led by PRI federal deputy César del Ángel, peacefully marched on their union's Acapulco headquarters on 20 August 1967 to prevent their leadership from incorporating the independent organization into the fold of the PRI-controlled National Campesino Confederation (CNC). A DFS intelligence memo produced by an undercover agent reported that during the coprero meeting "instructions were given that stated no one was to carry weapons during the protest and that they adopt a posture of prudence in case of provocative acts." The dissident copreros led by del Ángel planned to "demand the revocation of the $0.10 per kilo tax on copra and insist that Jesús Flores Guerrero, president of the URPC, provide a report on the current economic situation, a program of the work conducted until the current date, and his plans for the future of the union."[65]

Upon reaching the union building, state police officers, paramilitary forces, and paid gunslingers stationed within the headquarters opened fire on the unarmed, unsuspecting copreros. The gunfire stopped only when soldiers intervened and temporarily detained the aggressors. Between twenty-three and forty were killed, and dozens of injured copreros lay in the street.[66] Subsequent government investigations, like those for the earlier massacres, blamed the victims.[67] Impunity for the executioners reigned as the pacific democratic struggles of the 1960s ended bloodily.

"The Bad Government of Caciques" in Late 1967

Seven years of massacres committed by state forces revealed the rottenness of regional PRI rule in Guerrero. In the tense days after the 1962 Iguala massacre, Vázquez described a social atmosphere of terror and injustice homologous to the Guerrero of late 1967 after the Atoyac and Acapulco massacres:

> Various accusations were launched against the guerrerense People, identifying us as communists; then, of being a "rebellious People" ... repeating the old mantra that we are an "ungovernable People." Once again impunity and injustice produced grieving households, sacrificing the humble people of our communities, imprisoning and persecuting all ACG members who had committed no crime other than maintaining alive the 1910 revolutionary ideal of "effective suffrage" without impositions. To the exercise of [constitutional] rights, the government responded with violence.[68]

The exercise of state violence as a response to the popular exercise of rights characterized the gubernatorial tenure of Raymundo Abarca Alarcón (1963–9), characterized by CAP activists as the "bad government of caciques."[69] Indeed, Abarca Alarcón's assumption of power required not only the 1962 Iguala massacre of ACG members but also the military counter-cívico campaigns throughout 1963 that punished electoral inconformity with scorched earth policies. As governor, the Iguala military doctor-turned-politician criminalized social dissidence with the full support of local-regional caciques like Donato Miranda Fonseca, longtime politician, powerbroker, and passed over gubernatorial candidate in 1957. Decree 29, passed in May 1965 by the state legislature, represented a regional manifestation of Article 145 of the Federal Penal Code, the infamous law of "social dissolution" passed during the Second World War that severely punished those who "propagate ideas, programs, or conduct that tend to produce rebellion, sedition, riots, disorders, and the obstruction of the functioning of legal systems."[70] De facto application of Article 145, like Decree 29, targeted regime critics, leftists, and, in Guerrero, masses of citizens who attempted to exercise their constitutional rights. Yet by late 1967, Decree 29, and the massacres of Atoyac and Acapulco, signified the nearly "complete suspension of constitutional guarantees."[71]

The revelation of rotten cacique law paralleled the beginnings of a national agrarian crisis that brought the so-called economic Mexican Miracle to a close. An economic model that posited a polarized countryside (divided into an undercapitalized ejidal sector and a lavishly protected agrocapitalist sector designed for export) as the subsidizer of rapid industrial development and feeder of growing cities faced exhaustion. Population growth strained an ejidal economy meant to feed an internal market (and produce an exportable surplus) at artificially suppressed prices with minimal credit, technological support, and irrigation. The lack of meaningful land redistribution from 1940 to 1965 and rural population growth had produced large numbers of landless peasants in the countryside.[72] Lacking significant state support, those small and middling peasants who retained land necessarily turned to a rural commercial bourgeoisie that monopolized agricultural markets through its control over credit and exchange. They controlled access to markets, credit, water, processing plants, transportation, seeds, and fertilizers. These modern capitalist caciques—linked to national financial and industrial interests along with transnational corporations—remained firmly entrenched throughout the 1960s. Large-scale agrobusiness largely located in northern Mexico focused on export crops and producing livestock feed for a burgeoning internal and state-subsidized livestock business, also contributing to a dramatic decline in agricultural production and growth by 1965. By the early 1970s, Mexico's status as a nation that exported agricultural products ceased, and it became a nation dependent upon imported agricultural goods.[73]

The coastal regions of Guerrero experienced the national agricultural decline with the dramatic fall of international coffee and copra prices during the mid-1960s. While relatively high international prices for copra and coffee during the 1950s allowed ejidatarios a modicum of improvement in their lives, a regional rural commercial bourgeoisie linked to transnational corporations based in Acapulco checked their ability to obtain just returns for their labor. The drop in international prices only intensified the economic precariousness experienced by small and middling peasants subject to a rigid system of cacique domination. Intermediaries and merchants who provided credit to peasants at loan-shark rates and bought their harvests for low prices created a sort of debt-ejido system that forced indebted ejido owners to illegally sell their lands. By the late 1960s, this system had led to the reconcentration of land in the hands of a few wealthy regional caciques and their web of commercial intermediaries.[74] Peasants often supplemented ejido labor with alternative sources of wage labor. Or they could migrate to shantytowns that surrounded cities like Acapulco or Mexico City. In the end, the Mexican Miracle had pauperized them.[75]

Rural guerrerenses responded with resistance. Two decades of ejidatario and cívico attempts to democratize processes of cultivation, production, and exchange through union organizing and political means had exposed the violent determination of regional caciques to maintain existing relations of domination. Basing "protest and popular struggle...within the legal framework of the Constitution," in the words of an August 1967 CAP communiqué, resulted in continual political violence that intensified in proportion to the radicalization of popular demands.[76] Massacre after massacre revealed that the federal government not only failed to heed popular protest against injustice but also that it formed a double helix of power with local-regional caciques. Questions emerged about whether the PRI regime, like the state government, "had allied itself with exploitative cacique factions that repress the People."[77] The "bad government" label used to describe state governorships began to apply to the federal level as poor and middling guerrerenses experienced "the corruption of powerful elites [and] the decadence of a social system that no longer guaranteed the redistribution of land, schools, and security. People lived with fear."[78]

People also lived with anger. Campesino leader Hilario Mesino recalled widely held visions of retribution after the massacres of 1967.[79] Similarly, Cabañas remembered that rage spread throughout the Costa Grande region after the Atoyac massacre. Campesinos from the surrounding mountain communities wanted to descend on Atoyac with machetes in hand and exact revenge on the "rich" merchants they blamed for the massacre.[80] Such collective anger was marked by a sense of class solidarity. The rich-versus-poor or shoes-versus-sandals class dyads that had emerged after the anti-Caballero social movement and during the ACG electoral campaign gained new force with each massacre. Corridos, gossip, conversations over *metates*, and graffiti—those reliable public mediums of popular hidden transcripts—began to express an urgent need for change.[81] Radical black and red slogans appeared on the walls of Atoyac's main streets.[82] Rumors spread that an armed organization led by Cabañas would soon appear.[83] Many campesinos demanded the recovery of dignity and the end of humiliation. At their most violent, they talked about killing the rich.[84]

President Lázaro Cárdenas predicted this type of popular violence. In February 1966, the ex-president wrote in his personal notes, "these people live in desperation and if conditions continue they will kill those who steal their labor. And they, in turn, will be killed, accused of being murderers when it was the inexistence of justice that moved them to do so."[85] In addition to the imminent explosion of popular violence, he also predicted the reaction of PRI regime officials. Guerrero rebels were labeled assassins, bandits, thieves, criminals, and terrorists in the pages of intelligence reports, memorandums, and telegrams even when PRI officials knew otherwise—when they knew that the ACNR and PDLP counted on vast campesino support. To admit the legitimacy of armed popular struggle in this southern state would reveal the potential illegitimacy of a national regime self-proclaimed as the "Revolution turned into government." In the twilight of the Mexican Miracle, the PRI regime chose to violently repress a variety of popular wills. In Guerrero, state violence reinforced Leon Trotsky's and Max Weber's contention that without violence there is no state.[86]

"In April All the Hills are Bald"

The rains did not come early in 1968. A stifling, arid heat dominated Iguala and the surrounding hills during the month of April (Figure 4.1). Dryness,

Figure 4.1   Icatepec, Guerrero, on the outskirts of Iguala.

unrelenting sun, and incessant CAP activism characterized this part of Guerrero, known as the birthplace of the Mexican flag.[87] Almost a year and a half had passed since state police had detained Vázquez in Mexico City and transported him to Iguala's municipal jail. The ACG leader had reached various conclusions during his imprisonment. For one, revolution represented the only way to obtain profound political and socioeconomic change in Guerrero and throughout Mexico. Yet, to enact such a change required his immediate freedom. Despite the fact that "in April all the hills are bald . . . there is no water and anything green is [practically] nonexistent," Vázquez decided that it was time to escape.[88]

Imprisonment and the continued persecution of social activists—culminating in the Atoyac and Acapulco massacres—had convinced Vázquez that the PRI regime would allow or directly participate in the continued repression of dissidents committed to constitutionality and the legal arena. Thus, in August 1967 the ACG leader formulated a clear statement of political intent, addressed to ACG cadres, calling for "the development and consolidation of the Vanguard Proletarian Party [for] the Armed Political Combat of the Masses." National liberation, "the implementation of a popular democratic government and the installment of socialism" constituted the political ends for an ACG called to transform into a revolutionary vanguard organization. Entitled "Programmatic Principles of the ACG," the document represented both a declaration of reformulated principles and a plan of action meant for internal consumption. Combining national and international political and socioeconomic Leninist analyses under the rubric of "dialectical materialism," Vázquez argued that the time for revolution ("national liberation" in his terms) had arrived. The "contradictions" unleashed by the global war that posited socialism against imperialism (as "the most advanced stage of capitalism") favored "the forces of revolution against the decadent and reactionary forces of the exploiters." Only national liberation offered the possibility of escaping the yoke of an "oligarchic pro-imperialist and neocolonial" PRI regime that sided with the sponsor of global imperialism, the United States, and ruled its people under "a backward and feudal political autocracy."[89] The time had come, Vázquez concluded, for cívicos to become revolutionary.

For Vázquez, the bloody 1960s in Guerrero confirmed his prediction of an impending global revolution. Indeed his call for action, shaped by an evaluation of capitalism as decaying and dying, reveals profound Leninist influence.[90] For the schoolteacher, Marxism-Leninism, "as a scientific theory and interpretation of the world," allowed him to forge a political perspective that bridged the local and the global.[91] In contrast to the Menshevik postures of the MLN or PCM, the definition advanced by Vázquez exhibited urgency: an urgency to defeat the local-regional violent manifestation of imperialism in Guerrero to create the antechamber of national revolution; an urgency to capitalize on the "favorable conditions" for global revolution; an urgency to stop the massacres.

When Lenin wrote that the political face of "parasitic" imperialism consisted of reactionary violence, Vázquez could point to the various massacres that had occurred during the 1960s and a regional commercial bourgeoisie that controlled campesino production and exchange of crops.[92] As it had for the Mayan Marxists discussed by historian Greg Grandin in his study on Cold War Guatemala, Marxism "as a theory of how to understand and act in the world" gave Vázquez "a means to insist on [his] consequence."[93] How to generalize that experience among Guerrero's campesinos represented a key challenge in the transformation of the ACG from a civic organization to a revolutionary vanguard party.

At first glance, it seems that the imprisoned ACG leader had described yet another Latin American New Left guerrilla group that showed traces of the vanguardist structure faithful to Guevarist notions of the insurgent *foco*.[94] Yet Vázquez grounded his argument for revolution in seven years of local history and decades more of national history. As his wife Consuelo Solís Morales remarked, his interpretation of class struggle and exploitation displayed the deep influence "of José María Morelos, his 'Sentiments of a Nation,' and the Apatzingán Constitution."[95] Indeed, he would later use Morelos, Vicente Guerrero, and Juan Álvarez as names for his guerrilla camps and units. Vázquez straddled the line between a Marxist-Leninist historical determinism and the voluntarism of emancipatory action. Forming an armed organization responded to local exigencies, primarily the need for self-defense and to conduct the arduous political work required for cultivating popular support. The revolutionary cívicos would have to transform popular support from sympathy and passive identification with ACG demands into a willingness on the part of the rural masses to undertake insurrectionary tasks in the service of revolution.

Such were the prerequisites for a revolutionary organization in the process of development. In his critique of contemporary Mexican guerrilla groups, Vázquez elucidated his vision for developing the ACG into a revolutionary organization using Che Guevara's theories. Armed struggle waged through an insurrectional guerrilla foco, the ACG leader argued, succeeds only with popular support—a relationship cemented by "a revolutionary program of [popular] political and social demands." Previous 1960s guerrilla attempts in Mexico like the Revolutionary Movement of the People (MRP)[96]

> Violated what the principle of historical materialism that tells us...that the masses make revolutions, not heroes or select individuals. [They] succumbed to the error of adventurism, exposing the lack of revolutionary organization and their complete disconnection from the masses; circumstances that facilitated police infiltration and their repression by the government.[97]

In stark contrast, he described the ACG as an organization that had emerged from a series of popular movements that had forged an organic relation with the "masses" and had "proletarianized" ACG "petit bourgeois" cadres. To become "professional revolutionaries," Vázquez concluded, ACG militants needed to study Marxism-Leninism in order to help convince the masses that "only with armed struggle will it be possible to effectively defend the rights of the People under the existing political-social conditions."[98] Vázquez thus clearly enunciated and exposed the discursive specter that had haunted the 1963 "New Route" document. Armed revolutionary struggle directed by a revolutionary vanguard organization represented a new methodology that resolved earlier contradictions. Political work involved not Marxist-Leninist proselytizing missions among the masses, but convincing guerrerenses on the appropriate methods for waging a new revolution. Indeed, ACG ideas on "democracy, national liberation, and the installment of socialism" presupposed the types of demands made during the previous seven years of guerrerense social movements. Definitions of what constituted socialism certainly varied between campesinos and ACG professional revolutionaries, but they found common ground in shared histories of state repression. As Atoyac campesina Gregoria Nario later remarked, "If socialism ensured food, education, health, and recreation for our children, then the path was marked before us."[99] The Marxism-Leninism of Vázquez and the ACG developed in relation to underlying local-regional definitions of local democracy, economic justice, and land tenure—and campesino expectations of a state that could meet such demands.

After producing and distributing the document in late August 1967, Vázquez and the ACG commenced planning how to engineer his escape from the Iguala prison. Supposed attempts carried out by a number of National Polytechnic Institute (IPN) student leaders and "northerners" failed to free Vázquez at least three times.[100] After these failures, the ACG decided to directly participate in the planning and liberation of Vázquez, organizing a commando group of seven militants. Inexperienced yet among the most committed of ACG members—all but one or two emerged from the "Melchor Ocampo" study group and led the various organizations that constituted the CAP—the group began military training in the Atoyac sierra. José Bracho, Abelardo Velázquez Cabañas, Roque Salgado, Filiberto Solís (Vázquez's brother-in-law), Pedro Contreras, Donato Contreras, and Prudencio Casarrubias trained at the Contreras family coffee plot while passing as temporary laborers hired to clean the coffee trees.[101]

After months of training, the ACG's first guerrilla commando unit decided to exercise its military training by robbing Domingo Ponce, a rich coffee cacique who owned the region's coffee mill, to obtain money and weapons. In late February 1968, the unit attacked Ponce at his mill. During the exchange of gunfire, Ponce fell mortally wounded, along with one of his workers and the first ACG casualty, Casarrubias.[102] Fearing detection, the ACG commandos fled the Costa Grande to begin preparations for Vázquez's escape, while government agents sought out the "gang led by Cabañas [that] continues to ravage the mountains" in Atoyac, violently targeting caciques.[103] When they reached Iguala they encountered a robust support network comprising ACG members who had actively participated in the 1960 anti-Caballero movement and had helped reorganize the local municipal government as popular-democratic in 1961. They subsequently transformed the region into a fortress of cívico support during the electoral campaign and remained defiantly indignant about the 1962 massacre.[104] Militants like "Mamá Lipa" Pérez, an elderly campesina and ardent cívica who had long struggled to protect her ejidal lands, sustained the oppositional, direct democracy politics of the ACG in the midst of political violence and repression. She bravely smuggled secret messages and correspondence to Vázquez in prison. Iguala's radicalized and "politicized community," including committed people like Pérez, made the ACG possible.[105] Any future guerrilla successes would also depend on them.

Conclusion

Until recently, most scholars of Mexico generally marked 1968 as the year in which a vast student movement unmasked the PRI regime's pretensions to be a revolutionary and democratic state.[106] Yet, in the different regions of Mexico, "1968" occurred in 1943 (Morelos), 1946 (León), 1961 (San Luis Potosí), 1964 (Puebla), or 1965 (Chihuahua). Guerrero, perhaps adding to its singular reputation, experienced a regional variety of "1968s" between the democratic civic effervescence at the beginning of the decade and its bloodied, frustrated, and enraged state at the end. A guerrerense student at the IPN in Mexico City described popular sentiment at a student assembly in August 1967, as summarized by a regime spy:

> [In] Acatitla state police under orders from the Governor burned down campesino homes and raped women. The student said they need to inform the President of the Republic that they are tired of so much injustice that is committed in Guerrero and they are ready to take up arms if necessary. They can no longer wait for promises from the Federal Government. This was not a threat but a warning.[107]

Years after the Atoyac massacre, while encamped in the mountains surrounded by PDLP guerrillas, Cabañas remembered the time when such warnings of taking up arms permeated the region. He remarked that for an armed movement to begin it needed certain factors: "poverty, the existence of revolutionary orientation, a bad ruling government, a direct mistreatment of the populace at the hands of government authorities." Yet, he cautioned, the people can endure those factors. What they will not allow "is a massacre . . . that they will not silently endure."[108] Although the 1960 Chilpancingo massacre was largely interpreted as an isolated act of violence attributable to a single despot, the bloody outcome of the 1962 ACG electoral campaign and the subsequent campaigns of state terror that targeted dissidence helped expose the systemic inequalities and violence that made the PRI regime possible.

State violence unleashed against law-abiding citizens working within the legal system to achieve political and social reform (and undermine the power of local-regional caciques) thus led activists like Vázquez and Cabañas to a conclusion similar to one expressed years earlier by Arturo Gámiz, Pablo Gómez, and the Gáytan brothers during the 1964–5 Chihuahua guerrilla movement: "we are convinced that the time to talk to them [the PRI] in the only language they understand has come. The time to base ourselves on the 30-30 and 30-06 carbines, rather than the Agrarian Code or Constitution, is here."[109] From 1963 to 1968 guerrerenses witnessed and directly experienced the combination of dramatic acts of state terror and systemic violence, the everyday appropriation of campesino surplus-labor to subsidize PRI-led capitalist modernization, leading many to conclude that only emancipatory violence could bring justice, vengeance, and redemption.[110] The time for a new revolution was at hand. As entire sections of Guerrero refused to endure more massacres, men, women, students, elders, teachers, and campesinos decided to support two separate guerrilla insurgencies.

5

"There Was No Other Way"

I am a campesino
from the state of Guerrero
my rights were taken away
and they made me a guerrilla.
I left my mother and children
And my wife as well
the People have always suffered
I will have to defend them.

Rosendo Radilla,
"El Guerrillero," ca. 1970

Throughout Mexico's so-called *Pax Priísta*, men and women who took up arms against a violent, undemocratic state expressed a sentiment analogous to that of the corrido "El Guerrillero": "My rights were taken away and they made me a guerrilla." In Morelos, followers of Rubén Jaramillo passionately argued that "they made him into a rebel."[1] Just days before their 1965 attack on the Madera barracks in Chihuahua, Arturo Gámiz and Salomón Gaytán wrote in a communiqué that, after a long process of unfruitful, constitutionally based struggles against local caciques, "they embraced [armed struggle] as a means to obtain justice that is denied to the poor."[2] Urban insurgents who emerged during the 1970s after participating in a series of violently suppressed student movements expressed a similar reaction: "the state is the great maker of guerrillas."[3]

By the summer of 1967 both Vázquez and Cabañas had reached a similar conclusion. "There was no other way," remembered guerrillera Concepción Solís Morales.[4] After almost eight years of organizing democratic civic movements and social justice efforts that sought economic equity and the protection of community resources, both schoolteachers faced constant state persecution. While the imprisoned ACG leader survived assassination attempts with the help of fellow prisoners in Iguala's municipal jail, the communist teacher sought refuge, like his Zapatista great-uncles decades before him, in the imposing mountains that towered above Atoyac. Such persecution extended throughout guerrerense civil society as the state and federal PRI governments unofficially suspended constitutional rights and violently punished dissidence and criticism of the regime. By the 1970s Guerrero suffered what the late Mexican intellectual Carlos Montemayor termed an "experiment in military governance."[5]

State terror did not end popular attempts to reclaim constitutional rights; rather, it radicalized populations and political efforts. State terror made guerrillas and guerrilla supporters. It contributed to the development of a guerrilla New Left predicated on direct action capable of organizing bases of campesino support.[6] By the late 1960s, many poor and middling campesinos, women, students, teachers, and municipal officials shared a sentiment expressed by Cabañas: "if they kill one of us, we'll go to the mountains…we were tired of protesting and organizing peacefully [constitutionally] without achieving anything."[7] The emergence of the guerrilla National Revolutionary Civic Association (ACNR) represented one such radicalized expression of popular frustration and anger. Led by Vázquez, the ACNR sought the national liberation of Mexico and popular-democratic revolution as a prerequisite for establishing an anti-imperialist socialist regime.[8]

The ACNR and the Party of the Poor (PDLP), covered in Chapter 6, represented the culmination of a cycle of popular protest in Guerrero that linked violently repressed social movements working with the "Mexican Constitution in hand" with unredeemed rural promises stretching back to the Mexican revolution.[9] The fusion of a repressed present with an unredeemed past shaped the revolutionary praxis and programs of the ACNR and PDLP. As guerrilla organizations with one foot in the Latin American guerrilla New Left and the other in Guerrero's local-regional histories of insurrection, both exhibited a volatile coupling of Marxist-Leninist internationalist politics and local politics of vengeance and dignity. *Foquista* venues for anti-imperialist national liberation had to negotiate with local demands for "a new way of life";[10] a commitment to destroying the bourgeois state had to make room for a "let's take up arms and kill the state police that committed massacres" mentality.[11] Vázquez and PDLP leader Cabañas demonstrated an ability to make their differing notions of insurgent Marxism conversant with campesino political ideas defined by notions of local patriarchal democracy, land tenure, and economic democracy. Indeed this ability explains the guerrillas' capacity to recruit popular support and survive. To imagine a revolutionary future thus required the ACNR and PDLP to harness durable campesino utopias to mobilize revolution and use the anger and indignation provoked by state massacres as the foundation for revolutionary violence.[12]

Both rural guerrilla projects would emerge during a time of national crisis. In the aftermath of the bloody 1960s, including the 2 October 1968 student massacre in Mexico City, the PRI regime faced widespread social unrest. Even the urban middle classes, beneficiaries of the so-called Mexican Miracle, demonstrated significant political discontent. Exponential population growth strained state resources. In response the PRI attempted to resurrect revolutionary populism from the past. The party chose Luis Echeverría as presidential candidate for the 1970 elections, a man who could boast both conservative and leftist credentials. As minister of the interior in the previous administration, he at least tacitly participated in the 2 October massacre.[13] Married into a historically progressive Guadalajara family, he rhetorically would articulate a leftist, anti-imperialist political discourse—particularly in the international arena.[14]

Echeverría faced a daunting task in 1970. Although he traveled thousands of miles throughout the country during his presidential campaign, Mexicans refused to vote en masse.[15] To regain credibility and legitimacy, the president would enact a series of populist measures such as a large increase in urban public spending. The countryside witnessed rejuvenated agrarian reform efforts. New and reinvigorated state-owned companies (*paraestatales*) flourished, particularly in the rural sector.[16] Some high-profile political prisoners regained their freedom. Attempts to regain political legitimacy thus led to an Echeverría presidency characterized by democratic "openings," economic nationalism, and a strong state influence over the economy.[17] The Echeverría version of revolutionary populism would exhibit shades of counterinsurgency in Guerrero.

Before National Liberation, Personal Liberation

To initiate the national liberation of Mexico, a small commando group comprising ACG and CAP militants needed to liberate Vázquez from the state penitentiary located in Iguala. After their costly first armed action in February 1968, during which cacique gunslingers killed ACG militant Prudencio Casarrubias, the group prepared to free Vázquez while sheltered by a clandestine network of ACG supporters in Iguala and surrounding communities. The erroneous attributing of February's violent incident to the Cabañas-led PDLP by intelligence agents also allowed Vázquez's comrades to plan the prison escape relatively unimpeded on Iguala's streets.[18]

After intense preparation and the acquisition of a getaway car in the state of Hidalgo, the first ACG commando unit moved to rescue Vázquez on 22 April 1968.[19] A reconstituted group of seven that now included cafeticultor Ceferino Contreras (father of Donato and Pedro Contreras) ambushed a group of three police officers escorting Vázquez to a nearby medical clinic, after first giving the officers an opportunity to peacefully hand over the ACG president.[20] The brief skirmish left Roque Salgado, leader of the armed group, and two police officers gravely wounded. Another police officer lay dead in the street. During the gunfight the members of the guerrilla unit were separated, and when the engine of their getaway car failed to start, they were forced to improvise. With Vázquez in their custody, the group left the city on foot taking a difficult northwest route that led them to a series of dry hills that separate the small community of Icatepec from Iguala. Using a small plane that had managed to trace the escape route, Mexican soldiers ambushed the armed cívicos. Soldiers from the 49th Infantry Battalion killed Sólis Morales in the ensuing battle. Bracho received a bullet wound in the head that knocked him briefly unconsciousness, but he managed to hide under the cover of rocks. Wounded and with limited mobility, twenty-one-year-old Salgado, "an inexhaustible organizer, tabbed by Genaro as his successor," covered the retreat of the remaining four cívicos by firing upon dozens of soldiers. (Figure 5.1) [21] Campesinos from Icatepec later told Donato Contreras Javier that at least six soldiers died in their attempt to recapture Vázquez.

Vázquez and the remaining survivors, with the exception of Bracho, Donato Contreras, and Ceferino Contreras, escaped the Iguala region by traveling southwest into the Sierra Madre del Sur that separates the Tierra Caliente and Centro regions from the Costa Grande. After passing through the Rio Balsas region, they sought shelter in Chapultepec, a small community north of the city

Figure 5.1 Plaque in Icatepec that commemorates the fallen ACNR guerrillas Roque Salgado Ochoa and Filiberto Solís Morales.

of Tlacotepec. It was a grueling trip on foot through a region known for its lack of accessible water sources and its densely forested mountain ranges. The ACG leader and his comrades managed to escape only with the help of "numerous nuclei of ACG people and sympathizers."[22] Past ACG and CAP political organizers in the homeland of the old Zapatista General Heliodoro Castillo provided the fleeing group with a vigorous support network that provided shelter, food, and protection. Bracho recalled that months before the daring escape, he lived in Tlacotepec, passing out *El Cívico* newspapers and "reorganizing the cívico committees that Genaro [Vázquez] had left with [campesino] defenders of communally owned forests [during the ACG campaign]."[23] Donato Contreras asserted that the escape depended upon "clandestine armed self-defense committees" organized in 1965 throughout the Tierra Caliente, Centro, and Costa Grande regions during the emergence of the CAP. The committees, he remembered, "were formed with people who sympathized with the movement; with ACG people...the idea had been to elevate the political consciousness of the people."[24] Past political work and organization allowed the nascent guerrilla group to survive.

In contrast, intelligence agents from the DGIPS translated such popular support as "the total lack of civic valor among rural guerrerenses, not collaborating with any type of authority." Agents OFG, PLL, and RMP argued, "state investigations have failed, principally due to [rural] hermetic attitudes and practically nonexistent collaboration." Lack of cooperation did not translate into popular support for Vázquez. Rather, the agents concluded, "the few who have helped have done so out of fear of reprisal from the Cívicos."[25] Such unwillingness to recognize popular support for Vázquez and the ACG tended to characterize internal correspondence in the Mexican military, DGIPS, and DFS agencies. State recognition of the various factors that shaped the gradual development of two separate guerrilla movements in Guerrero would later be granted in relative proportion to the perceived military strength of the guerrillas. In April 1968, the PRI regime's discourse that tagged Vázquez and Cabañas as simple bandits largely paralleled pronouncements expressed in most regional and national newspapers. In the days after the escape, newspapers decried a "coming war of guerrillas" organized by a "delirious Left" and "Communists" who had waged earlier "holy wars" against a series of state governors. The reunion of Vázquez and Cabañas was a constant fear expressed in the regional press and state intelligence services. One Guerrero newspaper, *Trópico*, even asserted that Cuban guerrillas had kidnapped Vázquez.[26]

Unlike their miscalculation of popular support, intelligence agents correctly anticipated that the Costa Grande was the intended destination point for Vázquez and his companions. They recognized that the various independent sesame seed producers, coprero, cafeticultor, and other campesino unions that collectively formed the CAP derived political strength there. While the ACG leader sought refuge in mountainous Chapultepec, military units initiated a wide-ranging disarmament campaign in the Atoyac municipality in the days after the escape. General Juan Manuel Enriquez Rodríguez, commander of the 27th Military Zone based in Acapulco, asserted in an interview on 26 April 1968 that the campaign aimed "to prevent any sort of social disorder that expressed support for Vázquez by members of the [CAP]."[27] Internally, agents pursued an additional tactical goal: preventing "Vázquez from establishing contact with Cabañas."[28] In a city already polarized by the 18 May 1967 and coprero massacres and the armed anticacique actions carried out by the Cabañas-led PDLP, such military campaigns only increased popular discontent. Citizens in Atoyac complained that their city had been turned into a "fortress" where "people of renowned moral dignity" suffered intrusive searches at the hands of soldiers. DGIPS agents predicted an increase in negative popular reactions to military operations and "a loss of confidence in the armed Institution [the military]."[29]

As Atoyac militarized, Vázquez elaborated a new ideological program for the ACG in the mountains above Tlacotepec. Discarding the Seven-Point program, he created a Four-Point manifesto to serve as the ideological foundation for a guerrilla ACG committed to the overthrow of the PRI regime via guerrilla warfare. The new program stated its aims as:

(1) The overthrow of the ruling oligarchy formed by major capitalists and large landowners allied to the Yankee Imperialism that oppresses us; (2) The establishment of a coalition government composed of workers and campesinos, students and progressive intellectuals; (3) The achievement of complete political and economic independence for the nation; (4) The implementation of a just social order of life that benefits the working masses of Mexico.[30]

With his new program in place, Vázquez left Chapultepec in mid-July and traversed the Sierra Madre del Sur, reaching the Contreras' coffee ejido approximately fifteen to twenty miles northeast of Atoyac. They encountered a mountainous region highly politicized by previous ACG movements and local struggles to protect forestry resources against logging companies. After making the difficult trip, he called for high-ranking ACG militants to reunite in late August, and organized two separate guerrilla units stationed in the coffee-producing communities of San Vicente de Benítez and El Paraíso.[31]

From one of those locations, dubbed "Revolutionary Outpost 'José María Morelos,'" Vázquez sent a letter on 1 August 1968 to the expanding student movement in Mexico City. Expressing "decided and unmitigated" support for their movement, he advocated the use of "revolutionary violence" as the only way to achieve "a more just and free way of life" in the face of a "neo-Porfirian state...[that utilizes] a political methodology of systematized violence."[32] The solution, he argued, consisted of "creating an armed political vanguard in the countryside as the foundation for developing the People's armed struggle for its national liberation." Vázquez exhorted students to clarify tactical and political objectives without succumbing to the "masks of false bourgeois legality" or "mediating positions of the so-called PCM." Only an armed response to the "violence and repression exercised by the reactionary forces that govern" and the creation of an armed revolutionary organization sufficed as appropriate courses of action. Guerrillas in Guerrero, Vázquez concluded, had begun to forge the new path of revolution—one that "combatants throughout the nation, including revolutionary students, will have to travel, not by choice but forced by the brutal annihilation of democratic liberties carried out by the pro-imperialist oligarchy that governs the country."[33] Eight years of dealing with the Janus-faced PRI regime helped Vázquez provide a warning to the student movement months before that infamous October night in Tlatelolco.

Unlike previous letters sent to the press during the summer of 1968, which justified the escape operation and rejected the label of "bandits," the letter addressed to Mexico City students contained Vázquez's first public call for armed struggle.[34] Yet he announced the call to arms before the actual reorganization of the ACG into a guerrilla group took place. The transformation of the ACG into the National Revolutionary Civic Association (ACNR) occurred in subsequent weeks. Meeting in a site called "El Triángulo" (near Atoyac), the cívicos became "revolutionary cívicos," discussed and adopted the Four-Point program, and redefined the structure of the new ACNR. Vázquez emerged as leader of an ACNR defined as a broad political-military revolutionary structure, beholden to a guerrilla "Popular Armed Nucleus" camped in the mountains of Guerrero and sustained by two organizational levels. Committees of Clandestine Struggle (CLC), made up of three to six persons, were tasked with organizing secret support networks in communities and recruiting potential ACNR militants. Armed Liberation Committees (CAL) engaged in armed actions in rural and urban settings.[35] Campesinos, workers, and students—particularly those with old ACG ties—represented the ideal candidates for CLCs and potential commando recruits for CALs. Both CLCs and CALs would provide their best militants to the "Popular Armed Nucleus."[36] Clandestine activity, popular support, and the spread of rebellion beyond the borders of Guerrero were key factors in facilitating an ACG-ACNR transformation and waging a new national revolution against the PRI regime. As ex-ACNR guerrilla Bracho recalled, "the ACNR was formed with visions of national liberation."[37]

"Liberty Can Only Be Obtained with the Rifle…"

Making a new revolution proved arduous for the ACNR. Despite deep skepticism in the region of constitutionalist and legalistic attempts to obtain profound political reform, violent armed struggle was not the most appealing of political paths. Even for those who agreed with Vázquez's diagnosis of the country's maladies, a vast gulf separated rhetorical affinity or political sympathy from the proposed cure of national liberation through revolutionary direct action. For the ACNR leader, the decade-long terror unleashed regionally by a PRI regime defined as oligarchic, reactionary, and in the service of US capitalist imperialism produced the historical necessity of armed struggle as the only way to "achieve national liberation and construct a better country [*Patria*]" for the working masses.[38] Yet rural communities in Guerrero did not necessarily reach the same conclusion as Vázquez even after years of state terror. The ACNR thus needed to translate popular sympathy and moral authority gained from earlier instances of popular struggles into concrete popular support and solidarity for armed insurrection. Vázquez knew, as did Che Guevara, that "to attempt to carry out this type of [guerrilla] war without the population's support is the prelude to inevitable disaster."[39]

The ACNR, as evinced by documentation produced by intelligence agents, managed to develop an extensive network of rural and urban popular support during its armed tenure.[40] Vázquez and his ACNR guerrillas emerged from wide-ranging, yet violently suppressed, social movements that provided them with connection to the laboring classes they wanted to lead in revolution. Years of political organizing and consciousness-raising through civic movements, electoral campaigns, and union organizing had laid the foundation for the ACNR in this new phase of armed struggle. School teachers who graduated primarily from the Normal nacional in Mexico City, political ground zero for Vázquez during the 1950s, formed the guerrilla core of the ACNR. Antonio Sotelo, José and Ismael Bracho, Demóstenes Onofre, Roque Salgado, and Fausto Avila made the transition with Vázquez from ACG to ACNR. Some, like Elpidio Ocampo, had worked with Vázquez since the 1960 movement. Campesinos Santos Méndez and Samuel Adame helped organize and lead the independent unions that collectively formed the LARSEZ during the mid-1960s, suffering violent reprisals in the process.[41] Familial ties, too, brought schoolteachers Concepción and Filiberto Solís Morales and Jorge Mota González into the fold.

In the Guerrero countryside, older campesinos like "Mamá Lipa," Rosendo Radilla, Petronilo Castro, Juan Tabares, and José Martinez nourished the ACG, CAP, and ACNR struggles with their memories of the 1910 revolution and their struggles to consolidate Cardenismo and agrarian reform in Guerrero. Tabares and Martínez recounted their experiences as Zapatista revolutionaries.[42] Radilla had a long history of political and social activism. During the 1940s, he formed part of the Rural Defense unit that guarded coffee-producing ejidal lands in the Atoyac mountains granted by Cárdenas. He led independent syndical attempts to organize cafeticultores during the 1950s and prominently participated in the 1960 anti-Caballero social movement. As an ardent ACG militant, Radilla organized campesinos during the 1962 electoral campaign and later worked as a peasant representative for the LARSEZ.[43] Campesinos such as Radilla and "Mamá Lipa" made the emergence and survival of the ACNR possible.

From the end of 1968 until mid-1970, the ACNR experienced a transition from a popular-front civic organization to an underground political-military force that required a patient, clandestine restructuring of support networks. By the end of 1968, the ACNR depended heavily on the Costa Grande organization that previously comprised the CAP, namely, the Union of Coffee Producers (UPC), which at one time was organized and led by ACNR commando Pedro Contreras. With Contreras and the UPC, the guerrilla organization counted on a level of cafeticultor support in the mountains above Atoyac and potential collaborators that knew well the mountainous region. During these months, Vázquez and his twenty guerrillas attempted to establish contact with Cabañas but failed due to, as Bracho recalled, "the overwhelming presence of soldiers; in other words, the objective conditions of war prevented the possibility of unification."[44] Moreover, the guerrillas soon found themselves enmeshed in a local cacique power struggle that exposed the group's tenuous base of support in the Atoyac region. Offered money by one cacique to kill his rival, a man already targeted for execution by the ACNR, the guerrillas decided not to carry out the hit, most likely fearing popular reprisal and ever-increasing military patrols.[45]

Lack of military capacity and inaction led to internal conflicts within the ACNR. Unable to militarily assist the mountain coffee communities that sustained them or to continue the organizational political work that characterized the CAP, the group began to experience divisions and discipline problems. In January 1969, the ACNR convened an assembly to debate the problems and voted to punish Abelardo Velázquez Cabañas, Pedro Contreras Javier, and Donato Contreras Javier—all original members of the armed group that liberated Vázquez. According to Bracho, the three challenged Vázquez for the leadership position of the ACNR, arguing that they had participated in his escape and their coffee ejidos had served as the group's first base. Vázquez responded by asserting that the masses recognized his leadership status within the ACNR from past ACG and CAP struggles. After several tense moments that included the drawing of weapons, the three challengers decided to leave the group permanently.[46] Losing their primary link to the region's coffee producing communities, and thus the possibility of solidifying a support network fully invested in guerrilla warfare, the ACNR decamped from the Costa Grande for Vázquez's hometown of San Luis Acatlán in the Costa Chica region, though not before carrying out "economic activities" that assisted widows and orphans living in the region.[47] Longtime ACG and CAP militants Antonio Sotelo and Fausto Avila arrived to join the guerrilla group on a permanent basis.

In contrast to the initial rural failures and internal conflicts, ACNR urban militants managed to organize a "rearguard" supply cell in Mexico City by early 1969. Led by schoolteacher Concepción Solís Morales (Vázquez's sister-in-law), the urban cell was tasked with obtaining money and supplies for the main rural "Popular Armed Nucleus," which was then in transit to the Costa Chica. According to DFS intelligence memos, Solís Morales passed ACNR letters from Vázquez to leftist newspapers like ¿Por qué?, distributed communiqués to Mexico City activists and students, transported weapons, organized safe houses, maintained "expropriated" money funds, and organized other urban cells.[48] Solís Morales described her own role as that of a "supplier" responsible for obtaining funds and necessary supplies for the rural ACNR.[49] In April 1969, the urban cell carried out a procurement when at least five guerrillas attempted to rob a bank in Mexico City. Three managed to escape the ensuing gunfight, but police officers immediately detained two: Florentino Jaimes Hernández and Juan Galarza Antúnez. Both suffered brutal torture at the infamous Military Camp Number 1 (CM1) in Mexico City. Police officers or interrogators beat Galarza to death. The torture sessions produced information that led to the remaining members of the bank assault party in Guerrero. Members of the Mexican military detained Jorge Manuel Torres, Santos Galarza Millán, and Epifanio Avilés Rojas in May and June 1969 and sent them to CM1. The detention of Avilés Rojas, a rural schoolteacher in Coyuca de Catalán, inaugurated the Mexican Dirty War. He was the first disappeared casualty.[50]

Increased military presence and continuous search-and-destroy army patrols motivated Vázquez to leave the Atoyac region. Accompanied by three ACNR guerrillas, he reached the mountains north of San Luis Acatlán in May 1969. In Iliatenco and Tlaxcalixtlahuaca the ACNR encountered communities with limited prior contact with past ACG and CAP movements. To use then-contemporary guerrilla discourse, the ACNR failed to account for "objective" conditions when moving to an unknown region embroiled in indigenous campesinos-versus-cacique conflicts "objectively" different from other agrarian conflicts throughout Guerrero. They also failed to consider "subjective" conditions in entering a site previously not politically organized by ACNR cadres. After making a national call for armed revolution through a series of communiqués, Vázquez and his small remaining group were forced by local exigencies to travel the mountainous region trying to convince impoverished communities to risk everything in rebellion. For two months, according to the torture transcripts of ACNR militant Jorge Mota González, the guerrillas failed "to enact any armed actions... walking [through various communities], staying the night and dining in the homes of Genaro's friends... [Vázquez] paid for the food and lodging."[51]

Determined to implant an ACNR guerrilla foco in the region, the small group stayed in the Costa Chica mountains nearly a year, establishing an encampment near Tlaxcalixtlahuaca.[52] In late May and June, state authorities discovered ACNR literature that justified bank "expropriations" as revolutionary acts distributed in front of the state capitol in Chilpancingo and the women's normal rural in Palmira, Morelos (where Bracho's sister worked as an instructor).[53] Yet, Vázquez knew that the ACNR was floundering. The cultivation of popular support enacted through individual meetings with campesinos proceeded painstakingly slow. Thus, in July, the "Political-Central Central Directive" of the ACNR organized an assembly with the intent of re-directing the group's effort. The group collectively valued military actions over "political work with the masses" as the best method to capture popular support and create "an Insurrectional Center" from which to spread revolution. To that end, "solidifying a mobile Nucleus of Armed Combat," intensely studying Marxist-Leninist literature by guerrilla combatants, and "carefully and adequately strengthening the supply lines between rural and urban groups" emerged as essential prerequisites.[54] In sum, armed actions would serve the purpose of rapidly incorporating the mountain communities.[55] Targeting local caciques for revolutionary expropriations or execution offered the possibility of obtaining local popular support. Such actions also aimed at politicization, "a style of revolutionary work we direct in order to posit national liberation and Socialism as the goals of mass popular struggle."[56]

The change in political direction led to the expropriation of funds from a local usurer and the "revolutionary execution" of a cacique in late 1969. Yet such public actions only gained attention from local, regional, and federal authorities and mobilized repressive state apparatuses. While the Costa Grande and Tierra Caliente regions had suffered several counterguerrilla military campaigns by the end of 1969, until the ACNR violence the Costa Chica had remained relatively unmolested since the terror of 1963. The appearance of an ACNR-linked "Committee of Clandestine Struggle" in Jalisco and the armed actions of Cabañas initially helped conceal the location of the main ACNR guerrilla unit until someone revealed the location of the ACNR to local officials in the middle of 1970.[57] Days after the presidential elections that witnessed the ascendency of Luis Echeverría, the Mexican military organized "Operation Friendship" in the region of Iliatenco and Tlaxcalixtlahuaca to search for Vázquez, in the process carrying out torture, rape, extrajudicial executions, and illegal detentions. Avoiding the military operation by just days, the guerrilla group left the Costa Chica and returned to Atoyac.[58]

The scope and function of such counterinsurgent antiguerrilla military operations contradicted public declarations made by state and federal officials that characterized both Vázquez and Cabañas as simple bandit-criminals. As early as April 1969 Secretary of National Defense General Marcelino García Barragán declared to an assembled group of military officers in Acapulco that they faced "rural guerrillas [distinguished] by their radical ideology... [not unique to Guerrero] since similar situations exist throughout great parts of national territory."[59] General García Barragán suggested using military medics as a more effective counterinsurgency technique than the deployment of "rapid-deployment columns" that only raised "[popular] tension in the area [of operation]." In essence, the general provided a blueprint for the type of military operations realized in the coastal regions of Guerrero from 1968 to 1970: the employment of medical battalions in rural communities as a way to obtain popular support and intelligence; the reorganization of local rural defense auxiliaries suspected of collaborating with guerrillas; the deployment of infantry battalions to the most inaccessible mountain points of the Sierra Madre del Sur; the cooptation of community elders and leaders as intelligence sources; and the "arming and discreet supporting of the Torreblanca family of San Jeronimo in their hostile actions against the rival Cabañas family."[60] In conclusion, General García Barragán affirmed "the Mexican Revolution, fortunately, was the only vaccination against the Communist and Church viruses that bad Mexicans tenaciously sought to infect in the consciousness of the poor masses."[61]

"Operation Friendship" in the Costa Chica highlighted a change of attitude among the upper echelons of the Mexican military and ruling party between 1969 and 1970. Everyday campesinos in certain communities became the "bad Mexicans" targeted for counterinsurgent elimination regardless of constitutional rights. Yet General García Barragán had mistaken the malady for the cure. The metaphorical Mexican revolution "vaccine"—campesino adherence to the Constitution and memories of popular mobilization—had facilitated the emergence of the guerrilla ACNR when campesinos perceived its PRI betrayal. Thus, Vázquez and the ACNR continued to enjoy rural support throughout Guerrero despite numerous failed attempts to consolidate a guerrilla foco in both the Costa Chica and Costa Grande by 1970. Nonetheless, a logistical and political gap separated the sort of moral authority and sympathy accorded to the ACNR and the physical manifestation of that support in the form of a broad popular base capable of sustaining the incipient guerrilla group. ACNR attempts to bridge that gap, in the form of military actions and "armed propaganda," largely failed as the Mexican military forced them to leave the Costa Chica.

The ACNR guerrillas discovered a divided region rife with campesino discontent and anger directed against the increasingly violent military actions when they reentered the Costa Grande in the fall of 1970. While tens of thousands of

Mexicans jeered President Díaz Ordaz at the opening game of the 1970 World Cup in the Azteca Stadium, soldiers violently searched for the guerillas PRI officials publicly claimed did not exist.[62] Under the pretense of "antinarcotics" campaigns, military operations terrorized municipal capitals and mountain communities with extrajudicial assassinations, unjustified detainments, and widespread torture. Such practices polarized communities as wealthy merchants and caciques, directly threatened by the PDLP, tended to collaborate with the military. Military officials also enacted the practice of using (willing or coerced) campesino spies (*madrinas*) as sources of intelligence.

Repression provoked heterogeneous responses, particularly when military violence directly affected all sectors of Costa Grande society. PRI-linked rural organizations like the League of Agrarian Communities and Campesino Unions, local deputies, and ejido commissaries lodged persistent protests with state and federal authorities. Poor and middling campesinos sent letters to political and military authorities essentially begging for the return of disappeared loved ones. They also refused to vote *en masse* in the presidential elections of July 1970. As military repression intensified, numerous campesino communities came to support two separate guerrilla movements.[63] State terror had thus created a political topography amenable to political violence. A population of simultaneously frightened and enraged campesinos proved receptive to an ACNR communiqué's suggestion "that they denounce the bad deeds of the rich and imperialist authorities so that the guerrilla can dispense justice for them."[64]

Denunciation and the meting out of justice comprised two constant themes in the ACNR's communicative efforts to convince campesinos of the necessity (and inevitability) of armed struggle. The practice of "armed propagandizing" as a political recruitment and persuasion method involved the distribution, publication, and propagation of communiqués. Throughout 1970 the guerrilla group sent a number of documents to regional and national newspapers via their Mexico City urban cell that touched upon a number of themes: a revolution betrayed by the "bourgeois" victors of 1910; exposing the "antinational ruling oligarchic regime allied with North American monopoly imperialists"; the farcical 1970 presidential elections as part of a form of rule that also included extreme violence; the political and moral bankruptcy of the PRI and other political parties; the renewed claim that Mexico lacked a revolutionary vanguard party; denunciations of political repression and counterinsurgent violence; and the necessity of armed struggle as the only path capable of guaranteeing national liberation.[65] In these documents Vázquez, Bracho, and other ACNR authors attempted essentially to expose the violent core of the PRI regime, revealing what they identified as the coercive and illegitimate foundations of its political rule. In sum, they sought to unravel the political threads that connected an "oppressed" nation ("the Pueblo/People") and an oppressive PRI regime ("the government of the rich"):

> the Mexican People know that remaining subject to a social, political, and economic order ruled by a pro-imperialist oligarchy of capitalists and large landowners signifies an eternal defeat. Depending on a regime that constantly betrays and sells our national interests can lead to the loss of our nationality, our nation.[66]

Anti-imperialist national liberation provided the sole means through which to save Mexico (*patria*) from PRI "antinational" traitors (*vendepatrias*) at the service of foreign imperialists. The theme of a revolution betrayed, so prevalent in the cívico movements of the 1960s, thus vividly reappeared in the ACNR program, yet with major differences. Ten years of violently suppressed popular struggle in Guerrero had armed the guerrillas with a reinterpretation of post-revolutionary Mexican history that posited the betrayal of the revolution not in 1960, 1962, 1966, or 1968, but rather in the genesis of the postrevolutionary state itself:

> our combat (expressed with the honor, dignity and energy of free men) responds to the exploitation and political repression that so long has affected the working masses of the south and other regions of our country. The assassinations of 1910 revolutionary popular leaders Ricardo Flores Magón, Francisco Villa, and Emiliano Zapata remain fresh in our memory. As are the killings of Feliciano Radilla, Rubén Jaramillo and his family, Pedro Cortés Bustos, and many other social leaders, murdered by the rich rulers and their repressive apparatuses; the genocidal repression of railroad workers, teachers, telegraphers, oil workers, doctors, and many more; the bloody repression of university and polytechnic students in 1968 and 1971; the massacres of guerrerenses in 1960 and 1962.[67]

The 1910 revolution, according to the ACNR's revisionist account, failed to strike twice by leaving largely intact the capitalist form of the Porfirian state while deposing its ruling and economic elites.[68] Economic exploitation and state violence thus continued in the postrevolutionary historical period. In offering a potent historical critique of the PRI regime by exposing the "oligarchic dictatorial form of its political rule...concealed by tricks and lies," ACNR guerrillas sought to demolish foundational, legitimizing myths.[69]

Grounded in local-regional popular memories inhabited by martyred campesino leaders and defeated popular movements, the ACNR historical narrative simultaneously represented a call for justified revolutionary action in the face of state repression and a forceful reminder for potential revolutionaries of all stripes to reengage national traditions of struggle. In an interview he granted in 1971, Vázquez remarked to a *¿Por qué?* journalist that the ACNR's "[political] orientation was inspired by and grounded in the concrete realities of [Mexico], in its unresolved problems... [the ANCR] is neither pro-Soviet, pro-Chinese or pro-Cuban but pro-Mexican." At an earlier campesino assembly attended by the same journalist, Vázquez exhorted his audience, "to remember the feats of Morelos, Zapata, and Villa."[70] The Four-Point ACNR political program was similarly couched within broad nationalist terms that spoke of national liberation, social democracy, and the participation of campesinos, workers, students, progressive intellectuals, and "the working masses in general." The nonsectarianism of Vázquez's political thinking and his penchant for popular-front organizational structures carried over into this Marxist-Leninist guerrilla transformation. As in 1960 and 1962, leftist ideological purity or party orthodoxy mattered less than the specific path needed to reach an emancipatory goal. For the man described by his wife, Consuelo Solís Morales, as "admiring Che [Guevara] but [José María Morelos] even more," and who read *Sentiments of a Nation* to his children, the end goal proved quite clear.[71] By the end of 1970, the overthrow of the PRI regime via the proliferation of rural guerrilla warfare and "combat unity among revolutionaries" comprised "the correct method of armed struggle... to achieve the complete and definitive liberation of our Nation and a social order more just and truly beneficial for the majority of this country."[72]

Entering into Action

During the fall of 1970, the ACNR set up camp in the mountains east of Atoyac in a small community called El Refugio. In lieu of the assistance of the Contreras family in San Vicente de Benítez, Vázquez and the small number of guerrillas elicited the support of several local families including those of Piza Fierro, de Jesus, Adame, Garay, and Benítez.[73] In particular, the assistance of Samuel Adame, a local campesino leader and CCI member, proved crucial. He gave the ACNR entry to the region, organizing small assemblies during which he introduced the guerrillas and exhorted campesinos to "join the cause that takes from the rich and gives to the poor."[74] Such negotiated support enabled the guerrillas to operate in a mountainous area that contained small towns and hamlets and was populated largely by coffee-producing campesinos amid increased Mexican military surveillance. Daily activities, gleaned from ACNR guerrilla Justino Piza Fierro through torture, also included the daily cleaning of weapons; the organizing of small groups tasked with guarding the camp or dispensing disciplinary actions; weekly shooting practice; and the gathering of intelligence on military movements by Santos Méndez, Hilario Adame, and Jorge Mota González.[75] By early December, the group had planned the kidnapping of a local wealthy cacique with the intention of raising money and publicity. They targeted Donaciano Luna Radilla, manager of the Atoyac branch of the Bank of the South and alleged sharpshooter during the 18 May 1967 Atoyac massacre.[76]

Dressed as soldiers and using an "expropriated" taxi to follow the bank manager, an ACNR group dubbed the "Committee of Armed Liberation 'General Juan Álvarez'" (comprising Vázquez, Bracho, Méndez, and several others) kidnapped Luna Radilla on 29 December 1970. A week later, the ACNR released a communiqué to newspapers addressed "to the People of Mexico" that explained their motivation for kidnapping Luna Radilla, "general representative of the Bank of the South in the region and member of a group of wealthy families."[77] After noting that they demanded "a special tax" charged to the banker's family in exchange for his return, the authors denounced the images of domestic tranquility exported by the PRI for international consumption. In Guerrero reality proved different as the ACNR authors detailed the violent counterinsurgency campaigns launched by the military under the cover of counternarcotics operations. They denounced the military's use of napalm bombs, the assistance of "specialized American police (FBI, CIA)," and the "bestial murders committed by the 48th Infantry Battalion in indigenous mountain communities of [the Costa Chica]...Antonio Espinobarros, Irineo Juárez Castro, among others." With such repression causing popular suffering, the communiqué continued, "it should be no surprise that the impoverished masses and their armed group should charge special taxes on the same rich class that is the principal culprit of the situation that Mexico suffers." Should the repression continue, the authors concluded, "those of us in the revolutionary armed forces" will respond violently.[78]

After his family paid the "special tax," an unharmed Luna Radilla was released by the ACNR guerrillas. In addition to obtaining 500,000 pesos, the ACNR received the publicity that could potentially increase the visibility and political power of the guerrilla group beyond its limited military capacity. For instance, DFS agents discovered the distribution of the group's communiqué in the Residential Units of Tlatelolco in Mexico City and various university campuses.[79] Back in the Costa Grande, military units continued to pour into the region under the orders of new president Luis Echeverría and his Secretary of National Defense General Hermenegildo Cuenca Díaz in response to the ACNR kidnapping of Luna Radilla and various killings of local caciques and expropriations committed by the Cabañas-led PDLP since late 1969. By the spring of 1971, Echeverría, General Cuenca Díaz, and other high-ranking officials realized that the Costa Grande actively and clandestinely supported two separate guerrilla insurgencies. They deployed a multifaceted strategy of constant public declarations, social works, and increased repression. Echeverría used populist rhetoric and promises that posited his administration as "truly revolutionary [in contrast to] the impostor or dreamer of revolutions; the anarchist, provocateur, or traitor moved by foreign anti-Mexican forces or interests."[80] General Cuenca Díaz followed such "revolutionary" pronouncements by ordering a "social labor" military campaign for the Costa Grande in April 1971, described by local newspapers as vast and unprecedented. Three hundred doctors, dentists, barbers, social workers, veterinarians, and shoe cobblers were mobilized to the Costa Grande.[81] The ACNR greeted the social labor campaign with another kidnapping.

Many in Atoyac remembered Jorge Bautista as one of the town "rich" who directly participated in the 18 May 1967 massacre. Many more campesinos knew him as a wealthy regional coffee planter and merchant who did not hesitate to use violence as a method to suppress popular challenges. On 11 April 1971, the "Committee of Armed Liberation 'Emiliano Zapata'" expropriated sixty quintals of coffee from Bautista and kidnapped his son, Agustín Bautista Cabrera. The same day the ACNR cell released a letter claiming responsibility for the kidnapping and framing the action as a response to the deeds of Jorge Bautista: "an exploitative cacique, persecutor and assassin of campesinos; tracking guide for the military and [opium] poppy cultivator supported by official interests."[82] Targeting a specific and perceived class enemy of the cafeticultores that supported them in the Atoyac mountains allowed the ACNR to both present their analysis of national campesino exploitation and posit their group as a primarily rural organization. As such, the act aimed at reestablishing contact with campesino networks severed by military repression. After accusing Bautista of the recent murders of six campesinos, the authors of the communiqué directly called "poor campesinos...to maintain alive the ideals of Zapata to achieve liberty and justice for the People...a goal possible through Revolutionary Armed Struggle, the only path left to the Mexican People, for so long tricked and violently deprived of their rights." To ensure the safe return of Agustín Bautista, they demanded an undisclosed monetary sum, threatening to kill the son if the family refused. Bautista's lifeless body appeared days later.[83]

The Bautista kidnapping represented Mexico's first "formal political kidnapping" due to the widespread national media diffusion it received and Jorge Bautista's political connections.[84] The act undermined the social labor aspect of the military's counterinsurgency campaign designed only days prior to the kidnapping. Days before the abduction, General Cuenca Díaz had written that the "criminal groups," meaning ACNR and PDLP, "did not represent a threat from a military perspective...but a general plan designed to stimulate the state economy through literacy programs, electrification, diffusion of potable water, medical assistance, and reductions of foodstuff prices...aims to undermine the motivations of the supposed movement of bandits."[85] Yet, the killing of Bautista transformed "Operation Spider Web" into a search-and-destroy campaign that targeted real and imagined supporters of the guerrilla groups. Recently declassified daily reports confirm the detention of dozens of Costa Grande residents from April to June 1971, including a number of subsequently disappeared campesinos.[86] Certain last names—Cabañas, Barrientos, Fierro, and de Jesús—practically ensured detention. Military forces arrested the father of Vázquez, the ardent priísta Alfonso Vázquez, when the latter conducted business at the Atoyac offices of the Bank of the South.[87] The widespread repression and intensified military operations forced the ACNR to flee the region, traveling through the Sierra Madre del Sur to the Tierra Caliente, Mexico City, and ending at the home of Vázquez's in-laws in the state of Hidalgo.[88] Cabañas and the PDLP, too, felt the effects of "Operation Spider Web." During the Bautista kidnapping, the PDLP camp was located near the ACNR base: "we were on the other side [of the River Santiago] in La Pedregosa . . . we experienced the persecution."[89]

The ACNR returned to their Costa Grande base in El Refugio sometime in early May 1971. Yet, the small group of supporters was subjected to continued arrests and torture interrogations. After a small wedding celebration on 13 May 1971, for instance, soldiers managed to encircle El Refugio, effectively trapping the guerrillas. The ensuing battle left a local ACNR supporter dead but the group managed to escape the military operation. Harassed for eight days by bomb-dropping army helicopters and foot patrols, the ACNR abandoned their guerrilla camp and continued moving north into the most inaccessible section of the Atoyac mountains.[90] With the rural ACNR wing continually on the run, their Mexico City urban cell under the command of Concepción Solís Morales renewed its activities. At the end of May, the nine- to ten-person cell—"Urban Commando 22 April"—composed of teachers and university students, assaulted an "Azteca de México" commercial store in Mexico City, taking some 78,000 pesos. Demonstrating what ex-ACNR guerrilla Bracho described as the guerrilla group's "capacity for rural, urban, and suburban mobility of action," the urban cell struck again weeks later, attempting to rob a taxi revenue collecting site that shared office space with the Mexico City PRI committee.[91] One member failed to escape the assault and subsequently turned in the rest of the urban cell after a number of torture sessions. All suffered sadistic torture and interrogation led by the infamously cruel DFS agent Miguel Nazar Haro. By July 1971, the urban wing of the ACNR had collapsed.[92]

Meanwhile, in the mountains above Atoyac, military units persisted in their persecution of Vázquez and the few remaining ACNR guerrillas. In late June near the rural hamlet of San Vicente de Jesús, soldiers surprised the camped guerrillas who managed to escape after a brief gun battle. While Vázquez and four others made their way back to El Refugio, soldiers detained five campesinos from the region accused of supporting both the ACNR and PDLP. Contrary to local testimonies and declassified state documents, military correspondence subsequently alleged that the five detained campesinos—Eusebio Arrieta Memije, Miguel Cadena Diego, Cresencio Calderón Laguna, José Ramírez Samaycón, and Inocencio Calderón—died in combat. All five men, disappeared to this day, joined the ranks of an increasing number of victims in "Operation Spider Web."[93] In early July, soldiers detained nine campesinos in El Refugio after the ACNR had left the region and most likely headed to the safety of working-class neighborhoods in Acapulco. Allegedly finding high-powered rifles and leftist literature in several El Refugio homes, General Cuenca Díaz identified the campesinos as "common bandits that operated in the Costa Grande."[94] The language of counterinsurgency consistently used by Cuenca Díaz and the Secretariat of National Defense, which criminalized the ACNR and denied the existence of campesino guerrillas, provided an effective counterbalance to ACNR communiqués. Moreover, President Echeverría's recent announcement of a "democratic aperture" beginning throughout the country after the 10 June 1971 student massacre in Mexico City prompted the question of how guerrillas could exist in an already "revolutionary" nation experiencing a process of democratization. On 22 July, state governor Israel Nogueda Otero unequivocally stated to local newspapers: "the guerrillas don't exist . . . when you present me with pictures of guerrillas training in El Paraíso, San Vicente de Benítez or other towns, then I will believe that they exist."[95]

A beleaguered ACNR provided a much publicized response a day later through the leftist journal *¿Por qué?* For five days in June, the guerrilla group hosted a journalist who attended campesino assemblies, chronicled internal guerrilla life, and interviewed Vázquez. Published as a three-part series between late July and early August, the report publicized the existence of "Guerrillas in Guerrero" and catapulted Vázquez and the group into the national spotlight.[96] The ACNR became the revolutionary guerrilla vanguard of a new Mexican revolution. Vázquez's interview allowed the guerrilla leader to reconstruct the historical trajectory of the guerrilla movement, beginning with the cívico movement of 1960, as the legitimate social expression of repeatedly repressed popular movements. Explaining the *raison d'être* of the ACNR as a political option reached "after struggling through all possible and legal forms" challenged state declarations by simultaneously demonstrating the political (versus criminal) and organic (versus "outside" communist) origins of the guerrilla movement.[97] In addition to the interview, photographs revealed a small but determined campesino guerrilla force able to travel throughout the mountains of Guerrero with the active support of a peasantry weary of repression and exploitation.

The journalistic exposure also enabled the ACNR to disseminate a series of political arguments, justifying the necessity of rural guerrilla warfare in the national liberation of Mexico, disqualifying leftists attracted by pronounce-ments of "democratic aperture" and critical of armed struggle, and undermining Echeverría's self-styled populist government. Vázquez must have realized that Echeverría's recent comments about initiating a national "democratic aperture" and programs that promised the second coming of agrarian reform could fur-ther divide an already disarrayed Mexican Left.[98] Moreover, the reinvigoration of state revolutionary rhetoric and practice (in the form of increased public-social spending and land redistribution) potentially undermined the historical and ideological foundations upon which the ACNR armed struggle was based.

Vázquez thus used the interview as an opportunity to expose the rural, vio-lent underpinnings of Echeverría's "democratic opening" and to criticize left-ists attracted to the promise of democratic reforms. After describing how the Mexican military violently organized strategic hamlets in the Costa Chica, the ACNR leader undermined the self-proclaimed revolutionary nationalism of Echeverría as false: "Nothing exists concretely, in his actions...an absolute gap exists between what he says and what he does."[99] He repeated his wide-ranging call for national revolutionary unity—under the broad and nonsectarian Four-Point ACNR banner—while excluding those leftists who disagreed with violent rebellion as a political option. Political pragmatism and ideological flex-ibility did not extend to the question of praxis: "those [leftists who support Echeverria] do so by convincing themselves without concrete evidence gleaned from objective reality...we reject the hypothetical, the abstract." The ACNR, Vázquez concluded, desired to form alliances "with the sincere nationalist who maintains a combative political position and does not sign secret pacts or trea-ties [with the government]."[100]

Along with publicity and political capital came increased state repression and surveillance for ACNR militants. Throughout the summer of 1971 mili-tary detachments combed the small network of coffee-producing communities between Atoyac and San Vicente de Benítez who had supported the ACNR since 1970. In late August, Vázquez convened a small assembly during which he allowed most of the guerrilla group to disband and return to their communities. Spending only a few more days in the Costa Grande, the ACNR leader and three to four guerrillas (including Bracho and Samuel Adame) permanently left the region and headed north for Iguala, which represented a relatively safe haven for the ACNR guerrillas.[101] Bracho described Iguala and surrounding communi-ties as "a zone organized and won over by the cívicos [which still] possessed a solid political structure capable of helping the ACNR." An ACG and CAP politi-cal mainstay throughout the 1960s, the region offered logistical support, safety, militants, and potential kidnapping targets.[102] After Avila and Bracho recruited two local rural schoolteachers in October 1971, Arturo Miranda Ramírez and Gregorio Fitz García, the reconstituted guerrilla group selected a new target.

"The idea of kidnapping this man," Bracho recalled, "was to force the government into presenting disappeared detainees...alive."[103]

On the evening of 26 November 1971, Jacobo Zabludowsky, Mexico's most watched news anchor, read a communiqué from the "Armed Committee of Liberation 'Vicente Guerrero'" that announced the kidnapping of Dr. Jaime Castrejón Díez. Describing Castrejón Díez as the "rich owner of the Coca-Cola factories in Acapulco, Iguala, and Taxco, rector of the State University of Guerrero, and noted member of the pro-imperialist oligarchy that governs [Mexico]," the ACNR guerrillas demanded the release of nine ACNR comrades "to be sent to a country of their choice": Florentino Jaimes, Mario Menéndez, Demóstenes Onofre, Concepción Solís Morales, Ceferino Contreras, Antonio Sotelo, Rafael Olea, Santos Méndez, and Ismael Bracho. They also demanded that state authorities present before judicial courts a group of disappeared campesinos accused of cooperating with the ACNR.[104] Finally, they demanded that the family of Castrejón Díez provide 2.5 million pesos as a ransom fee, "money that will go to the victims of state repression." Such an act, the authors asserted, "constitutes the People's armed response to the grave and criminal repression exercised in the southern region of our Nation by police and army...and the indescribable tortures suffered by political prisoners."[105] Newspapers throughout the country published the ACNR communiqué the next morning.

Castrejón Díez, his wife, and driver had been stopped days earlier while traveling on the Taxco-Chilpancingo road early in the morning by four ACNR guerrillas dressed in military uniforms, who kidnapped the doctor (also the former municipal president of Taxco and close associate of Echeverría).[106] The kidnapping provoked a national media frenzy, with government officials denouncing it as a "criminal act" committed by "cow-thieves and bandits" motivated solely by monetary considerations. Governor Nogueda placed the blame not on guerrillas but on "simple bandits"—claims seconded by military authorities.[107] Amid the frantic media coverage and increased military operations in the mountains south of Iguala, the ACNR guerrillas established contact with the doctor's family five days after the kidnapping. By the time Zabludowsky read the ACNR communiqué, the Castrejón family was moving the ransom money to a mediator, Sergio Méndez Arceo, the liberation theology Bishop of Cuernavaca. The bishop paid the ransom money the next day while government officials prepared to exile nine ACNR militants to Cuba. Castrejón Diez safely returned to his home on 1 December. For the first time in national history, a guerrilla organization forced the PRI regime to free political prisoners and safely move them to another country.[108]

While the Castrejón Diez kidnapping produced important tangible results, it failed to stop state terror and persecution in Guerrero. Instead, military units and DFS agents intensified counterinsurgency operations that disrupted ACNR support networks and forced Vázquez to leave the state. With the help of the longtime cívico Elpidio Ocampo Mancilla, the small remaining group made their way to Mexico City via the state of Puebla.[109] They eventually reached a safe-house in Cuernavaca at the end of December but DFS agents had found the car used in the Castrejón Diez kidnapping and used it to track a number of other ACNR militants closely linked to Vázquez in the days before and after the abduction.[110] With militants coerced into providing information under torture, Vázquez and Bracho (along with two female schoolteachers) decided to leave Cuernavaca for the safety of Guerrero's mountains. The ACNR leader and his trusted lieutenant picked an inexperienced driver to take them back to the coastal mountains, however. Around the time they set out from Mexico City, Vázquez's wife, Consuelo Solís Morales, gave an exclusive interview to *Excélsior* after spending three days illegally detained with her daughter at the CM1. Solís prophetically told the reporter: "[Vázquez] will die for his struggle... I am resigned that I have lost him, that I will never see him again... and I am preparing my children for the possibility that their father will soon be a dead man."[111]

The automobile that transported Vázquez, Bracho, and three others crashed during the early hours of 2 February 1972 on the "Road of a Thousand Peaks" near the city of Morelia. Bracho recounted the experience:

> We took the female schoolteachers to lessen suspicions. A car with only three men would arouse too much suspicion plus one of the teachers was friends with a priest near Morelia that had agreed to house us on the way to Guerrero. We stopped in Toluca for gasoline but we felt that a car was following us... so we left the city headed to Morelia. Around midnight or one in morning we reached a place with many trees, cold, and with seemingly endless curves. Genaro thought we could reach Morelia and then the small town of Ipana [*sic*] where the priest lived. It was my turn to sleep since we took turns. I was in the passenger seat while Genaro was sitting in between the schoolteachers in the back. Suddenly the crash woke me from my sleep. I felt the crash, I felt something hot cloud my vision. I turned around to see Genaro. He was slumped over, along with the teachers. They did not demonstrate visible signs of life but Genaro was breathing... *no one died in the accident*... not Genaro or the schoolteachers... when I got out of the car to help Genaro he was alive.[112]

Driving inexperience, possibly lack of sleep, and a difficult, curvy road all contributed to Salvador Flores Bello losing control of the automobile and crashing into a bridge eave. Vázquez and the two schoolteachers, María

Aguilar Martínez and Blanca Ledesma Aguilar, were taken a Morelia hospital, while Flores Bello and Bracho escaped separately into the surrounding forest. Military authorities arrested the schoolteachers hours later, taking them and Vázquez's body to Morelia's Military Hospital. They created an official version describing the death of the ACNR leader: "at 1:30 am today on the México-Nogales road near the town of Bajúmparo, Michoacán, a car accident occurred in which a Dodge crashed into a bridge, resulting in the injuries of two women... one man died, he being Genaro Vázquez Rojas, identified by a wedding ring."[113] Military and state police also recovered a cache of weapons, ammunition, homemade bombs, leftist literature, documents, and a tape recorder (Figure 5.2). More importantly, they obtained large sums of money and a diary that contained the names and addresses of Vázquez's associates. Authorities captured Bracho two days later, severely injured and in need of medical attention.[114]

Surviving ACNR members never accepted the official version of the crash. When interviewed, Bracho remained convinced that soldiers killed Vázquez by striking him in the head with a rifle butt, and indeed, the official report describes a fractured cranium as cause of death (Figure 5.3). Flores Bello and Consuelo Solís

Figure 5.2 Weapons, leftist literature, and equipment recovered by government security forces from the wrecked car that transported Vázquez, Bracho, and three others. Archivo General de la Nación, Fondo Hermanos Mayo, concentrados sobre 363.

Figure 5.3   Ex-ACNR guerrilla José Bracho (center) at the thirty-fifth anniversary of
Genaro Vázquez's death in San Luis Acatlán, flanked by historian Andrés Zaldívar Rubio
(right).

also argued that the military killed Vázquez, presumably on orders given at the
upper echelons of the PRI. "Genaro did not die in an accident, my husband was
killed," Solís remarked in 2007.[115] Just two days after the automobile accident,
students from the combative University of Michoacán San Nicolás de Hidalgo in
nearby Morelia had already spread "rumors" (according to DFS agents) that members of the military killed Vázquez. They argued that they were "prevented from
seeing the cadaver in order to conceal wounds caused by gunfire."[116] State officials
and military authorities moved quickly to quell such rumors in the aftermath of
the accident. On 3 February a military convoy transported Vázquez's body from
Morelia through the Tierra Caliente, while 100 soldiers from the 48th Infantry
Battalion moved into San Luis Acatlán to ensure security and prevent "outsider
agitation."[117] The convoy arrived that same night in Vázquez's hometown amid a
climate of fear, heavy military presence, and profound sadness.

     That night, Solís remembered, military medics handed over the body of
the revolutionary leader. Surrounded by bayoneted rifles and tanks that kept
"outsiders" from entering San Luis Acatlán, the Vázquez and Solís families
organized a funeral and burial the next day. Photographs taken by government
agents depict a crowd much larger than the 600 officially reported in military

telegrams. People filled the streets, lined with soldiers, as Vázquez's body traveled from the church to the cemetery early in the morning of 4 February.[118] While military intelligence reported "popular indifference," Solís recalled a saddened and frightened populace mourning a great loss. Martin Vázquez, cousin to the guerrilla leader, told the crowd that "Vázquez had not died; rather he began to live permanently in the memories of the humble and poor people."[119] An inebriated older woman paid her respects to Vázquez in different fashion. Managing to break through the ranks of soldiers that contained the funeral procession, the woman began to angrily shout and denounce the military. "She began to shouting insults about the soldiers' mothers, 'sons of whores...you all wanted to see him [Vázquez] like this and look how scared you still are with your rifles and bayonets in case he awakens...I wish he would arise!'"[120]

In his famous 1971 *¿Por qué?* interviews, Vázquez had delineated a process of revolutionary development that stipulated first the establishment of popular or campesino support bases capable of sustaining the guerrilla ACNR, followed by the projection of armed actions onto the national level in collaboration with other organizations and, subsequently, the coordination of continental movement with other Latin American groups. Vázquez died in the midst of the first step. State terror continually disrupted support networks forged by the guerrilla group, limiting the military capacities of the ACNR to that of a small insurgent organization perpetually in gestation. Yet, for the PRI regime, the danger represented by the ACNR and Vázquez resided in the realm of ideas, political legitimacy, and popular support. For twelve years Vázquez labored to provide a better life for the working and impoverished rural masses of Guerrero and Mexico. Through a variety of political options and paths, he and the organizations he helped create exposed the PRI regime's "armor of coercion."[121] His death and the demise of the ACNR represented a military victory of sorts for the regime but failed to eradicate the subversive longings and memories in rural Guerrero that nourished the guerrilla group in the first place.

Moreover, Cabañas and the PDLP still roamed the Costa Grande mountains, as did surviving ACNR militants. Three days after Vázquez's death, the PDLP released a mournful but determined communiqué that expressed moral support and affection for the Vázquez family:

> It is very sad for us to recognize that comrade Genaro Vázquez has died. For the people who suffer starvation, jails, and massacres, the death of our comrade provokes much suffering because it represents a setback in the hope for redemption...[but] revolutionary groups will continue to form. The revolutionaries of tomorrow will emerge from the combative

groups of today, revolutionaries that will ensure a victorious final battle for the oppressed.[122]

The struggle for national liberation would, they promised, transform into an all-out class war in which the poor would seek to destroy the "dictatorial government of the rich." PDLP guerrillas would fight to create a political community "in which the poor govern everything."[123]

6

A Poor People's Revolution

Lucio spoke their language, Alejandra Cárdenas recalled about the charismatic schoolteacher. Originally from Baja California, Cárdenas attended the Patrice Lumumba University in Moscow during the early 1970s. After graduation she left the Soviet Union in 1974 to work as a university professor at the state university in Chilpancingo. She chose to live in Guerrero precisely because she wanted to participate in the guerrilla struggle waged by Cabañas and the Party of the Poor (PDLP). She had returned to Mexico from the Soviet Union with visions of socialist revolution, influenced by an international Marxist community at Lumumba University and repeated experiences of state repression in Mexico. After joining the PDLP in the early months of 1974, Cárdenas and her partner, Antonio Hernández, met Cabañas in the mountains above the Costa Grande. He asked both Cárdenas and Hernández to organize study circles for PDLP insurgents, and offered some suggestions for teaching Marxism and radical political theory to campesinos. "Help them understand, ok? Don't speak in your language but in theirs," he recommended, "because others [outsiders] have come before, talked, and no one understood them." Ever the "typical rural schoolteacher," treated as a moral and intellectual authority by the communities he served, Cabañas "wanted the people to understand and participate" in making a revolution on their terms (Figure 6.1).[1] In essence, he preached an insurgent and critical pedagogy of the oppressed.[2]

Cabañas also practiced the guerrilla critical pedagogy. During the winter of 1973–4, the PDLP traveled throughout the municipalities of Atoyac and Coyuca de Benítez organizing campesino assemblies to explain its reasons for revolution and to recruit potential guerrillas. PDLP guerrillas repeatedly explained that "a government of the rich" allied with regional "rich caciques" bore sole responsibility for campesino misery and poverty.[3] In the small mountain community of Yerba Santa, Cabañas broached the question of campesino impoverishment, like a Marxist guerrilla, by presenting a dialectical materialist analysis of the origins of rural poverty. Yet, to explain what dialectical materialism was in the first place, he used the metaphor of the growth cycle of maize: "maize plants have

Figure 6.1   Lucio Cabañas (left) and a PDLP guerrilla. AP Photo.

their beginning and their end...to get from beginning to the end the plants go through several stages."[4] In the face of injustice, hunger, and chronic illness that afflict rural communities, Cabañas explained, "we need to think in this [dialectical] manner: everything has its beginning and everything has its end." Such a way of thinking, the PDLP leader concluded, offered the opportunity to demystify why campesinos lived in poverty. "Why are we poor? Because the devil or some angel willed it so or because the wealthiest did?"[5] In remote Mexican backlands, Cabañas attempted to teach that revolutionary human agency could radically transform "man-made" inequitable systems of capitalist domination.

Cárdenas's testimony and the Santa Yerba anecdote offer windows onto how Cabañas and the PDLP managed to forge a broad base of popular support during the guerrilla struggle against the PRI regime. A social base consisting mainly of smallholding campesino communities, rural schoolteachers and students, and some migrant agricultural laborers (*jornaleros*) sustained the guerrilla group for seven years. After escaping the 18 May 1967 massacre in Atoyac, the rural schoolteacher fled to the surrounding mountains convinced that a violent PRI regime had suppressed all political options for social reform and redress. Revolutionary violence and terror, Cabañas concluded, remained the only options with which to overthrow an increasingly despotic government. From 1967 to 1974, Cabañas mobilized an angry Costa Grande rural populace into forming a serious political challenge to the postrevolutionary regime. This "regional problem," as a declassified July 1972 DFS document argued, showed signs "of expanding to the national level."[6] Using a revolutionary socialist discourse rooted in local-regional political peasant cultures, Cabañas and the PDLP waged the *revolución pobrista*, a campesino "war of the poor against the rich and the Government of the wealthy."[7] Part of a family with a long history of Zapatista resistance and agrarian mobilization, Cabañas was educated within a national network of rural teacher-training schools politically shaped by Cardenista, socialist, and Cuban revolutionary radicalism: politically formed by the Mexican Communist Party (PCM) within an Old Left rocked by the Cuban revolution and domestic state repression, and engaged in popular protest movements at the local, regional, and national levels. He led a homegrown peasant guerrilla movement integrated by people he intimately understood.

The poor people's revolution led by the PDLP thus represented an original and radical attempt to forge "a better world, a world called socialism," in the words of Alejandra Cárdenas.[8] Ricardo Flores Magón, Emiliano Zapata, Jesús H. Salgado, and Che Guevara were echoed in the politics and heterodox ideology of the PDLP project, as explained by Cabañas: "we the poor are resentful and angry at one class, a social class that has enriched itself off our labor. We can organize the revolution if we understand that everything owned by the rich was produced by our hands and hence should be returned to the rightful owners: the poor." This PDLP move from indignation and refusal to be exploited to waging popular revolutionary struggle—what political philosopher Antonio Negri terms "communist ethics"—exhibited multiple historical layers.[9] Like the Zapatistas, the PDLP constituted a poor people's militia closely linked to rural communities and moved by a definition of popular sovereignty as radically direct democracy. Campesino demands for equitable economic inclusion in a rapidly urbanizing and industrializing Mexico revealed the influence of more recent cycles of rural-agrarian struggles embodied by Cardenismo and Rubén Jaramillo. Cabañas's strategic emphasis on prolonged political organizing based on guerrillas "becoming the people" and prioritizing campesino political creativity paralleled influential Maoist tenets then circulating in parts of rural southern Mexico.[10]

During the summer of 1967 in the aftermath of two brutal massacres and years of state terror, Cabañas faced the challenge of how to harness campesino anger, indignation, and demands for vengeance within a broader revolutionary process. How could he help organize a "new revolution that will destroy the capitalist system, implement socialism in order to fulfill the ideals of justice that our people have fought for and defended in heroic battles of the past?"[11] How could the schoolteacher convince a rural population that initially wanted a guerrerense version of the Hampshire Blacks or Vehmgericht to rebalance a fragile moral economy by wreaking vengeance on unscrupulous caciques and state police forces?[12] In the last months of 1967, many poor and middling campesinos in the Costa Grande had vengeance on their minds.

Divine Violence, Campesino Style

Ominous signs of peasant class warfare appeared days before the 18 May 1967 Atoyac massacre. A movement formed by the parents of local schoolchildren who demanded the removal of an authoritarian school rector grew exponentially, drawing in ACG members, CCI campesinos, and teachers from other schools—including Cabañas. After local caciques and wealthy merchants issued death threats for those participating in the movement, the dissidents organized a clandestine nighttime assembly to discuss the possibility of violence, as they feared impending reprisal. Some at the assembly remembered the massacre of cívicos in 1960 and 1962. Others recalled how the local elites violently confronted the land invasions organized under the banner of Zapata after the 1960 fall of General Caballero. The assassinations of local peasant leaders such David Flores Reynada remained fresh in their memories.[13] Contingency plans and options soon emerged. Dissidents would resort to the Costa Grande tradition of fleeing into the nearly inaccessible surrounding mountain range for protection.[14]

Cabañas eventually took the floor. "We are tired of peacefully protesting, under the law, without accomplishing anything," the teacher remarked. Nothing, that is, except for drawing the ire of local caciques and their reactionary violence. Cabañas concluded with a dire warning: "if they kill or injure anyone of us, then we will finish off all of the rich townspeople."[15] Days later, when state police forces entered the main plaza of Atoyac to confront the protestors, the schoolteacher sarcastically announced the "arrival of repressive forces financed by the wealthy." Within minutes police forces opened fire on the protesting crowd. Seven people, including a pregnant woman and two state police agents, lay dead on the plaza floor. Arcadio Martínez was the first to fall, sacrificing himself to protect the main target of the firing police forces: Cabañas.[16] Popular rage spread throughout the Costa Grande. The next day, Cabañas told his host, fellow schoolteacher Hilda Flores, "the government has drastically reduced all pacific [constitutional] forms of struggle."[17]

Cabañas fled into the mountains with the help of activist rural schoolteachers linked to the MRM, ejido officials, local PCM militants, and campesinos. Rumors spread that he would flee to Cuba.[18] Days after the massacre, Cabañas and Flores appeared in the small community of El Ticuí, home to a textile cooperative organized by Flores's father decades earlier. Cabañas exhorted local residents to help him fulfill the promise he had made before the Atoyac massacre: kill off the rich. He identified several local wealthy merchants as the culprits responsible for the events of 18 May, encouraging enraged campesinos to attack "the commerce and property of Juvencio Luna, Wilfrido Fierro, Juan García, and Martín Salas Torres."[19] In essence, Cabañas advocated the using of violence for purposes beyond a simple settling of scores within a prolonged rich-versus-poor war. He sought to harness popular anger to finally end that rural class struggle and bring about revolution.

Throughout the rainy summer months of 1967, Cabañas traveled throughout the Atoyac mountains organizing daily political meetings in rural communities and speaking with campesinos enraged by the constant repression and massacres.[20] Despite increasing levels of military surveillance in the Costa Grande after a bombing attack on military vehicles by guerrillas linked to Chihuahua insurgents and Mexico City Maoists, he moved as "a fish" within water.[21] A network of extended family, independent campesino organizations organized by the PCM-allied CCI, radical rural schoolteachers, and local political officials aided the teacher. Relatives like his uncle Antonio Onofre Barrientos helped form the PDLP and served as guides for potential guerrilla recruits traveling to the mountains.[22] Cabañas's previous political experiences leading community struggles against logging companies and unpopular school rectors provided him with a trusted collection of local campesino allies. MRM schoolteachers throughout the Costa Grande region provided shelter and protection, including several later disappeared by state agents. Municipal and community authorities provided shelter and protection. A DFS memo dated 17 August 1967 noted that Cabañas and several allies armed with high-powered rifles traveled freely throughout the Atoyac municipality "without local authorities doing anything to prevent their indoctrination of peasants."[23] Community police forces (*defensas rurales*)—agrarian holdovers from the Cardenista years—refused to engage the guerrillas and also offered protection.[24] For Cabañas, the question soon became how to raise a broad base of rural support committed to sustaining and waging a campesino guerrilla revolution.

The mass killing of protesting copreros on 20 August 1967 in Acapulco further fanned the flames of popular protest. Cabañas later recalled:

> in those days there was much indignation in the region, much anger... and the people wanted to come down from the mountains with machetes in hand. They only wanted to momentarily express their anger, firing their weapons. They did not want to stay in the mountains, in the wild, like beasts [*brutitos*], as guerrilla warfare dictates. They did not yet believe in guerrilla warfare.[25]

Cabañas alluded to the political task that confronted his small group of two or three committed revolutionaries in late 1967: to convince the region's campesino communities to engage in the seeming "madness" of revolutionary insurrection via a methodology—guerrilla warfare—they initially rejected. Such a task required that the aspiring guerrilla leader personally travel through dozens of rural towns and hamlets on a sort of evangelizing mission and explain why he possessed the appropriate tactical response to elite cacique violence and massacre: "the people did not realize that [the wealthy] would finish us off if we attacked them frontally, that the appropriate form of struggle was guerrilla warfare…that using hit-and-run tactics provided the most effective way to attack caciques, or ambushing them at their merchant stores or properties."[26] To impart the revolutionary message, Cabañas organized rural meetings, his young student supporters distributed a newspaper entitled *The Huarachudo, Voice of the Poor*, and encouraged campesinos to hoard weapons and form self-defense guards. They also threatened and attacked the local-regional personification of power.[27] In the Costa Grande, state power was synonymous with individual wealthy caciques with last names like García, Luna, Gallardo, Rios, and Becerra.

The years 1967–8 were marked by extensive political proselytizing throughout the mountain ranges of the Costa, which involved what Sandinista guerrillas later described in Maoist terms as "the gathering of forces in silence."[28] Cabañas and one or two companions organized a vast clandestine support network operating across five Costa Grande municipalities capable of supporting a slowly growing rural guerrilla force.[29] Years later Cabañas would claim that 150 communities supported the guerrillas.[30] The schoolteacher courted the support of ejido commissaries and defensas rurales auxiliary guards.[31] Leftist students in Atoyac distributed his radical literature and responded to criminalizing cacique proclamations that portrayed the PDLP leader as a simple bandit.[32] By late September 1967, radical red and black antigovernment graffiti slogans appeared on the walls of homes and businesses in the city of Atoyac. In the minds of local-regional caciques, Cabañas represented a constant threat. Wealthy merchants began closing their businesses two hours early, scared by death threats and warnings "that in any moment campesinos would descend upon them and kill them since [caciques] did not agree with their ideals."[33] A day after Genaro Vázquez had dramatically escaped from Iguala's municipal prison on 22 April 1968, merchants and caciques in Atoyac discovered a pamphlet from Cabañas that exhorted campesinos to "take over the town and retake the wealth of the rich [*ricos*] since that wealth actually represented the sweat of the laboring exploited poor."[34]

With such statements Cabañas sought to channel popular rage and indignation into a rural class-struggle historically understood as the rich versus the poor. He sought to propagate a campesino definition of socialism "that was more a feeling than a theory,"[35] underscored by Costa Grande insurgent traditions and popular interpretations of 1910 and Cardenismo. In doing so, he employed polarized terms like the rich and the poor, exploiters and exploited, party of the rich (PRI) and party of the poor (PDLP), caciques and campesinos, "murderous" state police and "suffering" campesinos.[36] Using the experience he had gained as a rural schoolteacher and his personal knowledge of the region, Cabañas sought to reveal the core of revolutionary socialism that potentially moved people to risk everything in insurrection. George Orwell described this core as "justice and liberty... revolution and the overthrow of tyrants."[37] Walter Benjamin termed it workers' "hatred and spirit of sacrifice... nourished by the image of enslaved ancestors."[38] The schoolteacher-turned-guerrilla described the core in March 1969 as "the unity of [campesino] men and women prepared to kill the rich and state police... who are killing us... [Campesinos] be ready to defend your lives and fight for the justice of the poor."[39]

From the last months of 1967 to early 1969, public proclamations of an imminent peasant class-war against the rich complemented Cabañas's clandestine organizing of campesino communities. In documents produced by PRI state agents, he sporadically appears as a "professional agitator" leading a small criminal gang with "extremist tendencies" only when their activities, such as the "spread of subversive ideas" or the killing of a coffee cacique, are detected. The extortion of a wealthy merchant or the enunciation of public threats also attracted the PRI's attention.[40] A series of transcribed Cabañas speeches and interviews paints a portrait of the early formative days of the PDLP.[41] The schoolteacher engaged in a laborious everyday organizational effort that eventually forged an intricate network of auxiliary logistical support that connected urban centers like Acapulco and Chilpancingo to communities throughout the Costa Grande. He described the process as "being the people [*pueblo*], organizing the people, siding with the people"

> we proceeded to visit towns all over, to organize assemblies in towns, assemblies outside of towns, meetings in the countryside, in the mountains, in agricultural fields. We talked with everyone, at times on roads, in the mountains. That way we slowly, bit by bit, carried out a particular form of political instruction that eventually enabled us to provide revolutionary recommendations and orientation to the people. People eventually understood what guerrilla war meant but they still were not convinced.[42]

Military intelligence agents later identified these types of meetings as "study circles" that allowed Cabañas to "indoctrinate" campesinos in "subversive" political ideas.[43] Ex-PDLP militant Cárdenas remembered that such study circles in 1974 demonstrated,

> an internal democracy. Lucio told us to speak to campesinos in their language without fancy theory. He clearly said to us that campesinos didn't understand when spoken to about a dictatorship of the

proletariat, but they understood well when we told them that we were poor and there was an oppressive Party of the Rich.[44]

Though Cárdenas's description applies to study circles organized in March 1974, earlier study circles presumably followed a similar structural formula—a formula that posited a dialogic educational-political relationship between guerrillas and rural communities.

Cabañas envisioned aligned campesino communities forming the political base of the broader political-military movement and organization he dubbed the "Party of the Poor." The name simultaneously referred to the organizational structure, as a political party, and its fundamental compositional source—forged from the rural "poor."[45] Each rural community was to organize a "Committee of Struggle" that served to gather intelligence concerning the daily activities of the Mexican military and police for the PDLP, while also supplying the guerrillas with arms, food, and additional combatants. These committees functioned as the intermediaries between the PDLP and its rural base of popular support, essentially constituting—as said by a PDLP militant during an interrogation—the "eyes and heart" of the guerrilla organization.[46]

During the prolonged struggle waged against the PRI regime, the PDLP was thus meant to politically organize rural communities and logistically support its armed military wing, the Peasant Brigade of *Ajusticiamiento* (BCA). With its connotations of class terror and executions, the BCA also referred to the bringing of campesino justice. Cabañas and many campesinos in the aftermath of the 1967 massacres believed that only terror, the exercise of violence against the "rich," could bring forth justice. Dead victims of state violence, from ACG militants killed in 1960 and 1962 to the massacred copreros in 1967, demanded vengeance. Such a conceptualization of terror and justice recalled Robespierre's quote in the midst of the French revolutionary terror: "Terror is nothing but prompt, severe, inflexible justice."[47]

In late 1967 the addition of badly needed recruits, not the exercise of revolutionary class terror, primarily motivated the BCA. Cabañas remembered that early in the struggle, "me and one other [Clemente Hernández Barrientos]...we traveled around, we were the BCA."[48] That initial force of two slowly grew to include a dozen campesinos and schoolteachers by the first months of 1968. The PDLP leader divided the guerrilla force into two groups: guerrillas who joined the group on a temporary basis based on agricultural (cultivation and harvest) seasons and a smaller core of better-trained permanent fighters. The specific type of military action determined the size of BCA guerrilla columns.[49] By March 1968 unalarmed DGIPS agents reported that Cabañas, described as a "socialist disciple" of Vázquez, and his "group of bandits" included seventeen men who operated in a tiny region between the rural hamlets of La Remonta and

El Porvenir in the municipality of Atoyac. The PDLP represented just one gang of more than a dozen that operated in a state infamous for its supposed innate criminality.[50]

Securing and maintaining peasant support required more than study circles and meet-and-greets with BCA guerrillas. The BCA needed to carry out armed actions "to demonstrate to mountain [peasant] communities that guerrilla warfare was possible, and that the guerrilla could successfully combat and survive."[51] The small number of combatants, the lack of effective weapons and ammunition, and military inexperience limited the realm of possibilities for the nascent BCA to largely defensive actions. Take the issue of weapons, for example. Cabañas recalled that supportive campesino communities had financed and armed the BCA during the early days of the guerrilla struggle. In contrast to unnamed national political organizations that promised much but delivered little, "campesinos from here gave us our first weapons, the first automatic rifle, shotgun, and old carbine...all we had was a FAL [Belgian automatic rifle], an old 06 [Springfield .30-06], a single-shot shotgun, and a small pistol...yet we felt very brave."[52] Taking into account such limitations and the need to secure campesino support, the BCA took action for the first time in August 1968. DFS reports documented the BCA execution of a man named Tinito Villegas from the town of Cacalutla.[53]

In March 1969, a propaganda note appeared in the city of Atoyac in which the PDLP exhorted city residents to form a "party of poor" to violently overthrow the "party of the rich PRI that continued to kill students and campesinos."[54] The note's authors blamed the 18 May 1967 massacre on "the [city] rich and the traitors that supported them" and ended with a forceful call for revolution: "let's obtain justice with our own hands, death to state police forces, and *viva* the Party of the Poor!"[55] The BCA made its public appearance months later in May with a communiqué distributed en masse in Atoyac and plastered on principal buildings that thanked the community for providing crucial intelligence on army troop movements during a recent military counterinsurgency campaign.[56] The note vowed to continue the struggle to overthrow the PRI in memory of their fallen comrades:

> When we buried our comrades after the massacre an orator at the wake said, "We did not come here to bury them but to plant them...campesino justice will sprout from them." That was like a prophecy because the struggle has begun and no one will suppress it. We will not betray the cause.[57]

After the BCA authors had denied current newspaper reports that blamed them for a rash of assassinations, they forwarded a fateful warning: "when we begin to kill, tyrants will die, the same tyrants that ordered the massacres of campesinos and students...it's our generation's turn to exact demands from the Priísta government that betrayed the [1910] Revolution."[58]

State police forces (*judiciales*) represented one particularly odious local-regional node of priísta rule for the BCA and campesino communities. A BCA communiqué from March 1969 compared the judiciales to "the White Guards used by Porfirio Díaz to destroy the people's freedoms."[59] Months later, the BCA began to exact demands from the PRI regime by ambushing a truck caravan of state police forces. Ten "bearded men armed with automatic rifles" carried out the attack. The reporting IPS agent ventured an accurate assessment of the motives behind the ambush: "[the BCA guerrillas] blame the state police for the [May 1967] murder of Atoyac citizens."[60] Yet the popular hate dated back to the repressive gubernatorial regime of Caballero Aburto when some state police officers killed campesinos with impunity. "Nobody punished them," Cabañas remembered, "and we'd be full of rage witnessing such injustice and unable to do anything."[61] The revolution of the poor would thus begin by exacting vengeance and punishing caciques and judiciales.

Heaven-storming Attempts

The transformation of the PDLP-BCA from clandestine operations to overt guerrilla warfare can be generally divided into three phases: attacks on state police forces and local caciques (1969–72), ambushes of Mexican military forces (1972 to May 1974), and the kidnapping of Senator Rubén Figueroa and resulting fallout (May 1974 to December 1974). From 1969 to 1972 the Cabañas-led BCA carried out several executions of local caciques and ambushed state police patrols, with the extortion of wealthy merchants and landowners providing the necessary initial funding for the acquisition of weapons and supplies.[62] A small number of urban communists began to arrive in 1969 and joined the guerrillas. Schoolteachers Modesto Trujillo and Luis León Mendiola, who had known Cabañas from their activist normalista student days in the FECSM, joined the guerrillas, as did Trujillo's sister María Isabel.[63] A comrade from Ayotzinapa, schoolteacher Vicente Estrada Vega, arrived in late 1969 and served as a constant link to other radical organizations such as the Ho Chi Minh section of the Communist Sparticist League (LCE) and Jaramillista survivors in Morelos.[64] Medical student Ricardo Rodríguez González, a participant in the repressed 1964–5 medical workers' strike in Mexico City, arrived sometime in 1970 and agreed to serve as the organization's doctor. Upon arriving he was struck by the "immeasurable" level of popular support possessed by the PDLP.[65]

By May 1970 the BCA had taken credit in a communiqué sent to local and regional newspapers for a series of armed actions: the execution of two state police sergeants and two caciques whose gunmen had killed campesinos with impunity; the July 1969 ambush on state police forces; the coercing of a wealthy landowner to pay the salaries of his fifteen laborers; and the prevention of the presidential campaign of Luis Echeverría from visiting six of the seven municipalities that comprise the Costa Grande region. Indeed, a confidential DFS document written prior to Echeverría's campaign travels in Guerrero identified the ACNR and PDLP as real dangers to the presidential candidate.[66] In its communiqué, the BCA also related that "comrade Genaro Vázquez does not belong to our brigade yet he fights for the same motives as we do."[67]

Possibly more important than publicly revealing these actions, the communiqué disclosed the operation of four military counterinsurgency programs dating back to 1968 that aimed to suppress the guerrilla PDLP-BCA and Vázquez's ACNR. Such revelations contradicted the statements made by PRI officials and the Mexican military concerning the existence of guerrilla groups in Guerrero. In the aftermath of the 1968 Tlatelolco student massacre, the last thing the PRI regime wanted was to admit the existence of armed "subversives" in the impoverished sierras of southern Mexico. Additionally, the BCA authors decried the widespread violation of human rights committed by the Mexican army troops sent to Guerrero: "soldiers torture campesinos, asking them about us and the location of narcotics; they steal campesinos' clothes, money, and food, and they forcibly march them to Acapulco ... they also burn campesinos' chests with gasoline and brutally beat them."[68] DFS documents later backed BCA claims concerning the use of the gasoline in torture techniques; soldiers forced campesinos to drink gasoline and subsequently set them on fire.[69]

Facing two separate guerrilla movements, the military and PRI adopted a public lexicon of counterinsurgency in which bandits meant guerrillas, campesino support equaled the fear and coercion employed by armed criminals, and counterinsurgency signified, in the sarcastic words of the PDLP-BCA, "a social health campaign for the masses ... a campaign against the [opium] poppy farmers." BCA armed actions thus threatened the PRI regime's representation of its activities for domestic and international consumption. For instance, French newspapers *Le Monde* and *Le Figaro* published articles that respectively compared Cabañas to Emiliano Zapata and described the sending of 20,000 soldiers to coastal Guerrero to destroy the PDLP guerrillas.[70] *Le Figaro*'s report, sent to the military leadership in Mexico City by an attaché stationed at the Mexican embassy in France, prompted a press bulletin that forcefully refuted the article.[71] The PRI needed to maintain its national and international self-definition as a progressive and independent government with leftist inclinations and "revolutionary" heritage. Matching the government's counterinsurgency lexicon was the deployment of thousands of troops to Guerrero as early as 1971, sent initially to suppress the more famous ACNR. From 1968 to 1974, the military carried out sixteen different military campaigns in the coastal regions of Guerrero.[72]

Cabañas and the PDLP knew that their armed actions made them appear as bandits in the discourse of counterinsurgency utilized by the PRI. Moreover, they knew their Mexican history; how in the past Emiliano Zapata and Francisco Villa haunted "the rich class" as the nation's most dangerous "criminal bandits."[73] In communiqués sent to regional newspapers, the PDLP consistently countered official accusations that they stole money and livestock or that they killed without motive: "the thieves and murderers are others...those who have massacred campesinos...those who have the stolen the most are the ones that hate us the most; our cause is the cause of Juárez, Villa, and Zapata and like them we will be hated and slandered, but never defeated." Such responses indicated that the PDLP-BCA recognized the importance of this discursive contest waged between PRI officials and guerrilla fighters. Cabañas perceived that intelligent state-led counterinsurgency programs exercised on the nonmilitary fields of media discourse and socioeconomic assistance—as opposed to scorched-earth torture campaigns—potentially could unravel the political work carried out after the 1967 Atoyac massacre.[74] Yet, extortion and death threats issued against wealthy caciques financed the guerrilla movement. Such actions, even when couched in terms like "revolutionary expropriations" or the reclamation of "exploited campesino labor," required that the guerrillas tread carefully.

Cognizant of such dangers, the BCA added the kidnapping of wealthy landholders and bank robbery to their list of actions during the summer of 1970. Six BCA guerrillas, "armed with machine guns, wearing white tennis shoes and gray clothes, with covered faces," kidnapped Juan Gallardo Vega, a wealthy landowner and rancher from the coastal city of San Jerónimo.[75] After several days of captivity, the family of Gallardo Vega paid 100,000 pesos for his release. Gallardo Vega returned home unharmed while Cabañas distributed the money among fifteen BCA guerrillas. A subsequent bank robbery in Acapulco and the "expropriation" of 15,000 pesos from a cacique who mistreated his campesino workers joined the burgeoning list of BCA actions.[76] After the abductions of two regional doctors in early 1971, the guerrillas struck again with two high-profile kidnappings in the first months of 1972.[77] Jaime Farell worked as rector of a preparatory school in Acapulco and Cuauhtémoc García Teran was the son of one of the wealthiest coffee caciques in the Costa Grande.[78] García Teran returned to his family after the PDLP-BCA obtained a sizable ransom payment, while soldiers liberated Farell near Acapulco. As part of the ransom demands for the release of García Teran, regional and national newspapers published the political manifesto of the PDLP—the *Ideario Pobrista*—that outlined the guerrilla group's arguments for revolution and demands.[79]

The Farell abduction was also significant for revealing an expansion of PDLP military and political strategy. A student urban commando based in Acapulco organized and carried out the kidnapping, demonstrating for the first time the PDLP's ability and vision for organizing urban guerrilla units to complement the rural struggle.[80] Cabañas and the PDLP envisioned the development of multiple national urban guerrilla fronts that supported in auxiliary fashion the consolidation of various rural guerrilla columns. Captured PDLP documents revealed the role of urban guerrillas: "they needed to act as an extension of the BCA; enact sabotage campaigns, expropriate banks, and kidnap wealthy people to finance and supply the PDLP-BCA in Guerrero and, when ordered, carry out attacks on military/state police posts and/or barracks in order to distract state repressive campaigns."[81] The PDLP thus possessed a national vision of revolution with the countryside as the primary arena of struggle. In a letter sent to newspapers during the García Teran abduction, BCA guerrilla "Isidro Castro Fuentes" warned that the PDLP sought to overthrow the "government that has always belonged to the rich" through an armed struggle that extended throughout Mexico "until we destroy the current dictatorship and the poor govern the nation."[82]

PDLP practice matched the rhetoric. From 1970 to 1972, Cabañas utilized national networks forged during his years as FECSM student president, PCM militant, and MRM schoolteacher in an attempt to spread the guerrilla struggle beyond the mountains of Atoyac and Coyuca de Benítez. BCA guerrillas participated in "mixed brigades" with communist students from northern Mexico in urban bank expropriations.[83] In July 1971, Cabañas organized a meeting in Mexico City with a militant from the Maoist LCE and a schoolteacher from Aguascalientes named Filemón Bahena Román to discuss the possibility of forming an urban guerrilla unit in Bahena's home state.[84] One month later, PDLP literature distributed by a mysterious "Commission 'N' 13 '2 of October'" appeared in the city of Aguascalientes.[85] The commission soon morphed into the Armed Revolutionary Socialist Forces (FRAS) of Aguascalientes comprising professors and students. Like an earlier attempt to organize PDLP guerrilla fronts in Veracruz, the FRAS attempt failed when DFS agents detected the group and detained several members after a failed bank robbery.[86] Subsequent efforts in early 1972 to organize guerrilla fronts in Chiapas and Sonora (the latter led by Cabañas's younger brother Pablo) met a similar failed end.[87] Captured FRAS documents explained the purpose of extending the PDLP revolution beyond Guerrero: "In Mexico the only way to achieve the liberation of the poor is through armed struggle and that struggle needs to be conducted in the countryside and the urban front will act in service and support of the rural front."[88] Cabañas and the PDLP-BCA thus posited the campesino and the countryside as the revolutionary protagonist and context in the attempt to enact a new Mexican revolution. Such a posture would later create conflicts with the largest urban guerrilla group in Mexico, the Communist League 23 of September (LC23S).[89]

Following the high-profile Farrell and García Teran kidnappings during the first half of 1972, Cabañas and the PDLP started to debate the utility of an ambush directed against the Mexican Army. By mid-1972, the army had significantly increased its presence in the Atoyac region in response to the abductions conducted by PDLP and ACNR guerrillas. Military brass ordered the construction of barracks for additional battalions and continued to mount ineffective but violent counterinsurgency campaigns that resulted in illegal detentions, torture, and extrajudicial assassinations in the region's campesino communities.[90] At this point the PDLP-BCA, which numbered between thirteen and twenty permanent fighters, began to accept various urban guerrillas from other organizations who provided the necessary military training and support. Two militants, Arnulfo Ariza and normalista Wenceslao García José, initially arrived from the Movement of Revolutionary Action (MAR), an organization composed of Mexican communist university students who met at the Patrice Lumumba University in Moscow and received politico-military training in North Korea during the late 1960s.[91] A second wave of ten marineros (the nickname of MAR guerrillas) would subsequently arrive to provide training in guerrilla tactics, communications, weapons handling, and even judo and karate.[92]

The date 25 June 1972 marked a watershed moment for the PDLP-BCA, the Mexican military, and the campesino inhabitants of the Costa Grande region. A few kilometers from the small town of San Andrés de la Cruz, two military trucks transporting members of the 50th Infantry Battalion passed through a hailstorm of M-1 and M-2 bullets.[93] Ten soldiers died in an ambush that, according to the testimony of two surviving wounded soldiers, lasted less than fifteen minutes. For the PDLP, this attack consolidated their presence in the Costa Grande region as a guerrilla group able to inflict considerable military damage, a reputation further solidified with later, more costly, ambushes. An ambush enacted on 23 August 1972 resulted in eighteen military deaths, including several officers. Surviving soldiers claimed that 150 guerrillas attacked them, armed with automatic rifles and led by Cabañas (actually twenty or twenty-five BCA fighters participated).[94] The classic guerrilla-style attacks allowed the BCA to capture high-powered automatic weapons and ammunition. Both the army and the PRI regime recognized they now confronted a well-armed guerrilla organization versed in guerrilla warfare tactics and possessing a strong base of campesino support in the region.[95] A military intelligence report produced a day after the August ambush declared that the PDLP-BCA "constituted a strong and powerful threat for any military unit smaller than a battalion or regiment...sustained by either the voluntary or coerced support of campesinos as well as by their knowledge of operational terrain."[96]

Despite the ambushes the PDLP represented a limited military threat for the PRI regime but a potentially costly political risk. What would happen if the guerrillas managed to spread their struggle beyond the Costa Grande?[97] An internal report from the DFS produced after the first ambush proclaimed (somewhat hyperbolically) that the PDLP "accomplished what no other organization had achieved: the unification of clandestine leftist groups, currently active in the country, and throughout its area of operation, [the PDLP] spread and consolidated its network of intelligence, supply, and protection in both rural and urban sectors."[98] A subsequent analysis in September 1972 described the extent of peasant support for the PDLP, albeit in counterinsurgent prose: "due to the politicization campaigns conducted by Cabañas, he has obtained a great number of supporters in the mountains, with some exhibiting considerable fanaticism."[99] In response to the second ambush, the army mobilized five army battalions along with 10,000 state police on 25 August 1972. For campesinos, particularly those living in the towns in the immediate vicinity of the armed clashes, the ambushes resulted in increased repression and violence exercised by a simultaneously enraged and demoralized military.[100] 25 June 1972 thus represented a systematic shift in regime strategy.[101] Guerrero became an intensified hypertheater of counterinsurgency as the PRI attempted to discover, destroy and/or co-opt the invisible networks of rural communal support that sustained the guerrillas.

Blood and Coffee

The attacks on military caravans carried out by popularly backed rural guerrillas highlighted the need for the PRI regime to adopt a winning hearts-and-minds counterinsurgent strategy. In response to the second ambush, a colonel proposed in a classified report that the military "advise the President of the Republic... to implement a broad economic program in the region as a strategy to reduce [popular] discontent and, above all, to undermine the region's support for those who oppose the Government through illicit means."[102] A month later, state governor Israel Nogueda announced the implementation of "Plan Guerrero," which called for comprehensive irrigation programs, electrification, the construction of roads, schools, and hospitals, as well as the provision of drinking water, credit for small producers, and federal assistance for primary (agricultural) industrialization. Amid an increasingly savage theater of counterinsurgency and violent military actions directed at campesino communities, President Echeverría promised a more equitable rural social order.[103]

This new order depended primarily on heavy public spending. By 1974, the regime had vigorously recapitalized state-owned coffee and copra companies that purchased campesino products for higher prices than those offered by

local-regional caciques. In addition to reorganizing another state-owned company to regulate forestry and logging, the Plan also built more than seventy roads
in the mountains of Atoyac, ninety hydraulic works, and provided 180 million
pesos in credit to campesinos through the ejido bank, Banjidal. By 1980, the
state had spent over 400 million pesos on Guerrero alone.[104] That same year
marked the Mexican Institute of Coffee's (INMECAFE) purchase of 75 percent
of the region's annual coffee harvest. While ultimately failing to create a socialist
utopia through armed revolution, the PDLP and the statist public spending program financed primarily by foreign loans forced coastal caciques to cede much
of their regional political-economic power.[105]

Yet the counterinsurgent motives of Plan Guerrero attached the developmental program to the longevity of the guerrilla groups. When the PDLP reached
its peak of regional power between 1973 and the early months of 1974, creating
what political scientist Marco Bellingeri described as a type of "mobile parallel
power" to PRI rule, money poured into the coffers of the INMECAFE—sixteen million pesos in 1973 and twenty-one million in 1974—in order to provide
small coffee peasants with credit.[106] As caciques left the region, INMECAFE
purchased their processing plants in Atoyac and in the surrounding mountain
communities. After the killing of Cabañas in December 1974, though, the massive provision of credits to campesinos stopped. 1975 witnessed a decline with
the distribution of nine million pesos—a level of funding that remained stable
throughout the decade. As Atoyac campesino leader Hilario Mesino reflected
some thirty years later, "we fell into the trap of Plan Guerrero...what a coin-
cidence that when they capture Professor Lucio Cabañas, [the state] picks up
everything and leaves." [107]

Plan Guerrero formed part of a counterinsurgency program designed
to physically eliminate the insurgent guerrillas by militarily targeting their
base of popular support as Echeverría and state governors announced
wide-ranging structural reforms. The Mexican president understood that
historic socioeconomic inequality—sustained by cacique violence—generated widespread support for the PDLP. While compelled to ameliorate such
factors, Echeverría and his civilian administration could not tolerate, amid
significant peasant and worker unrest nationally, armed rebellion as a political option—particularly if that rebellion demonstrated an ability to spread.
Fausto Cantú Peña, head of INMECAFE during the 1970s, revealed that for
the PRI regime the Atoyac region represented a politically dangerous place,
"since there existed a fear that Lucio Cabañas could become the spokesman
for similar [campesino] demands in other parts of the country."[108] Thus, as
recently declassified documents show, Echeverría ordered the annihilation
of the PDLP in a military-led counterinsurgency characterized by the violent
targeting of the civilian population.[109]

Coerced disappearances of campesinos, detainment of entire communities, torture, and extralegal assassinations carried out by the military and state police forces became everyday occurrences. By late 1973, military restrictions on the transport of food and medicine into the Costa Grande inflicted dire hardships upon the region's impoverished communities. Such blockade tactics aimed to deprive the PDLP "fish" of its "water," being directed against supporting communities "with the sole purpose of destroying [the PDLP's] network of intelligence, supply, and recruitment."[110] A military report that announced the inauguration of "Plan Atoyac" in July 1974 explicitly stated that the authorities would exercise strict control over food supplies entering the region as an attempt to "starve out" PDLP guerrilla fighters.[111] Declassified documents also reveal the military's development of a "lexicon of terror" used to denote the unconstitutional practices of unlawful arrests, torture, and disappearance.[112] Within daily military correspondence, torture became "revision" or "interrogation," and an illegally detained person a "package." At times a long-held "archived package" possessed a name.[113] The fact that General Hermenegildo Cuenca Díaz, head of the Mexican military as Secretary of Defense, systematically used such language by mid-1973 in internal documentation addressed to high-ranking PRI officials suggests that orders for violations of constitutional and human rights came from the very top of the PRI regime.[114] Nearly 600 documented inhabitants, most from the Atoyac region, remain disappeared.[115] The disappeared most likely experienced torture and execution in the military camps of Acapulco, Pie de la Cuesta, Atoyac, and Mexico City. Countless others suffered illegal detention and torture. An unknown number of victims suffered "death flights." After being thrown off airplanes stationed near the port of Acapulco, they disappeared in the Pacific Ocean.[116]

An Enemy of Zapata

The period of June 1973 to December 1974 marked the zenith and then slow decline of the PDLP's military and territorial power in the Costa Grande region. By early 1974, an estimated 100–150 well-armed guerrillas regularly traversed large swaths of territory in at least six Costa Grande municipalities.[117] Robust urban networks existed in Acapulco and Chilpancingo. Low morale and desertion characterized federal army forces stationed in the region; they preferred the safety of barracks to search-and-destroy missions in the mountains.[118] Yet the group faced serious challenges. For one, the PDLP needed to expand its theater of operations beyond the Costa Grande to spread its poor people's revolution and avoid being besieged by the thousands of military troops that began to arrive by 1973. In addition to increased military operations that targeted rural communities, the PDLP faced a number of socioeconomic and political reforms initiated by President Echeverría and millions of dollars poured into the region by the federal government for developmental purposes. Cabañas noted that this latest counterinsurgency operation exhibited "more political acumen, and more technical support: helicopters, tanks, airplanes, many heavy trucks, a lot of army and even more FAL [automatic rifles] ... And new roads and spies and cows and CONASUPO [state-owned food stores]."[119]

The guerrilla leader thus recognized the potential effectiveness of the PRI regime's updated counterinsurgency program that violently attacked rural communities while offering them the trappings of economic development. Dozens of PDLP guerrillas and supporters suffered brutal attacks at the hands of the Mexican military throughout 1973 and 1974. Military bases in Mexico City and Acapulco operated as clandestine prisons and torture centers. While detainees in 1971 or 1972 occasionally faced formal legal proceedings and sentencing within the state's judicial system, new counterinsurgent tactics in 1973 followed a different methodology. Incensed by the release in early 1973 of dozens of campesinos accused of logistically supporting PDLP ambushes and the assassination of prominent businessman Eugenio Garza Sada in September 1973 by urban guerrillas, the military decided not to turn over suspects to judicial authorities.[120] The disappearance of suspects became a systematic technique to discipline real, imagined, and potential guerrilla supporters.

Internally, the PDLP-BCA suffered serious political divisions during the first half of 1973. The issue of explicitly defining a strict political line for the organization had produced sustained critical debates within the BCA leadership. Cabañas's insistence on maintaining an open socialist heterodoxy as articulated by the group's peasant base led to charges of *caudillismo* and "lack of political clarity" by two members of the five-person leadership directory.[121] Both members soon requested and received permission to leave the BCA. Though Cabañas emerged victorious—BCA guerrillas democratically elected him to continue as leader—the episode foreshadowed political conflicts. The PDLP leader received similar political criticisms in November 1972 during a national conference of armed revolutionary groups organized in the mountains of Guerrero with the goal of creating a unified national insurrectionary front. Future members of the LC23S (officially founded in March 1973) unequivocally defined revolution as the struggle led by the proletariat (including schoolteachers and students) against the bourgeoisie and capital. Any other definition smacked of "petit bourgeois reformism." Cabañas cleverly responded by asserting that almost everyone living in the mountainous Costa Grande assumed a proletarian identity since "the little piece of land they own fails to sustain them." They therefore had to engage in some form of supplemental agricultural employment.[122]

Another issue arose when Inocencio Castro, a member of the PCM-linked MRM and an old friend of Cabañas, joined the conference. Castro's presence highlighted the ambiguous historical relationship sustained throughout the years between Cabañas and his guerrilla group with a PCM that publicly rejected armed struggle as a political strategy. For urban guerrillas, that relationship inspired distrust and an ideological mistake. LC23S militants generally viewed the PCM as an inept organization, beholden to a reformist line that had failed to bring about revolutionary change in Mexico. For Cabañas, the ongoing contact with the PCM revealed his open tactical approach to other political organizations and methods of political struggle. Throughout his time as insurgent leader, he worked with multiple guerrilla and nonarmed organizations. Unlike LC23S militants, the guerrilla leader refused to define political ideology and revolutionary method in orthodox terms. Rather, he preferred a revolutionary methodology that encouraged "combining all possible forms of struggle."[123] As he later wrote, in a 1974 communiqué addressed to students at the Guerrero state university, "we believe that guerrilla warfare in the mountains and in the great cities constitutes the primary revolutionary struggle... [yet] the PDLP pronounces itself in favor of using all forms of struggle that help advance the broader revolutionary struggle... [excepting] electoral politics."[124] For Cabañas and the PDLP, historical and lived experience formed the basis for the development of revolutionary theory and praxis. Revolutionary theory derived from books, he once remarked, is dead theory.[125]

Yet for the LC23S, and some PDLP members, the lack of theoretical rigor and preparation within the insurgent group limited its revolutionary potential. If Cabañas looked to the people to obtain a political "mass line," the more orthodox Marxist-Leninist guerrillas believed in the necessity of orienting the popular classes to an ideological position of Marxism-Leninism. To that end, five future LC23S guerrillas joined the PDLP in the first days of 1973, harboring the clandestine goal of rectifying what they considered rampant "petit bourgeois reformism" within the guerrilla group.[126] They, along with internal BCA critics of Cabañas, got the opportunity to implement their political methods in early 1973 when the schoolteacher left Guerrero to seek medical treatment in Mexico City and reconnect with political contacts in several states. Carmelo Cortés, a former state university student leader and ex-member of the PCM-aligned Communist Youth (JCM) from the Atoyac region, assumed temporary leadership of the PDLP. From January to March 1973, Cortés would attempt to politicize and theoretically prepare the bases of popular support and BCA combatants.[127]

Such a task did not necessarily make Cortés and the LC23S guerrillas natural allies. During Cortés's short tenure as leader, an internal battle was waged against the visiting urban militants who inspired internal division. Like Cabañas, the former student leader believed the countryside was the primary arena of revolutionary struggle and recognized the importance of maintaining strategic alliances with other popular organizations that fought for revolutionary change. In contrast to the schoolteacher, Cortés believed in publicly and internally defining the PDLP's socialist orientation in more orthodox Marxist terms.[128] His demands that BCA guerrillas rigorously study Marxism-Leninism and engage in collective self-criticism to address internal failings signaled "that PDLP activities adopted a more dynamic character."[129] When Cabañas returned to the mountains of Guerrero in March or April 1973 he discovered an organization rife with internal divisions between Cortés's partisans and the LC23S militants. He also discovered a new, second PDLP *Ideario Pobrista* that defined the revolutionary struggle in Guerrero as Marxist, anti-capitalist, and internationalist: "to conquer political power; destroy the oppressive and exploitative bourgeois State; construct a proletarian State and form a government of all workers; to forge a new society, without exploiters or the exploited, oppressors or the oppressed."[130] Such political discourse demonstrated the influence of Cortés's work.

To resolve these political divisions and eradicate internal factionalism, Cabañas reaffirmed his role as the PDLP-BCA leader. He worked to undermine the popularity of Cortés by using a personal matter—the latter allegedly "stole" the female partner of an LC23S guerrilla—to arrange a disciplinary action. BCA and LC23S militants voted to temporarily expel both Cortés and his partner, Aurora de la Paz Navarro. They never returned, subsequently organizing an urban guerrilla group in Acapulco (taking with them a number of BCA guerrillas) that acted autonomously from the PDLP.[131] Cabañas then turned his attention to the LC23S members. At the second general assembly of the PDLP in June 1973, he openly attacked them as militaristic, charging them with exhibiting a "blind radicalism" and dogmatism "disconnected from reality." In other words, they "theorized much but failed to understand and connect with the people."[132] LC23S militants responded that the mere presence of "opportunist" Maoist, PCM, and Jaramillista activists at the assembly demonstrated the "degenerating," petit bourgeois politics of the PDLP.[133] Such "political divergences," DFS agents wrote on the typed interrogation transcripts of LC23S guerrilla Marisol Orozco Vega, sealed the fate of the urban militants.[134] The BCA expelled them in July 1973.

Amid these internal conflicts and mounting military repression in the summer of 1973, the PDLP worked to consolidate its support from communities throughout the Costa Grande. Following the high-profile military ambushes in 1972, the PDLP attempted to enact a strategic shift away from strictly military actions to the political organization of campesinos and rural communities and an expansion into other regions of Guerrero.[135] Working through their "Committees of Struggle" set up throughout the region's villages and towns, the guerrillas organized a series of popular assemblies in late 1973 and early 1974, during which they explained the motives behind their guerrilla struggle. In the small villages of Plan de los Molinos, El Porvenir,[136] Las Compuertas, San Cristobal, Santa Barbara, Santa Rosa (in the Chilpancingo region), San Juan de las Flores,[137] and San Miguel, 60–150 PDLP guerrillas organized day-long peasant assemblies.[138] To cite one example, an assembly in Rio Santiago on 17 March 1974, organized a day after the military occupied the town and tortured several residents in public, resulted in fourteen local youths joining PDLP ranks.[139] Saúl López de la Torre, a MAR guerrilla sent to work with the PDLP in August 1972, remembered that "all of them [the guerrillas] had a grievance, a personal thing that motivated them to fight the military." Such personal reasons for insurrectionary militancy, for de la Torre and other urban insurgents, demonstrated "the lack of political [i.e., Marxist] training."[140]

The guerrillas thus profited from a regional peasant structure of feeling characterized by antimilitary and anti-PRI hatred produced by state terror.[141] Even some local PRI militants decried such terror, as Atoyac PRI Youth cadre and student Jorge Radilla Galeana did in November 1972, recognizing that military violence only convinced "more campesinos to join the Party of the Poor" with vengeful aspirations.[142] If, by late 1973, the PDLP had not established a territorial liberated zone, the group did manage to partially circumvent military control of the region through the clandestine operation of its campesino "Committees of Struggle" network that included municipal authorities, army deserters,[143] rural schoolteachers, merchants, ejido commissaries, and even a Spanish Republican communist medic.[144] José Antonio Palós Palma served as medic to the BCA in a covert "security house" in Atoyac and provided military advice gained from his experiences in the Spanish Civil War and war studies in the Soviet Union.[145]

Continued attacks on military convoys and the executions of people identified by the BCA as military spies and informants (nicknamed *orejas*) further solidified the guerrillas' politico-military position.[146] In addition to the support of an estimated 150 rural communities, by 1974 the insurgent organization could also count on an urban network that linked the Costa Grande to Acapulco, Chilpancingo, and Mexico City.[147] With the organizational help of students, teachers, and PCM militants, the PDLP gained the support of urban workers. In Acapulco, taxi drivers, hotel workers, peddlers working the beaches, and market vendors joined the struggle. A number of leaders from the Metro (subway) workers union in Mexico City also participated with the PDLP. The rebels in the mountains could also count on logistical support from a considerable number of state university students and professors in Chilpancingo. Ex-PDLP militant Antonio Hernández estimated 1500 urban activists closely collaborated with the rural guerrillas.[148]

In the coastal countryside, the militarization of campesinos' daily lives mounted as the military restricted food and medical supplies and established curfews for the Costa Grande in a campaign that sought to starved nearly forty communities of the Atoyac region.[149] Realizing that increasing levels of repression could ultimately isolate them from their social base, the PDLP decided to carry out a spectacular act: the kidnapping of Rubén Figueroa Figueroa, a wealthy member of the PRI political elite, federal senator, and a close friend of President Echeverría. Since late 1972 Figueroa, also the leader of the PRI-controlled national truckers' union, had exhorted Cabañas to accept an amnesty offered by the federal government. As he began to position himself as a possible gubernatorial candidate, Figueroa repeatedly made calls to the guerrilla leader to set up an interview seeking a political solution to the conflict. In the midst of an intensified military occupation, the PDLP finally agreed to an audience with the future governor in May 1974. At the meeting in the mountains above Atoyac on 30 May, Cabañas informed Figueroa that the PDLP had decided to take him and his two companions as hostages until the federal government fulfilled a list of demands. For dialogue even to commence, the PDLP demanded the removal of military forces from the Costa Grande municipalities of Tecpan de Galeana, Coyuca de Benítez, San Jerónimo, and Atoyac de Álvarez, as well as fifty million pesos from the Figueroa family.[150]

The kidnapping gave the PDLP national exposure. National newspapers published the communiqués from the mountains of Guerrero and brought public attention to the military presence in the southern state. Yet the kidnapping also marked the beginning of the PDLP's decline. Rather than force the removal of military forces from the region, the act strengthened the resolve of the federal government to reject negotiation and annihilate the guerrilla group.[151] Illegal arrests, torture, and disappearances of individual guerrillas and supporters increased as the army combed the mountains for Figueroa. In the process they obtained intelligence that resulted in the rescue of the senator in September.[152] During the rescue operation military forces killed one guerrilla and destroyed one of two existing BCA combat columns charged with protecting the kidnapped.[153] Figueroa emerged as the courageous politician, denouncing Cabañas before the Federal Senate and soon after receiving the gubernatorial designation from the PRI. Scattered throughout the Costa Grande, the guerrillas who survived the rescue operation tried unsuccessfully to establish contact with the remaining Cabañas-led column.[154] Military forces soon recovered most of the millions of pesos delivered to the PDLP by the Figueroa family.[155] Declassified military documents reveal an intensified apprehension of key guerrilla contacts and fighters from September to November that produced the necessary intelligence to locate the Cabañas-led column.[156] Additional documents reveal high levels of popular discontent with continuing military operations that violently targeted civilians. The town of Cacalutla suffered what many other communities did in September 1974: "1500 inhabitants, living under the shadow of rifle bayonets, suffer a situation similar to concentration camps during war time ... no one does anything without the permission of the military."[157]

Some scholars and ex-guerrillas blame the failed kidnapping and unrealistic demands on Cabañas's limited political vision and horizon.[158] Yet tactical errors are not the same as broader evaluations of PDLP politics that reproduce traditional representations of "backward, localist" peasant political cultures. Cabañas and the PDLP leadership effectively miscalculated President Echeverría's willingness to negotiate (after previous high-profile kidnappings committed by the ACNR and urban guerrillas), the effectiveness of counterinsurgency operations, and the military capacities of other Mexican guerrilla groups from whom the PDLP expected aid.[159] From a military standpoint, the choice to kidnap Figueroa as a way to force concessions from the federal government seemed strange, even mad. But from a political standpoint, taking the cacique hostage represented an attempt to galvanize campesino support throughout the state by invoking history. In Guerrero, the Figueroa family historically represented the 1910 Madero-Carranza faction responsible for the assassination of Emiliano Zapata. In a communiqué sent during the kidnapping affair, the guerrillas responded to official accusations that they had tricked Figueroa:

> Recall, bourgeois Carrancistas, that you organized a worse trick against Emiliano Zapata. You called him to Chinameca claiming to join this cause but received him with bullets; the people's hope died there and that is why today we must wage a socialist revolution. Our path is illuminated by the great examples of [José María] Morelos, Francisco Villa, Ricardo Flores Magón, and Emiliano Zapata.[160]

The year 1910 and Zapata, in other words, necessitated revolutionary redemption as attempted in the mountains of Guerrero by BCA guerrillas. The specters of betrayed insurgent histories refused to disappear.

Last Stand

The military and scattered groups of BCA fighters continued to clash in late 1974, resulting in some considerable losses for the army.[161] Cabañas and three accompanying guerrillas were discovered and killed in combat on 2 December 1974 in El Otatal, a small community located in the municipality of Tecpan de Galeana.[162] A local campesino and alleged marijuana farmer had betrayed the location of the remaining guerrillas. This, at least, is the official story. Recent evidence suggests a range of different stories. According to a recently discovered letter written by a soldier who participated in the operation, Cabañas committed suicide to prevent his capture.[163] The extrajudicial execution of the insurgent leader by the Mexican military also is a possibility.[164] Soldiers most likely detained and executed the two rural schoolteachers, "Rene" (Lino Rosas Pérez) and "Arturo" (Esteban Mesino Martínez), who accompanied Cabañas.[165] Photographs taken by the military at the battle site and initial battle reports show a detained fourth fighter alive after the fighting: fifteen-year-old Marcelo Serafín Juárez ("Roberto").[166] Subsequent military records officially listed him as killed in combat. The young guerrilla remains disappeared.

Following the armed confrontation, the military transported Cabañas's body to Atoyac and filmed his autopsy in the presence of high-ranking military officers. The PRI regime reported the death of a "criminal and bandit," while the United States Embassy in Mexico announced the death of "the only terrorist known by name to the Mexican public." Meanwhile, students in Mexico City took over buses and spray-painted slogans honoring the fallen guerrilla leader and vowing to continue his fight.[167] Ayotzinapa normalistas stopped vehicles on the Tixtla-Chilpancingo road and painted them with slogans: "death to Rubén Figueroa!"[168] While military officials secretly buried Cabañas, his mother Rafaela Gervasio Barrientos and his guerrilla wife Isabel Ayala Nava languished in the main military prison in Mexico City, as did Micaela, the baby daughter Cabañas never met.[169]

Governments have a tendency to believe that killing charismatic leaders with subversive ideas and alternative imaginings of the world will ensure that their ideas will also die. Yet Cabañas was seemingly so subversive that the PRI government concealed the location of his burial plot for decades. His final three guerrilla companions, too, suffered the fate of clandestine burial sites hidden from their mourning families. Unlike Vázquez, the rural schoolteacher who led a peasant "war against the rich" would receive no public wake and funeral, only a secret burial.[170] Military officials subsequently denied that they possessed information on the whereabouts of the guerrilla leader's grave. General Eliseo Jiménez, commander of the final military operations that defeated the PDLP, proclaimed in a late 1970s interview, "everyone knew where the grave was." He also offered a final evaluation of Cabañas and the PDLP: "I qualify such guerrillas as deluded dreamers because they did not possess the support of the people."[171]

Campesinos in coastal Guerrero remember the movement and its leader differently. Some ardently believe that Cabañas is alive, waiting to return to finish the revolution.[172] The death of the popular hero and the military defeat of his revolutionary movement did not translate into the death of his radical ideals in collective popular memory. In large part, Cabañas succeeded in forming a guerrilla force of 100–240 combatants supported by dozens of peasant communities throughout the Costa Grande because, to quote George Orwell, he "made it clear that the essential aims of Socialism are Justice and Liberty."[173] For a region that experienced repeated state-sponsored massacres and terror, dignity could be added to Orwell's description. Cabañas became an improvised guerrilla leader but he never ceased being the rural schoolteacher. From teaching malnourished peasant children, he moved on to teaching campesinos something about guerrilla revolution. In turn he learned much about long-held peasant utopias imbued with historical demands for justice, liberty, and dignity. That revolutionary core moved hundreds of peasant guerrillas and thousands of collaborators to risk everything to create a better world. To defeat such popular passion and radical longings, the PRI regime enacted a military-led form of state terror that utilized the same violent practices and methods used by southern cone military dictatorships. Yet the utopias and longings persisted.

Conclusion: A Poor People's Utopia

Eleven-year-old Don Petronilo Castro Hernández joined the 1910 revolution alongside his mother. While his older cousin Silvestre Castro ("El Cirguelo") reached the rank of general, Don Petronilo ended the revolution as a lieutenant. He then returned to his native Atoyac de Álvarez, where he worked as a campesino and married Julia Molina Valdovinos. Together they raised a family of ten children. By the 1950s, Don Petronilo had spent decades organizing campesino communities to demand constitutionally mandated land-tenure rights and equitable access to forestry resources "because he believed the land belongs to those who work it."[1] Like campesinos elsewhere in post-1940 Mexico, he wanted PRI projects for political and economic modernization to benefit rural communities.[2] Elected as ejidal commissary and representative for his community, he would later participate in the civic struggles of the early 1960s.

After the 1967 massacre in Atoyac, Don Petronilo decided to become a revolutionary anew. Decades removed from 1910, the elderly campesino would make a new revolution since "campesinos needed justice."[3] Adopting the guerrilla pseudonym of "Elias," he helped Lucio Cabañas travel throughout the coastal mountains to escape detection after the massacre. "Elias" later participated in the formation of the PDLP-BCA, using his revolutionary experience to provide military training.[4] By the early 1970s he had led the organizing of guerrilla logistical support cells in Acapulco. Yet his participation in the new revolution proved costly. In late April 1972 military units detained Castro Hernández in Acapulco, dragging the seventy-six-year-old campesino out of his home by his belt. Days earlier his daughter Guadalupe, detained and tortured at the military base in the port city, had provided the names and addresses of PDLP supporters living in Acapulco.[5] On 25 April 1972, nine people arrived at Military Camp Number 1 (CM1) in Mexico City. Eight, including Don Petronilo and Guadalupe, would "disappear." The old campesino left behind etchings on his cell wall testifying to his detention.[6]

Why did people like Don Petronilo and Guadalupe risk their lives to make a new revolution? Why did schoolteachers, women, campesinos, children,

Catholic laypersons, students, municipal authorities, army deserters, and elderly persons participate in the PDLP insurrection? Don Petronilo's interrogation transcripts provide some hints about their motivations. When discussing the guerrillas' socialist vision for a post-PRI Mexico, the old campesino described "a government of campesino-popular extraction" focused on providing the countryside with jobs, economic advancement, hospitals, schools, subsidized health care, and educational opportunities through the university level.[7] Guerrilla socialism, as interpreted by Don Petronilo, harkened back to the promises of democratic and equitable economic modernization made by Lázaro Cárdenas during the 1930s or the social democratic visions that spread throughout Latin America immediately after the Second World War. Taking up arms to overthrow a violently authoritarian regime constituted an active and dangerous decision, underscored by a plethora of political and historical motivations—productive motivations that would shape the *pobrista* political community in case of revolutionary victory. Personal motives, too, shaped decisions to join and support the guerrillas. Indeed, two of Don Petronilo's children (and two sons-in-law) subsequently became urban guerrillas in Acapulco, seeking vengeance for the disappearance of their father and sister.[8] If vengeance powered the "poor people's" revolution, then the popular politics and memories of campesinos such as Don Petronilo provided the utopian hope for a postrevolutionary society.

This last section examines the PDLP's definition of campesino utopian hope: the creation of a poor people's state, grounded in the region's history of popular political mobilizations, imagined in the face of state terror, and influenced by the possibility of radical change represented by the Cuban revolution and an insurgent Third World amid a global Cold War. The poor people's state represented more than a simple inversion of the PRI government. Rather, it was an original project, or, perhaps, a project unfulfilled or betrayed in the eyes of campesino insurgents like Don Petronilo. The legacies of the 1910 revolution, Zapatista and Cardenista agrarianism in particular, loomed large in the region. Revolutionary Cuba and the emergence of a guerrilla New Left based on direct action influenced some Mexican leftists weary of state repression and the gradualist strategies espoused by the PCM. The region's guerrilla struggles of the 1920s for an equitable and democratic socioeconomic order without commercial and agricultural boss rule provided tactical suggestions and ideological propositions. In sum, the convergence of multiple political and geographic strands contributed to the creative, heterogeneous revolutionary imaginary of the Costa Grande guerrillas.

A gap did exist between the politics of the PDLP leaders and their campesino base. Despite the PDLP's arduous project of "being the people [*pueblo*], organizing the people, siding with the people" and its success in forging a popular base of support, doubts remain about whether the people actually accepted the

Marxist doctrines—despite Cabañas's rural schoolteacher ability to manifest and transmit such doctrines as "a critical knowledge of everyday life."[9] A radical definition of popular democracy, one that combined personal dignity and collective solidarity, constituted a crucial point of convergence between PDLP leaders and a rural base that had historically supported the radically social democratic Escudero, Vidales, and de la Cruz campesino movements of the 1920s.[10] That core of personal dignity and collective solidarity also galvanized the civic insurgencies of the 1960s.

Personal dignity and collectively solidarity underscored an additional point of convergence between guerrillas and rural communities: the elaboration of an alternative nationalism based on social justice and popular interpretations of Mexican history that posited the PRI as the "bad government," the betrayer of the 1910 revolution and 1917 Constitution. In a communiqué left behind at the scene of the 25 June 1972 ambush, the PDLP stated: "we want to remind the army and police that to defend the bad government means betraying the homeland [*patria*] of Cuauhtémoc, Morelos, and Zapata. Those of us who are patriots and lovers of liberty will unite our forces to violently overthrow the dictatorial government of Luis Echeverría."[11] Communiqués published several months prior to the first attack on military convoys also reaffirmed the nationalist and patriotic roots of the PDLP struggle: "this new revolution is inspired by the example of selfless defenders of the homeland like Cuauhtémoc, Hidalgo, and Juárez," and "Zapata is our guide and the people our support."[12] Overthrowing the PRI was simultaneously a matter of patriotic duty and a historical necessity to achieve social justice and national liberation.

The forging of community and neighborhood networks, extended familial ties, and friendships further cemented the negotiated political alliances between the PDLP and rural communities.[13] Shared historical experiences, memories, blood ties, and dialogue thus provided the common framework through which the PDLP and its campesino base communicated and understood one another. An urgent feeling of redemptive vengeance, nourished by decades of elite and state-sponsored reactionary violence, worked to fuse PDLP guerrillas and popular base in a common armed struggle against the PRI regime. As Cabañas remarked, "the only analysis we need is that they are screwing us [*fregando*] and we need to organize the people in order to respond."[14] Such redemptive vengeance cultivated and sustained a guerrilla movement that had promised to unleash a campesino war against the rich "who exploit the poor" and the "Government ruled by the wealthy."[15]

Cabañas represented the point of mediation between a rural peasantry steeped in centuries of popular Catholicism, decades of popular liberalism, and red agrarianism, and a generation of Marxists impacted by the possibility of radical change reflected by the Cuban revolution.[16] In the writings of Cabañas and the PDLP-BCA directive, the idea of a poor people's socialist state emerged amid a series of tensions, exemplified particularly by the existence of two drastically different *Idearios* (manifestos). Written and distributed in early 1973 during Cabañas's absence, the second Ideario contained the sort of orthodox Marxist-Leninist ideals espoused by contemporary urban guerrillas.[17] As provisional PDLP-BCA leader, Carmelo Cortés essentially codified in the second Ideario what he considered the prime weakness of the guerrilla organization, namely, the lack of a clear, doctrinaire Marxist-Leninist political line. For Cortés and a number of fellow guerrillas, such an absence permitted the proliferation of "social democratic" and "petit bourgeois" political thinking and tactics within the BCA combatants and PDLP bases of support. An absence of Marxist theoretical preparation signaled a lack of revolutionary discipline and praxis. How could the guerrillas, missing a proper ideological foundation, recruit additional support for the insurrectionary movement? The second Ideario thus intended to rectify existing "opportunism and petit bourgeois revolutionary romanticism" and introduce the "correct" definition of revolution.[18]

In contrast, the first PDLP Ideario, published earlier in 1972, had demonstrated intimate knowledge of a rural population the guerrillas had sought to lead in the making of a new revolution.[19] Containing fourteen points, the manifesto posited the defeat of the "government of the rich class" and its replacement with a popularly derived governance structure comprising campesinos, workers, and radicalized professionals. Several points addressed the parasitic nature and failure of the post-1940 rapid industrialization imposed by the PRI regime and demanded such hallmarks of modernity as education, health services, shelter, electricity, potable water, agricultural technology, and credit largely unavailable in the Mexican countryside. Demands for the actual manifestation of agrarian reform, labor rights, and national economic independence seemingly remained squarely within the legal framework of the 1917 Constitution and recalled Cardenismo. The call for the application of civic rights that legally ensured the formation of independent trade unions and political parties linked the PDLP guerrilla struggle to the ACG movements of 1960 and 1962. Calls for the liberation and equality of women (equal pay for equal work, access to higher education, the "right to associate freely and opine") and indigenous communities anticipated the later Central American and Chiapas guerrilla movements. Indeed, Cabañas's combat diary entries from March 1974 reveal that he was practicing speaking Nahuatl in order to extend the guerrilla insurgency to La Montaña region.[20]

In essence, the PDLP manifesto contained the historical motives and demands the guerrillas believed would move the Costa Grande's campesino population to armed insurrection, and forwarded concrete solutions to the latter's problems. Tasked with ensuring Mexico's economic independence from the United States, providing education for the masses, credit, infrastructure, and technology for ejidatarios, and democratic elections, the proposed pobrista state seemingly resembled a long-discarded Cardenista approach to statecraft. Or, at the very least, it looked like a Cardenista or somewhat Zapatista approach interpreted and imagined by the Guerrero countryside as a radically direct democracy in which peasant communities dictated political and economic organization. It was a world, as described by rebel protestor singer José de Molina, "without bosses or masters."[21] The omission of socialist or Marxist discourse from the Ideario did not signal ideological deficiency or petit bourgeois peasant leanings, but rather highlighted the PDLP's knowledge of a rural population that tended to equate socialism and communism with images of godlessness, immorality, and treason.[22] Though socialism represented the end goal of the PDLP, as ex-PDLP militants Alejandra Cárdenas and Luis León Mendiola recalled, Cabañas used rural assemblies and meetings to advance a campesino definition of socialism engaged with and determined by local political registers.[23] Rich versus poor represented the conflicted class structure, while the rural schoolteacher extracted the "true revolutionary" core of Christianity to posit Jesus Christ as a radical rebel who believed in social equality and justice and proclaimed "the equality the apostles wanted is the same equality fought for in revolutionary socialism."[24] In sum, the first PDLP Ideario—elaborated in direct relation to peasant political cultures—expressed a subaltern urgency for change forged in the face of constant state repression and the longing for an alternative political community organized by the needs and desires of exploited campesinos.

The form of radical democracy envisioned in the first Ideario paralleled the organizational form of the PDLP, the guerrilla BCA's internal life, and the decades-long struggle by Guerrero campesinos to achieve a real form of local democracy—a direct democracy that sought to radically transform entrenched cacique rule and organize a more just, equitable economic system. Democratic decision-making and the equal sharing of duty assignments characterized internal BCA life. If not on the move to another guerrilla base, permanent BCA fighters lived "a life characterized by routine: cooking, eating, sleeping... covering tracks and footprints, studying."[25] Study circles involved the teaching and reading of Marxist texts in an everyday "language" understood by campesino guerrillas. Equally distributed assignments like guard duty or traveling to nearby campesino communities for "politicization" conversations and to procure food supplies were handed out during early afternoon reunions. Night assemblies provided the opportunity for discussions about national or international news gleaned from shortwave radios, welcoming new recruits, and, most importantly, critically analyzing PDLP-BCA strategy and future actions.[26] BCA actions required group consensus as a guerrilla explained to an unidentified campesino community. After a discussion within the BCA leadership directive, "suggested actions are then presented to the rank-and-file, all of the comrades, and we discuss potential problems . . . and we collectively decide if the directive's proposals are correct."[27]

From a critical position, ex-BCA guerrilla and medic Ricardo Rodríguez González ("El Doc") remembered such nonhierarchical processes as an "excess of democracy" limited to daily tasks and not extended to questions of political ideology and military strategy. That excess, he argued, actually worked to conceal Cabañas's "caudillo" tendencies.[28] Yet the PDLP-BCA leader continuously refused the title of *comandante* (commander) and a yearly vote held by all BCA guerrillas decided the composition of the leadership after the previous group had engaged in self-critique and self-evaluation.[29] Political-military strategy, too, was discussed, debated, and voted upon. Entries from the insurgent schoolteacher's combat diaries dated 14 and 15 March 1974 reveal a sustained debate over course of action. A number of guerrillas had advocated a direct, frontal attack on the military barracks located in San Andrés de la Cruz while others had stressed the importance of visiting rural communities to "politicize" and organize popular support. The latter option won by a vote of forty-eight to three, with a noted abstention of eight.[30] Days later, DFS agents reported dozens of heavily armed rebels holding "town hall" meetings in three different communities. The meeting in San Juan de las Flores included "approximately 150" guerrillas, including several guerrilleras.[31]

Women in the PDLP-BCA combated and fulfilled daily chores assigned regardless of gender. As such, their participation in the armed struggle represented an initial challenge to rural patriarchy from within the guerrilla organization. Guillermina Cabañas recalled working several details—guard duty, cooking, and collecting food from allied communities—in which "all of us participated equally . . . it was a coexistence based on profound comradeship." She amusingly reminisced how the majority of male guerrillas, when assigned to cooking detail, produced horrendously disfigured tortillas.[32] Alejandra Cárdenas seconded such experiences of equality: "women took up arms, as did the men, who also had to make tortillas and prepare daily meals."[33] At least twenty women, including Guillermina Cabañas and María Isabel Ayala Nava ("Carmén," Lucio Cabañas's wife), fought in the BCA, serving in a combat role alongside their male comrades.[34] Hundreds more, like Romana Ríos de Roque ("Elena"), belonged to the PDLP's support network that linked coastal rural communities to urban centers like Acapulco, Chilpancingo, and Mexico City to provide food, medical services, messages, and weapons to the guerrillas in the mountains.[35] A thirty-six-year-old campesina at the time of her 1972 detention-disappearance by state police forces, Ríos de Roque had used her home in Acapulco as a safe house for the "May 18 Brigade" armed cell for several years and had also worked as a message courier.[36]

The participation of women in the armed struggle, particularly in combat-
ant roles, broadened the patriarchal boundaries of the popular democracy that
had underscored Guerrero's popular movements since 1960. Guerrilleras challenged, if implicitly, traditional gender roles based on male authority and female
subservience.[37] Moreover, their revolutionary praxis (simultaneously against the
PRI and social gender roles)[38] offered more radically democratic potential. The
attempt to create a daily existence within the BCA that challenged patriarchal
gender roles represented an idealized model society within the revolutionary
organization, an ongoing, contested process that did not necessarily extend to
the rural communities that supported the BCA.[39] Ríos de Roque, for instance,
had to ask her husband for permission to join the PDLP.[40] Yet for campesinas
who became guerrilleras, armed struggle facilitated the challenging of rural patriarchal norms in which women belonged to their fathers or husbands and needed
permission to act politically.[41] In fighting to overthrow the PRI regime "as a just
struggle," Guillermina also fought against a rural patriarchy that dictated that
she ask her parents for permission to join the PDLP (a movement her parents
supported) and have her brother accompany her in the guerrilla organization
"because it was dangerous for a woman to be alone and among so many men."[42]

Other young women who joined to avenge the abuse and killings of loved ones
or because they were moved by the "injustice suffered by the poor" challenged the
very idea that politics, revolution, and armed struggle comprised worlds strictly
limited to males.[43] They also transgressed moral codes predicated on the separa-
tion of public and private spheres as young women who freely traveled in the
mountains with a large number of men without familial patriarchal supervision.
During one rural assembly in the mountains, Cabañas had to assure the peasant community that the armed guerrilleras had joined for political and personal
motives—not through coercion or abduction: "one [*muchacha*] is here because
the army killed her first cousin; another because they beat her uncle... others
joined because they know we can end poverty through armed struggle and they
come to fight."[44] The participation and longings of women-guerrillas offered
alternative imaginings of liberation to the internal life of the guerrilla organization. Additionally, a demand for the rights and equality of women represented
one of the main points elaborated in the first PDLP Ideario.[45] Such a posture
challenged urban guerrilla groups' general characterization of women's rights as
a "bourgeois," and hence reactionary or secondary, concern.[46]

The first PDLP Ideario thus propagated an original campesino vision and
posited the peasantry as the revolutionary subject of Mexico—despite the accusations of "petit bourgeois" launched by contemporary urban guerrilla groups
such as the LC23S. Moreover, it demonstrated the fruit borne from the PDLP's
political practice of "forging community support." Such a process, as described
by Cabañas, involved "inserting oneself among the people... being with the

people, learning from them in order to provide revolutionary orientation using their language...the first phase is to proletarianize oneself, to become a part of the masses...learning from the people, not teaching the people."[47] Only after establishing this relationship with campesinos could the revolutionary group begin to suggest the necessity of socialist revolution in subaltern terms and concrete experiences. The roots of this political methodology derived from the many years Cabañas had spent in rural communities organizing, teaching, and learning as student, teacher, and PCM organizer. Though most likely coincidental, his ideas on political methodology paralleled some Maoist approaches: "To link oneself with the masses, we must act in accordance with the needs and wishes of the masses. All work done for the masses must start from their needs."[48]

Cabañas's misinterpreted disdain for "highbrow" Marxist theory arose from the latter's lack of relevance with the everyday experiences of campesinos and from its urban biases—not from his supposed "petit bourgeois" ideology or caudillo postures.[49] He had, after all, participated in the theory-obsessed PCM. Subaltern experiences, ideas, and visions, for Cabañas and the PDLP leadership, created the theories necessary for enacting the socialist guerrilla insurgency demanded by campesinos, on their terms and in their language. They "theorized from the concrete" in the midst of a revolutionary process.[50] Marxist-Leninist theory had its limits, as Cabañas argued: "Lenin's theory doesn't tell us how to form the masses [or] cultivate popular support."[51] In a separate instance, the guerrilla leader mentioned to a group of urban Marxist guerrillas, "revolutionary theory gleaned from a book is dead theory if not first extracted from the experiences of the masses." In essence, the PDLP envisioned the formation of guerrilla "theoreticians of the masses" closely connected to, and in egalitarian relationships with, "the poor masses" they fought for and defended.[52]

Yet, as Cabañas reminisced about the early days of the PDLP, "there are things the people want but that are not correct."[53] The group's tactical vanguardism was apparent in its military strategy and the principal form of armed struggle. Convincing the region's campesino population of the utility and necessity of guerrilla warfare involved transforming an essential aspect of the Costa Grande's subaltern culture of rebellion. Cabañas recalled that after the 1967 massacres in Atoyac and Acapulco, campesinos he encountered in the mountains had asked him what general would come to their aid, organize an insurgent army, proclaim a rebel manifesto or plan (*à la* Emiliano Zapata, Francisco Madero, and Amadeo Vidales), and set the date for insurrection. The PDLP needed to demonstrate that such a strategy would only result in their quick annihilation at the hands of well-organized state forces. As an alternative, guerrilla warfare waged in prolonged fashion required patient PDLP political work to convince the region's population of the necessity of clandestine organizing, the gradual buildup of politico-military forces and networks, the cultivation of popular support, and a gradualist military strategy that first targeted local caciques. "We had to cultivate popular support with deeds," Cabañas remarked:

> We needed to demonstrate to the people that here, in this terrain, with popular support and difficult topographical terrain on our side, we could escape from any government. When the people began to see that nothing happened to [me], they slowly started incorporating themselves into the group, one by one. And nothing happened to them. That way, comrades, we gained popular faith in our struggle.

As the PDLP and Cabañas continually reminded fellow urban comrades, "There is no struggle without popular support."[54] It was the key to poor people's revolution and the ensuing creation of a pobrista state.

Immersed in seven years of warfare, the PDLP-BCA did not complete the definition of the socialist pobrista state. The state, as a form of organized political community and power, remained largely unquestioned. Within the revolutionary imaginary of the PDLP appear the traces of another form of state in which historical notions of popular sovereignty as unmediated direct democracy—longings for justice, equity, and the redemption of betrayed revolutions—blended with a nonsectarian form of revolutionary socialism intimately connected to the quotidian, concrete experiences of its popular base. Yet, the lack of a Marxist conception of the state, orthodox class analysis, or mention of the proletariat's revolutionary vanguard role in the first Ideario brought forth sharp criticisms from contemporary Marxists and, subsequently, some scholars and ex-guerrillas.[55] The LC23S, for instance, viewed the PDLP's call to overthrow "the bad government" and not the bourgeois state as politically "petit bourgeois" and theoretically misguided. Cabañas grounded his clever response on historical experience, "the government is part and parcel of the bourgeois state... all revolutions have begun by fighting to overthrow the government."[56]

LC23S and scholarly accusations of PDLP "reformism," "populism," and "petit bourgeois" presupposed stereotypical assessments of peasant politics such as locality, lack of class-consciousness, lack of national perspective, and so on. In contrast, for the PDLP such shortcomings constituted the source of strength for their armed movement. The customs and folklore, which for some revealed peasant "backwardness" in need of modernizing, formed "the pillars of politics and of any collective action" for the PDLP's revolutionary struggle.[57] Those pillars, those long-held clandestine subaltern longings, and more recent experiences in the PRI's school of authoritarianism (and the Cuban example of redemptive hope) collectively constituted the pobrista revolution and the dream of "a regime of the poor and for the poor."[58]

The First Time as Tragedy, the Second Time as ... Tragedy

In Guerrero, guerrillas rarely leave. They go underground into a latent state, passing on experiences to younger generations and/or pursuing democracy and socioeconomic justice via other means. Violence represents a political tactic ultimately dependent on the support and willingness of peasant communities. After a decade of state terror during the 1970s, these rural communities chose other political paths—paths with a long regional history—for the subsequent decade. Throughout the 1980s, they actively participated in the formation of autonomous peasant cooperatives like the Coalition of Cafetalero Ejidos of the Costa Grande that demanded collective and democratic campesino control over all stages of coffee production. Maize- and banana-producing ejidos followed suit, as did peasant communities that leased forested property to logging companies.[59] The 1988 presidential campaign of Cuauhtémoc Cárdenas (son of Lázaro Cárdenas), under the banner of an independent political party, overwhelmingly attracted the participation of Guerrero's autonomously organized peasantry as they sought to gain political power through the vote. Well-versed in the PRI's electoral fraud strategy, campesinos angrily denounced the subsequent PRI "victory" in July 1988. One campesino wrote to Cárdenas, "we are with you in the good and the bad ... you are not alone and we will take you to the presidential chair with machine guns in hand if the PRI does not want to accept their defeat in peace."[60]

Cárdenas controversially lost the 1988 presidential election but his campaign signaled a resurgence of popular political mobilization previously suppressed by the 1970s Dirty War. Guerrerenses lost the fear to openly participate politically.[61] The center-left political party that Cárdenas helped create, the Revolutionary Democratic Party (PRD), later performed strongly in Guerrero's municipal and state elections. Nine municipalities, including Atoyac, flew the PRD's yellow flag in 1990, while PRD members occupied twenty-nine more after controversial electoral results. The PRI responded with violence. From 1989 to 1990, gunmen allied to the PRI killed at least fifty-six PRD members and disappeared eight more. State police and military forces forcibly recovered the PRD municipalities not recognized by the state legislature, leaving dozens of injured and detained.[62] The situation in 1990 thus resembled a political situation of about 1961–2. Popular democratic impulses, desires, and organizations would not trump the one-party ruling prerogative of the PRI. Only a massacre of unarmed, peaceful protestors separated the two historical contexts.

As state governor, Rubén Figueroa Alcocer, son of former state governor (and PDLP kidnapping victim) Rubén Figueroa and *compadre* to President

Ernesto Zedillo (1994–2000), ordered the type of action that gives the history of Guerrero a sense of déjà vu. In June 1995, he directed the state police to ambush a peasant caravan made up of members of the Campesino Organization of the Sierra of the South (OCSS), a peasant organization that included Dirty War survivors and veterans of 1980s autonomous campesino unions like Hilario Mesino.[63] The OCSS did not demand a democratic revolution of the relations of rural production but a series of limited reformist proposals that highlighted the level of impoverishment suffered by the Costa Grande in 1994: health care, adequate shelter, roads that remained travelable during the rainy season, schools, fertilizer, and credit. OCSS direct action—the blockading of roads, public protests, and the takeover of municipal government buildings—bothered Figueroa.[64] On 28 June 1995, state police forces attacked as an OCSS caravan traveling to a political demonstration in Atoyac near the village of Aguas Blancas (Coyuca de Benítez). Police agents killed seventeen OCSS members, wounded twenty-three more, and planted weapons on the dead to portray their ambush as an act of self-defense.[65] Days later 2500 enraged campesinos burned down a section of the municipal palace in Coyuca de Benítez. Atoyac's priest, Máximo Gómez Muñoz, prophetically commented that the same conditions that produced the PDLP during the 1970s existed in 1995 Guerrero.[66] Exactly one year later, amid popular rage and indignation, Popular Revolutionary Army (EPR) guerrillas reemerged to "take up arms" and proclaim a new revolution against the PRI. Once again, state terror made guerrillas and guerrilla supporters. Some EPR guerrillas directly traced their participation in armed revolutionary struggles to the 1970s.[67] The PDLP remained alive and the political option of armed struggle reemerged.

The idea of "taking up arms" is a significant part of Mexican campesino political cultures, rooted in and nourished by historical experiences and memories used against governing regimes popularly perceived as devoid of ruling legitimacy and constitutional legality.[68] Several historians have noted the unique ability of Mexican campesinos within Latin America to consistently "take up arms" and decisively impact every major social transformation in Mexican history.[69] Guerrero's campesinos prominently and crucially participated in all phases of Mexican national history: from the 1810 Independence movement and their continual defense of Republican-Federalist-Liberal principles during the mid-nineteenth century, to the 1910 Mexican revolution and their everyday battles to impose Cardenismo at the local-regional level. Each historical episode, each instance of "taking up arms," each process of everyday nonviolent protest that preceded violent action added layers of historical memories and experiences that collectively shaped a campesino political culture capable of galvanizing future mobilizations in rural Guerrero.

Additionally, new political forms that emerged in the course of struggle left a lasting imprint on nineteenth- and twentieth-century state-making attempts.[70]

Peasant federalist visions of universal male suffrage, municipal autonomy, and low taxes mobilized campesinos against centralist-conservative governments and facilitated the foundation of a nascent liberal state during the late 1850s.[71] During the 1910 revolution, alternative peasant definitions of local patriarchal democracy and land tenure that reached back to the nineteenth century forced their way into the 1917 Constitution. Rural popular imaginings of the Cardenista 1930s as a time when the postrevolutionary government provided land and encouraged campesino political participation melded with modern demands for agricultural technology, credit, education, and health services served as a point of reference when evaluating the failings of post-1940 national governments.[72] These longings and utopias nourished the various civic, electoral, and syndical movements of the 1960s and the later ACNR and PDLP guerrilla insurgencies.

For decades official versions of Mexican history that hailed economic miracles, exponential GDP growth rates, and political stability subsumed local-regional histories of popular protest. Such versions neglected the histories and processes of popular resistance, political radicalization, and state terror critically explored in *Specters of Revolution*. The history of Guerrero after 1940 reveals how popular protest consistently challenged the PRI regime's attempts to discard social reforms in favor of national and foreign capital and its political authoritarianism. Demanding agrarian reform, political democracy, and/or syndical democracy, popular movements from 1960 to 1967 fought to conserve, indeed to redeem, the progressive social tenets of the 1917 Constitution. While movements like the 1960 cívicos or the 1962 ACG electoral campaign initially worked within legal channels to achieve reformist demands, violent state reactions progressively drained the PRI of legitimacy and served to radicalize some popular groups. Vázquez, Cabañas, and hundreds more became guerrillas in the face of sustained state terror and the erasure of legal channels of protest and redress. The violent military counterinsurgency campaigns that followed the emergence of the guerrilla ACNR and PDLP reveal a modernization program thoroughly reliant on repression of protest, repeal of social reforms, and authoritarian rule and force a reconceptualization of post-1940 Mexican history. Violence enabled Mexican golden ages and economic miracles.

The story of the guerrilla ACNR and PDLP thus emerges from a series of frustrated, constitutionally based popular movements and reactive state massacres. Like Rubén Jaramillo before them, Genaro Vázquez and Lucio Cabañas initially sought the real application of political and socioeconomic reforms stipulated by the 1917 Constitution. Both men came of age during an era in which the revolutionary nationalist discourse of the PRI regime failed to match reality on the ground in their rural Guerrero homeland. Moved by a radically popular—even socialist—interpretation of the 1910 revolution that posited Zapatista agrarianism and Cardenista statecraft as its essential core, Vázquez and Cabañas initially worked within constitutional guidelines to obtain profound reform. Their prominent participation in the 1960 cívico movement and the 1962 ACG electoral campaign evinced a certain level of trust in the governing framework consolidated after 1910. Yet repeated acts of state and cacique violence gradually convinced both schoolteachers to search for alternative political paths in the face of intransigent regional political officials that proved unable to rule with resorting to terror and murder.

In search of new political options, both Vázquez and Cabañas navigated the political pathways of an Old Mexican Left battered and driven partially underground (with a brief Cardenista revival in the early 1960s) and a New Left that flirted with the possibility of revolutionary victory represented by Cuba during the mid-1960s. Continued state repression at the regional level, enacted by a governor who came to power immediately after the 1962 Iguala massacre, made it dangerous to even verbally express protest. In 1965, after the state legislature passed Decree 29, dissidence literally became a crime in Guerrero. After organizing independent peasant unions and local community-based resource movements, Vázquez and Cabañas personally experienced state violence. Vázquez evaded assassination attempts in Iguala's municipal prison and Cabañas barely escaped assassin bullets in 1967; such acts convinced both men that armed insurgency represented the only viable path to achieve fundamental change. At first, such an option was a response to the exigency of self-defense. Eventually, the political option of armed insurgency took the form of two separate peasant guerrilla movements with widespread campesino support that roamed Guerrero during the late 1960s and early 1970s, sought the overthrow of the PRI, and imagined the implementation of a revolutionary socialist regime. If state terror initially radicalized and pushed Vázquez and Cabañas to New Left rural guerrilla warfare, networks forged during their travels through the Old Mexican Left sustained the development of the nascent guerrilla organizations. Popular support ensured their survival.

The ACNR and PDLP ultimately failed in their respective attempts to overthrow the PRI regime and install a more just system of governance. Yet traditional explanations used to explain unsuccessful peasant insurgencies—localism and circumscribed political horizons—do not provide adequate answers;[73] nor do arguments that characterized New Left guerrillas as militarist, utopian, Cuban-derived, and responsible for provoking state terror,[74] or others that focused on the Guerrero guerrillas' use of socialist discourse "disconnected" from campesinos' dedication to the revolutionary principles of 1910.[75] Rather, state terror that violently targeted ACNR and PDLP bases of popular support ultimately defeated the guerrillas. Torture, rape, disappearances, death flights, strategic hamlets, the rationing of food and medicine, and the razing of villages turned coastal Guerrero into a counterinsurgent war zone. Key guerrilla shortcomings explored in *Specters of Revolution* pale in comparison to the type of terror unleashed by the Mexican military and police forces. The scope and furious intensity of the military counterguerrilla operations signaled the success Cabañas and the PDLP, in particular, enjoyed in recruiting support from dozens of Costa Grande communities. With a revolutionary socialism grounded in local-regional traditions of rebellion, rural understandings of class warfare, and sentiments of redemptive vengeance, the PDLP achieved high levels of peasant support noted by internal military documents. Yet terror eventually succeeded in physically isolating the guerrilla movements from broader nonviolent social movements and from their peasant support base. Terror secured a short-term military victory for the PRI regime but failed to defeat the political ideas and utopias of the ACNR and PDLP.

Both guerrilla organizations thus failed to actualize a militarily victorious revolution. Yet exploring the utopias that existed at the core of the revolutionary projects advanced by the guerrillas offers the possibility of obtaining insight into their rationales for organizing insurrections and attempting to seize state power. That they failed to do so, that they failed to create the revolutionary conditions necessary for organizing new societies, increases the importance of analyzing their utopias. In those utopias are glimpses of the different worlds imagined by the militarily defeated insurgents and their peasant supporters—worlds based on long political histories that continue to serve as inspirations. Their durability in Guerrero testifies to the counterhegemonic power of their radically egalitarian social visions contrasted with a series of social orders characterized by inequality, exploitation, and domination. In these organizations' ideas, history is not predestined or linear, and "the poor," in PDLP parlance, possess the potential to change the conditions of their everyday existence.

In his reformulation of Hegel's ideas on history and repetition, Karl Marx argued that the past, "the tradition of all dead generations," constituted a burden on the present, a "nightmare on the brains of the living" that prevented the successful enactment of proletarian revolutions. Yet the man who symbolized revolution failed to appreciate the insurgent power of pasts filled with alternative imaginings of how to organize social life. In particular, he misunderstood how memories of past injustice and elite violence serve as analytical referents for injustice and violence in the present and can potentially spark protest, resistance, and even revolution. ACNR and PDLP guerrillas reveal something about the way in which poor and oppressed peoples remember their histories and how those remembrances fuel attempts to drastically change the circumstances under which they live. Even if such attempts fail, they join the ranks of other specters.[76] And those specters at times demand vengeance.

Epilogue: "The Bones Will Tell Us What Happened"

The specter of Cabañas returned to Atoyac de Álvarez on 2 December 2002. With the help of forensic anthropologists and archeologists, family members had months earlier discovered the remains of the guerrilla leader in an unmarked tomb in Atoyac's municipal cemetery. Bloodied cotton balls (used during a military-supervised autopsy in 1974) found alongside human bones evinced the haste in which the military had secretly buried the body—and, crucially, helped confirm Cabañas's identity through DNA tests. At least one thousand people filled the streets to commemorate the return of an insurgent leader believed by some to have never died. In a way, those believers were right: the longings and utopias that had nourished the guerrilla PDLP, embodied in popular memories of Cabañas, proved to be alive and still inspirational. Family members placed his remains within an unfinished obelisk built in the central plaza of Atoyac—a monument erected without official authorization (Figure 8.1). Indeed, the entire commemoration provoked the ire of the ruling right-wing National Action Party (PAN). At the same time, radical EPR slogans appeared on buildings in Tixtla, the city that houses that educational "nest of reds [*rojillos*]," Ayotzinapa, once attended by Cabañas.[1] Elsewhere, guerrillas of the Revolutionary Army of the Insurgent People (ERPI) announced the creation of a national coordinating committee intended to combine the insurgent efforts of several guerrilla organizations.[2] The guerrilla past and the guerrilla present fused on the day that Cabañas returned to Atoyac.

An additional facet of Guerrero's recent past remains poignantly alive. The abandoned military base in Atoyac houses secrets and anguished silences. During the 1970s, the base served Mexican infantry battalions that spearheaded unconstitutional counterinsurgency efforts and confined suspected peasant guerrillas and their supporters. They all eventually left as military officers redeployed their soldiers to other turbulent Mexican and guerrerense regions with new counternarcotics missions. Much less is known about their prisoners.

Figure 8.1 The obelisk and statue of Lucio Cabañas in contemporary Atoyac de Álvarez.

Perhaps some suffered the fate of "death flights." Others probably experienced a move to different clandestine prisons and torture centers. Or, perhaps, they remain on the base, keeping secrets and silences from within their clandestine graves.

In July 2008, an assortment of human rights activists, officials from the federal Attorney General's Office, and Argentine forensic experts began excavating the base hoping to find traces of some 470 disappeared Atoyac residents.[3] For Tita Radilla, the excavations represented one more step in her decades-long search for her disappeared father Rosendo Radilla. Her legal proceedings against the Mexican government had forced the exhumation of the military base. When speaking with a journalist, Radilla expressed hope: "They say the bones talk…I know my father was at the military base. Witnesses who were there saw him, but they never saw him leave."[4] When asked about the secrecy surrounding Mexico's Dirty War, she responded, "the Mexican government has always been very careful to guard its image as a protector of human rights. That's why not much is known about this time period."[5] Excavations continue at the abandoned base.[6]

Tita Radilla's ongoing effort to find her father and the excavations to search for the hundreds more disappeared by the PRI regime poignantly demonstrate the very real and continuing aspects of this history. If guerrillas continue to emerge in the Guerrero countryside calling for new revolutions, the specters of Dirty War victims continue to hover. The impact of the Dirty War, or rather the counterinsurgent terror exercised by the Mexican military against civilian populations, thus persists. Such terror inspired a chronic and degenerative fear that permeated public spaces and ripped communities apart, and divided neighbors and families. While the majority of the Costa Grande's villages and towns supported the PDLP to varying degrees, they also housed military informers whose denunciations led to the detention of neighbors and even family members.[7] Military officials coerced others to identify fellow community members as "collaborators" or to guide military units to suspected guerrilla camps under threat of death. Having the last name of Cabañas or Iturio almost certainly guaranteed arrest and disappearance. David Cabañas Gervasio, Lucio's half-brother, estimated that the army killed or disappeared more than 100 people with his last name.[8] Cabañas's maternal relatives—the Barrientos—suffered the murder or disappearance of at least eighteen people.[9]

Families that experienced the disappearance of a loved one were often rejected or shunned by fellow terrorized neighbors. Radilla recalled how neighbors distanced themselves from her family after the 1974 disappearance of her father, Rosendo Radilla, a noted campesino activist, rural union organizer, and corrido composer linked to Genaro Vázquez. "No one wanted to get near you," she remembered, "even your closest relatives." A courageous activist who has led a decades-long campaign demanding justice for all of the disappeared, Radilla related another family's story:

> there is a family…Ramos Cabañas, that woman [the mother] had six sons, she was from the town of San Juan de las Flores. When the situation [military repression] started they managed to leave town and seek refuge in their coffee plot located up in the mountains. Well, the military went all the way up there to get them. They took five of her sons and her husband, leaving the remaining son because he was only six

years old. The poor woman went mad. She still lives but it is very hard for her.[10]

Countless stories evince the ongoing presence of the Dirty War in the everyday lives of residents. One in particular stands out. Don Chon, a campesino from Atoyac, poignantly remembers the day in the early 1970s when his son Lino Rosas Pérez vaguely insinuated that he wanted to join the PDLP. "Don't make any commitments to any of that," the concerned father told his son. "Those things [armed resistance] have to happen," Lino responded, though he told his father not to worry. As a rural schoolteacher, Rosas Pérez had been a student of Cabañas and came to believe in the ideals of the pobrista revolution. A year and half later army troops attacked Lino's school and community for supporting the PDLP, killing and capturing a large number of inhabitants. Lino apparently managed to escape and joined the ranks of the PDLP. Don Chon received news of the attack but none pertaining to his son. "I was left with many doubts and he never returned [to his home]; soon after, people from the mountains began telling me that he was up there with the group [PDLP]."[11]

Don Chon inadvertently received some information when in September 1974 soldiers detained and transferred him, blindfolded, to a clandestine military prison near Acapulco after a relative identified him as a guerrilla collaborator at a military checkpoint in Tecpan de Galeana. He suffered thirteen days of torture, physical beatings, and mock executions because army officers called him "a Cabañas" and "the father of the guerrillas."[12] Don Chon responded to such accusations by saying, "*cabrón*, I fathered only one guerrilla, not the whole lot!" He still remembers the endless cries and whimpers of pain that filled the prison, the certainty that he would die at any moment, torture sessions inflicted on detainees that seemingly never ended. Even on the day of his release, soldiers threatened him with execution, asking him if he was ready for death. The soldiers eventually released Don Chon, leaving him with twenty pesos and a warning to "behave and go to work."

After his release, Don Chon received little information about his guerrilla son. When soldiers killed Cabañas and three companions in December 1974, the campesino heard rumors that Lino had died fighting during the final battle near El Otatal. For the next three decades Don Chon received only rumors. He knew that Lino was probably dead but wanted conclusive evidence. It took decades of unrelenting activism, social organizing, and the electoral defeat of the PRI in 2000 for him to finally obtain information. He painfully recalled the day in February 2007 when "the delinquent government" (as he referred to the PRI regime) finally returned the remains of his guerrilla son. They did so in two separate cheap plastic boxes.[13] Don Chon sadly asked: "which one is my son?"[14] Despite the profound pain and sadness he felt the day he received Lino's remains, at least he finally knew.[15] He wanted the truth. Radilla expressed a similar sentiment: "we want the truth no matter how painful."[16]

The families of some 600 disappeared guerrerenses—all documented cases—have yet to obtain the truth about their loved ones, much less justice.[17] Given the scale of counterinsurgent terror in Guerrero, more disappearances most likely went unreported, fulfilling some of the goals of such terror: to discipline subjects, silence communities, and erase memories. The disappeared remain disappeared and soldiers and caciques to this day continue to violently harass peasant communities.[18] Another Dirty War against campesino leaders and social activists continues in contemporary Guerrero, cloaked by a national military offensive launched against powerful narco-trafficking organizations.[19]

There can be no end to the story with hundreds of disappeared Mexicans and their surviving families suspended in a vacuum characterized by government silence, impunity, and injustice. There can be no end to the story while the factors that prompted the emergence of two peasant guerrilla organizations in Guerrero decades ago—political authoritarianism, inequitable capitalist development, and state terror—continue to exist. "If an armed movement exists, it is because the conditions for it also exist: poverty, injustice, and repression. That is why guerrillas arise. It is not something we do for fun," Comandante Ramiro explained.[20] As a leader of ERPI, he made that statement in late 2009, some months after soldiers had tortured and shot young campesino men over the course of four days in the small mountain community of Puerto Las Ollas. The soldiers were looking for guerrillas. A column of ERPI fighters led by Comandante Ramiro later ambushed the torturous military unit. The past has never gone away in Guerrero.

In the meanwhile, many guerrerenses continue their decades-long search for justice and information about disappeared loved ones. They persevere in the face of government disinterest, cacique violence, and death threats. Like Tita Radilla, they hope "the bones will tell us what happened."[21]

NOTES

Introduction

1. Lucio Cabañas quoted in Suárez, *Lucio Cabañas,* 157. Unless otherwise noted all translations are my own.
2. Bartra, "Sur profundo."
3. "Guerrerense" is an adjective of or relating to Guerrero: its people, culture, and so on.
4. EPR, "Manifiesto de Aguas Blancas;" and the Revolutionary Army of the Insurgent People (ERPI), "Aguas Blancas: Una experiencia insurgente," 27 June 2005 (both found at http://www.cedema.org).
5. Letter from Karl Marx to Dr. Ludwig Kugelmann, 12 April 1871, http://www.marxists.org/archive/marx/works/1871/letters/71_04_17.htm.
6. My conception of utopia is influenced by Michael Lowy's definition of "revolutionary romanticism" in his discussion of Walter Benjamin's political and intellectual influences. See Lowy, *Fire Alarm,* 5.
7. Benjamin, "On the Concept of History," 395.
8. Guardino, *Peasants, Politics,* 95–96, 210.
9. Jacobs, *Ranchero Revolt.*
10. Padilla, *Rural Resistance,* 2.
11. José Téllez Sánchez, interviewed in Radilla Martínez, *Poderes, saberes y sabores,* 132.
12. My work contributes to a recent but expanding literature on post-1940 Mexico. A short list of works includes: Servín, *Ruptura y oposición;* Newcomer, *Reconciling Modernity;* Oikión Solano and García Ugarte, eds., *Movimientos armados;* Condés Lara, *Represión y rebelión;* Padilla, *Rural Resistance;* Smith, *Pistoleros and Popular Movements;* Navarro, *Political Intelligence;* Gillingham, "Maximino's Bulls;" Cedillo and Calderón, eds., *Challenging Authoritarianism;* Walker, *Waking from the Dream;* Pensado, *Rebel Mexico;* Rath, *Myths of Demilitarization;* and Gillingham and Smith, *Dictablanda.*
13. Blacker-Hanson, "Cold War in the Countryside," 206; and Archivo General de la Nación (hereafter AGN), Dirección Federal de Seguridad (hereafter DFS), 100-10-16-2-72, Legajo 5, 107.
14. Cacique refers to local or regional "boss" political rule and organization. Caciques usually managed to fuse political and economic power in rural Mexico—often in contravention of PRI policies and designs emanating from Mexico City.
15. Olcott, *Revolutionary Women,* 12. As Olcott notes, popular enfranchisement coexisted with, and usually depended upon, a hierarchical system of patronage fostered by the Cardenista postrevolutionary government—though the results of popular enfranchisement, of everyday Mexicans acting upon the revolutionary rhetoric of the government, often led to "surplus" democracy. For a "surplus" of democracy in 1940s Mexico, see Gillingham, "Maximino's Bulls," 175–211.

16. Olcott, *Revolutionary Women*, 7–15, 159–165.
17. Matthew 20:16.
18. Stern, "New Approaches," 12–13.
19. The corridos written and sung by campesino Rosendo Radilla Pacheco during the late 1960s and early 1970s expressed such sentiment. A veteran of 1930s agrarian reform and a former municipal president of Atoyac de Álvarez, Radilla Pacheco would be detained and disappeared by the Mexican military in August 1974. He was accused of producing proguerrilla corridos and supporting the guerrilla movements. Tita Radilla, interview with the author, Atoyac de Álvarez, Guerrero, 16 May 2007; and Andrea Radilla Martínez, *Voces acalladas*, 60–75.
20. The "newness" of the Latin American armed New Left should not be overstated. Direct action, national liberation, and anti-imperialism also recall the Comintern's "Third Period" of the late 1920s and early 1930s. Decades before the publication of the revolutionary manuals of Che Guevara and Carlos Marighella (and Vo Nguyen Giap, to a lesser extent), for instance, the Peruvian military officer Julio C. Guerrero had written *La lucha de guerrillas: ¿Una modelidad de la lucha armada del futuro?* (1932). Melgar Bao, "La memoria submergida," 36.
21. To understand this confluence of radical traditions and ideas, I draw from Raymond Williams's framework of cultural analysis. Williams, "Dominant, Residual, and Emergent," in *Marxism and Literature*, 121–127.
22. Ideological flexibility, pragmatism, and the use of radical nationalism also place the ACNR and PDLP alongside other Latin American guerrilla organizations like the Colombian M-19 and the Revolutionary Organization of the People in Arms (ORPA) in Guatemala. I would also include certain wings of the Nicaraguan Sandinista National Liberation Front (FSLN) during its struggle against the Somoza dictatorship and the Salvadoran Farabundo Martí National Liberation Front (FMLN). Manz, *Paradise in Ashes*, 74–80, 106–108; MacAllister, "Headlong Rush into the Future," 276–308; Castañeda, *Utopia Unarmed*, 87–94; Wickham-Crowley, *Guerrillas and Revolution*, 252–254; Gould, "On the Road," 111–116; Gould, *To Lead as Equals*, 270–291; and Chávez, "Pedagogy of Revolution."
23. Aranda, *Los cívicos guerrerenses*, 123–126.
24. Guha, "The Prose of Counter-Insurgency," 47.
25. Anthropologist Armando Bartra's 1996 *Guerrero bronco*—a historical essay that passionately traces popular efforts in Guerrero to forge a meaningful democratic society—represents a key initial work that engages the political visions of the Guerrero guerrillas without fully subscribing to a limiting binary. Marco Bellingeri's essays on the ACNR and PDLP represent the first scholarly effort to use a small sample of declassified government documents to contextualize the Guerrero guerrillas within a longer history of rural insurgency and resistance. Bellingeri, *Del agrarismo armado*, 109–158, 173–247.
26. See Aranda Flores, *Los cívicos guerrerenses*; Aroche Parra, *El Che, Genaro y las guerrillas*; Aroche Parra, *Los secuestros de Figueroa, Zuno*; de Mora, *Las guerrillas en México*; de Mora, *Lucio Cabañas*; Hipólito, *Guerrero*; López, *10 años de guerrilla*; Ortíz, *Genaro Vázquez*; Natividad Rosales, *La muerte de Lucio Cabañas*; Natividad Rosales, *¿Quien es Lucio Cabañas?*; and Reyes Serrano, *Trinchera…!* For important testimonial works produced by ex-guerrilla militants see: Gallegos Nájera, *La guerrilla en Guerrero*; Miranda Ramírez, *El otro rostro*; Solís Robledo and Cantú Lagunas, *Rescate para la historia*; and Sotelo Pérez, *Breve historia*. Montemayor, *Guerra en el Paraíso* represents a fictional yet historically researched novel on the Cabañas-led PDLP. Two additional works produced by PDLP militants that shed light on the internally fractious and violent history of the PDLP during the 1980s are Fierro Loza, *Los papeles de la sedición*, and Campos Gómez, *Lucio Cabañas y el Partido de los Pobres*.
27. Suárez, *Lucio Cabañas*, 7–12, 339; Mayo, *La guerrilla de Genaro y Lucio*, 9; and Castañeda, *Utopia Unarmed*, 87.
28. Hodges, *Mexican Anarchism*, 94–95; and Hodges and Gandy, *Mexico under Siege*, 127.
29. Suárez, *Lucio Cabañas*, 12. This work is valuable for its collection of primary sources related to the PDLP.
30. Ulloa Bornemann, *Surviving Mexico's Dirty War*, 34–35, 63–64.
31. Blacker-Hanson, "Cold War in the Countryside," 197–198, 207–208; and Blacker-Hanson, "The Intellectual Roots," 101–117.

32. Joseph, "What We Now Know and Should Know," 28–29.
33. For example see, McAllister, "Headlong Rush into the Future," 276–308; Wood, *Insurgent Collective Action and Civil War*; James, *Doña María's Story*; and Rodríguez, *Women, Guerrillas, and Love.*
34. Personal politics also highlight the generational continuities that tend to characterize rural guerrilla movements in Mexico. Montemayor, "La guerrilla recurrente," 24–30.
35. I borrow the term "moral economy of vengeance" (though understood in conceptually different ways) from Rabasa, *Writing Violence on the Northern Frontier*, 263.
36. Grandin, "Living in Revolutionary Times," 22.
37. ACNR communiqué, November 1969, in Aranda, *Los cívicos guerrerenses*, 141.
38. León Mendiola, interview in the documentary *La Guerrilla en México* (2004), DVD.
39. A campesino class forged in the midst of popular struggle with a sharpened political consciousness and identity "as well as by a collective history of oppression." Boyer, *Becoming Campesinos*, 2–6.
40. Bhadram, "Four Rebels of Eighteen-Fifty-Seven," 174.
41. Benjamin, "On the Concept of History," 394.
42. Žižek, *Violence*, 9–15, 178–205; and Benjamin, "Critique of Violence," 287–300. For a useful critical evaluation on the theorizing of violence see Scholl, *Two Sides of a Barricade*, 176–179.
43. Suárez, *Lucio Cabañas*, 83.
44. Gould, *To Lead as Equals*, 10, 305.
45. Grandin, *The Last Colonial Massacre*, 173. See also, Grandin, *Who is Rigoberta Menchú?*, 39–41; and Beverley, "Rethinking the Armed Struggle," 47–59. The most widely read historiography that I refer to includes: Castañeda, *Utopia Unarmed*; Stoll, *Between Two Armies*; Stoll, *Rigoberta Menchú*; and Brands, *Latin America's Cold War*. The "Cuban Crucible" refers to Castañeda's argument that places revolutionary Cuba as the ideological, logistical source and instigator for most Latin American guerrilla organizations after 1959 (though he excludes Mexico). The "Two Demons" thesis, elaborated in Argentina (and applied elsewhere in Latin America), posits a moral equivalence between the violence and political extremism deployed by military dictatorships and New Left guerrilla groups. State terror (and its ideological sources) equates with "left wing extremism"; the latter provoked the former. See Grandin, "The Instruction of Great Catastrophe," 50–54. For a Mexican version of this argument that allots equal blame to the Mexican government and guerrillas, see Scherer and Monsiváis, *Los patriotas*.
46. Castañeda, *Utopia Unarmed*, 51, 88; and Stoll, *Rigoberta Menchú*, 282. Castañeda does note that the Guerrero guerrillas did not receive any sort of Cuban assistance.
47. AGN, DGIPS, box 1195B, folder 3, 383–384.
48. Two of the most famous critics were journalist Victor Rico Galán and PCM militant Heberto Castillo. The PCM adopted this line of argument vis-à-vis the PDLP in October 1973 at its XVI National Congress. According to journalist Luis Suárez, President Echeverría expressed a similar argument when discussing Cabañas, "as victim of injustice," who chose the wrong path of armed struggle. Suárez, *Lucio Cabañas*, 342–343.
49. Mallon, *Peasant and Nation*, 5; and Hylton and Thomson, *Revolutionary Horizons*, 29–31.
50. Bartra, *Guerrero bronco*, 73.
51. Niblo, *Mexico in the 1940s*, 361–364.
52. Ibid., 363. See also Bartra, *Notas sobre la cuestión campesina*, 85–86; Sanderson, *The Transformation of Mexican Agriculture*, 40–48; Babb, *Managing Mexico*, 79–80; and Hansen, *The Politics of Mexican Development*, 71–90, 113–115.
53. Gramsci, *Selections from the Prison Notebooks*, 275–276.
54. These counterinsurgency campaigns exhibited tension between domestic tactics developed by the Mexican military in the countryside after 1940 and the commodified, rational-choice models taught by US military officials at the School of the Americas during the 1960s. Rath, *Myths of Demilitarization*, 167–172; and Veledíaz, *El general sin memoria*, 309–330. For a broader discussion on the emergence of rational choice counterinsurgency in the United States, see Robin, *The Making of the Cold War Enemy*, 185–205.
55. Beginning in 2002, the Mexican government created a special office to investigate human rights violations committed by the PRI regime from the 1960s to 1980s. The final

governmental report on the "Dirty War" produced by the Special Prosecutor for Social and Political Movements of the Past (hereafter FEMOSPP) in late 2006 proved to have been censored. Anticipating such censorship, investigators working for FEMOSPP released an 'unfiltered' version of the Dirty War report in February 2006 to Kate Doyle and the National Security Archive. That report can be viewed at http://www.gwu.edu/~nsarchiv/NSAEBB/NSAEBB180/index2.htm. Hereafter I will refer to the unfiltered report as *FEMOSPP Filtrado* and the final report as FEMOSPP, *Informe Histórico a la Sociedad Mexicana*.

56. "La Guerra Sucia en Guerrero," *FEMOSPP Filtrado*, 129–132; Victor Fuentes and Abel Barajas, "Vuelos de la madrugada," *Reforma*, 29 October 2002; and Gloria Leticia Díaz, "La 'foto del recuerdo' y al mar," *Proceso* 1356 (17 October 2002).

57. The final FEMOSSP report estimates nearly 600 cases of disappearances in Guerrero. FEMOSPP, *Informe Histórico a la Sociedad Mexicana*, 502. In 2002, protected government witness Gustavo Tarín Chávez testified that nearly 1500 suspected guerrillas were executed at the Pie de la Cuesta military aviation base near Acapulco. He also testified to the systematic operation of "death flights." Gustavo Castillo García, "Acosta y Quirós ordenaron asesinar a más de mil 500, dice testigo protegido," *La Jornada*, 18 November 2002; http://www.cesarsalgado.net/200211/021118b.htm.

58. A recent, growing literature on the Mexican Dirty War includes (not exhaustively) the following works: Cedillo and Calderón, *Challenging Authoritarianism*; Condés Lara, *Represión y rebelión*; Oikión Solano and García Ugarte, *Movimientos armados*; Castellanos, *México armado*; Glockner, *México Rojo*; Aviña, "We have returned to Porfirian Times"; Carey, *Plaza of Sacrifices*; Aguayo Quezada, *La charola*; Scherer and Monsiváis, *Los patriotas*; and both FEMOSSP reports.

59. Ascención Rosas Mesino (Don Chon), interview with the author, Atoyac de Álvarez, Guerrero, May 16, 2007. Certainly the Mexican military exhibited brutal tactics of repression prior to the 1960s, as it did in Chiapas in 1955 when an army captain beheaded five protestors. Military and state violence in Guerrero, beginning in the late 1960s, was different due to its systematic operation. Terror committed against guerrerense peasant communities was not an isolated phenomenon, but part of a series of systematic counterinsurgency operations. For the Chiapas incident, see Rath, *Myths of Demilitarization*, 119.

60. For current discussion on PRI authoritarianism, see Gillingham and Smith, *Dictablanda*.

61. Gramsci, *Selections from Prison Notebooks*, 106–124, 206–276; Williams, *Marxism and Literature*, 108–114, 115–127; Roseberry, "Hegemony and the Language of Contention," 358; Rubin, *Decentering the Regime*, 11–23; and Gillingham, "Maximino's Bulls," 181;

62. Hobsbawm, "The Machine Breakers," cited in Gillingham, "Maximino's Bulls," 189; Padilla, *Rural Resistance*, 106; Rath, *Myths of Demilitarization*, 54–80; Gillingham, "Ambiguous Missionaries," 331–360; and Smith, *Pistoleros and Popular Movements*, 289–327. For elite and middle-class forms of protest, see Zaragoza, *The Monterrey Elite*; Gauss, *Made in Mexico*; Walker, *Waking from the Dream*; and Newcomer, *Reconciling Modernity*.

63. The impact of such protest also depended on the historical moment. Gillingham's research on elections during the 1940s, from the village level to the presidency, demonstrates both the significant "veto" power of popular protests and electoral participation and the relative weakness of the central government. The power of popular protest via the ballot box tended to wane by the 1950s, though municipal politics remained sites of intense contestation. Even within the PRI, elections remained contested as the history of 1960s reformer Carlos Madrazo demonstrates. Gillingham, "Maximino's Bulls," 180–181; and Gillingham, "Baltasar Leyva Mancilla," 183–189. See also Newcomer, *Reconciling Modernity*, 143–176; Rubin, *Decentering the Regime*, 102–160; and Navarro, *Political Intelligence*, 121–149.

64. For recent works on the role of violence and coercion in twentieth-century Mexican state formation see the collection edited by Wil Pansters, *Violence, Coercion, and State-making*, especially the chapters by Pansters and Paul Gillingham.

65. For insightful and innovative discussions on these declassified documents see the dossier "Spy Reports," *Journal of Iberian and Latin American Research* 19:1 (2013).

66. Matsuda, *The Memory of the Modern*, 121–146; and Robertson, "Mechanisms of Exclusion," 70.

67. Scott, *Domination*, 10–16, 70–75.
68. Mallon, "The Promise and Dilemma of Subaltern Studies," 1506; and Guha, "The Prose of Counter-insurgency."
69. Portelli, "What Makes Oral History Different," 33–36. See also Portelli, *The Death of Luigi Trastulli*, 50–51.

Chapter 1

1. Estrada Castañón, *Guerrero*, 8–9.
2. López Miramontes, "Panorama historiográfica," 23.
3. *El Avisador* (25 November 1891), cited in Illades, *Breve historia de Guerrero*, 99. Guerrero's first railway would arrive in the city of Iguala in 1892.
4. Letter from Santa Anna to Juan Álvarez, 16 April 1843, in Díaz y Díaz, *Santa Anna y Juan*, 150, cited in Bartra, *Guerrero bronco*, 22. For a recent biography of Santa Anna, see Fowler, *Santa Anna of Mexico*.
5. Guardino, *Peasants, Politics*, 132. Alamán served as minister of the interior from 1830 to 1832 during the centralist/conservative presidency of Anastasio Bustamante.
6. Benjamin, "Convolute N: On the Theory of Knowledge," 463; García de León, *Resistencia y utopía*, 24–25; and Hylton and Thomson, *Revolutionary Horizons*, 29–31.
7. Guha, *Elementary Aspects of Peasant Insurgency*; and Durkheim, *The Elementary Forms of the Religious Life*.
8. Wickham-Crowley, *Guerrillas and Revolution*, 131.
9. Guardino, *Peasants, Politics*, 74–78.
10. Ibid., 79–80; and Illades, *Breve historia*, 33–35.
11. Carlos María de Bustamante, *Cuadro histórico de la revolución mexicana*, vol. 1, 620, cited in Illades and Ortega, *Guerrero*, vol. 1, 193. *Ediciones de la Comisión Nacional para la Celebración del Sesquicentenario*, 3 vols. Mexico City, 1961.
12. In response to the invasion of Spain in 1808 by Napoleon, Spanish rebel provinces united to militarily resist the French. In 1810, the rebel forces organized the Cortes and invited delegates from the American colonies to participate. By 1812, the Cortes had drawn up a new Spanish Constitution in Cádiz: a liberal document that contained a popular-national definition of sovereignty. See Rodríguez O., *"We Are Now the True Spaniards."*
13. Guedea, "The Process of Mexican Independence," 122–125.
14. The document also established Catholicism as the only religion of the land and limited the admission of foreigners into Mexico to artisans willing to teach their crafts. Lemoine, *Morelos y la Revolución de 1810*, 260–265.
15. Serulnikov, "Andean Political Imagination," 271.
16. Martínez, *Genealogical Fictions*, 42–60, 142–172.
17. Lemoine, *Morelos y la Revolución de 1810*, 289; Guardino, *Peasants, Politics*, 68; and de la Cueva, "La idea de la soberanía," 317. For an assessment of the importance of the document expressed by a nineteenth-century intellectual, see Luis Mora, "Discurso sobre la Independencia del Imperio Mexicano," 469.
18. Lemoine, *Morelos y la Revolución de 1810*, 264.
19. Guedea, "Los procesos electorales insurgentes," 222–248.
20. Guardino, *Peasants, Politics*, 68–71; and Lemoine, *Morelos y la Revolución de 1810*, 289–296.
21. Guardino, *Peasants, Politics*, 70–80; Archer, "La Causa Buena," 102–108; and Archer, "The Militarization of Politics," 209–218.
22. Guardino, *Peasants, Politics*, 87; and Hernández Chavez, "From *res publicae* to Republic," 54–55.
23. Rodríguez O., "The Struggle for the Nation," 2–10, 20–21; and Anna, *Forging Mexico*.
24. Guardino, *Peasants, Politics*, 95–96, 210.
25. Mallon, *Peasant and Nation*, 9–12.
26. Alamán, *Historia de Méjico Tomo V*, 812; cited in Rodríguez O., "The Struggle for the Nation," 22.
27. Guardino, *Peasants, Politics*, 108. See also Warren, "Elections and Popular Political Participation," 42–44.

28. Guardino, *Peasants, Politics*, 113–120.

29. Ibid.,121–130; Muñoz y Pérez, *General Don Juan Álvarez*, 11–12; and Anna, *Santa Anna of Mexico*, 115–116.

30. Gómezjara, *Bonapartismo y lucha campesina*, 67–69; and Muñoz y Pérez, *Don Juan Álvarez*, 31, 161–162.

31. Tenenbaum, *The Politics of Penury*, 46–56; Josefina Vázquez, "Iglesia, ejército y centralismo," 205–234; and Guardino, *Peasants, Politics*, 139–140, 144–146.

32. Luis Mora, *Obras Sueltas*, 168–169. By no means did Centralists possess a monopoly on fears of racial caste war. Many federalists, including Mora, tended to share a fear of the popular masses that expressed itself in calls for the limiting of suffrage to certain "propertied" classes. See Warren, "Elections and Popular Political Participation," 43–45; and Arrom, "Popular Politics in Mexico City," 248–249.

33. Peasant insurgents belonged to at least five main indigenous groups: tlapanecos, yopes, nahautlacas, amusgos, and mixtecos. See Reina, *Las rebeliones campesinas*, 94–95; and Hart, "The 1840s Southwestern Mexico Peasants' War," 250.

34. Guardino, "Barbarism or Republican Law," 194–203; Hart, "The 1840s Southwestern Mexico Peasants' War," 256–266; Reina, *Las rebeliones campesinas*, 85–98; and Jean Meyer, *Problemas*, 10.

35. Quoted in Reina, *Las rebeliones campesinas*, 97.

36. Guardino, *Peasants, Politics*, 150; and Guardino, "Barbarism or Republican Law?" 211.

37. Guardino, *Peasants, Politics*, 158–162; and Guardino and Walker, "The State, Society, and Politics," 35–37.

38. Reina, *Las rebeliones campesinas*, 118; and Bartra, *Guerrero bronco*, 21–23.

39. Guardino, *Peasants, Politics*, 175.

40. Ibid., 174–175; and *Ley orgánica provisional para el arreglo interior del estado de Guerrero*, 3–55, reproduced in Illades and Ortega, *Guerrero*, vol. 1, 318–357.

41. Guardino, *Peasants, Politics*, 180–190.

42. O'Gorman, "Precedentes y sentido de la revolución de Ayutla," 176–178; and "El Plan de Ayutla Reformado en Acapulco [1854]," included in Muñoz y Pérez, *Don Juan Álvarez*, 183–186.

43. Guardino, *Peasants, Politics*, 184–185; and Reina, *Las rebeliones campesinas*, 17–20.

44. Álvarez, "Don Juan Álvarez a sus soldados," 14 March 1854; Álvarez, "El Manifiesto del general Don Juan Álvarez lanzado en Cuernavaca el 2 de Octubre de 1855"; both included in Muñoz y Pérez, *Don Juan Álvarez*, 187, 195–200. See also Mallon, *Peasant and Nation*, 137–175.

45. Muñoz y Pérez, *Don Juan Álvarez*, 92–93; and Bushnell, *La carrera política y militar de Juan Álvarez*, 235–336.

46. Guardino, *Peasants, Politics*, 178–189.

47. Carranco Cardoso, *Acciones militares en el estado de Guerrero*, 45–75; Illades, *Breve historia*, 51–53; and Martínez Carbajal, *Diego Álvarez y Vicente Jimenez*, 8–22.

48. Mallon, *Peasant and Nation*, 312–316; Thomson, *Patriotism, Politics, and Popular Liberalism*, 73–88; and Thomson, "Bulwarks of Patriotic Liberalism," 34–44.

49. According to historian John Coatsworth, such elite unwillingness and failure represented a disavowal "of the only Mexican institutions where democracy possessed a deep ideological, economic, and social significance": indigenous and mestizo peasant communities. Such democracy, as Florencia Mallon's work on late nineteenth-century Puebla and Morelos demonstrates, possessed internal communal hierarchies structured along gendered and generational lines. Coatsworth, "Los orígenes sociales del autoritarismo," 226; and Mallon, *Peasant and Nation*.

50. Mallon, *Peasant and Nation*, 313–314; and Meyer, *Problemas campesinos*, 18–19.

51. Díaz displayed a crafty ability to play off rival regional caciques against one another while bringing in military outsiders to rule the state as governors. Jacobs, *Ranchero Revolt*, 8–14; and Illades, *Breve historia*, 52.

52. Falcón, "Force and the Search for Consent," 107–134.

53. Bartra, *Guerrero bronco*, 26–27; and Falcón, "Force and the Search for Consent," 111–112.

54. Adame Salazar, "Movimientos populares durante el porfiriato," 107–111, 123–124.

55. From 328 to 901 ranchos in that period. Salazar Adame, "Periodo 1867–1910," 67; Illades, *Breve historia*, 68–69; and Jacobs, *Ranchero Revolt*, 29–39.

56. Bartra, *Guerrero bronco*, 28–29. Bartra describes three Spanish-owned merchant companies based in Acapulco as the most important landowners in the Costa Grande. Two American companies also owned extensive land: Roberto Silberber Sucesores, with 40,000 hectares of forested land, and the Guerrero Land and Timber Company, with 150,000 hectares that extended over the municipalities of Tecpan de Galeana, Coyuca de Benítez, and Atoyac de Álvarez.

57. Jacobs, *Ranchero Revolt*, 17; Illades, *Breve historia*, 60; Bartra, *Guerrero bronco*, 24–25; and de Paul Andrade, "Un viaje a Chilapa leído en la sesión del 22 de abril de 1911," 304–307, included in Illades and Ortega, *Guerrero*, vol. 2, 168–169.

58. Jacobs, *Ranchero Revolt*, 18.

59. Ibid.; and Illades, *Breve historia*, 59–61. For Huerta's actions in Yucatán against the Mayan rebels, see Reed, *The Caste War of Yucatán*, 302–303.

60. Bartra, *Guerrero bronco*, 27.

61. Ambrosio Figueroa, letter to Francisco Madero, 12 December 1911, reproduced in Martínez Martínez and López Miramontes, *Figueroismo versus Zapatismo*, 15.

62. Bartra, *Guerrero bronco*, 32–33; Jacobs, *Ranchero Revolt*, 98–101; Gilly, *La revolución interrumpida*, 96–101; Womack, *Zapata and the Mexican Revolution*, 400–404; and Ravelo Lecuona, *La revolución Zapatista*, 202–205.

63. Ravelo Lecuona, "Periodo 1910–1920," 128–129; and Ravelo Lecuona, *La revolución Zapatista*, 203.

64. Ravelo Lecuona, *La revolución Zapatista*, 87–88.

65. Ravelo Lecuona, "Periodo 1910–1920," 120.

66. Bartra, *Guerrero bronco*, 34; and González Bustos, *El general Jesús H. Salgado*, 67–80, included in Illades and Ortega, *Guerrero*, vol. 2, 217–219.

67. Illades and Ortega, *Guerrero*, vol. 2, 224–225.

68. Gilly, *The Mexican Revolution*, 330–332.

69. Radilla Martínez, *Poderes, saberes y sabores*, 104; and Radilla Martínez, *Voces Acalladas*.

70. Carmen Téllez, interviewed by Andrea Radilla Martínez, September 1988, in Radilla Martínez, *Poderes, saberes y sabores*, 104.

71. Martínez Carbajal, *Juan Escudero y Amadeo Vidales*, 53–59; Gill, "Los Escudero de Acapulco," 295–300; Gómezjara, *Bonapartismo y lucha campesina*, 100–107; Bartra, *Guerrero bronco*, 45–48; and Reyes, "El jefe agrarista costeño Valente de la Cruz," 145–150.

72. Blacker-Hanson, "La Lucha Sigue!" 75.

73. Bartra, *Guerrero bronco*, 47; Reyes, "El jefe agrarista," 155–159; and Jacobs, *Ranchero Revolt*, 115–119.

74. In 1923, General Adolfo de la Huerta and half of the federal army rebelled against President Álvaro Obregón when the latter attempted to install Plutarco Elías Calles as his presidential successor. See Purnell, *Popular Movements and State Formation*, 197–202; and Fuentes Díaz, *Historia de la Revolución*, 185–202. Escudero had already survived several assassination attempts, including one in 1922 that left him paralyzed.

75. Bartra, *Guerrero bronco*, 47–51.

76. Ibid., 53.

77. Martínez Carbajal, *Juan R. Escudero y Amadeo S. Vidales*, 153–167; and Gómezjara, *Bonapartismo y lucha campesina*, 108–115.

78. Bartra, *Guerrero bronco*, 55–56; and Gómezjara, *Bonapartismo y lucha campesina*, 115.

79. Molina Álvarez, "Periodo 1910–1920," 271–272.

80. Padilla, *Rural Resistance*, 5–6.

81. José Téllez Sánchez, interviewed in Radilla Martínez, *Poderes, saberes y sabores*, 132; and Padilla, "'Por las buenas no se puede,'" 278.

82. Bartra, *Guerrero Bronco*, 70–73. For critical analyses of Cárdenas's failures and role in institutionalizing political centralization, see: Hamilton, *The Limits of State Autonomy*; Becker, *Setting the Virgin on Fire*; and Bantjes, *As if Jesus Walked on Earth*.

83. Padilla, *Rural Resistance*, 5–7; and Radilla Martínez, *Poderes, saberes y sabores*, 110–113. See also Radilla Martínez, *Voces Acalladas*.

84. Radilla, interview, 16 May 2007.
85. Cárdenas, quoted in Radilla Martínez, *Poderes, saberes y sabores*, 110.
86. Ibid., 59–70; Radilla Martínez, *Voces Acalladas*; and "La Guerra Sucia en Guerrero," *FEMOSPP Filtrado*, 3–5.
87. Gilly, *El cardenismo, una utopía mexicana.*
88. Radilla Martínez, *Poderes, saberes y sabores*, 115–116.
89. Carr, *Marxism and Communism in Twentieth-century Mexico*, 143.
90. Hodges and Gandy, *Mexico under Siege*, 29–30; Servín, *Ruptura y oposición*, 16. Henriquista refers to a follower of General Miguel Henríquez Guzmán, an opposition presidential candidate who ran in the elections of 1952 for the Federation of People's Party (FPPM). Having mobilized to protest what they considered as the fraudulent election of PRI candidate Adolfo Ruiz Cortines in Mexico City on 7 July 1952, Henriquistas were attacked by riot police and federal troops. While later official declarations posted a casualty list of seven dead (and 500 detained), competing accounts place the number of dead between 100 and 500. Padilla, *Rural Resistance*, 135.
91. Suárez, *Lucio Cabañas*, 59–61.

Chapter 2

1. Olcott, *Revolutionary Women*, 7–22. This model of citizenship proved similar to the gendered "revolutionary citizenship" described by Olcott for 1930s Mexico.
2. Sandoval Cruz, *El movimiento social de 1960*, 65. Unless otherwise noted all translations are my own.
3. Archivo General de la Nación, Dirección Federal de Seguridad (hereafter AGN, DFS) 48-52-60, Legajo 1, 147.
4. In 1953, women obtained the right to vote in presidential contests, and did so for the first time in 1958. Olcott, *Revolutionary Women*, 234.
5. Vaughan, "Modernizing Patriarchy," 194–214; Olcott, *Revolutionary Women*, 22–23; and Padilla, *Rural Resistance*, 161.
6. Concepción Solís Morales, interview, 25 May 2007; Bracho, interview, 9 March 2007. For 1950s student movements, see Blacker-Hanson, "La lucha sigue!" 165–188; and Pensado, *Rebel Mexico*, 83–99, 129–146.
7. Padilla, "Rural Education, Political Radicalism."
8. Suárez, *Lucio Cabañas*, 53.
9. Consuelo Solís Morales, interview, 30 May 2007. Consuelo Solís Morales is the widow of Genaro Vázquez.
10. Other sources posit 1933 as Vázquez's birth year. See Ortíz, *Genaro Vázquez*, 73, 79; and Hodges and Gandy, *Mexico under Siege*, 108.
11. Vázquez also briefly studied law at the National University (UNAM) after completing his teaching credential. Bracho, interview, 9 March 2007; Ortíz, *Genaro Vázquez*, 73–74; Gómezjara, "El proceso político de Jenaro Vázquez," 88–89; and de Mora, *Las guerrillas en México*, 26–27.
12. Vázquez served at the MRM's secretary general of western Mexico City during the labor struggles of the late 1950s. The MRM was formed during the late 1950s by Othón Salazar as an independent, autonomous teacher's union that demanded better wages, improved healthcare, cheaper medicine, and union autonomy. See Castellanos, *México armado*, 112; and Consuelo Solís Morales, interview, 30 May 2007.
13. Ortíz, *Genaro Vázquez*, 74.
14. Consuelo Solís Morales, interview, 30 May 2007; and Bracho, interview, 9 March 2007. Baloy Mayo claimed that Vázquez once belonged to the PRI, as did ex-ACG member Blas Vergara. Both Solís and Bracho refuted that claim during their interviews with the author. See Mayo, *La guerrilla de Genaro y Lucio*, 35–36; and Román Román, *Revuelta cívica en Guerrero*, 175.
15. Revueltas, *Ensayo sobre un proletariado sin cabeza.*
16. Gramsci, *Selections from Prison Notebooks*, 168, 229–247, 418; and Miranda Ramírez, interview, 14 May 2007.

17. From 1940 to 1960 some thirteen million hectares of generally marginal and unproductive land was redistributed by the government—compared to the twenty million distributed by Lázaro Cárdenas during his presidential tenure. See Leal and Huacuja R., "Los problemas del campo mexicano," 17.

18. Padilla, *Rural Resistance*, 166; and Becker, *Setting the Virgin on Fire*, 28–31.

19. Industrial uses for copra include industrial lubricants and oils, cosmetics, and soap.

20. Bartra, *Guerrero bronco*, 75.

21. Bartra, *Guerrero bronco*, 77, 84; Paz Paredes and Cabo, "Café caliente," 131; Salgado Cortés, *Caciquismo y campesinado*, 35–66; Hoyos and Cárdenas, "Desarrollo del capitalismo," 84–87, 91–95; Restrepo Fernández, *Costa Grande*, 91.

22. While not necessarily owning large swaths of land, caciques did own the most fertile properties with superior access to irrigation. For instance, in 1971 only six out of seventy-eight ejidos in the Costa Grande owned land classified as "with irrigation [*de riego*]." Also, in a region that lacked reliable all-weather roads, caciques also controlled the means of transporting coffee beans and processed copra by air or sea. They also owned the processing plants. Restrepo Fernández, *Costa Grande*, 89–90; and Paz Paredes and Cabo, "Café caliente," 131–133.

23. Servín, *Ruptura y oposición*, 345.

24. Castellanos, *México armado*, 47; and Padilla, *Rural Resistance*, 135.

25. José Bracho and Santos Méndez, interviews, 9 March and 15 May 2007. For specifics on Caballero's military career, see Gutiérrez Galindo, *Y el pueblo se puso de pie*, 100; Roderic Ai Camp, *Mexican Political Biographies*, 97; Miranda Ramírez, *La violación de los derechos humanos*, 100–102; and Rodríguez Saldaña, *La desaparición de poderes*, 134–135.

26. Giner Durán, a large landholder in Chihuahua, protected other cacique landholders and did not hesitate to use violence as a principal form of ruling. Castellanos, *México armado*, 65–67, 80–81.

27. Dr. Pablo Sandoval Cruz, quoted in Miranda Ramírez, *La violación de derechos humanos*, 99.

28. AGN, DFS 100-10-1, Legajo 7, 93. This internal DFS memorandum lists former state governors General Baltazar Leyva Mancilla (1945–51), Alejandro Gómez Maganda (1951–4), and Darío L. Arrieta (1954–7, interim) as having formed two separate political groups that challenged, possibly even clandestinely worked against, the administration of Caballero Aburto. The general also faced pressure from passed-over candidates, a group that included: Ruffo Figueroa, elder member of the Figueroa cacicazgo; Donato Miranda Fonseca; and Fernando Roman Lugo.

29. A list sent by the ACG to the federal senate in 1960 included thirty public positions occupied by Caballero's relatives—a list that contained the names of persons from the two Costa Chica cacicazgos that most supported the general: the Flores and Añorve families. AGN, DFS 48-54-1960, Legajo 1, 119–120.

30. AGN, DFS 100-10-1, Legajo 7, 90, 93–94.

31. AGN, DFS 48-54-60, Legajo 1, 1–3. For a similar case in Tlacotepec (Centro region), see AGN, DFS 48-54-60, Legajo 1, 17.

32. 30 January 1960, AGN, DFS 48-54-60, Legajo 1, 23.

33. In contrast, corporations usually received preferential treatment. A decreed "Law of Protection of Industry #29" reduced or removed taxes for a period of five to ten years for tourism-based businesses deemed necessary by the governor. One particularly blatant example was the ten-year tax exemption allotted to Cementos del Sur, S.A., a Caballero-owned company. AGN, DFS 48-54-60, Legajo 1, 121–123; Estrada Castañón, *El movimiento anticaballerista*, 57–59; and Román Román, *Revuelta cívica en Guerrero*, 58–59.

34. The Mercantile Union was to receive 75 percent of the copra taxes, while the URPC received the remaining funds. The cafeticultores operated on a similar distribution model. Bartra, *Guerrero bronco*, 80–86; and Román Román, *Revuelta cívica en Guerrero*, 60–61.

35. AGN, DFS 100-10-1, Legajo 3, 113; AGN, DFS 100-10-1, Legajo 7, 90–108; Gómezjara, "La experiencia cooperativa coprera," 135–138; Radilla, *Poderes, saberes y sabores*, 185–187; and Sotelo Pérez, *Breve historia*, 46–47.

36. Ignacio de la Hoya, director of *La Verdad*, cited in Román Román, *Revuelta cívica en Guerrero*, 181.

37. The Trozadura refers to an area where the Atoyac road joined the Acapulco-Zihuatanejo free-way. Former ACNR guerrilla Antonio Miranda Ramírez wrote that the trees of the Trozadura often served as gallows for dissident campesinos who refused to cede their land, or those accused of livestock theft. Miranda Ramírez, *La violación de derechos humanos*, 9–10, 110.

38. PDLP guerrillas, in their words, "brought to justice" (ajusticiamiento) and executed Paco in early 1974. Campos Gómez, *Lucio Cabañas y el Partido de los Pobres*, 141.

39. AGN, DFS 100-10-1, Legajo 7, 94; and Sandoval Cruz, *El movimiento social de 1960*, 76–78.

40. AGN, DFS 100-10-1, Legajo 7, 94.

41. AGN, DFS 48-54-60, Legajo 1, 19; and Niblo and Niblo, "Acapulco in Dreams and Reality," 39–44. For the case of Tuncingo, this document fails to demonstrate if community members died in the attack on their homes. Historian Salvador Román Román demonstrates that in December 1959 state police officers under the orders of Francisco "La Guitarra" Bravo Delgado arrived in Tuncingo and "machine-gunned" various members of the Pino family—nephews of a veteran general of the Mexican revolution. Román Román, *Revuelta cívica en Guerrero*, 146–148.

42. Sandoval Cruz, *El movimiento social de 1960*, 77; Sotelo Pérez, *Breve historia*, 46; and Castellanos, *México armado*, 105–106.

43. Sotelo Pérez, *Breve historia*, 41. Article 145 of the Mexican Constitution, passed during the Second World War, punished those who "propagate ideas, programs, or conduct that tend to produce rebellion, sedition, riots, disorders, and the obstruction of the functioning of legal systems." Bellingeri, "La imposibilidad del odio," 53, quoted in Zolov, *Refried Elvis*, 122.

44. AGN, DFS 44-17-60, Legajo 1, 27–28.

45. Williams, *Marxism and Literature*, 128–135.

46. Sandoval Cruz, *El movimiento social de 1960*, 65.

47. AGN, DFS 48-54-1960, Legajo 1, 29.

48. AGN, DFS 100-10-1, Legajo 7, 94; AGN, DFS 100-10-1, Legajo 2, 47–48; and AGN, DFS 48-54-60, Legajo 1, 1-3, 5. A letter published in January 1961 by a group of expelled ACG members, including López Carmona, signals 14 November 1959 as the organization's founding date. See AGN, DFS 100-10-1, Legajo 7, 29.

49. Sotelo Pérez, *Breve historia*, 53; and Román Román, *Revuelta cívica en Guerrero*, 120–122. Gómezjara identified 10 September 1959 as the ACG's founding date. Gómezjara, *Bonapartismo y lucha campesina*, 264.

50. AGN, DFS 58-54-60, Legajo 1, 17.

51. Ortíz, *Genaro Vázquez*, 74; and Román Román, *Revuelta cívica en Guerrero*, 122.

52. In 1950 expelled militants from the PCM joined to form the POCM as a "new" communist party. Lombardo Toledano formed the Popular Party (PP) in 1948 as a broad, leftist front party that included independent leftists and progressive PRI members. The PP changed its name to PPS (adding Socialist) in 1960. Carr, *Marxism and Communism*, 179, 188–201.

53. AGN, DFS, 48-52-60, Legajo 1, 186; and AGN, DFS 100-10-1, Legajo 4, 161.

54. AGN, DFS 48-54-60, Legajo 1, 161–162. Additional anti-Vázquez rumors, repeated within DFS circles, included one that identified Caballero as Vázquez's godfather. AGN, DFS 100-10-1, Legajo 2, 124.

55. Sotelo Pérez, *Breve historia*, 54; and AGN, DFS 48-54-60, Legajo 1, 1.

56. The local cacique, Candelario Ríos, was a personal friend of former president Miguel Alemán and commanded a paramilitary force that confiscated campesino lands and coprero products. Sotelo Pérez, *Breve historia*, 55–56; and Bartra, *Guerrero bronco*, 85.

57. Sotelo Pérez, *Breve historia*, 57; and Román Román, *Revuelta cívica en Guerrero*, 138–139.

58. Sotelo Pérez, *Breve historia*, 59; and AGN, DFS 48-54-60, Legajo 1, 1.

59. AGN, DFS 48-54-60, Legajo 1, 23–24.

60. Suárez, *Lucio Cabañas*, 53.

61. Sotelo Pérez, *Breve historia*, 58; and Estrada Castañón, *El movimiento anticaballerista*, 64–65.

62. *La Prensa*, 3 February 1959, cited in Estrada Castañón, *El movimiento anticaballerista*, 64.

63. AGN, DFS 44-17-60, Legajo 1, 27; AGN, DFS 48-54-60, Legajo 1, 31; and AGN, DFS 48-54-60, Legajo 1, 46. The first report states that prior to the automobile attack, armed persons

arrived at Lacunza's small ranch and peppered it with submachine gun fire. Lacunza was the son of General Albino Lacunza Pino, veteran of the Mexican revolution.

64. *Trópico*, 22 February 1960, quoted in Román Román, *Revuelta cívica en Guerrero*, 142.

65. Sotelo Pérez, *Breve historia*, 43.

66. AGN, DFS 48-54-60, Legajo 1, 29.

67. AGN, DFS 48-54-60, Legajo 1, 72–73; and Sotelo Pérez, *Breve historia*, 76.

68. *Diario de Acapulco*, 26 March 1960, quoted in Román Román, *Revuelta cívica en Guerrero*, 150.

69. *La Prensa*, 19 June 1960, quoted in Estrada Castañón, *El movimiento anticaballerista*, 66.

70. AGN, DFS 48-54-60, Legajo 1, 72–73.

71. Sotelo Pérez, *Breve historia*, 60–61.

72. AGN, DFS 100-10-1, Legajo 2, 99; DFS 48-54-60, Legajo 1, 57; and Sotelo Pérez, *Breve historia*, 61.

73. Sandoval Cruz, *El movimiento social de 1960*, 29–30. In 1958 students lifted the black and red flag of strike to protest Caballero's choice for school rector. See García Cerros, *Historia de la Universidad*, 59–60.

74. Román Román, *Revuelta cívica en Guerrero*, 189; and García Cerros, *Historia de la Universidad*, 63–74.

75. AGN, DFS 48-54-60, Legajo 1, 60; AGN, DFS 48-54-60, Legajo 1, 66, 94; and AGN, DFS 100-10-1, Legajo 2, 149–150.

76. AGN, DFS 100-10-1, Legajo 2, 112–124.

77. AGN, DFS 100-10-1, Legajo 2, 149.

78. AGN, DFS 48-54-60, Legajo 1, 101, 105–106.

79. *Diario de Acapulco*, 24 June 1960, quoted in Román Román, *Revuelta cívica en Guerrero*, 235.

80. AGN, DFS 48-54-60, Legajo 1, 118–123.

81. AGN, DFS 48-54-60, Legajo 1, 118–129.

82. Gómezjara, *Bonapartismo y lucha campesina*, 181–186; and Niblo and Niblo, "Acapulco in Dreams and Reality," 39.

83. Martínez Carbajal, *Juan Escudero y Amadeo Vidales*, 53. Joseph also studied in Ayotzinapa at the Normal Rural in 1926, worked as "youth secretary" of the Socialist Party of the South headed by Governor Adrián Castrejón in 1929, and worked a number of years as a journalist in Mexico City during the 1950s—culminating in a press position on the campaign staff of President López Mateos. Estrada Castañón, *El movimiento anticaballerista*, 76.

84. AGN, DFS 100-10-1, Legajo 3, 113; Román Román, *Revuelta cívica en Guerrero*, 259–262; and Vázquez Garzón, *El ciudadano Jorge Joseph*, 52.

85. AGN, DFS 100-10-1, Legajo 2, 123; and DFS 100-10-1, Legajo 7, 96.

86. Gómezjara, *Bonapartismo y lucha campesina*, 210–217.

87. *Trópico*, 18 October 1960, quoted in Román Román, *Revuelta cívica en Guerrero*, 267. See also Gutiérrez Galindo, *Y el pueblo se puso de pie*, 202–203; and García Cerros, *Historia de la Universidad*, 79–81.

88. AGN, DFS 48-54-60, Legajo 1, 153–154; Sotelo Pérez, *Breve historia*, 62, 69; Vázquez Garzón, *El ciudadano Jorge Joseph*, 118–119; and Gutiérrez Galindo, *Y el pueblo se puso de pie*, 202–203. The discussion in which Vázquez aired his idea took place on 25 October 1960 according to Sotelo. Vázquez took control of the ACG sometime after his release from jail in mid-May. Sotelo remembers that after his release from prison, López Carmona left Guerrero and the ACG along with his closest sympathizers.

89. *La Prensa*, 22 October 1960, quoted in Estrada Castañón, *El movimiento anticaballerista*, 80.

90. AGN, DFS 48-52-60, Legajo 1, 154. Castro was disappeared by the Mexican Military in 1974.

91. AGN, DFS 48-54-60, Legajo 1, 177–178, 183.

92. Estrada Castañón, *El movimiento anticaballerista*, 80; and AGN, DFS 48-54-60, Legajo 1, 161–162, 169.

93. Sotelo Pérez, *Breve historia*, 70; Hodges and Gandy, *Mexico under Siege*, 108; and Bellingeri, *Del agrarismo armado*, 120.

94. Sotelo Pérez, *Breve historia*, 70.

95. AGN, DFS 48-54-60, Legajo 1, 183; "La Guerra Sucia en Guerrero," *FEMOSSP Filtrado*, 15; Miranda Ramírez and Valencia, *La violación de derechos humanos*, 106; and Sotelo Pérez, *Breve historia* 70–71.

96. Before relocating to the Alameda "Francisco Granados Maldonado" on 3 November after another police attack, the ACG had moved to a kiosk near the central plaza that faced the state capitol. *Excélsior*, 3 November 1960, quoted in Román Román, *Revuelta cívica en Guerrero*, 314.

97. *Excélsior*, 1 November 1960, quoted in Román Román, *Revuelta cívica en Guerrero* 308; and García Cerros, *Historia de la Universidad*, 80–100.

98. Miranda Ramírez, interview, 14 May 2007; Bracho, interview, 9 March 2007; and Sandoval Cruz, *El movimiento social de 1960*, 34–35. A selective list of the groups included: the Union of State and Municipal Workers (SUTSEMID), the Delegation of Communication and Transport, teachers from Section 7 of the National Union of Education Workers (SNTE), Chilpancingo Chamber of Commerce, State Breeders Association, Association of Fathers, Regional Campesino Committees of Atoyac, San Jeronimo, Taxco, Tecpan, San Pedro and San Pablo, Tlapa, and La Unión, National Teachers Training School, Union of Electrical Workers, Association of Cafeticultores of Guerrero, Union of Authentic Copreros of both Coasts of Guerrero, and various preparatory and university student groups. AGN, DFS 48-54-60, Legajo 1, 165, 183–187.

99. Under Article 76 of the Mexican Constitution, only the Senate has the power to remove state governors from power and name interim governors.

100. Published in *Excélsior*, the petition included sixteen demands, with the removal of Caballero as the first one listed. The others included: the legal prosecution of Caballero and his functionaries for crimes committed; the absolute respect for the federal Constitution in the state of Guerrero, most especially that of Article 115 that deals with municipal autonomy; the derogation of taxes imposed by Caballero; the abolition of latifundios; the improvement of primary and secondary education; the protection of small and big commerce from high tax rates; the prohibition of the "irrational" exploitation of forests and the implementation of a reforestation plan; and the prosecution of caciques. *Excélsior*, 12 November 1960, cited in Gutiérrez Galindo, *Y el pueblo se puso de pie*, 52–54.

101. AGN, DFS 100-10-1, Legajo 4, 183–185. The three politicians were Herón Varela, Enrique Salgado Sámano, and Moisés Ochoa Campos.

102. AGN, DFS 48-54-60, Legajo 1, 223. Before the 20 November march, police in Acapulco violently repressed a protest on 16 November leaving twenty-three injured and over 200 detained.

103. COP leader Pablo Sandoval Cruz, quoted in Estrada Castañón, *El movimiento anticaballerista*, 85; and Sandoval Cruz, *El movimiento social de 1960*, 52.

104. Ibid., 55–56.

105. Castellanos, *México Armado*, 108–109; and Sotelo Pérez, *Breve historia*, 77–80.

106. AGN, DFS 48-54-60, Legajo 1, 255; Sandoval Cruz, *El movimiento social de 1960*, 5859; Estrada Castañón, *El movimiento anticaballerista*, 88–89; and Radilla Martínez, *Poderes, saberes y sabores*, 194–197.

107. Gómezjara, "El proceso político de Jenaro Vázquez Rojas," 90.

108. Sandoval Cruz, *El movimiento social de 1960*, 27.

109. Karl Marx, letter to Frederic Engels, 7 September 1864. Other translations refer to "democratic swindle."

110. Gómezjara, "El proceso político de Jenaro Vázquez Rojas," 94, 99–101; Gómezjara, *Bonapartismo y lucha campesina*, 290–294; and Mayo, *La guerrilla de Lucio y Genaro*, 34–39.

111. Bartra, *Guerrero bronco*, 90.

112. AGN, DFS 48-54-60, Legajo 1, 161–162, 177, 185–186, 240; and AGN, DFS 100-10-1, Legajo 4, 161.

113. Moscovici, *Gender and Citizenship*, 112.

114. Olcott, *Revolutionary Women*, 240; and Cano, "Una Cuidadana igualitaria," 73, cited in Olcott, *Revolutionary Women*, 234.

115. Gregoria Nario, interviewed by Andrea Radilla Martínez, in Radilla Martínez, *Poderes, saberes y sabores*, 191.

116. Castellanos, *México armado*, 113; and Consuelo Solís Morales, interview, 30 May 2007.
117. Román Román, *Revuelta cívica en Guerrero*, 664; and AGN, DFS 100-10-1, Legajo 4, 185–186.
118. Estrada Castañón, *El movimiento anticaballerista*, 87–88.
119. Sandoval Cruz, *El movimiento social de 1960*, 124, 153, 156, 165.
120. Differing numbers of casualties exist depending on the source. Román's study of the 1960 social movement, the most exhaustive to date, lists twenty-three dead and forty wounded. Government sources at the time listed a lower number and blamed the victims for having provoked the massacre. My reconstruction of the events is based on: a 21 February 1961 DFS analysis report; the testimonies of participants Antonio Sotelo, Pablo Sandoval Cruz, and Mario García Cerros; and the works produced by scholars Román, Castellanos, and Estrada Castañón. AGN, DFS 100-10-1, Legajo 7, 102–104; Sotelo Pérez, *Breve historia*, 81–84; Sandoval Cruz, *El movimiento social de 1960*, 64–70; García Cerros, *Historia de la Universidad*, 123–124; Román Román, *Revuelta cívica en Guerrero*, 555–569; and Estrada Castañón, *El movimiento anticaballerista*, 89–91.
121. Sotelo Pérez, *Breve historia*, 85.
122. Gutiérrez Galindo, *Y el pueblo se puso de pie*, 35.
123. Gillingham, "Baltasar Levya Mancilla," 183.
124. AGN, DFS 100-10-1, Legajo 7, 92; and Estrada Castañón, *El movimiento anticaballerista*, 96–97.
125. Consuelo Solís Morales, interview, 30 May 2007.

Chapter 3

1. Radilla Martínez, *Poderes, saberes y sabores*, 201. For the definition of acaparadores, see López, *Crafting Mexico*, 164.
2. Padilla, "From Agraristas to Guerrilleros," 76.
3. AGN, DFS 100-10-16-2, Legajo 1, 8–10, 106–107, 144.
4. Gillingham, "Maximino's Bulls," 210–211.
5. Sotelo Pérez, *Breve historia*, 91
6. AGN, DFS 100-10-1, Legajo 7, 104; and Bracho, interview, 9 March 2007.
7. Tavira Urióstegui, "Proceso Revolucionario y Democrático en Guerrero," 159.
8. AGN, DFS 100-10-1, Legajo 6, 107.
9. Public Version [hereafter PV], "Lucio Cabañas Barrientos [hereafter LCB]," DFS File 1, 100-10-1, Legajo 7, 77–78.
10. PV, "LCB," DFS File 1, 100-10-1, Legajo 5, 328.
11. Estrada Castañón, *El movimiento anticaballerista*, 97–98.
12. AGN, DFS 100-10-1, Legajo 7, 29.
13. AGN, DFS 100-10-1, Legajo 6, 141.
14. Ezcurdia, *Análisis teórico del Partido Revolucionario Institucional*, 146.
15. AGN, DFS 48-54-60, Legajo 1, 222.
16. AGN, DFS 100-10-1, Legajo 4, 161.
17. AGN, DFS 48-52-60, Legajo 1, 240. For the struggles between López Carmona and Vázquez, see AGN, DFS 48-54-60, Legajo 1, 185–186, 222–223; and DFS 100-10-1, Legajo 7, 29.
18. AGN, DFS 100-10-1, Legajo 6, 141; and DFS 100-10-1, Legajo 7, 29. The DFS identifies Vázquez as president of the ACG and Sotelo Pérez as vice-president by 10 January 1961. López Carmona and his cadres either were expelled or willingly left the group sometime later that month.
19. Estrada Castañón, *El movimiento anticaballerista*, 106. Sandoval Cruz worked with the ACG throughout 1961.
20. Bracho, interview, 9 March 2007; and Zaldívar Rubio, "ACNR, PDLP, y GPG," 8, included in the Movimiento Armado Socialista Digital Archive [hereafter MAS], Folder "Trabajos de Investigación," José Luis Moreno Borbolla, ed., Centro de Investigaciones Históricas de los Movimientos Sociales A.C. (A CD-ROM copy of this Mexican Guerrilla digital archive was provided to the author by ex-guerrilla José Luis Moreno Borbolla in February 2007.)
21. Jurado Guízar, *Revista de América*, 12 February 1972, included in Ortíz, *Genaro Vázquez*, 42–48.

22. "La Guerra Sucia en Guerrero," *FEMOSPP Filtrado*, 17; and Consuelo Solís Morales, interview, 30 May 2007.
23. López Limón, "Historia de las organizaciones," 637–640.
24. Carr, *Marxism and Communism*, 221–223; Bartra, *Blood, Ink, and Culture*, 204; Pensado, *Rebel Mexico*, 147–180; Cohn, "The Mexican Intelligentsia," 141–182; and Zolov, "Expanding our Conceptual Horizons," 56–61. Under the leadership of Lombardo Toledano, the PPS never fully adopted the call for a new revolution.
25. Carr, *Marxism and Communism*, 200–201; and Henson, "Madera 1965," 19–39. Gámiz was a normalista rural schoolteacher and secretary general of the PPS in Chihuahua during the early 1960s. Earlier he participated in the 1956 student movement at the National Polytechnic Institute (IPN) while attending school there.
26. Alegre, *Railroad Radicals in Cold War Mexico*, 176–214.
27. Carr, *Marxism and Communism*, 224; and Revueltas, *Ensayo sobre un proletariado sin cabeza*, 83.
28. Such dogmatism also led to frequent purges of PCM militants. Revueltas, "Sobre la crisis del Partido [1943]," 33; and Carr, *Marxism and Communism*, 223.
29. Carr, *Marxism and Communism*, 223–226, 253; Martínez Verdugo, ed., *Historia del comunismo en México*, 277–279.
30. Additional international events that impacted the PCM included the 1956 Soviet invasion of Hungary, the anti-Stalin revelations of the XX Congress of the Communist Party of the Soviet Union in 1956, and, to a lesser extent, the Sino-Soviet split.
31. With some important exceptions like the Colombian Communist Party and the Guatemalan Party of Labor (PGT) that supported armed insurgencies during the 1960s.
32. Guevara, "Cuba: ¿Excepción histórica o vanguardia en la lucha anticolonialista?" 264. In highlighting the tendency of Latin American communist parties to follow Moscow's line, we should not overemphasize the Latin America-Moscow connection to detriment of analyzing how communists in nations like Mexico necessarily engaged and were influenced by local traditions and politics. Carr, "The Fate of the Vanguard under a Revolutionary State," 10.
33. Zolov, "Expanding our Conceptual Horizons," 49–53.
34. Arturo Gámiz, quoted in Castellanos, *México armado*, 69.
35. Miranda Ramírez, *El otro rostro de la guerrilla*, 19; Glockner, *Memoria roja*, 96–97; and Zolov, "¡Cuba sí, Yanquis no!" 175–214.
36. The conference was partly sponsored by the World Peace Council in which Cárdenas served as one of the organization's three Latin American leaders. Pellicer de Brody, *México y la revolución cubana*, 96; Zolov, "Expanding our Conceptual Horizons," 71; and Colmenero, "El Movimiento de Liberación Nacional," 13.
37. Semo, "El ocaso de los mitos," 64–65; Pellicer de Brody, *México y la revolución cubana*, 96–100; Condés Lara, *Represión y rebelión en México*, vol. 1, 198–204; and Zolov, "¡Cuba sí, Yanquis no!" 187–188. For interviews and speeches given by Cárdenas before and during the Conference, see Vázquez Gómez, Valcarce, and Alonso, eds., *Palabras y documentos públicos de Lázaro*, vol. 3, 105–115.
38. Cárdenas, *Ideario político*, 285.
39. Semo, "El ocaso de los mitos," 57; Zolov, "¡Cuba sí, Yanquis no!" 176.
40. Colmenero, "El Movimiento de Liberación Nacional," 12.
41. Cárdenas, *Ideario político*, 34–37; and Zolov, "¡Cuba sí, Yanquis no!," 216–218.
42. Accounts differ on whether Vázquez actually participated both in the Conference and the founding of the MLN as an official representative of the ACG. Gómezjara argues that the ACG, represented exclusively by Blas Vergara, officially participated in the elaboration of the Conference's final document but not in the founding of the MLN in August 1961. Gómezjara, *Bonapartismo y lucha campesina*, 282; and Gómezjara, "El proceso político de Jenaro Vázquez Rojas," 102–103. For accounts that place Vázquez at both events, see Glockner, *Memoria Roja*, 114–119; and Castellanos, *México armado*, 70. In any case the MLN included the participation of a score of future guerrilla leaders including Vázquez, Cabañas, Arturo Gámiz, Pablo Gómez, and César Yáñez.
43. Arguedas, "El movimiento de liberación nacional," 232; and Semo, *México: Un pueblo en la historia*, 64–67.

44. The CEM was founded in 1954 by a group of leftist public intellectuals and scholars that defined the group as "independent leftist" in political orientation. Zolov described the organization as a type of "left-wing think tank" that sponsored conferences with heavy emphasis on political economy. Zolov, "Expanding our Conceptual Horizons," 60–61; and Semo, *México: Un pueblo en la historia*, 66.

45. AGN, DFS 100-10-1, Legajo 8, 52.

46. AGN, DFS 100-10-1, Legajo 7, 102, 107.

47. Arguedas, "El movimiento de liberación nacional," 233; and Movimiento de Liberación Nacional, *Programa y Llamamiento*, 70–71. The MLN did include some dissident campesino groups affiliated with the CNC and the UGOCM. Important campesino leaders included Jacinto López and later on, Rubén Jaramillo.

48. Arguedas, "El movimiento de liberación nacional," 234; and Movimiento de Liberación Nacional, *Programa y Llamamiento*, 62–69.

49. Servín, *Ruptura y oposición*, 16.

50. Vázquez Gómez and Alonso, eds., *Palabras y documentos*, vol. 3, 120, 134; and MLN, *Programa y Llamamiento*, 5. The first quote from Cárdenas referred to a speech he gave on 10 March 1961 at the Workers University of Mexico to commemorate that institution's twenty-fifth anniversary.

51. AGN, DFS 32-16, Legajo 1, 102. Vázquez also participated in the failed Political Movement of Mexican Youth (MPJM) in December 1961. The MPJM was organized by independent leftists and Marxists intent on moving beyond the "quotidian Stalinism" that had permeated traditional Left parties in Mexico. Gómezjara, "El proceso político de Jenaro Vázquez Rojas," 103–104.

52. AGN, DFS 100-10-1, Legajo 9, 265; and Gómezjara, "El proceso político de Jenaro Vázquez Rojas," 104–105.

53. Consuelo Solís Morales, interview, 30 May 2007; Gómezjara, "El proceso político de Jenaro Váquez Rojas," 104–105; and Padilla, *Rural Resistance*, 209, 216–218.

54. AGN, DFS 63-3, Legajo 7, 108.

55. PV, "LCB," DFS File 1, 63-3, Legajo 17, 164.

56. Suárez, *Lucio Cabañas*, 53. The children of rural schoolteachers could also attend normales rurales.

57. Padilla, "Rural Education, Political Radicalism."

58. PV, "LCB," DFS File 1, 100-10-1, Legajo 9, 287.

59. León Mendiola, "El Partido de los Pobres," 3.

60. López Limón, "Los mártires de Madera," 264; and PV, "LCB," DFS File 1, 40-1, Legajo 30, 6. Gámiz and Quiñónez would form the GPG in Chihuahua and launch a failed attack on the Madera military barracks on 23 September 1965. Martínez Pérez later became a leader of the guerrilla Movement of Revolutionary Action (MAR).

61. "La Guerra Sucia en Guerrero," *FEMOSPP Filtrado*, 27.

62. Pansters, "Social Movement and Discourse," 88–96.

63. PV, "LCB," DFS File 1, 100-26-1 Legajo 6, 66; 100-19-1, Legajo 4, 129–130, 134; 40-1, Legajo 30, 6; 100-10-1, Legajo 9, 287; and 40-1, Legajo 31, 267–268.

64. The congress took place in July 1961. PV, "LCB," DFS File 1, 100-26-1, Legajo 6, 66.

65. PV, "LCB," 100-10-1, Legajo 9, 287.

66. PV, "LCB," DFS File 1, 100-10-1, Legajo 11, 245.

67. Servín, "Hacia el levantamiento armado," 307–332; and Semo, *México: Un pueblo en la historia*, 82–83.

68. Sotelo Pérez, *Breve historia*, 101–102; Bartra, *Guerrero bronco*, 93–94; and Miranda Ramírez and Valencia, *La violación de los derechos humanos*, 114.

69. DFS memo quoted in Condés Lara, *Represión y rebelión*, 158–184, esp. 180. In 1958 Nava helped create the Potosí Civic Union (UCP) as a political party that challenged the decades-long boss rule of Gonzalo N. Santos and his cronies. Dr. Nava ran for the office of municipal president of San Luis Potosí, and the UCP organized a massively supported tax strike as a tactic to force an end to the Santos cacicazgo. In December 1958, Nava won the elections and after a successful two-year stint as municipal president, he attempted to run for governor in 1961. The PRI responded by violently attacking Navista supporters, prevented

Nava from running, and used the Gasca uprising to arrest him in September 1961. See also Pansters, "Citizens with Dignity," 244–266.

70. Miranda Fonseca enjoyed a long career in public service prior to his post in the López Mateos administration. As a former local and federal deputy, senator, state and federal judge, diplomatic representative, and head of Miguel Alemán's presidential campaign in 1946, the lawyer and former mayor of Acapulco lost out on his bid to become governor of Guerrero in 1956—to General Caballero Aburto. His personal relationship with López Mateos extended back to their law studies during the late 1920s and their subsequent participation in a 1929 student strike. In 1964 he lost the presidential *dedazo* (pick) to Gustavo Díaz Ordaz, despite the initial wishes of López Mateos to designate him as the next president of Mexico. Camp, *Mexican Political Biographies*, 472–473.

71. AGN, DFS 100-10-1, Legajo 9, 82; and AGN, DFS 100-10-16-2, Legajo 1, 8.

72. I have been unable to obtain details on the meeting between Vázquez and Jaramillo. Gómezjara makes a brief reference to the meeting in "El proceso político de Jenaro Vázquez," 104.

73. *La Verdad*, 5 March 1961, quoted in, AGN, DFS 100-10-1-16-2-62, Legajo 10, 215.

74. Miranda Ramírez, *La violación de los derechos humanos*, 116; "La Guerra Sucia en Guerrero," *FEMOSSP Filtrado*, 17; and Bellingeri, *Del agrarismo armado*, 124.

75. Gómezjara, "El proceso político de Jenaro Vázquez," 105–107. Since the 1920s, Suárez Tellez had worked in land redistribution efforts and regional agrarian parties in Guerrero. During the late 1920s and 1930s, he joined the PCM and participated in a series of popular movements that earned him the wrath of Guerrero caciques, including that of Miranda Fonseca. During the 1940s, the combative agrarian leader abandoned the PCM, worked as a federal deputy for the PRI, and joined the POCM after his stint within the PRI.

76. AGN, DFS 100-10-16-2-62, Legajo 10, 204; and DFS 100-10-1-16-2-62, Legajo 10, 215.

77. Consuelo Solís Morales, interview, 30 May 2007.

78. AGN, DFS 100-10-16-2-62, Legajo 1, 8–10.

79. Ibid. The program's land-tenure demands also included: an expansion of agrarian reform; the reduction of property units to thirty hectares; and an increase in the creation of industrial, forestry, and livestock ejidos.

80. Otero, *Farewell to the Peasantry*, 1, 26, quoted in Padilla, *Rural Resistance*, 53. For the 1970s campesino movements, see Bartra, *Los herederos de Zapata*.

81. Escárcega López, *Historia de la cuestión agraria mexicana*, vol. 5, 27.

82. Radilla Martinez, *Poderes, saberes y sabores*, 114–115.

83. AGN, DFS 100-10-16-2-62, Legajo 1, 9.

84. Padilla, *Rural Resistance*, 165–166; and Warman, *We Come to Object*, 253.

85. Becker, *Setting the Virgin on Fire*, 101; Olcott, *Revolutionary Women*, 8, 234; Molyneux, "Twentieth-Century State Formation in Latin America, 50–57; and Vaughan, "Modernizing Patriarchy," 208–210.

86. Concepción Solís Morales, interview, 25 May 2007.

87. Padilla, *Rural Resistance*, 161–168; Olcott, *Revolutionary Women*, 15–22; and Carey, *Plaza of Sacrifices*, 4–7.

88. AGN, DFS 100-10-16-2-62, Legajo 1, 42.

89. Ibid.; AGN, DFS 100-10-16-2-62, Legajo 1, 55; and DFS 100-10-16-2-62, Legajo 1, 86–87.

90. PV, "LCB," DFS File 1, 100-10-1, Legajo 11, 250.

91. AGN, DFS 100-10-16-2-62, Legajo 1, 1, 38.

92. AGN, DFS 100-10-16-2-62, Legajo 1, 71–72. Maldonado also served as governor of Baja California from 1953 to 1959.

93. PV, "LCB," DFS File 1, 100-10-1, Legajo 11, 250.

94. US Embassy in Mexico, Confidential Airgram to the Department of State, 3 January 1963, National Archives, National Security Archives, RG 59, 1960-63, Box 1511, Folder 712.00/12-362. (Document obtained from Doyle, "After the Revolution.")

95. An ACG pamphlet distributed in May 1962 included the names of the following supporting organizations: Revolutionary Bloc of Guerrerense Students, State Miners Union, State Association of Small Merchants, Union of Silver Workers, Acapulco Hotel and Restaurants Workers Union, and a number of independent coprero unions. AGN, DFS 100-10-16-2-62, Legajo 1, 42.

96. At the time there were more than seventy municipalities in Guerrero. A *regidor* is a community representative that serves before the municipal government within the ayuntamiento.
A *diputado* serves in the federal Camara de Diputados (analogous to the United States House
of Representatives). Gómezjara, *Bonapartismo y lucha campesina*, 288–289; and Miranda
Ramírez and Valencia, *La violación de los derechos humanos*, 117–118. See also, AGN, DFS
100-10-16-2-62, Legajo 1, 70–71, 79, 86.

97. AGN, DFS 100-10-16-2-62, Legajo 1, 106–108.

98. Ixcateopan was disproved as the burial site of Cuauhtémoc. Gillingham, *Cuauhtémoc's
Bones*, 44–82.

99. AGN, DFS 100-10-16-2-62, Legajo 1, 116-118; and PV, "LCB," DFS File 1, 100-10-1, Legajo
11, 249.

100. Gómezjara, *Bonapartismo y lucha campesina*, 289.

101. Bracho, interview, 9 March 2007.

102. AGN, DFS 100-10-16-2-62, Legajo 1, 144–145.

103. Concepción Solís Morales, interview, 25 May 2007

104. AGN, DFS 100-10-16-2-62, Legajo 1, 144–145.

105. AGN, DFS 100-10-16-2-62, Legajo 1, 162, 194.

106. AGN, DFS 100-10-16-2-62, Legajo 1, 144, 185. For the Vázquez interview and victory prediction, see *Correo de Iguala*, (18 November 1962) and *El Día* (2 December 1962), quoted
in Gómezjara, *Bonapartismo y lucha campesina*, 289–290.

107. Sotelo Pérez, *Breve historia*, 106–107.

108. AGN, DFS 100-10-16-2-62, Legajo 1, 267.

109. AGN, DFS 100-10-1-62, Legajo 1, 79

110. AGN, DFS 100-10-16-2-62, Legajo 1, 161–162.

111. AGN, DFS 100-10-16-2-62, Legajo 1, 241–242.

112. AGN, DFS 100-10-1, Legajo 13, 33; and "La Guerra Sucia en Guerrero," *FEMOSPP
Filtrado*, 19.

113. AGN, DFS 100-10-16-2-62, Legajo 1, 262.

114. AGN DFS 100-10-16-2-62, Legajo 1, 264, 266, 268–270.

115. "La Guerra Sucia en Guerrero," *FEMOSPP Filtrado*, 19; Gómezjara, *Bonapartismo y lucha
campesina*, 290–291; and Sotelo Pérez, *Breve historia*, 108–109.

116. AGN, DFS 100-10-16-2-62, Legajo 1, 279, 281–290. The reports fail to mention any dead
casualties, citing only the number of detained.

117. AGN, DFS 100-10-16-2-62, Legajo 1, 292.

118. Bellingeri, *Del agrarismo armado*, 125.

119. US Embassy in Mexico, Confidential Airgram to the Department of State, 3 January 1963.

120. AGN, DFS 100-10-1-63, Legajo 13, 92.

121. AGN, DFS 100-10-16-2-63, Legajo 1, 323.

Chapter 4

1. *¿Por qué?* (10 February 1972), included in Ortíz, *Genaro Vázquez*, 213–214. Published days
after his death in Michoacán, Vázquez's letter blasted the editorials written by Victor Rico
Galan (a radical journalist jailed during the late 1960s, accused of plotting a guerrilla insurgency) and Heberto Castillo (a longtime socialist activist).

2. *¿Por qué?* (17 August 1972), included in de la Mora, *Lucio Cabañas, su vida*, 91–95.

3. In a recent study on student political activism in 1950s and 60s Mexico City, historian Jaime
Pensado convincingly traces the cultural and political beginnings of a student New Left to
the 1956 student strike at the National Polytechnic Institute (IPN) and the 1958 student
movement in support of striking bus drivers. Pensado, *Rebel Mexico*, 83–99, 129–146.

4. Historical works on Cold War Latin America tend to define "New Left" as mainly encompass-
ing the urban and rural guerrilla movements that emerged after the 1959 Cuban Revolution.
For works that provide a broader definition, to highlight the role of the intellectual, student,
and countercultural New Left, see Zolov, "Expanding our Conceptual Horizons," 47–73;
Melgar Bao, "La memoria submergida" 29–67; the articles on the various Colombian Lefts

during the Cold War in Archila Neira et al., *Una historia inconclusa;* and Pensado, *Rebel Mexico,* 129–180.

5. AGN, DFS 100-10-16-2-63, Legajo 1, 323; Sotelo Pérez, *Breve historia,* 109; Ortíz, *Genaro Vázquez,* 73–74; and Castellanos, *México armado,* 112–113.

6. "Terror en Guerrero," *Política,* 15 May 1963, 28, quoted in Bartra, *Guerrero bronco,* 99–100.

7. Ibid. El Ticuí also hosted a textile factory that, in October 1963, was closed. Factory workers' leaders were soon thereafter assassinated. Miranda Ramírez and Valencia, *La violación de los derechos humanos,* 133–134.

8. Gómezjara, *La explotación del hombre y los bosques,* 12–13, 21–23.

9. AGN, Secretaría de Defensa Nacional (hereafter SDN) box 74, folder 229, 388–390.

10. Anacleto Ramos Ramírez, quoted in Gómezjara, *La explotación del hombre y los bosques,* 43. In late 1974, Ramos Ramírez (or his brother, José Isabel Ramos Ramírez) revealed the secret location of Cabañas and his remaining three guerrillas to soldiers, resulting in their killing on 2 December 1974. In 1986, PDLP members executed Anacleto in Cuidad Nezahualcóyotl. José had been executed in 1981. Ramírez, "Los orígenes, las huellas, la evolución del EPR," *Proceso* (24 August 1996).

11. Gómezjara, *Bonapartismo y lucha campesina,* 292; Sotelo Pérez, *Breve historia,* 111, Colmenero, "El Movimiento de Liberación Nacional," 18–23; Carr, *Marxism and Communism,* 225–230; and Castellanos, *México armado,* 113.

12. *Política,* (15 September 1963), quoted in Gómezjara, *Bonapartismo y lucha campesina,* 293.

13. They included José and Ismael Bracho, Pedro and Donato Contreras Javier, Fausto Avila, and Demóstenes Lozano Valdovinos. Bracho, interview, 9 March 2007; and Sotelo Pérez, *Breve historia,* 120–122.

14. According to Sotelo Pérez, Leonel Padilla, Carlos Farias, and Augusto Velasco—members of the PCM(b)—aided the ACG president throughout the electoral campaign. In addition to texts like Karl Marx's *Eighteen Brumaire of Louis Napoleon* and Lenin's *What is to be Done?* Vázquez also read contemporary literature on Third World national liberation movements—while also studying Mexican history and revolutions. Sotelo Pérez, *Breve historia,* 102–103.

15. Concepción Solís Morales, interview, 25 May 2007; and Consuelo Solís Morales, interview, 30 May 2007.

16. By the time Vázquez encountered the "heretical" Marxists in 1963, the LLE had split in two: the LLE and PCB. The PCB was previously known as the PCM(b). Cedillo, "El fuego y el silencio," 80; Crespi, "José Revueltas," 103–108; Fernández Christlieb, *El espartaquismo,* 70–82; Carr, *Marxism and Communism,* 210; and, López Limón, "Historia de las organizaciones," 637–640.

17. Concepción Solís Morales, interview, 25 May 2007; and Bellingeri, *Del agrarismo armado,* 127–128.

18. For the quotations, see "The New Route," in Gómezjara, "El proceso político de Jenaro Vázquez Rojas," 111–114.

19. Ibid., 113.

20. Ibid., 114.

21. Carr, *Marxism and Communism,* 222; and Bellingeri, *Del agrarismo armado,* 128.

22. By 1939, 90 percent of rural schoolteachers in Guerrero belonged to the PCM. Bustamante Álvarez, "Periodo 1934–1940," 407, cited in Carr, "The Fate of the Vanguard," 337.

23. Serafín Núñez Ramos, interviewed in Tort, *The Guerrilla and the Hope;* and "La Guerra Sucia en Guerrero," *FEMOSPP Filtrado,* 27.

24. Shanin, "The Question of Socialism," 72, quoted in Carr, "The Fate of the Vanguard," 329.

25. José Revueltas uses the term "red priests [*curas rojos*]" in his 1949 novel, *Los días terrenales.*

26. Carr, *Marxism and Communism,* 2; and Padilla, *Rural Resistance,* 10–11. Hodges and Gandy posit a similar, though overstated, thesis in *Mexico under Siege,* xii, 23–26.

27. Suárez, *Lucio Cabañas,* 53.

28. PV, "LCB," IPS File 7, 238, 247.

29. PV, "LCB," IPS File 7, 246, 249

30. Quintero Romero, "La lucha difícil lucha," 165–171; and the documentary *El Edén bajo el Fusil,* directed by Salvador Díaz (1986), DVD. Such communities included Jaleaca,

Mazcaltepec, Agua Fría, San Andrés, Rincón de las Parotas, Rio Chiquito, El Camarón, and Pie de la Cuesta.

31. Hipólito, *Guerrero, amnistía y represión*, 52, cited in "La Guerra Sucia en Guerrero," *FEMOSPP Filtrado*, 24. Former PCM militant Arturo Martínez Nateras marks 1963 as the year that Cabañas joined the party. Martínez Nateras, *El secuestro de Lucio Cabañas*, 32.

32. Padilla, *Rural Resistance*, 100.

33. Felix Bautista, interviewed in Tort, *The Guerrilla and the Hope*.

34. Suárez, *Lucio Cabañas*, 53.

35. Particularly the Chihuahua normales. A number of these students and teachers would go on to form the guerrilla GPG. Padilla, "Rural Education, Political Radicalism."

36. Padilla, *Rural Resistance*, 100.

37. PV, "LCB," DFS File 1, 40–1, Legajo 36, 202–203.

38. PV, "LCB," DFS File 1, 63–19, Legajo 1, 19–20.

39. PV, "LCB," DFS File 1, 100-10-1, Legajo 16, 132.

40. PV, "LCB," DFS File 1, 100-10-1, Legajo 18, 246–247.

41. Serafín Núñez Ramos, interviewed in Tort, *The Guerrilla and the Hope*; Bartra, *Guerrero bronco*, 105; "La Guerra Sucia en Guerrero," *FEMOSPP Filtrado*, 21; and Quintero Romero, "La lucha difícil lucha," 165–170.

42. AGN, DGIPS box 447, 190–199.

43. PV, "LCB," IPS File 7, 235.

44. Serafín Núñez, interviewed in Tort, *The Guerrilla and the Hope*; and PV, "LCB," DFS File 1, 100-8-1 Legajo 4, 19.

45. PV, "LCB," DFS File 1, 100-8-1, Legajo 4, 435. The local steel plant struggle refers to the Movement of the Cerro del Mercado. See Haber, *Power from Experience*, 129–130.

46. Years later while recounting his path to becoming a guerrilla leader, Cabañas recalled that the remaining members of the Gámiz-led GPG visited Guerrero to meet with him (1965–6): "after the death of Gámiz they visited us...they were here scouting and reconnoitering the mountains well before us." Suárez, *Lucio Cabañas*, 70.

47. Suárez, *Lucio Cabañas*, 35–36; "La Guerra Sucia en Guerrero," *FEMOSPP Filtrado*, 25; and Martínez Nateras, *El secuestro de Lucio Cabañas*, 36. As head of the JCM, Ramos Zavala would break from the PCM in 1970 after disagreeing with the party's unwillingness to engage in armed struggle. Though killed before its official creation in 1973, Ramos Zavala helped forge the material, political, and theoretical foundations of the Communist League of September 23rd (LC23S).

48. PV, "LCB," IPS File 7, 249; and Suárez, *Lucio Cabañas*, 45–46.

49. Radilla, interview, 16 May 2007. Radilla's father, Rosendo Radilla, participated in the ACG and helped create LARSEZ.

50. AGN, DFS 100-10-16-2-64, Legajo 1, 390–392; and Aranda, *Los cívicos guerrerenses*, 72–77, 92-93.

51. AGN, DFS 100-10-16-2-64, Legajo 1, 392; and AGN, DFS 11-136-65, Legajo 8, 59.

52. "La Guerra Sucia en Guerrero," *FEMOSPP Filtrado*, 21; and Bartra, *Guerrero bronco*, 105. For examples of state terror directed against CAP members, see AGN, DFS 100-10-1, Legajo 21, 31, 64; and Aranda, *Los cívicos guerrerenses*, 96–99.

53. AGN, DFS 100-10-3-4-66, Legajo 1, 136.

54. AGN, DFS 100-10-1-66, Legajo 20, 326–327, 334–336; and AGN, DGIPS, box 500, file 5, 53–55.

55. Aranda, *Los cívicos guerrerenses*, 58; Castellanos, *México armado*, 115–116; and López Limón, "Historia de las organizaciones," 683.

56. AGN, DGIPS box 500, file 5, 283–284, 294, 309.

57. AGN, DFS 100-10-1-67, Legajo 24, 67–69; and PV, "LCB," DFS File 1, 100-10-1, Legajo 24, 32–33, 38. The teacher was Alberto Martínez Santiago. His father, Arcadio Martínez, was later killed in the 18 May 1967 massacre.

58. AGN, DGIPS box 549, file 3; and DGIPS box 462, file 1, 263–264.

59. PV, "LCB," DFS File 1, 100-10-1, Legajo 24, 42.

60. PV, "LCB," DFS File 1, 100-10-1, Legajo 24, 44.

61. Suárez, *Lucio Cabañas*, 57.

62. Radilla, interview, 15 May 2007; AGN, DFS 100-10-1-67, Legajo 24, 99–101; DFS 100-10-3-67, Legajo 1, 202; AGN, DGIPS box 462, file 1, 3–4, 265–267, 535–536, 688. Subsequent intelligence reports placed the entire blame on the activists: AGN, DFS 100-10-1, Legajo 24, 99–101.

63. PV, "LCB," DFS File 1, 100-10-1, Legajo 24, 167; and Campos Gómez, *Lucio Cabañas y el Partido de los Pobres*, 180.

64. Suárez, *Lucio Cabañas*, 53–56. Government documents dated 18 May 1967 reveal that the state's attorney general planned to hold Cabañas responsible for the Atoyac movement: AGN, DGIPS box 462, file 1, 265.

65. AGN, DFS 100-10-1-67, Legajo 25, 12.

66. AGN, DGIPS box 1488A, file 3, 57–67; "La Guerra Sucia en Guerrero," *FEMOSPP Filtrado*, 26; and Bellingeri, *Del agrarismo armado*, 133–134.

67. AGN, DFS 100-10-1-67, Legajo 25, 12.

68. Internal ACNR document, 19 January 1963, quoted in Miranda Ramírez and Valencia, *La violación de los derechos humanos*, 131.

69. AGN, DFS 100-10-1-67, Legajo 24, 175.

70. Bellingeri, "La imposibilidad del odio," 53, quoted in Zolov, *Refried Elvis*, 122. The definition for Decree 29 is the following: "any person who propagates or distributes an idea, program, or plan through whatever medium that tends to disturb the public peace and order of the state or subverts juridical and social institutions will face a prison term of 2-10 years and a fine ranging between 10 and 10,000 pesos." "La Guerra Sucia en Guerrero," *FEMOSPP Filtrado*, 21.

71. "La Guerra Sucia en Guerrero," *FEMOSPP Filtrado*, 21.

72. That is, the distribution of arable, quality land. Both the López Mateos and Díaz Ordaz administrations redistributed land, but mostly of poor quality. Only 10 percent of land distributed by Díaz Ordaz was arable. Otero, *Farewell to the Peasantry*, 58–59.

73. The problem was not one exclusively related to land tenure and depended on specific regions. From 1940 to 1960, the PRI regime redistributed thirteen million hectares (32,110,000 acres) while 1960–1976 witnessed the redistribution of thirty million hectares (74,100,000). Other key factors to consider include: the superexhaustion of land provoked by agrobusiness utilization of ecologically corrosive fertilizers and insecticides and the emergence of superplagues caused by the overuse of insecticides and herbicides. Bartra, "Crisis agraria y movimiento campesino," 19–27; Bartra, "Sobre las clases sociales," 25–28; Leal and Huacuja R., "Los problemas del campo mexicano," 20–28;; Hansen, *The Politics of Mexican Development*, 77–83; and Wright, *The Death of Ramón González*, 10–50.

74. Restrepo Fernández, *Costa Grande de Guerrero*, 87–104, 196–200.

75. Otero, *Farewell to the Peasantry*, 56–73.

76. AGN, DFS 100-10-1, Legajo 25, 203.

77. CAP letter to President Gustavo Díaz Ordaz, September 1967. AGN, DFS 100-10-1-67, Legajo 26, 117–119.

78. Radilla Martínez, *Poderes, saberes y sabores*, 207.

79. Hilario Mesino, interviewed in Tort, *The Guerrilla and the Hope*; and Mesino, interview, 17 May 2007. See also, AGN, 100-10-1-67, Legajo 26, 31.

80. Suárez, *Lucio Cabañas*, 58; and AGN, DGIPS box 462, folder 2, 16.

81. Scott, *Domination and the Arts of Resistance*, 183–201.

82. AGN, DFS 100-10-1-67, Legajo 26, 3. DFS agents first reported the appearance of black and red slogans in Atoyac that attacked the state governor on 9 September 1967.

83. PV, "LCB," DFS File 1, 100-10-1, Legajo 24, 187–188; and 100-10-1, Legajo 25, 338.

84. AGN, DFS 100-10-1-67, Legajo 26, 31; DFS 100-10-1-67, Legajo 29, 10-11; and AGN, DGIPS box 463, folder 1, 836.

85. Cárdenas, *Obras 1: Apuntes 1913–1940*, vol. 1, 118–119, quoted in Bartra, *Guerrero Bronco*, 123.

86. Weber followed his oft-quoted assertion with an additional insight applicable to 1960s and 70s Guerrero: "Violence is, of course, not the normal or sole means used by state." The PRI regime exhibited a variety of "means" throughout the most violent phases of the Dirty War in Guerrero. Weber, *The Vocation Lectures*, 310; and Buck-Morss, *Dreamworld and Catastrophe*, 1–11.

87. AGN, DGIPS box 462, folder 2, 94, 425–426, 690, 977–978; DGIPS box 463, folder 1, 205; and AGN, DFS 100-10-1-67, Legajo 24, 147–148, 202–203.

88. Bracho, interview, 9 March 2007. Thirty-nine years later the landscape and climate displayed a strong resemblance with Bracho's description. I traveled there to chronicle the anniversary of Vázquez's escape on 23 April 2007.

89. Méndez and Bracho, interviews, 9 March and 15 May 2007; and "Lineamientos Programaticos de la A.C.G.," 22 August 1967, in Aranda, *Los cívicos guerrerenses*, 107–122.

90. Concepción Solís Morales, interview, 25 May 2007. For a helpful analysis of Lenin's writings on imperialism, see Harding, *Leninism*, 113–141.

91. Harding, *Leninism*, 107–109.

92. Lenin, *El imperialismo*, 115, 125–136.

93. Grandin, *The Last Colonial Massacre*, 182.

94. As defined by Guevara, the "insurrectional foco" referred to a small group of revolutionary guerrillas dedicated to the harassment of state military forces through hit-and-run actions. Guevara envisioned a dialectical relationship between the guerrilla foco and a broader popular struggle, the former aiding in the development and strengthening of the latter. In 1963, he wrote that guerrilla warfare, "was a war of the People, a struggle of the People . . . waging guerrilla warfare without popular support is the prelude to an inevitable disaster." Moreover, the guerrilla foco represented a defensive measure, the first stage of a mass popular revolution in gestation. Guevara, "Guerra de guerrillas: Un método," 391–397; and Guevara, *Guerrilla Warfare*, 50.

95. Consuelo Solís Morales, interview, 30 May 2007.

96. The MRP was an incipient guerrilla group disarticulated by state security forces in August 1966 before it went into action. Noted leftists like journalist Víctor Rico Galán, Raúl Ugalde (leader of the FEP), leaders from the 1964–5 medical workers' strike, and other MLN and FEP militants formed part of the group. Castellanos, *México armado*, 83–84; and Aguayo, *La charola*, 125–131.

97. "Lineamientos Programaticos de la A.C.G.," 22 August 1967, in Aranda, *Los cívicos guerrerenses*, 120.

98. Ibid., 122.

99. Gregoria Nario, interviewed by Andrea Radilla Martínez in Radilla Martínez, *Poderes, saberes y sabores*, 195.

100. Ex-ACG and commando member Donato Contreras Javier propagated this version. Solís Robledo and Cantú Lagunas, *Rescate para la historia*, 51–52.

101. Prudencio Casarrubias was an ACG member from Chilpancingo who had joined the organization during the 1962 electoral campaign.

102. Miranda Ramírez, *La violacion de los derechos humanos*, 150; and "La Guerra Sucia en Guerrero," *FEMOSPP Filtrado*, 32–33.

103. State officials knew little if anything about the ACG group. AGN, DGIPS box 473, folder 2, 296.

104. Bracho, interview, 9 March 2007; and Solís Robledo and Cantú Lagunas, *Rescate para la historia*, 133. At one point Vázquez helped Pérez protect her lands from an ejidal commissary.

105. Concepción Solís Morales, interview, 25 May 2007.

106. Abrams, "Notes on the Difficulty of Studying the State, 77.

107. AGN, DFS 63-3-67, Legajo 25, 168–171; and Williams, *Marxism and Literature*, 128.

108. Suárez, *Lucio Cabañas*, 55.

109. "Resolución Cuarta, II Encuentro en la Sierra 'Heraclio Bernal,'" Folder Grupo Guerrilla Popular, MAS Archive, ed. Moreno Borbolla.

110. Žižek, *Violence*, 1–8, 12–15; Benjamin, "Critique of Violence," 277–300; and Negri, *Insurgencies*, 253–258.

Chapter 5

1. Padilla, *Rural Resistance*, 139.

2. "Hablan los jefes de la guerrilla," *Indice* 11 (September 1965), in MAS Archive, Folder "Grupo Popular Guerrillero," ed. Moreno Borbolla.

3. José Luis Moreno Borbolla, ex-member of the LC23S, quoted in "Confesiones de un joven guerrillero," *Diario Monitor* (31 July 2007).

4. Concepción Solís Morales, interview, 25 May 2007.

5. Montemayor, interviewed in Tort, *The Guerrilla and the Hope.*

6. For critical analyses of the racialized and gendered model of the "heroic" revolutionary subjectivity advanced by the Latin American guerilla New Left see, Saldaña-Portillo, *Revolutionary Imagination in the Americas*, 63–108; Beverley, "Rethinking the Armed Struggle," 47–59; and Mallon, "*Barbudos*, Warriors, and *Rotos*," 179–215.

7. Suárez, *Lucio Cabañas*, 57.

8. Bracho, interview, 9 March 2007.

9. ACG, March 1962, quoted in AGN, DFS 100-10-1-16-2, Legajo 11, 245.

10. Ex-PDLP guerrilla Juan Martínez, interviewed in Tort, *The Guerrilla and the Hope.*

11. Cabañas quoted in Suárez, *Lucio Cabañas*, 55.

12. Suárez, *Lucio Cabañas*, 323.

13. In March 2009 Mexicans courts exonerated Echeverría on the charge of genocide related to the 1968 massacre. Yet much remains unknown about his participation due to governmental intransigence and secrecy, and missing declassified documents. Doyle and Savala, "2 de octubre: Verdad Bajo Resguardo."

14. Walker, *Waking from the Dream*, 25–27.

15. Echeverría was elected by a vote of 21 percent of eligible voters with 58 percent abstaining. See Schmidt, *The Deterioration of the Mexican Presidency*, 32–33.

16. The state could exercise majority or minority control in the companies. Other paraestatales were trusts or decentralized entities. A few examples include: INMECAFE (coffee), Forestal Vicente Guerrero (logging and forestry conservation), and Proquivemex (steroids). Soto Laveaga, "Searching for Molecules," 87–95.

17. Knight, "Cárdenas and Echeverría," 22–26.

18. AGN, DGIPS box 473, folder 2, 296.

19. To reconstruct the escape of Vázquez, I utilize oral interviews, public talks, published testimonies, and declassified DFS and DGIPS documents. Bracho, interview, 9 March 2007; Santos Méndez, interview, 9 March 2007; Concepción Solís Morales, interview, 25 May 2007; José Bracho, talk with the Icatepec community, 21 April 2007; Santos Méndez, talk with the Icatepec community, 21 April 2007; Solís Robledo and Cantú Lagunas, *Rescate para la historia*, 58–77; AGN, DFS 100-10-16-2-68, Legajo 2, 36–37, 44; AGN, DGIPS box 2946A, 1–8; and DGIPS box 530, folder 3, 205–226, 229–247.

20. As José Bracho remembers, "we did not want them to die." José Bracho, talk with the Icatepec community, 21 April 2007. Vázquez expressed a similar opinion in a letter he sent to national newspapers in early June 1968. AGN, DFS 100-10-16-2-68, Legajo 2, 110.

21. Santos Méndez, talk with the Icatepec community, 21 April 2007.

22. AGN, DGIPS box 530, folder 3, 218.

23. José Bracho, talk with the Icatepec community, 21 April 2007.

24. Solís Robledo and Cantú Lagunas, *Rescate para la historia*, 55–57, 71–73.

25. AGN, DGIPS box 530, folder 3, 242.

26. AGN, DGIPS box 530, folder 3, 207, 211, 213, 231–234.

27. AGN, DGIPS box 530, folder 3, 235–236, 243.

28. AGN, DFS 100-10-1-68, Legajo 30, 384–386.

29. AGN, DGIPS box 530, folder 3, 218–219; and AGN, DFS 100-10-1-68, Legajo 30, 420.

30. AGN, DFS 100-10-16-2-70, Legajo 2, 289–291; and Miranda Ramírez and Valencia, *La violación de los derechos humanos*, 164.

31. Méndez, interview, 15 May 2007; and Miranda Ramírez, *El otro rostro de la guerrilla*, 42–45.

32. Ortíz, *Genaro Vázquez*, 194–195.

33. Ibid., 196–198.

34. See Aranda, *Los cívicos guerrerenses*, 123–126; AGN, DFS 100-10-1-68, Legajo 30, 375–377, 384–386; DFS 100-10-16-2-68, Legajo 2, 121–122; and AGN, DGIPS box 530, folder 3, 231–232.

35. Bracho, interview, 9 March 2007.

36. Ortíz, *Genaro Vázquez*, 129–134; Zaldívar Rubio, *El movimiento social guerrerense*, 24–25; Bellingeri, *Del agrarismo armado*, 136–138; and Miranda Ramírez and Valencia, *La violación de los derechos humanos*, 163–165.

37. Bracho, interview, 9 March 2007.
38. Aranda, *Los cívicos guerrerenses*, 173.
39. Guevara, *Guerrilla Warfare*, 148.
40. AGN, DGIPS box 1195B, folder 4, 6–9.
41. Adame was the CCI (noncommunist faction) leader in the Costa Grande during the late 1960s. He continually faced death threats from local caciques and military forces. AGN, SDN box 81, file 244, 29; and SDN box 76, folder 231, 182.
42. For a brief biography of Petronilo Castro see this volume, Conclusion. Méndez, interview, 9 March 2007; Gallegos Nájera, *La guerrilla en Guerrero*, 243; Solís Robledo and Cantú Lagunas, *Rescate para la historia*, 46–47; and Sotelo Pérez, *Breve historia*, 133.
43. Radilla, interview, 16 May 2007.
44. Bracho, interview, 9 March 2007.
45. Zaldívar Rubio, *El movimiento social guerrerense*, 26–27. The rival caciques were incidentally Cabañas's uncles.
46. Bracho, interview, 15 May 2007; and Miranda Ramírez, *La violación de los derechos humanos*, 170. Donato Contreras argued that Vázquez wanted to execute his brother Pedro Contreras for having an affair with a married woman. This incident led to a major dispute over tactics. Solís Robledo and Cantú Lagunas, *Rescate para la historia*, 175–177, 181–182.
47. Bracho, interview, 9 March 2007; and AGN, DFS 100-10-1-69, Legajo 33, 201–202.
48. Miranda Ramírez casts doubt on the large number of duties assigned to one militant, arguing that the DFS fabricated some as to incriminate Solís Morales with more criminal charges. Miranda Ramírez, *La violación de los derechos humanos*, 180.
49. Concepción Solís Morales, interview, 25 May 2007. In the transcript of his "interrogation," Jorge Mota González asserted that he worked with Solís Morales in receiving and mimeographing communiqués sent by Vázquez. He also mentioned that she sent money, medicines, and clothes. AGN, DGIPS box 2492, folder 1, 251–253, 255.
50. "La Guerra Sucia en Guerrero," *FEMOSPP Filtrado*, 35–36; and DFS 100-10-16-2-70, Legajo 2, 315.
51. AGN, DGIPS box 2492, folder 1, 252–253.
52. AGN, DGIPS box 2492, folder 1, 438–439, "Interrogation of Fausto Avila Juárez (a) 'Alejandro.' " Avila Juárez declared that he joined Vázquez in the Costa Region in 1969 "[helping him] by talking with campesinos from the region and convince them to help Vázquez... when he had free time he taught local campesinos how to read."
53. AGN, DFS 100-10-1-69, Legajo 33, 407; and DFS 63-19-69, Legajo 6, 212.
54. "Conclusiones llevadas a cabo por la A.C.N.R. en las Montañas del Sur," in Aranda, *Los cívicos guerrerenses*, 127–128.
55. Zaldívar Rubio, *El movimiento social guerrerense*, 29.
56. "Conclusiones llevadas a cabo por la A.C.N.R. en las Montañas del Sur," in Aranda, *Los cívicos guerrerenses*, 127–128.
57. AGN, DGIPS box 550, folder 1; and AGN, DFS 100-10-16-2-70, Legajo 2, 287–291, 295–306.
58. AGN, SDN box 93, folder 279, 49–50; and "La Guerra Sucia en Guerrero," *FEMOSPP Filtrado*, 36. Using torture, interrogators obtained the date of Vázquez's departure from Costa Chica residents and ACNR supporters Sixto Flores and Marcial Juárez. For "Operation Friendship," see Aviña, " 'We Have Returned to Porfirian Times,' " 106–107.
59. AGN, DGIPS box 549, folder 3, 1–2.
60. Ibid. The general essentially called for the arming of a paramilitary family or clan unit to combat the Cabañas-led PDLD and the ACNR. Since early 1968, the Torreblanca and Cabañas families had clashed over the death of a Torreblanca man—brother to the municipal president of San Jerónimo. The family accused Manuel García Cabañas, municipal president of Atoyac and Lucio Cabañas's cousin, of the murder. AGN, DGIPS box 473, folder 2, 379–380, 450, 558–559.
61. AGN, DGIPS box 549, folder 3, 3–4.
62. Krauze, *Mexico*, 728; and Scherer García and Monsiváis, *Los patriotas*, 79–85.
63. AGN, DGIPS box 550, folder 1; DGIPS box 586, folder one; DGIPS box 2364, folder 1, 324–325; DGIPS box 2364, folder 1, 556–557; and DGIPS box 586, folder 3.

64. AGN, DGIPS box 550, folder 1.

65. AGN, DFS 100-10-16-2-70, Legajo 2, 301–306; and Aranda, *Los cívicos guerrerenses*, 149–157. The various documents are dated, respectively: February, March, and November–December 1970.

66. AGN, DFS 100-10-16-2-70, Legajo 2, 301–302.

67. Aranda, *Los cívicos guerrerenses*, 171.

68. Such analysis bears the influence of Revueltas (particularly *Ensayo sobre un proletariado sin cabeza*) and Lenin's 1917 writings. See Žižek, "Introduction: Between Two Revolutions," in Lenin, *Revolution at the Gates*, 7–9.

69. ACNR communiqué, AGN, DFS 100-10-16-2-70, Legajo 2, 301.

70. "Guerrillas en Guerrero," *¿Por qué?* 160 (22 July 1971), and "Seguiremos la lucha. . ." *¿Por qué?* 161 (29 July 1971), included in Ortíz, *Genaro Vázquez*, 67–78.

71. Consuelo Solís Morales, interview, 30 May 2007.

72. ACNR communiqué, AGN, DFS 100-10-16-2-70, Legajo 2, 303.

73. AGN, DGIPS box 586, folder 3.

74. This information was obtained from campesino Sulpicio de Jesús de la Cruz by military and police interrogation through the use of torture. De Jesús was detained days after the Agustín Bautista Cabrera kidnapping in mid-April 1971. He was later re-detained on 27 June 1972 and disappeared. National Commission on Human Rights (CNDH), *Informe especial*, folder PDS/95/GRO/S00111.000, number 162-R.

75. Miranda Ramírez, *La violación de los derechos humanos*, 217–218.

76. AGN, DGIPS box 2492, folder 1, 256–258, "Interrogation of Jorge Mota González."

77. Hipólito, *Guerrero, amnistía y represión*, 42.

78. AGN, DGIPS box 586, folder 3; DGIPS box 2492, folder 1, 257–258; and AGN, DFS 100-10-16-2-71, Legajo 2, 345.

79. AGN, DFS 100-10-16-2-71, Legajo 2, 345; and DFS 11-4-71, Legajo 128, 159–172.

80. AGN, DGIPS box 1195B, folder 3, 68.

81. AGN, DGIPS box 1195B, folder 3, 92–93.

82. ACNR communiqué, 11 April 1971, in Aranda, *Los cívicos guerrerenses*, 161–162.

83. Aranda, *Los cívicos guerrerenses*, 161–162; AGN, DGIPS box 1195B, folder 3, 102–104, 170–173; and Bellingeri, *Del agrarismo armado*, 144–145.

84. Zaldívar Rubio, *El movimiento social guerrerense*, 36.

85. AGN, SDN box 93, folder 279, 26–31; and, SDN box 93, folder 286, 3.

86. AGN, SDN box 93, folder 286, 3–65.

87. Bracho, interview, 9 March 2007; AGN, DFS 100-10-16-2-71, Legajo 3, 15; and DGIPS box 1195B, folder 3, 487. Alfonso Vázquez was taken to Military Camp Number 1 (CM1) in Mexico City where he spent more than three months detained. Bracho's brother Ismael was detained during this time. AGN, DFS 100-10-16-2-71, Legajo 3, 157.

88. AGN, DGIPS box 2492, folder 1, 259–261,"Interrogation of Jorge Mota González"; AGN, DFS 100-10-16-2-71, Legajo 4, 279–280, "Interrogation of Raúl Pano Mercado"; and DFS 100-10-16-2-71, Legajo 5, 1–3.

89. Suárez, *Lucio Cabañas*, 62.

90. Miranda Ramírez, *El otro rostro de la guerrilla*, 113–114; "La Guerra Sucia en Guerrero," *FEMOSPP Filtrado*, 39–40; and AGN, DFS 100-10-16-2-71, Legajo 3, 19.

91. Bracho, interview, 9 March 2007.

92. Concepción Solís Morales, interview, 25 May 2007.

93. "La Guerra Sucia en Guerrero, *FEMOSPP Filtrado*, 40; CNDH, *Informe especial*, case numbers 014-R, 047-R, 048-R, 235-R, and 407-R.

94. AGN, SDN box 91, folder 276, 16.

95. "Versión oficial: No hay guerrillas," *El Trópico* (21 July 1971), reproduced in AGN, DGIPS box 1195B, folder 3, 383–384.

96. The articles are reproduced in Ortíz, *Genaro Vázquez*, 67–83.

97. Ibid., 71.

98. Schmidt, *The Deterioration of the Mexican Presidency*, 71; Castellanos, *México armado*, 172; and Saldívar, "Una decada de crisis y luchas," 219–220.

99. Ortíz, *Genaro Vázquez*, 78–79.

100. Ibid., 80–81.

101. Miranda Ramírez, *La violación de los derechos humanos*, 256–261; and AGN, SDN box 91, folder 276, 106.

102. Bracho, interview, 9 March 2007.

103. Ibid.; Miranda Ramírez, interview, 14 May 2007; and Miranda Ramírez, *La violación de los derechos humanos*, 260.

104. These included campesinos from the Costa Chica, Costa Grande, and at least one school-teacher: José Garay (disappeared in 1974), Francisco Garay, Sixto Flores, Cliserio de Jesús, Efrén Gutiérrez, Miguel García Martínez, José Ramírez, Crecencio Calderón (disappeared), Mellado Martínez, Juan de Jesús, Hilda Flores, Eusebio Armenta (disappeared), Marcos Saldaña, Angel Piza (disappeared), and Justino Piza. López Limón, "Concentrado General Desaparecidos [Excel Worksheet]," *FEMOSPP Filtrado*.

105. Aranda, *Los cívicos guerrerenses*, 167–168; AGN, DGIPS box 1195B, folder 3, 654–659; and Bellingeri, *Del agrarismo armado*, 148–149.

106. AGN, DFS 80-9-71, Legajo 1, 1; DGIPS box 1195B, folder 3, 624–626; AGN, SDN box 122, folder 371, 3; and Castellanos, *México armado*, 132.

107. *El Día* (22 November 1971); *El Sol de México* (24 November 1971); *El Día* (27 November 1971); and *El Sol de México* (1 December 1971); all reproduced in Ortíz, *Genaro Vázquez*, 91, 100, 109–110, 146.

108. Castellanos, *México armado*, 133; Bracho, interview, 9 March 2007; and AGN, DGIPS box 1195B, folder 4, 3, 6–9.

109. Ocampo was detained on 20 January 1972 in Puebla. He was last seen alive at CM1 in late January 1972 by Concepción and Consuelo Solís Morales. Concepción Solís Morales, interview, 25 May 2007; and Consuelo Solís Morales, interview, 30 May 2007.

110. Bracho, interview, 9 March 2007; and Miranda Ramírez, *El otro rostro*, 67–69.

111. *Excélsior* (2 February 1972), quoted in Castellanos, *México armado*, 135; and Consuelo Solís Morales, interview, 30 May 2007.

112. Bracho, interviews, 9 March and 15 May 2007.

113. AGN, DFS 100-10-16-2-72, Legajo 5, 107; and AGN, DGIPS box 673, folder 2. The initials GVR were engraved on the wedding ring found on Vázquez. Consuelo Solís Morales told me that the jeweler (in 1958) had mistakenly engraved the couple's wedding rings, switching the rings with the appropriate engraved initials; interview, Mexico City, 30 May 2007.

114. Bracho, interview, 9 March 2007; "La Guerra Sucia en Guerrero," *FEMOSPP Filtrado*, 47; and AGN, DFS 100-10-16-2-72, Legajo 5, 168.

115. Consuelo Solís Morales, interview, 30 May 2007.

116. AGN, DFS 100-10-16-2-72, Legajo 5, 224.

117. AGN, SDN box 94, folder 281, 90.

118. AGN, DGIPS box 2493 contains the photographs.

119. AGN, DFS 100-10-16-2-72, Legajo 5, 226–227.

120. Consuelo Solís Morales, interview, 30 May 2007.

121. Gramsci, *Selections from the Prison Notebooks*, 263.

122. AGN, DFS 100-10-16-4, Legajo 4, 365–366.

123. AGN, DFS 80-21-72, Legajo 1, 105–106.

Chapter 6

1. Cárdenas, interview, 23 April 2007.

2. Freire, *Pedagogy of the Oppressed*; and McLaren, *Che Guevara, Paolo Freire*, 184–186.

3. AGN, DFS 100-10-16-4, Legajo 8, 14–16, 23.

4. Suárez, *Lucio Cabañas*, 131.

5. Ibid., 132.

6. AGN, DFS 100-10-16-4-72, Legajo 5, 96.

7. Cárdenas, interview, 23 April 2007.

8. Ibid.

9. Negri, "Communism," 163–164.

10. Meza Velarde and Rubio Zaldívar, "Luchas sociales en el estado de Guerrero," 76. A group of Mexican Maoists attempted to establish contact with the PDLP in early 1970. This group, led by Javier Fuentes Gutiérrez and included Florencio Medrano, had traveled to China in 1967 and received military and political training. Cabañas was also friends with a group of Maoists from the state of Morelos—some connected to the earlier Jaramillista struggle—that visited him throughout the PDLP insurgency. PV, "LCB," DFS File 1, 11-94-70, Legajo 2, 107–109, 128–133; AGN, DFS 100-10-16-4, Legajo 6, 257; and Padilla, *Rural Resistance*, 216–219.

11. PDLP communiqué, 27 November 1974, DGIPS box 2743, file 1, 251–255.

12. Thompson, *Whigs and Hunters*, 160–161; Marx, "Speech at the anniversary of the *People's Paper*," 500. Marx described the Vehmgericht as a secret tribunal that existed in Germany during the Middle Ages that punished overbearing or criminal members of the ruling class. The Hampshire Blacks were deer poachers in southern England during the 1720s that challenged the loss of peasant forest rights.

13. Flores Reynada was a long-time peasant and labor leader in the Atoyac region, assassinated by anti-worker gunslingers during the early 1930s.

14. Suárez, *Lucio Cabañas*, 56–57.

15. Ibid., 57.

16. Survivors recalled the deaths of five people, including Martínez, Isabel Gómez Romero, Prisciliano Téllez, Regino Rosales de la Rosa, and Feliciano Castro. DGIPS documents included an additional casualty: the death of María de Jesús González. I have not been able to cross-check or reference the veracity of the report. Hilda Flores, interviewed by Felipe Fierro Santiago, in Fierro Santiago, *El último disparo*, 23–25; Suárez, *Lucio Cabañas*, 58; AGN, DGIPS box 462, file 2, 266–267; and Radilla, interview, 16 May 2007.

17. Hilda Flores, interview with Felipe Fierro Santiago, in Fierro Santiago, *El último disparo*, 28.

18. PV, "LCB," DFS File 1, 100-10-1, Legajo 24, 167.

19. AGN, DGIPS box 463, file 1, 836.

20. PV, "LCB," DFS File 1, 100-10-1, Legajo 24, 187–188.

21. Mao, *On Guerrilla Warfare*, 93; and "Archivos de Bucareli," *Nexos* (1 June 1998), 11–12.

22. Onofre Barrientos also headed the PDLP support cell in the community of El Quemado. He was detained and disappeared by the Mexican military in September 1972. AGN, DGIPS box 2547, file 1, 1–2.

23. AGN, DFS 100-10-1-67, Legajo 25, 12.

24. AGN, DGIPS box 549, file 3; and PV, "LCB," DFS File 2, Legajo 38, 1–4.

25. Suárez, *Lucio Cabañas*, 58–59.

26. Ibid.

27. "La Guerra Sucia en Guerrero," *FEMOSPP Filtrado*, 29–30; and AGN, DGIPS box 473, file 2, 296.

28. Wright, *Latin America in the Era of the Cuban Revolution*, 170–171.

29. PV, "LCB," DFS File 2, 187–189, "Estado de Guerrero, Agosto 25 de 1972."

30. Fierro Loza, *Los papeles de la sedición*, 17.

31. PV, "LCB," DFS File 1, 100-10-1, Legajo 29, 233–234.

32. AGN, DGIPS box 474, file 1, 638–639.

33. AGN, DFS 100-10-1-67, Legajo 26, 31; DFS 100-10-1-67, Legajo 26, 1–6; and DFS 100-10-1-67, Legajo 29, 10–11, 126–128.

34. AGN, DFS 100-10-16-2-68, Legajo 2, 45.

35. Doña Socorro Meléndez, quoted in Vaughan, "Implementation of National Policy," 7, cited in Knight, "Popular Culture and the Revolutionary State in Mexico, 1910-1940," 430.

36. AGN, DGIPS box 549, file 3.

37. Orwell, *Road to Wigan Pier*, 178–180.

38. Benjamin, "On the Concept of History," 394.

39. AGN, DFS 100-10-1-69, Legajo 33, 179–180.

40. AGN, DGIPS box 530, file 3, 95; and PV, "LCB," DFS File 1, 100-10-1, Legajo 25, 336–338, 362–363.

41. Suárez, *Lucio Cabañas*, 54–60.

42. Ibid., 60–61.
43. "La Guerra Sucia en Guerrero," *FEMOSPP Filtrado*, 29–30.
44. Cárdenas, interview, 23 April 2007.
45. An additional meaning for *partido* is the act of taking sides—in this case, taking the side of the poor. Bellingeri, *Del agrarismo armado*, 198.
46. AGN, DFS 100-10-16-4, Legajo 8, 58–59, "Interrogation of Raúl Castañeda Peñaloza." Castañeda Peñaloza, was tortured and subsequently disappeared.
47. Robespierre, *Virtue and Terror*, ed. Slavoj Žižek, viii.
48. Suárez, *Lucio Cabañas*, 61; and López Limón, "Historia de las organizaciones," 699.
49. "La Guerra Sucia en Guerrero," *FEMOSPP Filtrado*, 29–31.
50. AGN, DGIPS box 474, file 1, 640–642; and DGIPS box 2946A, 1–8. Other estimates range from nine to thirteen fighters. Bellingeri, *Del agrarismo armado*, 180; and Fierro Loza, *Los papeles de la sedición*, 10.
51. Bellingeri, *Del agrarismo armado*, 179.
52. Suárez, *Lucio Cabañas*, 71. PCM militants claim they provided the first high-powered rifles. Martínez Nateras, *El secuestro*, 30–31.
53. "La Guerra Sucia en Guerrero," *FEMOSPP Filtrado*, 31.
54. AGN, DGIPS box 549, file 3.
55. Ibid.
56. AGN, DFS 100-10-1-69, Legajo 33, 179–180.
57. AGN, DGIPS box 549, file 3; and AGN, DFS 100-10-1-69, Legajo 33, 371–372.
58. Ibid.
59. PV, "LCB," DFS File 1, 100-10-1, Legajo 33, 179–180.
60. AGN, DGIPS box 549, file 3.
61. Suárez, *Lucio Cabañas*, 177.
62. AGN, DGIPS box 550, file 1; and AGN, DFS 100-10-16-2, Legajo 2, 148.
63. Modesto Trujillo, "Testimonio;" and León Mendiola, "Mi Testimonio," in Testimonios o Entrevistas Folder, MAS Archive, ed. Borbolla Moreno.
64. PV, "LCB," DFS File 5, 81–87.
65. Ricardo Rodríguez González, inteview with the author, Mexico City, 5 May 2007; and Rodríguez González, "Testimonio," Testimonios o Entrevistas Folder, MAS Archive, ed. Borbolla Moreno.
66. PB, "LCB," DFS File 1, 10–26, Legajo 17, 194, 4 March 1970.
67. AGN, DFS 100-10-16-2, Legajo 2, 285; AGN, DGIPS, box 550, file 1; and Bracho, interview, 9 March 2007.
68. AGN, DFS 100-10-16-4, Legajo 1, 8–9.
69. "La Guerra Sucia en Guerrero," *FEMOSPP Filtrado*, 86. A vigilante paramilitary group named "Group Blood," allegedly led by high-ranking military officials, carried out such acts against perceived PDLP supporters. AGN, DGIPS box 1067, file 3, 18–19.
70. Natividad Rosales, *¿Quien es Lucio Cabañas?* 80; and AGN, SDN box 99, file 294, 332.
71. AGN, SDN box 99, file 294, 327–329.
72. AGN, DFS 100-10-16-4 L1, 12–13. Estimates regarding the number of troops deployed to Guerrero range from 10,000 to 24,000 (one-third of the entire Mexican Army). Thousands of state police forces also participated in the counterinsurgency campaigns, as did plainclothed DFS agents. A military report dated September 1974 has the number at nearly 4500—an improbably low number that probably only counts troops in the Atoyac region. AGN, SDN box 100, file 298, 45.
73. AGN, DFS 100-10-16-4, Legajo 1,1.
74. Suárez, *Lucio Cabañas*, 154–155.
75. AGN, SDN box 93, file 278, 110–111.
76. Suárez, *Lucio Cabañas*, 318–320.
77. BCA guerrillas abducted the two doctors for their close links to caciques: Dr. Telésforo Andalón and Dr. Juan Becerra Luna. Becerra Luna, accused of paying state police officers for the 1967 Atoyac massacre, was executed 25 June 1971. AGN, DGIPS box 673, file 2; AGN, SDN box 94, file 281, 227; and AGN, DFS 100-10-16-4, Legajo 4, 396, 404; and Fierro Santiago, *El último disparo*, 36.

78. AGN, DFS 80-21-72, Legajo 1, 41, 44–45, 103, 187; DFS 100-10-16-4, Legajo 5, 30–32, 37–38, 41, 46–49; AGN, DGIPS, box 1195B, file 4, 235–236, 264–266; and DFS 100-10-16-4, Legajo 5, 46–49.

79. AGN, 100-10-16-4, Legajo 6, 230–231; and Bellingeri, *Del agrarismo armado*, 182.

80. University, preparatory, and normalista students comprised the self-dubbed "Armed Commandos of Guerrero." AGN, DFS 80-16-72, Legajo 1, 17, 22, 114; and Bellingeri, *Del agrarismo armado*, 181.

81. AGN, DFS 100-10-16-4, Legajo 1, 127.

82. AGN, DFS 80-21-72, Legajo 1, 105.

83. Cabañas dubbed the northern students "Los Guajiros" (The Peasants). Led by Leopoldo Angulo Luken ("The General"), the Guajiros operated mainly in Chihuahua and later formed part of the LC23S. "La Guerra Sucia en Guerrero," *FEMOSPP Filtrado*, 43.

84. AGN, DFS 100-10-16-4, Legajo 1, 109–113, 124–130, 163; and "La Guerra Sucia en Guerrero," *FEMOSPP Filtrado*, 43. See also García, *Fulgor rebelde*.

85. AGN, DFS 100-10-16-4, Legajo 1, 18–21; and DFS 100-1-18, Legajo 2, 59–60.

86. AGN, DFS 100-10-16-4, Legajo 1, 109–113, 124–130; and DFS 100-10-16-4, Legajo 1, 141–142.

87. AGN, DFS 100-10-16-4, Legajo 1, 170–171; and DGIPS box 2490, file 1, 1–10. Attempts in 1973 to establish a mixed PDLP-MAR guerrilla front in Hidalgo by university students and teachers also failed. Nine Hidalgo guerrillas remain disappeared. Pineda, *En las profundidades*, 201–209; and PV, "LCB," DFS File 5, 11–238, Legajo 4, 196–199 (153–156).

88. AGN, DFS 100-10-16-4, Legajo 1, 127.

89. The LC23S formed in March 1973, fusing a series of radical urban groups mostly composed by students from throughout Mexico (especially Mexico City, Guadalajara, and Monterrey) into one national guerrilla organization. A number of militants from armed groups like the MAR and the M23S also joined. The Communist Youth (JCM) was also an important source of LC23S theoreticians and militants, as were Monterrey university students trained by liberation theology Jesuits. Ramírez Salas, "La relación de la Liga Comunista," 527–547; and Robinet, "A Revolutionary Group," 129–145.

90. AGN, SDN, box 77, file 232, 96; and SDN box 93, file 278, 147–148, 152, 154, 181–182.

91. AGN, DFS 100-10-16-4 L1, 12; PV, "LCB," DFS File 4, 11-235-74, Legajo 19, "Interrogation of Marisol Orozco Vega;" PV, "LCB," DFS File 5, 11–235, Legajo 23, 66–69, "Interrogation of Wenceslao García José;" and Pineda, interview, 20 April 2007.

92. Pineda, *En las profundidades*, 163–165.

93. Rodríguez González, interview, 5 May 2007. Rodríguez González was part of the BCA leadership directive.

94. AGN, DFS 100-10-16-4, Legajo 5, 226.

95. AGN, SDN box 98, file 292, 16–17; SDN box 98, file 292, 19–21; and Rodríguez González, interview, 5 May 2007.

96. AGN, SDN box 98, file 292, 16–17, 19–21.

97. AGN, SDN box 93, folder 279, 26.

98. AGN, DFS 100-10-16-4 Legajo 5, 94–106.

99. AGN, DFS 100-10-16-4, Legajo 6, 188–189. The report also provided a list of twenty-seven communities that organized PDLP support committees "with others that have yet to be determined."

100. AGN, SDN box 94, file 281, 503 and "La Guerra Sucia en Guerrero," *FEMOSPP Filtrado*, 54–55.

101. AGN, DFS 100-10-16-4 Legajo 5, 59–60, 73–74, 78–79; AGN, SDN box 92, file 277, 221; SDN box 96, file 285, 493–95; and "La Guerra Sucia en Guerrero," *FEMOSPP Filtrado*, 54–56.

102. AGN, SDN box 92, folder 292, 16–17.

103. Bartra, *Guerrero bronco*, 117; and AGN, DFS 100-10-16-4, legajo 5, 313–318.

104. Cárdenas created Banjidal in 1935, tasked with providing credit to ejidatario peasants.

105. Bartra, *Guerrero bronco*, 124–126; and AGN, DGIPS box 723, file 3.

106. Bellingeri, *Del agrarismo armado*, 215; and Bartra, *Guerrero bronco*, 121.

107. Mesino, interview, 17 May 2007.

108. Carbot, *Café para todos*, 97–98.
109. "La Guerra Sucia en Guerrero," 73, and "Crímenes de Guerra," 11 in *FEMOSPP Filtrado*.
110. AGN, DFS 100-10-16-4, L5, 313–318.
111. AGN, SDN box 100, folder 299, 158–168; and AGN, SDN box 83, folder 248, 125.
112. Feitlowitz, *A Lexicon of Terror*, 50–62.
113. AGN, SDN box 99, folder 294, 185–186, 396.
114. According to the FEMOSPP report, the first time military correspondence used the term "package" occurred in late November 1973. See AGN, SDN box 97, folder 288, 43 (no. 17136); and "La Guerra Sucia en Guerrero," *FEMOSPP Filtrado*, 73. For more examples of military radiograms that utilized the lexicon see AGN, SDN box 100, folder 299. Declassified documents reveal that military and political leaders knew about the "revision" of "packages," including General Cuenca Díaz, President Echeverría, and Minister of the Interior Mario Moya Palencia.
115. Citlal Giles Sánchez, "Hay en el AGN 600 casos," *La Jornada Guerrero* (8 September 2012).
116. Castellanos, *México armado*, 160–163. A former military pilot testifying before a military tribunal in 2000 estimated that he witnessed some fifteen "death flights" that dumped an estimated 120–150 mostly male cadavers—some still alive—into the Pacific Ocean.
117. Rafael Aréstegui Ruiz estimated 240 guerrillas at the height of PDLP military power. General Mario Acosta Chaparro estimated 347. Aréstegui Ruiz, "Campesinado y lucha política," cited in Bartra, *Guerrero bronco*, 171; and Acosta Chaparro, *Movimiento subversivo*, 97–105.
118. PV, "Secuestro de Rubén Figueroa Figueroa," DFS File 1, 80–85, Legajo 1, 82.
119. Suarez, *Lucio Cabañas*, 75; and AGN, DGIPS box 713, file 3. CONASUPO provided essential food products at subsidized prices.
120. "La Guerra Sucia en Guerrero," *FEMOSPP Filtrado*, 70.
121. Rodríguez González, interview, 5 May 2007; and Fierro Loza, *Los Papeles de la sedición*, 16–20.
122. Fierro Loza, *Los Papeles de la sedición*, 46–47.
123. I borrow the term from the politico-military strategies elaborated by both the Colombian Communist Party and the Guatemalan Labor Party (PGT).
124. AGN, DFS 100-10-16-4, Legajo 8, 294–298.
125. Suárez, *Lucio Cabañas*, 137.
126. AGN, DFS 11-235, Legajo 19, 138–140.
127. AGN, DGIPS box 500, file 5, 157–160, 166–170; DGIPS box 462, file 1, 936–940; Fierro Loza, *Los Papeles de la sedición*, 48; and Evangelista Muñoz, *Carmelo Cortés Castro*, 55–75.
128. Bellingeri, *Del agrarismo armado*, 202–208.
129. Fierro Loza, *Los papeles de la sedición*, 54.
130. AGN, DFS 100-10-16-4, Legajo 7, 216–220, "Ideario del Partido de los Pobres," 25 March 1973.
131. Fierro Loza, *Los Papeles de la sedición*, 55–63; and AGN, DFS 100-10-16-4, Legajo 9, 150. Cortés and de la Paz organized the Revolutionary Armed Forces (FAR) in early 1974.
132. Fierro Loza, *Los Papeles de la sedición*, 63; and, Suárez, *Lucio Cabañas*, 197.
133. PV, "LCB," DFS File 4, 11-235-74, Legajo 19, 106; and AGN, DFS 11-235, Legajo 19, 140.
134. PV, "LCB," DFS File 4, 11-235-74, Legajo 19, 103–107.
135. The BCA did attack a military base in Tepetixtla during the second half of 1973. AGN, SDN box 97, file 287, 1–10; SDN box 97, file 289, 158; SDN box 122, file 372, 147–148; and Suárez, *Lucio Cabañas*, 167–168.
136. AGN, DGIPS box 1067, file 3, 169–170.
137. AGN, DFS 100-10-16-4, Legajo 9, 72.
138. AGN, DFS 100-10-16-4, Legajo 7, 378–380; and AGN, SDN box 97, file 288, 14–15, 20, 23–31.
139. Fierro Loza, *Los Papeles de la sedición*, 66–69.
140. Saúl López de la Torre, interviewed in Tort, *The Guerrilla and the Hope*.
141. Williams, *Marxism and Literature*, 128.
142. AGN, DFS 100-10-16-4, Legajo 7, 25.
143. I have located several references made to military deserters helping the PDLP. One such deserter, Humberto Espino Barros, was considered a close ally and advisor to Cabañas. Another, Heriberto Valle Adame ("Heraclio"), allegedly stole weapons from the elite

Presidential Guards and formed part of the BCA leadership. AGN, DFS 100-10-16-4, Legajo 1, 129; and DFS 100-10-16-4, Legajo 4, 378; DFS 100-10-16-4, Legajo 8, 39; AGN, DGIPS box 1066, file 2, 84-86; and PV, "LCB," DFS File 4, 100-10-16-4, Legajo 9, 26–27.

144. León Mendiola, "Testimonio." BCA guerrillas carried out two additional ambushes of army patrols in late 1973. For a November 1973 ambush near the village of Yerba Santa see AGN, DGIPS box 1182A, file 2, 266–267; AGN, DFS 100-10-16-4, Legajo 8, 23; AGN, SDN box 97, file 289, 158; and SDN box 122, file 372, 147–148.

145. PV, "LCB," DFS File 2, 138, "Interrogation of Romana Ríos Roque;" and Hernández Navarro, "Antonio Palós Palma," *La Jornada* (5 January 2010).

146. PV, "LCB, DFS File 4, 100-10-16-4, Legajo 9, 19–22.

147. Fierro Loza, *Los Papeles de la sedición*, 17.

148. Castellanos, *México armado*, 138–139; and AGN, DFS 100-10-16-4, Legajo 9, 266.

149. AGN, SDN box 41, 115–117; AGN, DGIPS, box 1066, file 2, 144–145; and, DGIPS box 1182B, file 2, 39–40.

150. AGN, DFS 80-84-74, Legajo 1, 4, 12, 23; AGN, DGIPS boxes 1934A and 1934B; DGIPS box 1066, file 1, 277–279, 331–333; AGN, SDN box 100, file 299, 3; and SDN box 98, file 291. Other PDLP demands included: the liberation of all political prisoners nationally; the liberation of all prisoners in Guerrero; 100 M-1 rifles and fifty 9 mm handguns with ammunition; national diffusion of PDLP literature and corridos; and the legalization of lands recently invaded by campesinos across Mexico

151. AGN, SDN box 100, file 299, 159–168.

152. AGN, SDN box 100, file 299, 702, 705; and SDN box 100, file 298, 26–28.

153. AGN, SDN box 100, file 298, 26–28; and SDN box 99, file 295, 15, 20, 32.

154. Cabañas had taken a smaller force (ten to fourteen guerrillas) with the intention of attracting the military's attention away from the area by launching attacks. AGN, DGIPS 2737, file 1, 2; and PV, "LCB," DFS File 5, 152–166, "Interrogation of Pedro Hernández Gomez."

155. PV, "LCB," DFS File 5, 80–85, Legajo 1, 297. At least twelve million pesos found their way to the PCM via PCM and PDLP militant Felix Bautista. That money provoked a series of ugly episodes during the 1980s between surviving PDLP guerrillas and the PCM.

156. AGN, SDN box 100, 298, 68, 183, 206–207, 245, 248, and 256.

157. "En una población," *El Diario de Acapulco* (17 September 1974), reproduced in AGN, DGIPS box 1066, file 2, 218–219.

158. Hodges and Gandy, *Mexico under Siege*, 125; Ulloa Bornemann, *Surviving Mexico's Dirty War*, 33–35; and Mayo, *La guerrilla de Genaro y Lucio*, 101–102.

159. Ex-PDLP guerrillas David Cabañas and Juan Martínez admitted such failures when interviewed in Tort, *The Guerrilla and the Hope*.

160. PV, "Secuestro de Rubén Figueroa Figueroa," DFS File 1, 80–85, Legajo 1, 71–74.

161. In his last communiqué, dated 29 November 1974, Cabañas outlined several confrontations from August to October claiming that the guerrillas had killed an estimated 76 soldiers. AGN, DGIPS box 2743, file 1, 251–255.

162. AGN, SDN box 98, file 293, 118–119, 153; and SDN box 100, file 298, 289. AGN, DGIPS box 2744, file 1 contains pictures of Cabañas's cadaver.

163. Leticia Díaz, "El suicidio de Lucio," *Proceso* (20 October 2002).

164. Castellanos, *México armado*, 159, fn. 43.

165. Silvia Otero, "Identifican a dos maestros," *El Universal* (15 November 2006).

166. AGN, SDN box 98, file 293, 153, radiogram no. 15596. Three of Marcelo's cousins would also be disappeared by the military.

167. AGN, SDN box 98, file 293, 154; and "The Death of Lucio Cabañas Barrientos," National Security Archive, Freedom of Information Request No. 18971 (Doyle, "The Dawn of Mexico's Dirty War.")

168. AGN, DGIPS, box 2744, file 1, 522.

169. Gloria Leticia Díaz, "La familia de Lucio Cabañas," *Proceso* (27 May 2001).

170. AGN, DGIPS box 2744, file 1, 329; and "La Guerra Sucia en Guerrero," *FEMOSPP Filtrado*, 119. The DGIPS document stated that the burial of Cabañas took place on 3 December at 6:20 a.m. "without incident."

171. Ignacio Ramírez, "Del cadaver de Lucio," *Proceso* (14 November 1992).

172. AGN, DGIPS box 1066, file 3, 68; and "En la sierra de Guerrero," *La Jornada* (13 October 2005).

173. Orwell, *Road to Wigan Pier*, 178.

Conclusion

1. Gallegos Nájera, *La guerrilla en Guerrero*, 243.

2. Padilla, *Rural Resistance*, 115–121.

3. Gallegos Nájera, *La guerrilla en Guerrero*, 13. Castro also collaborated with Vázquez and the ACNR. Méndez, interview, 9 March 2007.

4. Victor Ballinas, "Desaparecidos: Artugo Gallegos relata la captura de Petronilo Castro," *La Jornada*, 30 August 2001.

5. PV, "LCB," DFS File 2, 100-10-16-4, Legajo 4, 380; and Gallegos Nájera, *La guerrilla en Guerrero*, 81.

6. PV, "LCB," DFS File 2, 100-10-16-4, Legajo 5, 63–72. The etchings on the wall were discovered by a detained urban guerrilla from Guadalajara named Rubén Ramírez González. Gallegos Nájera, *La guerrilla en Guerrero*, 244.

7. PV, "LCB," DFS File 2, 100-10-16-4, Legajo 5, 65.

8. Fabiola and Eleazar Castro Molina joined the FAR, led by Carmelo Cortés Castro and Aurora de la Paz Navarro del Campo. Both Fabiola and Eleazar were captured and disappeared in 1975 and 1976. Two of Don Petronilo's sons-in-law, Daniel Martínez García and Benito Flores Silva (married to Fabiola), also joined the FAR and were detained and disappeared in January 1975. "Crímenes de lesa humanidad," *FEMOSPP Filtrado*, 21; and CNDH/PDS/95/GRO/S00094.000, number 67-R.

9. Henri Lefebvre, quoted in Bartolovich and Lazarus, *Marxism, Modernity*, 5; Suárez, *Lucio Cabañas*, 131–132; and Cárdenas, interview, 23 April 2007.

10. Grandin, *The Last Colonial Massacre*, xv, 191–196.

11. AGN, DFS 100-10-16-4, Legajo 5, 59.

12. AGN, DFS 100-10-16-4, Legajo 4, 365; and AGN DFS 80-21-72, Legajo 1, 106.

13. Rangel Lozano and Sánchez Serrano, "Las guerrillas de Genaro Vazquéz y Lucio Cabañas," 517; and "La Guerra Sucia en Guerrero," *FEMOSPP Filtrado*, 84, 95.

14. Suárez, *Lucio Cabañas*, 56.

15. AGN, DGIPS box 1067, file 3, 169–170; and AGN, DFS 100-10-16-4, Legajo 8, 303–304.

16. The Cuban revolution proved influential but not determinative of PDLP tactics and ideology. During the summer of 1973, Cabañas told an assembled group of urban and rural guerrillas: "the way to make a revolution will not be taught by Cuba…China, the Soviet Union, or any other country." *Un hombre llamado: Lucio Cabañas*; and AGN, DFS 11-207-73, legajo 10, 205.

17. Orthodox ideals like: "the conquest of political power and destruction of the Bourgeois state; destruction of the capitalist system and the abolition of private property; and the destruction of bourgeois culture." AGN, DFS 100-10-16-4, Legajo 7, 259–261.

18. Evangelista Muñoz, *Carmelo Cortés Castro*, 56–61.

19. For the first Ideario Pobrista, see AGN, DFS 100-10-16-4, Legajo 6, 230-31.

20. Suárez, *Lucio Cabañas*, 211. Survivors and guerrilla heirs of the PDLP would accomplish this extension into La Montaña during the 1980s and 90s.

21. AGN, DFS 100-10-16-4, legajo 6, 230–31. Bellingeri, *Del agrarismo armado*, 191–192; Warman, "The Political Project of Zapatismo," 330–335; and Molina, "De la Sierra de Guerrero."

22. Indeed, Cabañas cites such beliefs as the result of PRI propaganda. Suárez, *Lucio Cabañas*, 191–192.

23. Cárdenas, interview, 23 April 2007; and León Mendiola, "Mi Testimonio," 69.

24. José Arturo Gallegos Nájera, former PDLP and FAR guerrilla, described Cabañas's interpretation of Jesus Christ during a 1971 Christmas talk the teacher gave to the armed group. Gallegos Nájera, *La guerrilla en Guerrero*, 66; and Suárez, *Lucio Cabañas*, 175. This sounds

similar to some tenets of liberation theology but I cannot find evidence to suggest that it influenced Cabañas.

25. Ricardo Rodríguez González, interview, 5 May 2007.
26. Fierro Loza, *Los papeles de la sedición*, 40–46; and PV, "LCB," DFS File 5, 164, "Interrogation of Pedro Hernández Gómez."
27. Suárez, *Lucio Cabañas*, 116.
28. Rodríguez González, interview, 5 May 2007.
29. Trujillo Miranda, "Testimonio"; and Fierro Loza, *Los papeles de la sedición*, 82–83.
30. Suárez, *Lucio Cabañas*, 213–217.
31. AGN, DFS 100-10-16-4, Legajo 8, 14–16; DFS 100-10-16-4, Legajo 9, 70, 72; AGN DGIPS, box 1066, folder 1, 45–48; and "La Guerra Sucia en Guerrero," *FEMOSPP Filtrado*, 81.
32. Guillermina Cabañas Alvarado, presentation at the conference "Primer Encuentro Nacional de Mujeres Ex Guerrilleras," Mexico City, 13 December 2003; reproduced in "Encuentros de Mujeres Ex Guerrilleras," Encuentros de Ex Militantes Folder, 91–92, MAS Archive, ed. Borbolla Moreno; and Cabañas Alvarado, "Testimonio Personal."
33. Cárdenas, interview, 23 April 2007.
34. AGN, DFS 100-10-16-4, Legajo 8, 14–16, 23; AGN, SDN box 97, folder 288, 14, 20, 23–26; and García Estrada, "La persecución heredada," *La Jornada Guerrero*, 13 July 2011.
35. AGN, DFS 100-10-16-4, Legajo 2, 231; Castellanos, *México armado*, 138–139; and Suárez, *Lucio Cabañas*, 122–124.
36. PV, "LCB," DFS File 2, 100-10-16-4, Legajo 5, 66, 69–71. Romana's husband, Margarito Roque Texta, was also disappeared. They met Cabañas in 1964 when their children attended the primary school in Atoyac de Álvarez where the teacher worked. Her siblings, Salomón (detained and disappeared in 1977) and Ana María Ríos García, also joined the PDLP.
37. Rayas, "Subjugating the Nation," 168.
38. This dual struggle engaged by guerrilleras thus made them even more subversive in the eyes of the PRI regime. Indeed, as historian Lucía Rayas suggests, guerrilleras committed a dyadic transgression against the paternalistic state "that protects them" and gender roles that confined women to the private sphere. Such double subversion, for guerrilleras captured by state agents, led to torture, sexual assaults and/or rape meant to dehumanize "the woman being tortured…rape represents putting patriarchal power in place"; "Subjugating the Nation," 174–177. See also Cedillo, "Mujeres, guerrilla y terror de Estado."
39. The expression of female sexuality remained an internal patriarchal limit, as evidenced by the incident that led to the departure of Carmelo Castro Cortés and Aurora de la Paz Navarro del Campo in 1973. Also, unlike urban guerrilla organizations, no women occupied leadership positions in the PDLP-BCA.
40. PV, "LCB," DFS File 2, 100-10-16-4, Legajo 5, 66, 69–71
41. Cedillo, "Mujeres, guerrilla y terror de Estado."
42. Cabañas Alvarado, "Primer Encuentro Nacional de Mujeres Ex Guerrilleras"; see note 32.
43. Suárez, *Lucio Cabañas*, 122–123.
44. Ibid.
45. AGN, DFS 100-10-16-4, Legajo 6, 230–31.
46. Rayas, "Subjugating the Nation," 169; and Cárdenas Montaño, "La participación de las mujeres," 615.
47. Suarez, *Lucio Cabañas*, 136.
48. Mao, "The United Front in Cultural Work" (October 1944), 185–187; and Meza Velarde and Rubio Zaldívar, "Luchas sociales en el estado de Guerrero," 76. For an intriguing analysis of Maoism in Cold War Mexico see Rothwell, *Transpacific Revolutionaries*. Guerrillas who directly emerged from the PDLP after Cabañas's death would later explicitly adopt Maoist precepts (such as "prolonged popular struggle" or "prolonged people's war") after fusing with other guerrilla organizations. Castellanos, *México armado*, 310–311, 327–333.
49. AGN, DFS 11-235, Legajo 19, 138–140. This document is a letter addressed from the LC23S to the PDLP (dated 14 July 1973) in which the urban guerrillas denounced the expulsion of their militants, criticized Cabañas, and promised to politically challenge the PDLP by "orienting the masses and bringing them over to [true] revolutionary Marxism." For the LC23S perspective, see Ramírez Salas, "La relación de la Liga Comunista 23 de Septiembre," 527–547.

50. Bartra, *Regeneración*, 16, cited in Rabasa, *Without History*, 101.
51. Vicente Estrada Vega, interviewed in Tort, *The Guerrilla and the Hope*.
52. Suárez, *Lucio Cabañas*, 137.
53. Ibid., 59–61.
54. Ibid., 59–61, 120, 127. Cabañas used Che Guevara's fatal Bolivian experiences to evince his argument about the inexistence of revolutionary struggle without popular support.
55. Mayo, *La guerrilla de Genaro y Lucio*, 52–55; Hodges and Gandy, *Mexico under Siege*, 116–120, 126–127; Saúl López de la Torre interviewed in Tort, *The Guerrilla and the Hope*; Ulloa Bornemann, *Mexico's Dirty War*, 34–35; and Castañeda, *La negación del número*, 89.
56. AGN, DFS 100-10-16-4, Legajo 8, 294–298.
57. Antonio Gramsci, quoted in Guha, *Elementary Aspects of Peasant Insurgency*, 12; and Vicente Estrada Vega, interviewed in Tort, *The Guerrilla and the Hope*.
58. AGN, DFS 100-10-16-4, Legajo 5, 59–60.
59. Bartra, *Guerrero bronco*, 130–135; Bartra, "Sur profundo," 36–37; Paz Paredes and Cabo, "Café caliente," 172–195; and Radilla Martínez, *La organización en las nuevas estrategias*, 47–76.
60. Gilly, *Cartas a Cuauhtémoc Cárdenas*, 55.
61. Jacobo Silva Nogales, interview, *Radio Regeneración*, 27 May 2012. Nogales, a PDLP militant during the late 1970s and 1980s, also cites 1988 and the "Cardenista struggle" as moments that led to a "real growth" of the clandestine guerrilla movement due to a popularly perceived electoral fraud. Silva Nogales would later participate in the EPR and lead the Revolutionary Army of the Insurgent People (ERPI) during the late 1990s.
62. Bartra, *Guerrero bronco*, 147–155.
63. Mesino, interview, 17 May 2007. In 1996 the Mexican Supreme Court determined that Governor Figueroa Alcocer, the secretary general of the state, and the state attorney general were responsible for the massacre. Solomon and Brett, *Implausible Deniability*, 24–25; and CNDH, Recommendation No. 104, 1995 (http://www.cndh.org.mx/node/909168).
64. Bartra, *Guerrero bronco*, 160; and Bartra, "Historias de los otros Chiapas," 143.
65. Police agents also videotaped the massacre. A subsequent leaking of the video to journalist Ricardo Rocha in February 1996 undermined Figueroa's assertions that his forces had acted in self-defense against attacking campesinos. He resigned in March 1996 but to date has never been brought to justice. See the documentary produced by Canal 6 de Julio, *La matanza de Aguas Blancas* (1996).
66. Martínez Carbajal, *Masacre en el vado de Aguas Blancas*, 61–75, 91–93.
67. PDLP guerrillas who continued the struggle after Cabañas's death in 1974 would recruit a new generation of future revolutionaries during the late 1970s. Silva Nogales joined the PDLP in 1977 at the age of nineteen. Silva Nogales, interview, *Radio Regeneración*, 27 May 2012.
68. Gilly, *Chiapas: la razón ardiente*, 32; and Gilly, ed., *Cartas a Cuauhtémoc Cárdenas*, 55.
69. Coatsworth, "Patterns of Rural Rebellion in Latin America," 65–66; and Katz, *Riot, Rebellion and Revolution*, 522–523.
70. Mallon, *Peasant and Nation*, 316–317.
71. Guardino, *Peasants, Politics*, 95–96.
72. Radilla Martínez, *Poderes, saberes y sabores*, 108–116.
73. Castañeda, *Utopia Unarmed*, 86–88.
74. Ibid., 51–89; Harnecker, *Haciendo posible lo imposible*, 20–22; Suárez, *Lucio Cabañas*, 339; and Stoll, *Rigoberta Menchú*, 273–302.
75. Blacker-Hanson, "Cold War in the Countryside," 197–198, 207–208.
76. Scott, *Domination and the Arts of Resistance*, xiii, 19, 183–184.

Epilogue

1. AGN, DGIPS box 549, folder 3.
2. Patricia Muñoz Rios, "Identifican los restos de Lucio Cabañas," *La Jornada*, 13 August 2002; Sergio Flores, "Vuelve a Atoyac Lucio Cabañas," *Reforma*, 2 December 2002; Sergio Flores, "Inhuman restos óseos de Cabañas," *Reforma*, 3 December 2002; Jesús Guerrero, "Anuncia

ERPI fusión," *Reforma*, 3 December 2002; and Misael Habana de los Santos and Jesús Saavedra Lezama, "Rinden nuevo homenaje a Lucio Cabañas," *La Jornada*, 3 December 2002.

3. The abandoned base now forms part of the city and municipal government compound in Atoyac.

4. Gerardo Torres, "Mexico Looks for 'Dirty War' Graves on Army Base," *Reuters*, 8 July 2008.

5. Ibid. The search for Rosendo Radilla is portrayed in the documentary *12.511 Caso Rosendo Radilla: Herida abierta de la guerra sucia en México*, directed by Berenisse Vásquez Sansores and Gabriel Hernández Tinajero (2008).

6. Eugenia Jiménez, "Continúa búsqueda de restos de Rosendo Radilla," *Milenio*, 22 May 2013.

7. Some of whom were executed in 1973–4 by BCA guerrillas. Suárez, *Lucio Cabañas*, 161–165; and PV, "LCB," DFS File 4, 100-10-16-4, Legajo 9, 19–22.

8. David Cabañas, interviewed in Tort, *The Guerrilla and the Hope*.

9. Bartra, *Guerrero bronco*, 130; Bartra, "Sur profundo," 30–32; "La Guerra Sucia en Guerrero," *FEMOSPP Filtrado*, 87–88; and Alberto Guillermo López Limón, "Concentrado General Desaparecidos [Excel Worksheet]," *FEMOSPP Filtrado*.

10. Radilla, interview, 16 May 2007. Human rights activists have documented the disappearance of four men with the last names of Ramos Cabañas on 9 February 1975 along with their father—all identified as having belonged to the FAR guerrilla group led by Cortés and de la Paz Navarro. López Limón, "Concentrado General Desaparecidos [Excel Worksheet]," *FEMOSPP Filtrado*.

11. Ascención Rosas Mesino (Don Chon), interview with the author, Atoyac de Álvarez, 16 May 2007.

12. Ibid.

13. Ibid.

14. Cedillo, "El sepelio de Lino y Esteban," *emeequis* (9 April 2007), 20.

15. Ascención Rosas Mesino (Don Chon), interview, 16 May 2007.

16. Tita Radilla, interviewed in Tort, *The Guerrilla and the Hope*.

17. López Limón, "Concentrado General Desaparecidos [Excel Worksheet]," *FEMOSPP Filtrado*.

18. AGN, SDN box 101, file 301, 9–39.

19. Since the 1990s, hundreds of campesino leaders, indigenous community activists, PRD militants, and campesino ecologists have been persecuted and/or assassinated in Guerrero. Recently, in 2012, a campesina ecological leader, Juventina Villa Mojica, and her teenage son were ambushed and murdered by thirty to forty gunslingers, presumably because she had led dozens of campesino communities in efforts to protect forests against illegal logging. In August 2013 communist peasant leader Raymundo Velázquez Flores and two fellow activists were kidnapped, tortured, and killed. Velázquez Flores was president of LARSEZ, the peasant organization that Genaro Vázquez had helped create in the mid-1960s. Sergio Ocampo Arista, "Asesinan a dirigente ecologista," *La Jornada*, 29 November 2012; Arturo de Dios Palma, "Hay guerra de baja intensidad," *La Jornada Guerrero*, 10 August 2013; and, Schatz, *Murder and Politics*, 143–173.

20. John Gibler, "The Hidden Side of Mexico's Drug War" *ZMagazine* (October 2009). Comandante Ramiro, also a member of the PDLP during the 1980s, was killed by military troops in November 2009.

21. Gerardo Torres, "Mexico Looks for 'Dirty War' Graves on Army Base."

REFERENCES

Archives

Archivo General de la Nación (AGN)
Ramo Dirección Federal de Seguridad (DFS)
Ramo Dirección General de Investigaciones Políticas y Sociales (DGIPS)
Ramo Secretaria de la Defensa Nacional (SDN)
Moreno Borbolla, José Luis, ed. Centro de Investigaciones Históricas de los Movimientos Sociales A.C. CD-ROM Digital Archive (MAS). Mexico City.
Versiones Públicas (PV) (AGN)
    "Lucio Cabañas Barrientos" Dirección Federal de Seguridad
    "Lucio Cabañas Barrientos" Dirección General de Investigaciones Políticas y Sociales
    "Asociación Cívica Nacional Revolucionaria" Dirección Federal de Seguridad
    "El Secuestro de Rubén Figueroa Figueroa" Dirección Federal de Seguridad

Interviews

Aragón, Benjamin [researcher and student, ex-guerrilla]. Interview with the author, 18 April 2007, Mexico City.

Bracho, José [teacher]. Interview with the author, 9 March and 15 May 2007, Acapulco, Guerrero.

Cárdenas, Alejandra [university professor]. Interview with the author, 23 April 2007, Chilpancingo, Guerrero.

Méndez, Santos [campesino, former ACNR militant]. Interview with the author, 9 March and 15 May 2007, Acapulco, Guerrero.

Mesino, Hilario [campesino]. Interview with the author, 17 May 2007, Atoyac de Álvarez, Guerrero.

Miranda Ramírez, Arturo [university professor, former ACNR militant]. Interview with the author, 14 May 2007, Chilpancingo, Guerrero.

Nava, Gregoria [campesina]. Interview with Andrea Radilla Martínez, 1989, Atoyac de Álvarez, Guerrero.

Pineda, Fernando [professor and writer, former MAR militant]. Interview with the author, 20 April 2007, Chilpancingo, Guerrero.

Radilla, Tita [human rights activist]. Interview with the author, 16 May 2007, Atoyac de Álvarez, Guerrero.

Rodríguez González, Ricardo [medical worker, former PDLP militant]. Interview with the author, 5 May 2007, Mexico City.

Rosas Mesino, Ascención [campesino]. Interview with the author, 16 May 2007, Atoyac de Álvarez, Guerrero.

Solís Morales, Concepción [teacher, former ACNR militant]. Interview with the author, 25 May 2007, Mexico City.

Solís Morales, Consuelo [teacher]. Interview with the author, 30 May 2007, Mexico City.

Téllez, Carmen [campesina]. Interviewed by Andrea Radilla Martínez, September 1988, Atoyac de Álvarez.

Téllez Sánchez, José [campesino]. Interviewed by Andrea Radilla Martínez, 1989, Atoyac de Álvarez.

Newspapers and Periodicals

Así (Guerrero)
Diario Monitor (Mexico City)
Emeequis (Mexico City)
Excélsior (Mexico City)
Indice (Chihuahua)
La Jornada (Mexico City)
La Prensa (Mexico City)
Los Angeles Times
Milenio (Mexico City)
New York Times
Política (Mexico City)
¿Por Qué? (Mexico City)
Proceso (Mexico City)
Punto Crítico (Mexico City)
Reforma (Mexico City)
Reuters
Siempre (Mexico City)
Trópico (Guerrero)

Published Reports and Investigations

Comisión Nacional de Derechos Humanos. Caso de los hechos ocurridos el 28 de junio de 1995 en las cercanías de Aguas Blancas, municipio de Coyuca de Benítez, estado de Guerrero, y su investigación por las autoridades locales. Mexico City, 1995.

Comisión Nacional de Derechos Humanos. Informe de la investigación sobre presuntos desaparecidos en el estado de Guerrero, 1971–1974. Mexico City, 1992.

Doyle, Kate. "After the Revolution: Lázaro Cárdenas and the Movimiento de Liberación Nacional" (electronic briefing book no. 124). National Security Archive, 2004.

——. "The Dawn of Mexico's Dirty War: Lucio Cabañas and the Party of the Poor" (electronic briefing book). National Security Archive, 2003.

——. Draft Report Documents Eighteen Years of "Dirty War" in Mexico. National Security Archive, 2006.

——. Official Report Released on Mexico's "Dirty War" (electronic briefing book no. 209). National Security Archive, 2006.

Fiscalía Especial para Movimientos Sociales y Políticos del Pasado (FEMOSPP). Informe Histórico a la Sociedad Mexicana. Mexico: Procuraduría General de la República, November 2006.

Fiscalía Especial para Movimientos Sociales y Políticos del Pasado, José Sotelo Marbán et al. Informe ¡Que No Vuelva a Suceder! (FEMOSPP Filtrado). Mexico, released February 2006.

Speeches, Public Presentations, and Conference Proceedings

Bracho, José. Speech given at the 35th Commemoration of the death of Genaro Vázquez Rojas. San Luis Acatlán, Guerrero, 2 February 2007.

——. Speech given at the 39th Commemoration of Genaro Vázquez Rojas's escape from Iguala Prison. Icatepec, Guerrero, 23 April 2007.

Cabañas Alvarado, Guillermina. "Testimonio Personal." Testimony presented at the II Encuentro Nacional de Mujeres Ex Guerrilleras "Mujeres de Armas Tomar." Universidad Autónoma de Sinaloa, Mazatlán, 7 March 2008.

Fernández Brito, Gregorio. Speech given at the 39th Commemoration of Genaro Vázquez Roja's escape from Iguala Prison. Icatepec, Guerrero, 23 April 2007.

Gaytán, Salvador. Talk given in Fundición, Sonora, 5 April 2007.

López Limón, Alberto, and Edna Nevárez. "Commentary on Fernando Pineda's book *En las profundidades del MAR*." Commentary for the Homenaje al Movimiento de Acción Revolucionario. Asamblea Legislativa del Distrito Federal, Mexico City, 11 April 2007.

Méndez, Santos. Speech given at the 39th Commemoration of Genaro Vázquez Roja's escape from Iguala Prison. Icatepec, Guerrero, 23 April 2007.

Montemayor, Carlos. "La guerrilla recurrente." Paper presented at the II Encuentro Nacional de Mujeres Ex Guerrilleras "Mujeres de Armas Tomar." Universidad Autónoma de Sinaloa, Mazatlán, 7 March 2008

Santos, Gabriel, and Carlos Salcedo. "Commentary on Salvador Castañeda's book *La negación del número*." Commentary for the Homenaje al Movimiento de Acción Revolucionaria. Asamblea Legislativa del Distrito Federal, Mexico City, 11 April 2007.

Solís Morales, Consuelo. Speech given at the 35th Commemoration of the death of Genaro Vázquez Rojas. San Luis Acatlán, Guerrero, 2 February 2007.

Zaldívar Rubio, Andrés. Lecture given at the 35th Commemoration of Genaro Vázquez Rojas at the Preparatoria 14 de la Universidad Autónoma de Guerrero. San Luis Acatlán, Guerrero, 2 February 2007.

Documentaries

12.511 Caso Rosendo Radilla: Herida abierta de la guerra sucia en México. Directed by Berenisse Vásquez Sansores and Gabriel Hernández Tinajero. Mexico City, 2008. DVD.

El Edén bajo el Fusil. Directed by Salvador Díaz. Mexico City, 1986. DVD.

La guerrilla en México. Canal 11 del Instituto Politecníco Nacional. Mexico City, 2004. DVD.

La Matanza de Aguas Blancas. Canal 6 de Julio. Mexico City, 1996. DVD.

The Guerrilla and the Hope: Lucio Cabañas. Directed by Gerardo Tort. Mexico City: Facets Video/ Macondo Cine/CONACULTA, 2007. DVD.

Published Primary Sources

Acosta Chaparro, Mario A. *Movimientos subversivos en México*. Mexico, 1990.

Aranda Flores, Antonio. *Los cívicos guerrerenses*. Mexico City: Luysil, 1979.

Campos Gómez, Eleazar. *Lucio Cabañas y el Partido de los Pobres: Una experiencia guerrillera en México*. Mexico City: Editorial Nuestra América, 1987.

Cárdenas, Lázaro. *Ideario Político*. Mexico City: Serie Popular Era, 1972.

———. *Palabras y documentos públicos de Lázaro Cárdenas: Mensajes, discursos, declaraciones, entrevistas y otros documentos, 1928–1940*. 3 vols. Eds. Elena Vázquez Gómez, Carmen Valcarce, and Domingo Alonso. Mexico City: Siglo XXI, 1978.

———. *Obras 1. Apuntes, 1913-1940, Volume 1*. Mexico City: UNAM, 1972.

Convergencia Democrática Universitaria (Universidad Autónoma de Guerrero). *Comandante Genaro Vázquez Rojas*. San Luis Acatlán, Guerrero, 1993. In possession of the author.

———. *Periódico Pueblo de Chilpancingo*. Chilpancingo: EPMAT, Universidad Autónoma de Guerrero, 1994.

de Molina, José. "De la Sierra de Guerrero." In *Se Acabó*. Mexico: Nueva Voz Latinoamericana, 1976.

de Mora, Juan Miguel. *Las guerrillas en México y Jenaro Vázquez Rojas (su personalidad, su vida y su muerte)*. Mexico: Editora Latino America, 1972.

———. *Lucio Cabañas: Su vida y su muerte*. Mexico: Editores Asociados, 1974.

El Camarada "Ernesto." *El Guerrillero*. Guadalajara: Graphos, 1974.

Fierro Loza, Francisco. *Los papeles de la sedición y la verdadera historia político militar del Partido de los Pobres*. Chilpancingo: Unedited document, 1984.

Gallegos Nájera, José Arturo. *La guerrilla en Guerrero: Testimonios sobre el Partido de los Pobres y las Fuerzas Armadas Revolucionarias (FAR): proyectos, anécdotas, datos biográficos, fotos y documentos históricos*. Guadalajara: La Casa del Mago, 2007.

Ibarra Chávez, Héctor, ed. *La guerrilla de los 70 y la transición a la democracia*. Mexico City: Centro de Estudios Antropológicos, Científicos, Artísticos, Tradicionales y Lingüísticos "Ce-Acatl," 2006.

Jaramillo, Rubén M., and Froylán C. Manjarrez. *Autobiografía: La matanza de Xochicalco*. 4th ed. Mexico: Editorial Nuestro Tiempo, 1981.

"La Guerra Sucia en Guerrero." In *Fiscalía Especial para Movimientos Sociales y Políticos del Pasado (FEMOSPP), Reporte Filtrado*. Mexico City, 2006.

León Mendiola, Luis. "El Partido de los Pobres." In the accompanying CD-ROM to *La guerrilla de los 70s y la transición a la democracia*, ed. Héctor Ibarra Chávez, 1–48. Mexico City: Ce-Acatl, A.C., 2006.

—. "Mi Testimonio Acerca del Partido de Los Pobres en Guerrero." In Movimiento Armado Socialista Digital Archive, Folder "Testimonio o entrevistas," ed. José Luis Moreno Borbolla, 1–92. Mexico City: Centro de Investigaciones Históricas de los Movimientos Sociales A.C., 2004.

Martínez Carbajal, Alejandro, ed. "Plan del Veladero." In *Juan R. Escudero y Amadeo S. Vidales*, 153–167. Mexico: Editorial Revolución, 1961.

Martínez Martínez, Guillermo, and Álvaro López Miramontes. *Figueroismo versus Zapatismo*. Chilpancingo: Universidad Autónoma de Guerrero/Centro de Investigaciones Sociales, 1976.

Miranda Ramírez, Arturo. *El otro rostro de la guerrilla: Genaro, Lucio, y Carmelo, experiencias de guerrilla*. Mexico City: El Machete, 1996.

Miranda Ramírez, Arturo. *La violación de los derechos humanos en el Estado de Guerrero durante la guerra sucia: una herida no restañada*. Chilpancingo: Universidad Autónoma Guerrero, 2006.

Movimiento Nacional de Liberación. *Programa y Llamamiento*. Mexico City: El Movimiento, 1961.

Ortíz, Orlando. *Genaro Vázquez*. Mexico: Diógenes, 1972.

Osorio Cruz, Zacarias. *Obligado a matar: Fusilamientos de civiles en México*. Mexico City: Libros Proceso, 1993.

Pineda, Fernando. *En las profundidades del MAR (El oro no llego de Moscú)*. Mexico City: Plaza y Váldes, 2003.

Rubio Zaldívar, Andres. *El movimiento social Guerrerense y la lucha armada de Genaro Vázquez Rojas*. Movimientos y Protagonistas Sociales, Equipo Profesional Multidisciplinario de Apoyo Técnico, A.C. Chilpancingo, Guerrero: EPMAT, 1994.

——. "ACNR, PDLP, y GPG." In *Movimiento Armado Socialista Digital Archive, Folder "Trabajos de Investigación,"* ed. José Luis Moreno Borbolla. Mexico City: Centro de Investigaciones Históricas de los Movimientos Sociales A.C.

Sandoval Cruz, Pablo. *El movimiento social de 1960*. 2nd ed. Chilpancingo: Universidad Autónoma de Guerrero, 1999.

Solís Robledo, Jaime, and Carlos Cantú Lagunas. *Rescate para la historia: La fuga de Genaro Vázquez, narrada por Donato Contreras Javier, integrante del comando que lo liberó*. Mexico: Los Reyes, 2003.

Sotelo Pérez, Antonio. *Breve historia de la Asociación Cívica Guerrerense: Jefaturada por Genaro Vázquez Rojas*. Chilpancingo: Universidad Autónoma de Guerrero/Instituto de Investigaciones Científicas, 1991.

Suárez, Luis. *Lucio Cabañas: El guerrillero sin esperanza*. Mexico: Grijalbo, 1985.

Trujillo Miranda, Modesto. "Mi Testimonio." In *Movimiento Armado Socialista Digital Archive, Folder "Testimonio o entrevistas,"* ed. José Luis Moreno Borbolla, 1–34. Mexico City: Centro de Investigaciones Históricas de los Movimientos Sociales A.C., 2001.

Un Hombre Llamado: Lucio Cabañas. 2 Compact Disks. Mexico: Discos Pueblo Rebelde.

Womack, John, ed. "The Plan de Ayala." In *Zapata and the Mexican Revolution*, 400–404. New York: Alfred A. Knopf, 1968.

Secondary Sources

Abrams, Philip. "Notes on the Difficulty of Studying the State." *Journal of Historical Sociology* 1:1 (1988): 58–89.

Agamben, Giorgio. *Homo Sacer: Sovereign Power and Bare Life*. Translated by Daniel Heller-Roazen. Stanford: Stanford University Press, 1998.

——. *State of Exception*. Translated by Kevin Attell. Chicago: University of Chicago Press, 2005.

Aguayo Quezada, Sergio. *La charola: Una historia de los servicios de inteligencia en México*. Mexico City: Grijalbo, 2001.

——. *1968: Los archivos de la violencia*. Mexico City: Grijalbo/Reforma, 1998.

Aguilar Mora, Manuel and Carlos Monsiváis. "Sobre el Henriquismo: el populismo de derecha y la historia escamoteada." La cultura en México: Suplemento de *Siempre*, 557, 11 October 1972: II–III.

Aguirre Benítez, Adan. *Guerrero: Economía campesina y capitalismo*. Chilpancingo: Universidad Autónoma de Guerrero, 1996.

Alamán, Lucas. *Historia de Méjico*. Mexico: Editorial Jus, 1968.

Alcantará, Carlos Durand. *La lucha campesina en Oaxaca y Guerrero (1978–1987)*. Mexico City: Universidad Autónoma de Chapingo/Editores Costa Amic, 1989.

Alegre, Robert. *Railroad Radicals in Cold War Mexico: Gender, Class, and Memory*. Lincoln: University of Nebraska Press, 2014.

Alvarez, Sonia E., Evangelina Dagnino, and Arturo Escobar, eds. *Culture of Politics Politics of Culture: Re-visioning Latin American Social Movements*. Boulder, CO: Westview, 1998.

Amith, Jonathan. *The Mobius Strip: A Spatial History of Colonial Society in Guerrero, Mexico*. Stanford: Stanford University Press, 2005.

Anderson, Leslie, and Mitchell A. Seligson. "Reformism and Radicalism among Peasants: An Empirical Test of Paige's Agrarian Revolution." *American Journal of Political Science* 38:4 (November 1994): 944–972.

Anguiano, Arturo. *El estado y la política obrera del cardenismo*. Mexico City: Era, 1975

Anna, Timothy. *Forging Mexico: 1821–1835*. Lincoln: University of Nebraska Press, 1998.

Archer, Christon. "La Causa Buena: The Counterinsurgency Army of New Spain and the Ten Years War." In *The Independence of Mexico and the Creation of the New Nation*, ed. Jaime Rodríguez O., 85–102. Los Angeles: UCLA Latin American Center Publications, 1989.

——. "The Militarization of Politics or the Politicization of the Army? The Novohispano and Mexican Office Corps, 1810–1830." In *The Divine Charter: Constitutionalism and Liberalism in Nineteenth-Century Mexico*, ed. Jaime Rodríguez O., 205–234. Lanham, MD: Rowman and Littlefield Publishers, 2005.

Archila Neira, Mauricio, et al. eds. *Una historia inconclusa: izquierdas políticas y sociales en Colombia*. Bogota: Centro de Investigación y Educación Popular/Cinep, 2009.

Arguedas, Ledda. "El movimiento de liberación nacional: Una experiencia de la izquierda mexicana en los setentas." *Revista Mexicana de Sociología* 39:1 (1977): 229–249.

Aroche Parra, Miguel. *El Che, Genaro y las guerrillas: Estrategia y táctica de revolución*. Mexico City: Federación Editorial Mexicana, 1974.

——. *Los secuestros de Figueroa, Zuno y la muerte de Lucio Cabañas*. Mexico City: Editorial de los Estados, 1976.

Arnold, David. "Gramsci and Peasant Subalternity in India." *Journal of Peasant Studies* 11:4 (1984): 155–177.

Arrom, Silvia. "Popular Politics in Mexico City: The Parian Riot, 1828." *Hispanic American Historical Review* 68:2 (May 1988): 245–268.

——. *The Women of Mexico City, 1790–1857*. Stanford: Stanford University Press, 1985.

Aviña, Alexander. "An Archive of Counterinsurgency: State Anxieties and Peasant Guerrillas in Cold War Mexico." *Journal of Iberian and Latin American Research* 19:1 (July 2013): 41–51.

——. "Seizing Hold of Memories in Moments of Danger: Guerrillas and Revolution in Guerrero, Mexico." In *Challenging Authoritarianism in Mexico: Revolutionary Struggles and the Dirty War, 1964–1982*, ed. Fernando Herrera Calderón and Adela Cedillo, 40–60. London: Routledge, 2012.

——. "'We Have Returned to Porfirian Times': Neopopulism, Counterinsurgency, and the Dirty War in Guerrero, Mexico, 1969–1975." In *Populism in 20th Century Mexico: The Presidencies of Lázaro Cárdenas and Luis Echeverría*, ed. Amelia Kiddle and María Muñoz, 106–121. Tucson: University of Arizona Press, 2010.

Babb, Sarah. *Managing Mexico: Economists from Nationalism to Neoliberalism*. Princeton: Princeton University Press, 2001.

Bantjes, Adrian A. *As If Jesus Walked on Earth: Cardenismo, Sonora, and the Mexican Revolution*. Wilmington: Scholarly Press, 1998.

Bartolovich, Crystal, and Neil Lazarus, eds. *Marxism, Modernity, and Postcolonial Studies*. Cambridge, UK: Cambridge University Press, 2002.

Bartra, Armando. "Crisis agraria y movimiento campesino en los setenta." Cuadernos Agrarios 11 (December 1980): 19–27.

——. *Guerrero bronco: Campesinos, cuidadanos y guerrilleros en la Costa Grande*. Mexico City: Era, 2000.

——. *Los herederos de Zapata: Movimientos campesinos posrevolucionarios en México, 1920–1980*. Mexico City: Era, 1985.

——. "Historias de los otros Chiapas: Los Mesino del Escorpión." *Chiapas* 3 (1996): 141–143.

——. "Postdata." In *Crónicas del sur: Utopías campesinas en Guerrero*, ed. Armando Bartra, 413–428. Mexico City: Era, 2000.

——. *Regeneración: 1900–1918: La corriente más radical de la revolución mexicana de 1910 a través de su diario de combate*. Mexico City: Era, 1977.

——. "Sobre las clases sociales en el campo mexicano." *Cuadernos Agrarios* 1 (1976): 25–28.

——. "Sur profundo." In *Crónicas del sur: Utopías campesinas en Guerrero*, ed. Armando Bartra, 13–74. Mexico City: Era, 2000.

——, ed. *Crónicas del sur: Utopías campesinas en Guerrero*. Mexico City: Era, 2000.

——. *Notas sobre la cuestión campesina, México 1970–1976*. Mexico City: Editorial Macehual, 1979.

Bartra, Roger. *Agrarian Structure and Political Power in Mexico*. Baltimore: Johns Hopkins University, 1993.

——. *Blood, Ink, and Culture: Miseries and Splendors of the Post-Mexican Condition*. Durham, NC: Duke University Press, 2002.

——. *Campesinado y poder político en México*. Mexico City: Era, 1982.

——. *Estructura agraria y clases sociales en México*. Mexico City: Era, 1974.

——. *La jaula de la melancolía: Identidad y metamorfisis del mexicano*. Mexico City: Grijalbo, 1987.

——. *Las redes imaginarias del poder político*. Mexico City: Era, 1981.

——, ed. *Caciquismo y poder político en el México rural*. Mexico: Siglo XXI/Instituto de Investigaciones Sociales de UNAM, 1975.

Becker, Marjorie. "As though they meant her no harm, María Enríquez remade the friends who abandoned her—their intentions, their possibilities, their worlds—inviting them (perhaps, it is true) to dance." *Rethinking History* 12:2 (June 2008): 153–164.

——. *Setting the Virgin on Fire: Lázaro Cárdenas, Michoacán Peasants, and the Redemption of the Mexican Revolution*. Berkeley: University of California Press, 1995.

——. "Torching La Purísima, Dancing at the Altar: The Construction of Revolutionary Hegemony in Michoacán, 1934–1940." In *Everyday Forms of State Formation: Revolution and the Negotiation of Rule in Modern Mexico*, ed. Gilbert Joseph and Daniel Nugent, 247–264. Durham, NC: Duke University Press, 1994.

——. "'When I was a child, I danced as a child, but now that I am old, I think about salvation:' Concepción González and a past that would not stay put." In *Experiments in Rethinking History*, ed. Alun Munslow and Robert A. Rosenstone, 17–29. Abingdon, UK: Routledge, 2004.

Bellingeri, Marco. *Del agrarismo armado a la guerra de los pobres: Ensayos de guerrilla rural en el México contemporáneo, 1940–1974.* Mexico City: Ediciones Casa Juan Pablos/Secretaría de Cultura de la Ciudad de México, 2003.

———. "La imposibilidad del odio: La guerrilla y el movimiento estudiantil en México, 1960– 1974." In *La transición interrumpida: México 1968–1988,* ed. Ilán Semo, 49–73. Mexico City: Departamento de Historia, Universidad Iberoamericana/Nueva Imagen, 1993.

Benjamin, Walter. "Convolute N: On the Theory of Knowledge, Theory of Progress." In *The Arcades Project,* trans. Howard Eiland and Kevin McLaughlin, 456–488. Cambridge, MA: Belknap, 1999.

———. "Critique of Violence." In *Reflections: Essays, Aphorisms, Autobiographical Writings,* ed. Peter Demetz, 277–300. New York: Schocken, 1978.

———. "On the Concept of History." In *Selected Writings,* vol. 4, *1938–1940,* ed. Howard Eiland and Michael W. Jennings, 389–400. Cambridge, MA: Belknap, 2003.

Berger, Mark T. "Romancing the EZLN: International Intellectuals and the Chiapas Rebellion." *Latin American Perspectives* 28:2 (2001): 149–170.

Beverley, John. "Rethinking the Armed Struggle in Latin America. *Boundary 2* 36:1 (2009): 47–59.

Bhadram, Gautam. "The Four Rebels of Eighteen-Fifty-Seven." In *Selected Subaltern Studies, eds.,* Ranajit Guha and Gayatri Chakravorty Spivak, 129–175. New York: Oxford University Press, 1988.

Blacker-Hanson, O'Neill. "Cold War in the Countryside: Conflict in Guerrero, Mexico." *The Americas* 66:2 (October 2009): 181–210.

———. "The Intellectual Roots of Guerrero's Cold War Rebellion." *Journal of Iberian and Latin American Research* 18:2 (December 2012): 101–117.

———. "'La lucha sigue! (The Struggle Continues!)' Teacher Activism in Guerrero and the Continuum of Democratic Struggle in Mexico." PhD diss., University of Washington, 2005.

Bonilla Machorro, Carlos. *Ejercicio de guerrillero.* 2nd ed. Mexico City: Editorial Gaceta, 1983.

Boils, Guillermo. *Los militares y la política en México (1915–1974).* Mexico City: Ediciones "El Caballito," 1975.

Boostels, Bruno. "Hegel in Mexico: Memory and Alienation in the Posthumous Writings of José Revueltas." *South Central Review* 21:3 (fall 2004): 46–69.

Boyer, Christopher R. *Becoming Campesinos: Politics, Identity, and Agrarian Struggle in Postrevolutionary Michoacán, 1920–1935.* Stanford: Stanford University Press, 2003.

Brands, Hal. *Latin America's Cold War.* Cambridge, MA: Harvard University Press, 2010.

Buck-Morss, Susan. *Dreamworld and Catastrophe: The Passing of Mass Utopia in East and West.* Cambridge, MA: MIT Press, 2002.

Bushnell, Clyde Gilbert. *La carrera política y militar de Juan Álvarez.* Mexico City: Porrúa, 1988.

Bustamante Álvarez, Tomás. "Los campesinos en la reinvención de Guerrero." *In El sur en movimiento: La reinvención de Guerrero del siglo XXI,* ed. Tomás Bustamante Álvarez and Sergio Sarmiento Silva, 157–169. Chilpancingo: Universidad Autónoma de Guerrero/ CIESAS, 2001.

———. "Periodo 1934–1940." In *Historia de la cuestión agraria mexicana: Estado de Guerrero, 1867–1940,* ed. Jaime Salazar Adame, Renato Rabelo Lecuona, Daniel Molina Álvarez, and Tomás Bustamante Álvarez, 337–534. Mexico City: Gobierno del Estado de Guerrero/ Universidad Autónoma de Guerrero, 1987.

Bustamante Álvarez, Tomás, and Sergio Sarmiento Silva, eds. *El sur en movimiento: la reinvención de Guerrero del siglo XXI.* Chilpancingo: Universidad Autónoma de Guerrero/CIESAS, 2001.

Camp, Roderic Ai. *Generals in the Palacio: The Military in Modern Mexico.* New York: Oxford University Press, 1992.

———. *Mexican Political Biographies, 1935–1993.* Austin: University of Texas Press, 1995.

Cano, Gabriela. "Una Ciudadana Igualitaria: El Presidente Lázaro Cárdenas y el Sufragio Femenino." *Desdeldiez: Boletín del Centro de Estudios de la Revolución Mexicana, Lázaro Cárdenas A.C.* (December 1995): 69–116.

Carbot, Alberto. *Fausto Cantú Peña: Café para todos.* Mexico City: Grijalbo, 1989.

Cárdenas Montaño, Macrina. "La participación de la mujeres en los movimientos armados." In *Movimientos armados en México, siglo XX*, vol. 2, ed. Veronica Oikión Solano and Marta Eugenia García Ugarte, 609–624. Zamora: El Colegio de Michoacán/CIESAS, 2006.

Carey, Elaine. *Plaza of Sacrifices: Gender, Power, and Terror in 1968 Mexico*. Albuquerque: University of New Mexico Press, 2005.

Carr, Barry. "The Fate of the Vanguard under a Revolutionary State: Marxism's Contribution to the Construction of the Great Arch." In *Everyday Forms of State Formation: Revolution and the Negotiation of Rule in Modern Mexico*, ed. Gilbert Joseph and Daniel Nugent, 326–354. Durham, NC: Duke University Press, 1994.

———. *Marxism and Communism in Twentieth-Century Mexico*. Lincoln: University of Nebraska Press, 1992.

Carranco Cardoso, Leopoldo. *Acciones militares en el estado de Guerrero*. Mexico City: Sociedad Mexicana de Geografía y Estadística, 1963.

Castañeda, Jorge. *Utopia Unarmed: The Latin American Left after the Cold War*. New York: Vintage, 1994.

Castañeda, Salvador. *La negación del número: la guerrilla en México, 1965–1996: una aproximación crítica*. Mexico City: Consejo Nacional para la Cultura y las Artes/Ediciones Sin Nombre, 2006.

Castellanos, Laura. *México armado: 1943–1981*. Mexico City: Era, 2007.

Castillo García, Gustavo. "Acosta Chaparro y Quirós, acusados de 143 asesinatos." *La Jornada*, 31 October 2003.

———. "Acosta Chaparro, libre: Recobrará el grado militar." *La Jornada*, 30 June 2007.

Cedillo, Adela. "El fuego y el silencio: Historia de las Fuerzas de Liberación Nacional Mexicanas (1969–1974)." Licenciatura Tesis, Universidad Autónoma de México, 2008.

———. "Mujeres, guerrilla y terror de Estado en la época de la revoltura en México." *La guerra sucia en México* [blog], 9 March 2010. http://guerrasuciamexicana.blogspot.com/2010/03/mujeres-guerrilla-y-terror-de-estado.html.

Cedillo, Adela, and Fernando Herrera Calderón, eds. *Challenging Authoritarianism in Mexico: Revolutionary Struggles and the Dirty War, 1964–1982*. London: Routledge, 2012.

Chakrabarty, Dipesh. "Postcoloniality and the Artifice of History: Who Speaks for 'Indian' Pasts?" In *Postcolonialism: Critical Concepts in Literary and Cultural Studies*, vol. 4, ed. Diana Brydon, 1491–1518. London: Routledge, 2000.

Chatterjee, Partha. *Nation and its Fragments: Colonial and Postcolonial Histories*. Princeton: Princeton University Press, 1993.

Chávez, Joaquín. "The Pedagogy of Revolution: Popular Intellectuals and the Origins of the Salvadoran Insurgency, 1960–1980." PhD diss., New York University, 2010.

Chust Calero, Manuel. "De esclavos, encomenderos y mitayos. El anticolonialismo de las Cortes de Cádiz." *Mexican Studies/Estudios Mexicanos* 11:2 (Summer 1995): 179–202.

Coatsworth, John. "Patterns of Rural Rebellion in Latin America: Mexico in Comparative Perspective." In *Riot, Rebellion and Revolution: Rural Social Conflict in Mexico*, ed. Friedrich Katz, 21–62. Princeton: Princeton University Press, 1988.

———. "Los orígenes sociales del autoritarismo en México." *In Los orígenes del atraso: nueve ensayos de historia económica de México en los siglos XVIII y XIX*, ed. John Coatsworth, 214–275. Mexico City: Alianza Editorial Mexicana, 1990.

Cohn, Deborah. "The Mexican Intelligentsia, 1950–1968: Cosmopolitanism, National Identity, and the State." *Mexican Studies/Estudios Mexicanos* 21:1 (Winter 2005): 141–182.

Colmenero, Sergio. "El Movimiento de Liberación Nacional, la Central Campesina Independiente y Cárdenas." *Estudios Políticos* 2:2 (1975): 11–28.

Condés Lara, Enrique. *Represión y rebelión en México (1959–1985)*. Mexico City: Editorial Porrúa, 2007.

———. *Los últimos años del Partido Comunista Mexicano (1969–1981)*. Puebla: Universidad Autónoma de Puebla, 1990.

Cook, Maria Lorena. *Organizing Dissent: Unions, the State, and the Democratic Teachers' Movement in Mexico*. University Park: Pennsylvania State University Press, 1996.

Córdova, Arnaldo. *La política de masas del cardenismo*. Mexico City: Era, 1974.

Corrigan, Philip, ed. *Capitalism, State Formation, and Marxist Theory*. London: Quartet, 1980.

Corrigan, Philip, Harvie Ramsay, and Derek Sayer. *Socialist Construction and Marxist Theory: Bolshevism and its Critique*. New York: Monthly Review Press, 1978.

Corrigan, Philip, and Derek Sayer. *The Great Arch: English State Formation as Cultural Revolution*. Oxford: Basil Blackwell, 1985.

Crespi, Simon. "José Revueltas (1914–1976): A Political Biography." *Latin American Perspectives* 6:3 (1979): 93–113.

Cuevas Díaz, J. Aurelio. *El Partido Comunista Mexicano, 1963–1973: La ruptura entre las clases medias y el Estado fuerte en México*. Mexico City: Editorial Linea, 1984.

Darwish, Mahmoud. *The Butterfly's Burden*. Translated by Fady Joudah. Port Townsend, WA: Copper Canyon, 2007.

Das, Veena. "Subaltern as Perspective." In *Subaltern Studies IV*. Delhi: Oxford University Press, 1987.

de la Cueva, Mario. "La idea de la soberanía." In *Estudios sobre el decreto constitucional de Apatzingán*, 245–334. Mexico City: Universidad Autónoma de México, 1964.

de la Torre Villar, Ernesto. "El constitucionalismo mexicano y su origen." In *Estudios sobre el decreto constitucional de Apatzingán*, 167–212. Mexico City: Universidad Autónoma de México, 1964.

Derrida, Jacques. *Archive Fever*. Chicago: University of Chicago Press, 1998.

Dore, Elizabeth, and Maxine Molyneux, eds. *Hidden Histories of Gender and the State in Latin America*. Durham, NC: Duke University Press, 1999.

Durkheim, Emile. *The Elementary Forms of the Religious Life*, trans. Karen E. Fields. Oxford: Oxford University Press, 2001.

Eley, Geoff. *Forging Democracy: The History of the Left in Europe, 1850–2000*. New York: Oxford University Press, 2002.

Encarnación Ursua, Florencio. *Las luchas de los copreros guerrerenses*. Mexico City: Editora y Distribudora Nacional de Publicaciones, 1977.

Engels, Frederick. *The Peasant War in Germany*. New York: International, 2000 [1926].

Escárcega López, Everardo. *Historia de la cuestión agraria mexicana. Vol. 5: El cardenismo: un parteaguas histórico en el proceso agrario nacional, 1934–1940 (primera parte)*. Mexico City: Siglo XXI, 1990.

Estrada Castañón, Alba Teresa. *Guerrero: sociedad, economía, política y cultura*. Mexico City: Centro de Investigaciones Interdisciplinarias en Humanidades/UNAM, 1994.

———. *El movimiento anticaballerista: Guerrero 1960, Crónica de un conflicto*. Chilpancingo: Universidad Autónoma de Guerrero, 2001.

Evangelista Muñoz, Agustín. *Carmelo Cortés Castro y la guerrilla urbana: Las Fuerzas Armadas Revolucionarias (FAR)*. Mexico City: Centro de Investigaciones Históricas de los Movimientos Armados, 2007.

Ezcurdia, Mario. *Análisis teórico del Partido Revolucionario Institucional*. Mexico City: Costa Amic, 1968.

Falcón, Romana. "Force and the Search for Consent: The Role of the Jefaturas Políticas of Coahuila in National State Formation." In *Everyday Forms of State Formation: Revolution and the Negotiation of Rule in Modern Mexico*, ed. Gilbert Joseph and Daniel Nugent, 107–134. Durham, NC: Duke University Press, 1994.

Feitlowitz, Marguerite. *A Lexicon of Terror: Argentina and the Legacies of Terror*. New York: Oxford University Press, 1998.

Fernández-Santamaría, J. A. *Natural Law, Constitutionalism, Reason of State, and War: Counter-Reformation Spanish Political Thought*, vol. 2. New York: Peter Lang, 2006.

Fierro Santiago, Felipe. *El último disparo: Versiones de la guerrilla de los setentas*. Atoyac de Álvarez: Colección ATL, 2006.

Flores Magón, Ricardo. *¿Para qué sirve la autoridad? y otros cuentos*. Mexico City: Ediciones Antorcha, 1976.

Foucault, Michel. *Discipline and Punish: The Birth of the Modern Prison.* New York: Vintage, 1995.
———. *Power/Knowledge: Selected Interviews and Other Writings, 1972–1977.* Ed. Colin Gordon. New York: Pantheon, 1980.
———. "Subject and Power." *Critical Inquiry* 8:4 (1982): 777–795.
Fowler, Will. *Santa Anna of Mexico.* Lincoln: University of Nebraska Press, 2007.
———. "Dreams of Stability: Mexican Political Thought during the 'Forgotten Years.' An Analysis of the Beliefs of the Creole Intelligentsia (1821–1853)." *Bulletin of Latin American Research* 14:3 (September 1995): 287–312.
Frazier, Lessie Jo, and Deborah Cohen. "Defining the Space of Mexico '68: Heroic Masculinity in the Prison and 'Women' in the Streets." *Hispanic American Historical Review* 83:4 (November 2003): 617–660.
Freire, Paolo. *Pedagogy of the Oppressed.* New York: Continuum, 1993.
Fuentes Díaz, Vicente. *Historia de la Revolución en el estado de Guerrero.* Mexico City: Instituto Nacional de Estudios Históricos de la Revolución Mexicana, 1983.
García, Carlos. "Inventorio de las organizaciones campesinas." In *Crónicas del sur: Utopías campesinas en Guerrero,* ed. Armando Bartra, 103–128. Mexico City: Era, 2000.
García, Daniel Carlos. *Fulgor rebelde: la guerrilla en Aguascalientes.* Aguascalientes: Filo de Agua, 2006.
García Cerros, Mario. *Historia de la Universidad Autónoma de Guerrero, 1942–1971.* Chilpancingo: Universidad Autónoma de Guerrero, 1991.
García de León, Antonio. *Resistencia y utopía: Memorial de agravios y crónicas de revueltas y profecías acaecidas en la Provincia de Chiapas durante los últimos quinientos años de su historia.* Mexico City: Era, 1984.
Garza, David T. "Factionalism in the Mexican Left: The Frustration of the MLN." *Western Political Quarterly* 17:3 (1964): 447–460.
Gauss, Susan. *Made in Mexico: Regions, Nation, and the State in the Rise of Mexican Industrialism, 1920s–1940s.* University Park: Pennsylvania State University Press, 2010.
Gill, Mario. "Los Escudero de Acapulco." *Historia Mexicana* 3:4 (1953): 291–308.
Gillingham, Paul. "Ambiguous Missionaries: Rural Teachers and State Facades in Guerrero, 1930–1950." *Mexican Studies/Estudios Mexicanos* 22:2 (summer 2006): 331–360.
———. "Baltasar Leyva Mancilla of Guerrero: Learning Hegemony." In *State Governors in the Mexican Revolution, 1910–1952: Portraits in Conflict, Courage, and Corruption,* ed. Jurgen Buchenau and William Beezley, 177–196. Lanham, MD: Rowman and Littlefield, 2009.
———. *Cuauhtémoc's Bones: Forging National Identity in Modern Mexico.* Albuquerque: University of New Mexico Press, 2011.
———. "Maximino's Bulls: Popular Protest after the Mexican Revolution, 1940–1952. *Past and Present* 206 (February 2010): 175–211.
———. "Who Killed Crispín Aguilar? Violence and Order in the Postrevolutionary Countryside." In *Violence, Coercion and State-Making in Twentieth Century Mexico: The Other Half of the Centaur,* ed. Wil Pansters, 91–114. Stanford: Stanford University Press, 2012.
Gillingham, Paul, and Benjamin T. Smith, eds. *Dictablanda: Politics, Works, and Culture in Mexico, 1938–1968.* Durham, NC: Duke University Press, 2014.
Gilly, Adolfo. *El cardenismo, una utopía mexicana.* Mexico City: Cal y Arena, 1994.
———. *Cartas a Cuauhtémoc Cárdenas.* Mexico City: Era, 1989.
———. *Chiapas: la razón ardiente.* Mexico City: Ediciones Era, 1997.
———. *Historia a contrapelo: Una constelación.* Mexico City: Era, 2006.
———. *La revolución interrumpida.* Edición Corregida y Aumentada. Mexico City: Era, 1998.
———. *El siglo del relámpago: Siete ensayos sobre el siglo XXI.* Mexico City: Itaca/La Jornada Ediciones, 2002.
Gilly, Adolfo, and Subcomandante Marcos. *Discusión sobre la historia.* Mexico City: Taurus, 1995.
Gil Velasco, Mario. *Los ferrocarrileros.* Mexico City: Editorial Extemporáneos, 1971.
Glockner, Fritz. *Memoria roja: Historia de la guerrilla en México (1943–1968).* Mexico City: Ediciones B, 2007.

Gómezjara, Francisco. *Bonapartismo y lucha campesina en la Costa Grande de Guerrero.* Mexico City: Editorial Posada, 1979.

——. "La experiencia cooperativa coprera de Costa Grande, Guerrero." *Revista del México Agrario* 9:4 (1976): 131–140.

——. *La explotación del hombre y los bosques de Guerrero.* Mexico City: Editorial Tlacuilo, 1976.

——. *El movimiento campesino en México.* Mexico City: Editorial Campesina, 1970.

——. "El proceso político de Jenaro Vázquez Rojas hacia la guerrilla campesina." *Revista Mexicana de Ciencias Políticas y Sociales* 88 (April–June 1977): 87–127.

Gould, Jeffrey. "On the Road to 'El Porvenir': Revolutionary and Counterrevolutionary Violence in El Salvador and Nicaragua." In *A Century of Revolution: Insurgent and Counterinsurgent Violence during Latin America's Long Cold War*, ed. Greg Grandin and Gilbert Joseph, 88–120. Durham, NC: Duke University Press, 2010.

——. *To Lead as Equals: Rural Protest and Popular Consciousness in Chinandega, Nicaragua, 1912–1979.* Chapel Hill: University of North Carolina Press, 1990.

Gould, Jeffrey, and Aldo A. Lauria-Santiago. *To Rise in Darkness: Revolution, Repression, and Memory in El Salvador, 1920–1932.* Durham, NC: Duke University Press, 2008.

Gramsci, Antonio. *Selections from Prison the Notebooks.* Edited and translated by Quintin Hoare and Geoffrey Nowell Smith. New York: International, 1971.

Grandin, Greg. *Blood of Guatemala: A History of Race and Nation.* Durham, NC: Duke University Press, 2000.

——. "The Instruction of Great Catastrophe: Truth Commissions, National History, and State Formation in Argentina, Chile, and Guatemala." *American Historical Review* 110 (2005): 46–67.

——. *The Last Colonial Massacre: Latin America during the Cold War.* Chicago: University of Chicago Press, 2004.

——. "Living in Revolutionary Times: Coming to Terms with the Violence of Latin America's Long Cold War." *In a Century of Revolution: Insurgent and Counterinsurgent Violence during Latin America's Long Cold War*, ed. Greg Grandin and Gilbert Joseph, 1–44. Durham: Duke University Press, 2010.

——. *Who is Rigoberta Menchú?* London: Verso, 2012.

Grandin, Greg, and Gilbert Joseph. *A Century of Revolution: Insurgent and Counterinsurgent Violence during Latin America's Long Cold War.* Durham, NC: Duke University Press, 2010.

Guardino, Peter. "Barbarism or Republican Law? Guerrero's Peasants and National Politics, 1820–1846." Hispanic *American Historical Review* 75:2 (1995): 185–213.

——. *Peasants, Politics, and the Formation of Mexico's National State: Guerrero, 1800–1857.* Stanford: Stanford University Press, 1996.

——. *The Time of Liberty: Popular Political Culture in Oaxaca, 1750–1850.* Durham, NC: Duke University Press, 2005.

Guardino, Peter, and Charles Walker. "The State, Society, and Politics in Peru and Mexico in the Late Colonial and Early Republican Periods." *Latin American Perspectives* 19:2 (1992): 35–37.

Guedea, Virginia. "The Process of Mexican Independence." *American Historical Review* 105:1 (2000): 116–130.

——. "Los procesos electorales insurgentes." *Estudios de Historia Novohispana* 11 (1991): 222–248.

——, ed. *La independencia de México y el proceso autonomista novohispano, 1808–1824.* Mexico City: Instituto de Investigaciones Doctor José María Luis Mora/Universidad Autónoma de México, 2001.

Guevara, Che. *Guerrilla Warfare.* Ed. Brian Loveman and T. M. Davies. Lincoln: University of Nebraska Press, 1985.

——. "Cuba ¿Excepción histórica o vanguardia el la lucha anticolonialista?" In Ernesto Che Guevara, *América Latina: Despertar de un continente*, ed. María del Carmen Ariet García, 257–271. Melbourne: Ocean Press, 2003.

——. "Guerra de guerrillas: Un método." In Ernesto Che Guevara, *América Latina: Despertar de un continente*, ed. María del Carmen Ariet García, 390–406. Melbourne: Ocean Press, 2003.

Guha, Ranajit. "Chandra's Death." In *Subaltern Studies V*, ed. Ranajit Guha, 135–165. Delhi: Oxford University Press, 1986.

———. *Dominance without Hegemony: History and Power in Colonial India*. Harvard: Harvard University Press, 1999.

———. *Elementary Aspects of Peasant Insurgency in Colonial India*. Durham, NC: Duke University Press, 1999.

———. "The Prose of Counter-Insurgency." In *Subaltern Studies II*, ed. Ranajit Guha, 1–42. Delhi: Oxford University Press, 1983.

———, ed. *Subaltern Studies I: Writings on South Asian History and Society*. Delhi: Oxford University Press, 1982.

Guha, Ranajit, and Gayatri Chakravorty Spivak, eds. *Selected Subaltern Studies*. New York: Oxford University Press, 1988.

Gutiérrez, Maribel. "Irrumpe grupo armado en Aguas Blancas." *La Jornada*, 29 June 1996.

———. *Violencia en Guerrero*. Mexico City: Ediciones La Jornada, 1998.

Gutiérrez Galindo, José Catalino. *Yel pueblo se puso de pie: La verdad sobre el caso Guerrero*. Mexico City: Self-published, 1961.

Haber, Paul Lawrence. *Power from Experience: Urban Popular Movements in Late Twentieth-Century Mexico*. University Park, PA: Pennsylvannia State University Press, 2006.

Hale, Charles. "The Liberal Impulse: Daniel Cosío Villegas and the *Historia moderna de México*." *Hispanic American Historical Review* 54:3 (1974): 479–498.

———. *The Transformation of Liberalism in Late Nineteenth Century Mexico*. Princeton: Princeton University Press, 1991.

Hall, Stuart. "Notes on Deconstructing 'The Popular.'" In *People's History and Socialist Theory*, ed. Raphael Samuel, 227–239. London: Routledge and Kegan Paul, 1981.

Hamilton, Nora. *The Limits of State Autonomy: Post-revolutionary Mexico*. Princeton: Princeton University Press, 1982.

Hamnett, Brian. *Roots of Insurgency: Mexican Regions, 1750–1824*. Cambridge, UK: Cambridge University Press, 1986.

Hansen, Roger. *The Politics of Mexican Development*. Baltimore: Johns Hopkins University Press, 1971.

Harding, Neil. *Leninism*. Durham, NC: Duke University Press, 1996.

Harnecker, Marta. *Haciendo possible lo imposible: la izquierda en el umbral del siglo XXI*. Mexico City: Siglo XXI, 1999.

Harris, Richard. "Marxism and the Agrarian Question in Latin America." *Latin American Perspectives* 5:4 (1978): 2–26.

Hart, John. "The 1840s Southwestern Mexico Peasants' War: Conflict in a Transitional Society." In *Riot, Rebellion, and Revolution: Rural Social Conflict in Mexico*, ed. Friedrich Katz, 249–268. Princeton: Princeton University Press, 1988.

Harvey, David. *The Limits to Capital*. London: Verso, 2007 [1999].

———. *Spaces of Global Capitalism: Towards a Theory of Uneven Geographical Development*. London: Verso, 2006.

Harvey, Neil. *The Chiapas Rebellion: The Struggle for Land and Democracy*. Durham, NC: Duke University Press, 1998.

Hellman, Judith Adler. *Mexico in Crisis*. 2nd ed. New York: Holmes and Meier, 1983.

Henson, Elizabeth. "Madera 1965: Primeros Vientos." In *Challenging Authoritarianism in Mexico: Revolutionary Struggles and the Dirty War, 1964–1982*, ed. Adela Cedillo and Fernando Herrera Calderón, 19–39. London: Routledge, 2012.

Herrejón Peredo, Carlos. "Hidalgo: La justificación de la insurgencia." *Cuadernos Americanos* 42 (1983): 162–180.

———. *Morelos: Documentos inéditos de vida revolucionaria*. Zamora: El Colegio de Michoacán, 1987.

Hewitt de Alcántara, Cynthia. *La modernización de la agricultura mexicana, 1940–1970*. Mexico City: Siglo XXI, 1978.

Hipólito, Simón Castro. *Guerrero, amnistía y represión*. Mexico: Grijalbo, 1982.

Hodges, Donald. *Mexican Anarchism after the Revolution*. Austin: University of Texas Press, 1995.

Hodges, Donald, and Ross Gandy. *Mexico under Siege: Popular Resistance to Presidential Despotism*. London: Zed, 2002.

Hoyos, José Felix, and Olga T. Cárdenas. "Desarrollo del capitalismo agrario y lucha de clases en la costa y sierra de Guerrero." *Coyoacán* 13 (1981): 81–109.

Huizer, Gerrit. "Land Invasions as Non-violent Strategy of Peasant Resistance: Some Cases from Latin America." *Journal of Peace Research* 9:2 (1972): 121–132.

——. *La lucha campesina en México*. Mexico City: Centro de Investigaciones Agrarias, 1970.

Hylton, Forrest, and Sinclair Thomson. *Revolutionary Horizons: Past and Present in Bolivian Politics*. London: Verso, 2007.

Illades, Carlos. *Breve historia de Guerrero*. Mexico: El Colegio de México/Fondo de Cultura Económica, 2000.

Illades, Carlos, and Martha Ortega, eds. *Guerrero: Textos de su historia*. 2 vols. Mexico City: Gobierno del Estado de Guerrero/Instituto de Investigaciones Dr. José María Luis Mora, 1989.

Jacobs, Ian. *Ranchero Revolt: The Mexican Revolution in Guerrero*. Austin: University of Texas Press, 1982.

James, Daniel. *Resistance and Integration: Peronism and the Argentine Working Class, 1946–1976*. Cambridge, UK: Cambridge University Press, 1988.

——. *Doña María's Story: Life History, Memory, and Political Identity*. Durham: Duke University Press, 2000.

Joseph, Gilbert. "On the Trail of Latin American Bandits: A Reexamination of Peasant Resistance." *Latin American Research Review* 25:3 (1990): 7–53.

——. "What We Now Know and Should Know: Bringing Latin America More Meaningfully into Cold War Studies." In *In from the Cold: Latin America's New Encounter with the Cold War*, ed. Gilbert Joseph and Daniela Spenser, 3–46. Durham, NC: Duke University Press, 2008.

Joseph, Gilbert, and Daniel Nugent, eds. *Everyday Forms of State Formation: Revolution and the Negotiation of Rule in Modern Mexico*. Durham, NC: Duke University Press, 1994.

Joseph, Gilbert, and Daniela Spenser, eds. *In from the Cold: Latin America's New Encounter with the Cold War*. Durham, NC: Duke University Press, 2008.

Kaplan, Temma. "Community and Resistance in Women's Political Cultures." *Dialectical Anthropology* 15 (1990): 259–267.

Katz, Friedrich, ed. *Riot, Rebellion, and Revolution: Rural Social Conflict in Mexico*. Princeton: Princeton University Press, 1988.

Katz, Friedrich and Jane-Dale Lloyd, eds. *Porfirio Díaz frente al descontento popular regional (1891–1893)*. Mexico City: Universidad Iberoamericana, 1986.

Knight, Alan. "Cárdenas and Echeverría: Two 'Populist' Presidents Compared." In *Populism in 20th Century Mexico: The Presidencies of Lázaro Cárdenas and Luis Echeverría*, ed. Amelia Kiddle and María Muñoz, 15–37. Tucson: University of Arizona Press, 2010.

——. "Caciquismo in Twentieth-Century Mexico." In *Caciquismo in Twentieth-Century Mexico*, ed. Alan Knight and Wil Pansters, 3–48. London: Institute for the Study of the Americas, 2005.

——. "Cardenismo: Juggernaut or Jalopy?" *Journal of Latin American Studies* 26:1 (February 1994): 73–107.

——. "Historical Continuities in Social Movements." In *Popular Movements and Political Change in Mexico*, ed. Joe Foweraker and Ann Craig, 78–102. Boulder, CO: Westview, 1990.

——. *The Mexican Revolution*. Cambridge, UK: Cambridge University Press, 1986.

——. "Popular Culture and the Revolutionary State in Mexico, 1910–1940." *Hispanic American Historical Review* 74: 3 (August 1994): 393–444.

Knight, Alan, and Wil Pansters, eds. *Caciquismo in Twentieth-Century Mexico*. London: Institute for the Study of the Americas, 2006.

Krauze, Enrique. *Mexico: A Biography of Power*. New York: Harper Perennial, 1998.

Laclau, Ernesto, and Chantal Mouffe. *Hegemony and Socialist Strategy: Toward a Radical Democratic Politics*. New York: Verso, 1989.

Leal, Juan Felipe. "Guerrero: Economía y violencia, un análisis de las condiciones objetivas." *Punto Crítico* 10 (October 1972): 26–31.

Leal, Juan Felipe and Mario Huacuja R. "Los problemas del campo mexicano." *Estudios Políticos: Revista del Centro de Estudios Políticos* 5 (January–March 1976): 5–34.

Lemoine, Ernesto. *Morelos y la Revolución de 1810*. Mexico City: Gobierno del Estado de Michoacán, 1984.

Lenin, V. I. *El Imperialismo: Fase Superior del Capitalismo*. Mexico City: Ediciones Quinto Sol, 2004.

——. *Revolution at the Gates: A Selection of Writings from February to October 1917*, ed. Slavoj Žižek. London: Verso, 2002.

Lewis, Paul. *Guerrillas and Generals: The Dirty War in Argentina*. Westport, CT: Praeger, 2001.

Lipsky, William E. "Comparative Approaches to the Study of Revolution: A Historiographic Essay." *Review of Politics* 38:4 (October 1976): 494–509.

Lomnitz-Adler, Claudio. "Barbarians at the Gate? A Few Remarks on the Politics of the 'New Cultural History of Mexico.'" *Hispanic American Historical Review* 79:2 (1999): 367–385.

——. *Deep Mexico, Silent Mexico: An Anthropology of Nationalism*. Minneapolis: University of Minneapolis Press, 2001.

——. *Exits from the Labyrinth: Culture and Ideology in the Mexican National Space*. Berkeley: University of California Press, 1992.

——. "What was Mexico's Cultural Revolution?" In *The Eagle and the Virgin: Nation and Cultural Revolution in Mexico, 1920–1940*, ed. Stephen Lewis and Mary Kay Vaughan, 335–350. Durham, NC: Duke University Press, 2006.

López Miramontes, Alvaro. "Panorama historiográfica del estado de Guerrero." In *Ensayos para la historia del estado de Guerrero*, ed. Alvaro López Miramontes, 17–40. Chilpancingo: Instituto Guerrerense de la Cultura, 1985.

López, Jaime. *10 años de guerrilla en México, 1964–1974*. Mexico City: Editorial Posada, 1974.

López Limón, Alberto Guillermo. "Los mártires de Madera, rebeldía en el estado de Chihuahua, México (1965)." In *El rebelde contemporáneo en el Circuncaribe: Imágenes y representaciones*, ed. Enrique Camacho Navarro, 257–322. Mexico City: Universidad Autónoma de México, 2006.

——. "Historia de las organizaciones político militares de izquierda en México (1960–1980)." PhD diss., Universidad Autónoma de México, 2010.

López, Rick. *Crafting Mexico: Intellectuals, Artisans, and the State after the Revolution*. Durham, NC: Duke University Press, 2010.

Lowy, Michael. *Fire Alarm: Reading Walter Benjamin's "On the Concept of History."* London: Verso, 2006.

Loyo, Brambila, Aurora. *El movimiento magisterial de 1958*. Mexico City: Era, 1979.

MacAllister, Carlota. "A Headlong Rush into the Future: Violence and Revolution in a Guatemalan Indigenous Village." In *A Century of Revolution: Insurgent and Counterinsurgent Violence during Latin America's Long Cold War*, ed. Greg Grandin and Gilberto Joseph, 276–308. Durham, NC: Duke University Press, 2010.

Macías Cervantes, César Federico. *Genaro Vázquez, Lucio Cabañas y la guerrillas en México entre 1960–1974*. Guanajuato: Universidad de Guanajuato/Benemérita Universidad Autónoma de Puebla, 2008.

Mallon, Florencia. "Patriarchy in the Transition to Capitalism: Central Peru, 1830–1950." *Feminist Studies* 13:2 (summer 1987): 379–407.

——. *Peasant and Nation: The Making of Postcolonial Mexico and Peru*. Berkeley: University of California Press, 1995.

——. "The Promise and Dilemma of Subaltern Studies: Perspectives from Latin American History." *American Historical Review* 99:5 (1994): 1491–1515.

———. "Barbudos, Warriors, and *Rotos*: The MIR, Masculinity, and Power in the Chilean Agrarian Reform, 1965–1974." In *Changing Men and Masculinities in Latin America*, ed. Matthew Gutmann, 179–215. Durham, NC: Duke University Press, 2003.

Manz, Beatriz. *Paradise in Ashes: A Guatemalan Journey of Courage, Terror, and Hope.* Berkeley: University of California Press, 2005.

Mao Tse-tung. "The United Front in Cultural Work." In *The Selected Works of Mao Tse-tung, Volume 3*, 185–187. Peking: Foreign Languages Press, 1967.

———. *On Guerrilla Warfare*, ed. Samuel B. Griffith. New York: Praeger, 1962.

Márquez, Enrique. "Political Anachronisms: The Navista Movement and Political Processes in San Luis Potosí, 1958–1985." In *Electoral Patterns and Perspectives in Mexico*, ed. Arturo Alvarado. Monograph Series, 22. San Diego: Center for US-Mexican Studies, University of California, San Diego, 1987.

Martínez, María Elena. *Genealogical Fictions: Limpieza de Sangre, Religion, and Gender in Colonial Mexico.* Stanford: Stanford University Press, 2008.

Martínez Carbajal, Alejandro. *Diego Álvarez y Vicente Jiménez: Panteras del sur.* Acapulco: Comisión Editorial Municipal/Ayuntamiento de Acapulco, 1992.

———. *Ejército Popular Revolucionario: Guerrero.* Acapulco: Editorial Sagitario, 1998.

———. *Juan Escudero y Amadeo Vidales.* Mexico City: Editorial Revolución, 1961.

———. *Masacre en el vado de Aguas Blancas.* Acapulco: Editorial Sagitario, 1996.

Martínez M., Guillermo. "El movimiento zapatista en Guerrero." In *Movimientos populares en la historia de México y América Latina: memoria del primer encuentro nacional de historiadores*, 229–242. Mexico: Universidad Autónoma de México, 1987.

Martínez Nateras, Arturo. *El secuestro de Lucio Cabañas.* Mexico City: Altalena, 1986.

———. "Guerrero: Violencia y cambio, de Atoyac a Jaleaca." In *La transición democrática en Guerrero*, 127–138. Mexico City: Editorial Diana, 1992.

Martínez Rescalvo, Mario O., and Jorge R. Obregón Téllez. *La Montaña de Guerrero: Economía, historia y sociedad.* Chilpancingo: Universidad Autónoma de Guerrero.

Martínez Verdugo, Arnoldo, ed. *Historia del comunismo en México.* Mexico City: Grijalbo, 1985.

Marx, Karl. *Capital: A Critique of Political Economy*, vol. 1. New York: Penguin, 1992 [1867].

Matsuda, Matt. *Memory of the Modern.* New York: Oxford University Press, 1996.

Mayo, Baloy. *La guerrilla de Genaro y Lucio: Análisis y resultados.* Mexico City: Diogenes, 1980.

McCormick, Gladys. "The Political Economy of Desire in Rural Mexico: Revolutionary Change and the Making of a State, 1935–1965." PhD diss., University of Wisconsin-Madison, 2009.

McDowell, Roger. *Poetry and Violence: The Ballad Tradition of Mexico's Costa Chica.* Urbana: University of Illinois Press, 2000.

McGee, Sarah Deutsch. "Gender and Sociopolitical Change in Twentieth-Century Latin America." *Hispanic American Historical Review* 71:2 (1991), 259–306.

McLaren, Peter. *Che Guevara, Paolo Freire, and the Pedagogy of Revolution.* Lanham, MD: Rowman and Littlefield, 2000.

Medin, Tzvi. *El sexenio alemanista.* Mexico City: Era, 1990.

Medina, Luis. "Origen y circunstancia de la idea de unidad nacional." In *La vida política en México, 1970–1973*, ed. El Colegio de México, Centro de Estudios Internacionales, 5–32. Mexico City: El Colegio de México, 1974.

Melgar Bao, Ricardo. ""La memoria submergida: Martirologio y sacralización de la violencia en las guerrillas latinoamericanas." In *Movimientos armados en México, Siglo XX*, ed. Veronica Oikión Solano and Marta Eugenia García Ugarte, 29–67. Zamora, Michoacán: El Colegio de Michoacán/CIESAS, 2007.

Meyer, Jean. *Problemas campesinas y revueltas agrarias (1821–1910).* Mexico City: SEP, 1973.

Meza Velarde, Adriana and Andrés Rubio Zaldívar. "Luchas sociales en el estado de Guerrero. Los movimientos radicales." Mimeograph. Chilpancingo, Guerrero, 1982-86.

Middlebrook, Kevin. *The Paradox of Revolution: Labor, the State, and Authoritarianism in Mexico.* Baltimore: Johns Hopkins University Press, 1995.

Molina Álvarez, Daniel. "Periodo 1920–1940." In *Historia de la cuestión agraria mexicana: Estado de Guerrero, 1867–1940*, ed. Jaime Salazar Adame et al., 221–333. Chilpancingo: Universidad Autónoma de Guerrero/Gobierno del Estado de Guerrero, 1987.

Moscovici, Claudia. *Gender and Citizenship: The Dialectics of Subject-Citizenship in Nineteenth-Century French Literature and Culture*. Lanham, MD: Rowman and Littlefield Publishers, 2000.

Montemayor, Carlos. *Guerra en El Paraíso*. Mexico City: Editorial Joaquin Mortíz, 2003.

——. *La guerrilla recurrente*. Ciudad Juárez: Universidad Autónoma de Ciudad Juárez, 1999.

——. *La guerrilla recurrente/recurrente guerrilla*. Mexico City: Editorial Debate, 2007.

Molyneux, Maxine. "Twentieth Century State Formations in Latin America." In *Hidden Histories of Gender and the State in Latin America*, ed. Elizabeth Dore and Maxine Molyneux, 33–84. Durham, NC: Duke University Press.

Mora, José María Luis. *México y sus revoluciones*. 3 vols. Mexico City: Editorial Porrúa, 1965 [1836].

——. *Obras Sueltas de José María Luis Mora, Cuidadano Méjicano*. Mexico City: Porrúa, 1963 (1837).

——. "El discurso sobre la independencia del imperio Méjicano." In *Obras Sueltas de José María Luis Mora, Cuidadano Méjicano, Tomo 2*, ed. José María Luis Mora, 7–22. Mexico City: Porrúa, 1963 [1837].

Muñoz y Pérez. *El General Don Juan Álvarez*. Mexico City: Editorial Academia Literaria, 1959.

Natividad Rosales, José. *¿Quién es Lucio Cabañas? ¿Qué pasa con la guerrilla en México?* Mexico City: Editorial Posada, 1974.

——. *La muerte (?) de Lucio Cabañas*. Mexico City: Editorial Posada, 1975.

Navarro, Aaron. *Political Intelligence and the Creation of Modern Mexico, 1938–1954*. University Park: Pennsylvania State University Press, 2010.

Negri, Antonio. "Communism: Some Thoughts on the Concept and Practice." In *The Idea of Communism*, ed. Costas Douzinas and Slavoj Žižek, 155–166. London: Verso, 2010.

——. *Insurgencies: Constituent Power and the Modern State*. Minneapolis: University of Minnesota Press, 1992.

Newcomer, Daniel. *Reconciling Modernity: Urban State Formation in 1940s León, Mexico*. Lincoln: University of Nebraska Press, 2004.

Niblo, Stephen R. *Mexico in the 1940s: Modernity, Politics, and Corruption*. Wilmington, DE: Scholarly Resources Press, 1990.

——. *War, Diplomacy, and Development: The United States and Mexico, 1938–1954*. Wilmington, DE: Scholarly Resources Press, 1995.

Niblo, Diane, and Stephen R. Niblo. "Acapulco in Dreams and Reality." *Mexican Studies/Estudios Mexicanos* 24:1 (winter 2008): 31–51.

Núñez Ramos, Serafín. "Raíces históricas de la transición democrática en Guerrero." In *La transición democrática en Guerrero*, 177–188. Mexico City: Editorial Diana.

Ochoa Campos, Moisés. *Historia del estado de Guerrero*. Mexico City: Porrúa, 1968.

O'Gorman, Edmundo. "Precedentes y sentido de la revolución de Ayutla." In *Plan de Ayutla: Conmemoración de su primer centenario*, ed. Mario de la Cueva et al., 169–204. Mexico City: Facultad de Derecho, Universidad Autónoma de México, 1954.

Oikión Solano, Verónica, and Marta Eugenia García Ugarte, eds. *Movimientos armados en México, siglo XX*. 3 vols. Zamora, Michoacán: El Colegio de Michoacán/CIESAS, 2007.

Olcott, Jocelyn. *Revolutionary Women in Postrevolutionary Mexico*. Durham, NC: Duke University Press, 2006.

Ortiz Rivera, Alicia. *Alejandro Cervantes Delgado: Un guerrero sin violencia*. Mexico City: Grijalbo , 1999.

Orwell, George. *The Road to Wigan Pier*. New York: Berkley Medallion, 1961 [1937].

Otero, Gerardo. *Farewell to the Peasantry? Political Class Formation in Rural Mexico*. Boulder, CO: Westview Press, 1999.

Padilla, Tanalis. "From Agraristas to Guerrilleros: The Jaramillista Movement in Morelos." *Hispanic American Historical Review* 87:2 (2007): 255–292.

——. "'Por las buenas no se puede': Rubén Jaramillo's Campaigns for Governor of Morelos, 1946 and 1952." *Journal of Iberian and Latin American Research* 7:1 (July 2001): 21–48.

——. *Rural Resistance in the Land of Zapata: The Jaramillista Movement and the Myth of the Pax Priísta, 1940–1962*. Durham, NC: Duke University Press, 2008.

——. "Rural Education, Political Radicalism, and Normalista Identity in Post-1940 Mexico." In *Dictablanda: Politics, Work, and Culture in Mexico, 1938–1968*, ed. Benjamin Smith and Paul Gillingham, 341–359. Durham, NC: Duke University Press, 2014.

Pandey, Gyanendra. "In Defense of the Fragment: Writing About Muslim-Hindu Riots in India Today." *Representations* 37 (1992): 27–55.

Pansters, Wil, ed. *Violence, Coercion and State-Making in Twentieth-Century Mexico: The Other Half of the Centaur*. Stanford: Stanford University Press, 2012.

——. "Citizens with Dignity: Opposition and Government in San Luis Potosí, 1938–1993." In *Dismantling the Mexican State?*, ed. Rob Aitken, Nikki Craske, Gareth A. Jones, and David E. Stansfeld, 244–266. New York: St. Martin's Press, 1996.

——. "Social Movement and Discourse: The Case of the University Reform Movement in 1961 in Puebla, Mexico." *Bulletin of Latin American Research* 9:1 (1990): 79–101.

Parry, Benita. "Liberation Theory: Variations on Themes of Marxism and Modernity." In *Marxism, Modernity, and Postcolonial Studies*, ed. Crystal Bartolovich and Neil Lazarus, 125–149. Cambridge, UK: Cambridge University Press, 2002.

Pavía Miller, María Teresa, and Jaime Salazar Adame. *Historia General de Guerrero: Formación y modernización*, vol. 3. Chilpancingo: Asociación de Historiadores de Guerrero/Instituto Nacional de Antropología e Historia/Gobierno del Estado de Guerrero, 1998.

Paz Paredes, Lorena, and Rosario Cabo. "Café caliente." In *Crónicas del sur: Utopías campesinas en Guerrero*, ed. Armando Bartra, 129–274. Mexico City: Era, 2000.

Pellicer de Brody, Olga. *México y la revolución cubana*. Mexico City: El Colegio de México, 1972.

Pellicer de Brody, Olga, and José Luis Reyna. *El afianzamiento de la estabilidad política (1952–1960)*, vol. 22 of Historia de la Revolución Mexicana. Mexico City: El Colegio de México, 1978.

Pensado, Jaime. *Rebel Mexico: Student Unrest and Authoritarian Political Culture During the Long 1960s*. Stanford: Stanford University Press, 2013.

Portelli, Alessandro. *The Death of Luigi Trastulli and Other Stories: Form andMeaning in Oral History*. Albany: State University of New York Press, 1991.

——. "What Makes Oral History Different." In *The Oral History Reader*, ed. Robert Perks and Alistair Thomson, 63–75. London: Routledge, 1998.

Purnell, Jennie. *Popular Movements and State Formation in Revolutionary Mexico: The Agraristas and Cristeros of Michoacán*. Durham, NC: Duke University Press, 1999.

Quevado Castro, Gustavo. *La industrialización de la copra en la Costa Grande de Guerrero*. Mexico City: Logos, 1963.

Quintero Romero, Dulce María. "La lucha difícil lucha por la defense de los bosques de Guerrero a tráves de la sociedad civil organizada." *Redhes: Revista de Derechos Humanos y Estudios Sociales* 5 (July 2010): 163–181.

Rabasa, José. *Without History: Subaltern Studies, the Zapatista Insurgency, and the Specter of History*. Pittsburgh: University of Pittsburgh Press, 2010.

——. *Writing Violence on the Northern Frontier: The Historiography of Sixteenth Century New Mexico and Florida and the Legacy of Conquest*. Durham, NC: Duke University Press, 2000.

Radilla Martínez, Andrea. *La organización en las nuevas estrategias campesinas: La Coalición de Ejidos en la Costa Grande de Guerrero, 1980–2003*. Mexico: UNORCA, 2004.

——. *Poderes, saberes y sabores: Una historia de resistencia de los cafeticultores, Atoyac, 1940–1974*. Chilpancingo: Self-published, 1998.

——. *Voces Acalladas (vidas truncadas)*. Mexico City: Nueva Visión, 2007.

Ramírez Salas, Mario. "La relación de la Liga Comunista 23 de Septiembre y El Partido de los Pobres en el estado de Guerrero en la década de los sententa." In *Movimientos armados en*

México, siglo XX, vol. 2, ed. Verónica Oikión Solano and Marta Eugenia García Ugarte, 527–548. Zamora, Michoacán: Colegio de Michoacán/CIESAS, 2006.

Rangel Lozano, Claudia and Evangelina Sánchez Serrano. "La guerra sucia en los setentas y las guerrillas de Genaro Vázquez y Lucio Cabañas en Guerrero." In *Movimientos armados en México, siglo XX*, vol. 2, ed. Verónica Oikión Solano and Marta Eugenia García Ugarte, 495–525. Zamora, Michoacán: Colegio de Michoacán/CIESAS, 2006.

Rath, Thomas. *Myths of Demilitarization in Postrevolutionary Mexico, 1920–1960*. Chapel Hill: University of North Carolina Press, 2013.

Ravelo Lecuona, Ravelo. *La revolución zapatista en Guerrero*. Chilpancingo: Universidad Autónoma de Guerrero, 1990.

———. "Periodo 1910–1920." In *Historia de la cuestión agraria mexicana: Estado de Guerrero, 1867–1940*, ed. Jaime Salazar Adame et al., 81–219. Chilpancingo: Universidad Autónoma de Guerrero/Gobierno del Estado de Guerrero, 1987.

Ravelo Lecuona, Ravelo, and Tomás Bustamante Álvarez. *Historia General de Guerrero: Revolución y reconstrucción*, vol. 4. Chilpancingo: Asociación de Historiadores de Guerrero/Instituto Nacional de Antropología e Historia/Gobierno del Estado de Guerrero, 1998.

Rayas, Lucía. "Subjugating the Nation: Women and the Guerrilla Experience." In *Challenging Authoritarianism in Mexico: Revolutionary Struggles and the Dirty War, 1964–1982*, ed. Fernando Herrera Calderón and Adela Cedillo, 167–181. London: Routledge, 2012.

Reed, Nelson. *The Caste War of Yucatán*. Revised Edition. Stanford: Stanford University Press, 2001.

Reif, Linda. "Women in Latin American Guerrilla Movements: A Comparative Perspective." *Comparative Politics* 18:2 (January 1986): 147–169.

Reina, Leticia. *Las rebeliones campesinas en México (1819–1906)*. Mexico City: Siglo XXI, 1998 [1980].

Restrepo Fernández, Ivan. *Costa Grande de Guerrero: Estudio socio-económico*. Mexico City: Imprenta Venecia, 1975.

Revueltas, José. *Ensayo sobre un proletariado sin cabeza*. Mexico City: Ediciones Era, 1980.

———. "Sobre la crisis del Partido [1943]." In *Escritos políticos (Tomo I)*, 32–36. Ediciones Era: Mexico City, 1980.

Reyes Serrano, Angel. *Trinchera...! Lucio Cabañas, Genaro Vázquez y su guerrilla*. Mexico City: Costa-Amic, 1985.

Reyes, Cayetano. "El jefe agrarista costeño Valente de la Cruz." In *Ensayos para la historia del estado de Guerrero*, 146–165. Chilpancingo: Instituto Guerrerense de la Cultura, 1985.

Robertson, Craig. "Mechanisms of Exclusion: Historicizing the Archive and the Passport." In *Archive Stories: Facts, Fictions, and the Writing of History*, ed. Antoinette Burton, 68–86. Durham, NC: Duke University Press, 2005.

Robespierre, Maximilien. *Virtue and Terror*, ed. Slavoj Žižek. London: Verso, 2007.

Robin, Ron T. *The Making of the Cold War Enemy: Culture and Politics in the Military-Intellectual Complex*. Princeton: Princeton University Press, 2003.

Robinet, Romain. "A Revolutionary Group Fighting Against a Revolutionary State: The September 23rd Communist League against the PRI-State (1973–1975)." In *Challenging Authoritarianism in Mexico: Revolutionary Struggles and the Dirty War, 1964–1982*, ed. Adela Cedillo and Fernando Herrera Calderón, 129–147. London: Routledge, 2012.

Rodríguez, Ileana, ed. *Latin American Subaltern Studies Reader*. Durham, NC: Duke University Press, 2002.

———. *Women, Guerrillas, and Love: Understanding Love in Central America*. Minneapolis: University of Minnesota Press, 1996.

Rodríguez O., Jaime. *"We Are Now the True Spaniards": Sovereignty, Revolution, Independence, and the Emergence of the Federal Republic of Mexico, 1808–1824*. Stanford: Stanford University Press, 2012.

———, ed. *The Divine Charter: Constitutionalism and Liberalism in Nineteenth-Century Mexico*. Lanham, MD: Rowman and Littlefield, 2005.

———. "The Struggle for the Nation: The First Centralist-Federalist Conflict in Mexico." *The Americas* 49:1 (July 1992): 1–22.

Rodríguez Saldaña, Marcial. *La desaparición de poderes en el estado de Guerrero.* Chilpancingo: Universidad Autónoma de Guerrero, 1992.

Román Román, Salvador. *Revuelta cívica en Guerrero (1957–1960): La democracia imposible.* Mexico City: Instituto Nacional de Estudios Históricos de la Revolución Mexicana, 2003.

Roseberry, William. *Anthropologies and Histories.* New Brunswick, NJ: Rutgers University Press, 1989.

———. "Hegemony and the Language of Contention." In *Everyday Forms of State Formation: Revolution and the Negotiation of Rule in Modern Mexico*, ed. Gilbert Joseph and Daniel Nugent, 355–366. Durham, NC: Duke University Press, 1994.

Rothwell, Matthew. *Transpacific Revolutionaries: The Chinese Revolution in Latin America.* London: Routledge, 2012.

Roxborough, Ian. "Mexico." In *Latin American between the Second World War and the Cold War, 1944–1948*, ed. Leslie Bethell and Ian Roxborough, 190–216. Cambridge, UK: Cambridge University Press, 1992.

Rubin, Jeffrey W. *Decentering the Regime: Ethnicity, Radicalism, and Democracy in Juchitán, Mexico.* Durham, NC: Duke University Press, 1997.

Rubio, Blanca. *Resistencia campesina y explotación rural en México.* Mexico City: Era, 1987.

Salazar Adame, Jaime. "Movimientos populares durante el porfiriato en el estado de Guerrero." In *Porfirio Díaz frente al descontento popular regional (1891–1893)*, ed. Friedrich Katz and Jane-Dale Lloyd, 97–184. Mexico: Universidad Iberoamericana, 1986.

Salazar Adame, Jaime, Renato Revalo, Daniel Molina Álvarez, and Tomás Bustamante Álvarez, eds. *Historia de la cuestión agraria, 1867–1940.* Chilpancingo: Universidad Autónoma de Guerrero, 1987.

———. "Periodo 1867–1910." In *Historia de la cuestión agraria mexicana: Estado de Guerrero, 1867–1940*, ed. Jaime Salazar Adame et al., 9–80. Chilpancingo: Universidad Autónoma de Guerrero/Gobierno del Estado de Guerrero, 1987.

Saldaña-Portillo, María Josefina. *Revolutionary Imagination in the Americas and the Age of Development.* Durham, NC: Duke University Press, 2003.

Saldívar, Américo. "Una decada de crisis y luchas (1969–1978)." In *México: Un pueblo en la historia*, vol. 4, ed. Enrique Semo, 155–245. Puebla: Universidad Autónoma de Puebla/Editorial Nueva Imagen, 1982.

Salgado Cortés, Ernesto. *Caciquismo y campesinado en Guerrero.* Chilpancingo: Universidad Autónoma de Guerrero, 2009.

Sánchez Ortega, Jorge Alberto. "Los escenarios y los actores actuales: de la metáfora a la cultura: la invención política del Guerrero bronco." In *El sur en movimiento: La reinvención de Guerrero del siglo XXI*, ed. Tomás Bustamante Álvarez and Sergio Sarmiento Silva, 223–244. Chilpancingo: Universidad Autónoma de Guerrero/CIESAS, 2001.

Sanderson, Steve. *The Transformation of Mexican Agriculture.* Princeton: Princeton University Press, 1986.

Sandoval Cruz, Pablo. *El movimiento social de 1960 en Guerrero.* 2nd ed. Chilpancingo: Universidad Autónoma de Guerrero, 1999.

———. "Participación ciudadana en la vida del municipio." In *La transición democrática en Guerrero*, 171–176. Mexico City: Editorial Diana, 1992.

Sanford, Victoria. "Between Rigoberta Menchú and La Violencia: Deconstructing David Stoll's History of Guatemala." *Latin American Perspectives* 26:6 (1999): 38–46.

Sayer, Derek. "Everyday Forms of State Formation: Some Dissident Remarks on 'Hegemony.'" In *Everyday Forms of State Formation: Revolution and the Negotiation of Rule in Modern Mexico*, ed. Gilbert Joseph and Daniel Nugent, 367–377. Durham, NC: Duke University Press, 1994.

Schatz, Sara. *Murder and Politics in Mexico: Political Killings in the Partido de la Revolución Democrática and its Consequences.* New York: Springer, 2011.

Scherer García, Julio, and Carlos Monsiváis. *Los patriotas de Tlatelolco a la guerra sucia.* Mexico: Nuevo Siglo Aguilar, 2004.

Schmidt, Arthur. "Making it Real Compared to What? Reconceptualizing Mexican History since 1940." In *Fragments of a Golden Age: The Politics of Culture in Mexico Since 1940*, ed. Gilbert Joseph, Anne Rubenstein, and Eric Zolov, 23–70. Durham, NC: Duke University Press, 2001.

Schmidt, Samuel. *The Deterioration of the Mexican Presidency: The Years of Luis Echeverría.* Tucson: University of Arizona Press, 1991.

Scholl, Christian. *Two Sides of a Barricade: (Dis)Order and Summit Protest in Europe.* Albany: State University of New York Press, 2013.

Scott, David. *Conscripts of Modernity: The Tragedy of Colonial Enlightenment.* Durham, NC: Duke University Press, 2004.

Scott, James C. *The Art of Not Being Governed: An Anarchist History of Upland Southeast Asia.* New Haven: Yale University Press, 2010.

——. *Domination and the Arts of Resistance: Hidden Transcripts.* New Haven: Yale University Press, 1990.

——. "Protest and Profanation: Agrarian Revolt and the Little Tradition, Part I." *Theory and Society* 4:1 (1977): 1–38.

——. *Weapons of the Weak: Everyday Forms of Peasant Resistance.* New Haven: Yale University Press, 1985.

Scott, Joan Wallach. *Gender and the Politics of History.* New York: Columbia University Press, 1999.

Segovia, Rafael. "La reforma política: el ejecutivo federal, el PRI y las elecciones de 1973." In *La vida política en México, 1970–1973*, ed. El Colegio de México, Centro de Estudios Internacionales, 49–76. Mexico City: El Colegio de México, 1974.

Semo, Enrique. *The History of Capitalism in Mexico: Its Origins, 1521–1763.* Austin: University of Texas Press, 1993.

——, ed. *México: Un pueblo en la historia*, vol. 4. Puebla: Universidad Autónoma de Puebla/ Editorial Nueva Imagen, 1982.

Semo, Ilán. "El ocaso de los mitos (1958–1968)." In *México: Un pueblo en la historia*, vol. 4, ed. Enrique Semo, 9–154. Puebla: Universidad Autónoma de Puebla/Editorial Nueva Imagen, 1982.

Serulnikov, Sergio. *Subverting Colonial Authority: Challenges to Spanish Rule in Eighteenth-Century Southern Andes.* Durham, NC: Duke University Press, 2003.

——. "Andean Political Imagination in the Late Eighteenth Century." In *Political Cultures in the Andes, 1750–1950*, ed. Nils Jacobsen and Cristóbal Aljovín de Losada, 257–277. Durham, NC: Duke University Press, 2005.

Servín, Elisa. "Algunas ramas de un árbol frondoso: el cardenismo a medianos del siglo XX." *Historias* 69 (2008): 1–27.

——. "Hacia el levantamiento armado: Del henriquismo a los federacionistas leales en los años cincuenta." In *Movimientos armados en México, siglo XX*, vol. 1, ed. Verónica Oikión Solano and Marta Eugenia García Ugarte, 321–324. Zamora, Michoacán: El Colegio de Michoacán/ CIESAS, 2007.

——. *Ruptura y oposición: El movimiento Henriquista, 1945–1952.* Mexico City: Cal y Arena, 2001.

Shanin, Teodor. "*The Question of Socialism: A Development Failure or an Ethical Defeat?*" History Workshop Journal 30 (1990): 68–74.

Skocpol, Theda. "What Makes Peasants Revolutionary?" *Comparative Politics* 14:3 (April 1982): 351–375.

Smith, Benjamin. *Pistoleros and Popular Movements: The Politics of State Formation in Postrevolutionary Oaxaca.* Lincoln: University of Nebraska Press, 2009.

Solomon, Joel, and Sebastian Brett. *Implausible Deniability: State Responsibility for Rural Violence in Mexico*. Human Rights Watch/Americas, 1997.

Soto Laveaga, Gabriela. "Searching for Molecules, Fueling Rebellion: Echeverría's 'Arriba y Adelante' Populism in Southeastern Mexico." In *Populism in 20th Century Mexico: The Presidencies of Lázaro Cárdenas and Luis Echeverría*, ed. Amelia Kiddle and María Muñoz, 87–105. Tucson: University of Arizona Press, 2010.

Stephen, Lynn. *Zapata Lives! Histories and Cultural Politics in Southern Mexico*. Berkeley: University of California Press, 2002.

Stern, Steve. "Feudalism, Capitalism, and the World-System in the Perspective of Latin America and the Caribbean." *American Historical Review* 93:4 (October 1988): 829–872.

——. "New Approaches to the Study of Peasant Rebellion and Consciousness: Implications of the Andean Experience." In *Resistance, Rebellion, and Consciousness in the Andean Peasant World: 18th to 20th Centuries*, ed. Steve Stern, 3–28. Madison: University of Wisconsin Press, 1987.

Stoll, David. *Between Two Armies in the Ixil Towns of Guatemala*. New York: Columbia University Press, 1999.

——. *Rigoberta Menchú and the Story of all Poor Guatemalans*. Boulder, CO: Westview, 1999.

Subcomandante Insurgente Marcos. *Our Word is Our Weapon: Selected Writings*, ed. Juana Ponce de León. New York: Seven Stories, 2002.

Tenenbaum, Barbara. *The Politics of Penury: Debts and Taxes in Mexico, 1821–1856*. Albuquerque: University of New Mexico Press, 1986.

Terán, Marta. "El levantamiento de los campesinos gasquistas." *Cuadernos Agrarios* 5:10–11 (1980): 115–138.

Thompson, E. P. *The Making of the English Working Class*. New York: Vintage, 1966.

——. *The Poverty of Theory and Other Essays*. New York: Monthly Review, 1978.

——. *Whigs and Hunters: The Origin of the Black Act*. New York: Pantheon, 1975.

Thomson, Guy P. C. "Bulwarks of Patriotic Liberalism: The National Guard, Philharmonic Corps and Patriotic Juntas in Mexico, 1847–1888." *Journal of Latin American Studies* 22:1 (1990): 31–68

——. *Patriotism, Politics, and Popular Liberalism in Nineteenth Century Mexico: Juan Francisco Lucas and the Puebla Sierra*. Wilmington, DE: Scholarly Resources Press, 1999.

——. "Popular Aspects of Liberalism in Mexico, 1848–1888." *Bulletin of Latin American Research* 10:3 (1991): 265–292.

Trevizo, Dolores. "Dispersed Communist Networks and Grassroots Leadership of Peasant Revolts in Mexico." *Sociological Perspectives* 45:3 (autumn 2002): 285–315.

Trouillot, Michel-Rolph. *Silencing the Past: Power and the Production of History*. Boston: Beacon, 1995.

Tucker, Robert, ed. *The Marx-Engels Reader*. 2nd ed. New York: W. W. Norton, 1978.

Tutino, John. *From Insurrection to Revolution in Mexico: Social Bases of Agrarian Violence, 1750–1940*. Baltimore: Johns Hopkins University Press, 1989.

Ulloa Bornemann, Alberto. *Surviving Mexico's Dirty War: A Political Prisoner's Memoir*. Translated by Arthur Schmidt and Aurora Camacho de Schmidt. Philadelphia: Temple University Press, 2007.

Valdés, Rafael Catalán. "Guerrero, estado ingobernable…¿el fin de un mito?" In *La transición democrática en Guerrero*, 21–32. Mexico City: Editorial Diana, 1992.

Valdez, Norberto. *Ethnicity, Class, and the Indigenous Struggle for Land in Guerrero*. New York: Garland, 1998.

Vázquez, Josefina. "Iglesia, ejército y centralismo." *Historia Mexicana* 39 (1989): 205–234.

Vázquez Garzón, Emilio. *El ciudadano Jorge Joseph*. Mexico: Self-Published, 1962.

Van Young, Eric. *The Other Rebellion: Popular Violence, Ideology, and the Mexican Struggle for Independence, 1810–1821*. Stanford: Stanford University Press, 2001.

Vaughan, Mary Kay. *Cultural Politics in Revolution: Teachers, Peasants, and Schools in Mexico, 1934–1940*. Tucson: University of Arizona Press, 1997.

——. "The Implementation of National Policy in the Countryside: Socialist Education in Puebla in the Cárdenas Period." Paper presented to the 7th Conference of Mexican and US Historians, Oaxaca, October 1985.

——. "Modernizing Patriarchy: State Policies, Rural Households, and Women in Mexico, 1934–1940." In *Hidden Histories of Gender and the State in Latin America*, ed. Elizabeth Dore and Maxine Molyneux, 194–214. Durham, NC: Duke University Press, 2000.

Vázquez, Josefina. "Iglesia, ejército y centralismo." *Historia Mexicana* 39 (1989): 205–234.

Vázquez, Josefina, and Caroline Fowler. "Political Plans and Collaboration between Civilians and the Military, 1821–1846." *Bulletin of Latin American Research* 15:1 (1996): 19–38.

Veledíaz, Juan. *El general sin memoria: una crónica de los silencios del ejército mexicano*. Mexico City: Debate, 2010.

Vernant, Jean Pierre, and Pierre Vidal-Naquet. *Myth and Tragedy in Ancient Greece*. New York: Zone, 1988.

Walker, Louise E. *Waking from the Dream: Mexico's Middle Classes after 1968*. Stanford: Stanford University Press, 2013.

Warman, Arturo. *Los campesinos, hijos predilectos del régimen*. Mexico City: Editorial Nuestro Tiempo, 1972.

——. *Ensayos sobre el campesinado en México*. Mexico City: Editorial Nueva Imagen, 1980.

——. "The Political Project of Zapatismo." Translated by Judith Brister. In *Riot, Rebellion, and Revolution: Rural Social Conflict in Mexico*, ed. Friedrich Katz, 321–337. Princeton: Princeton University Press, 1988.

——. *"We Come to Object:" The Peasants of Morelos and the National State*. Baltimore: Johns Hopkins University Press, 1980.

Warren, Richard. "Elections and Popular Political Participation in Mexico, 1808–1836." In *Liberals, Politics, and Power: State Formation in Nineteenth-Century Latin America*, ed. Vincent C. Peloso and Barbara A. Tenenbaum, 30–58. Athens: University of Georgia Press, 1996.

Weber, Max. *The Vocation Lectures: Science as a Vocation, Politics as a Vocation*. Ed. David Owen and Tracy B. Strong. Indianapolis: Hackett, 2004.

Weller, Robert, and Scott E. Guggenheim. *Power and Protest in the Countryside: Rural Unrest in Asia, Europe, and Latin America*. Durham, NC: Duke University Press, 1989.

Westad, Odd Arne. *The Global Cold War: Third World Interventions and the Making of Our Times*. Cambridge, UK: Cambridge University Press, 2007.

White, Hayden. *The Content of the Form: Narrative Discourse and Historical Representation*. Baltimore: Johns Hopkins University Press, 1990.

Wickham-Crowley, Timothy. *Exploring Revolution: Essays on Latin American Insurgency and Revolutionary Theory*. New York: M. E. Sharpe, 1991.

——. *Guerrillas and Revolution in Latin America: A Comparative Study of Insurgents and Regimes since 1956*. Princeton: Princeton University Press, 1992.

Williams, Raymond. *Marxism and Literature*. Oxford: Oxford University Press, 1978.

Winn, Peter. *Weavers of Revolution: The Yarur Workers and Chile's Road to Socialism*. Oxford: Oxford University Press, 1989.

Wolf, Eric. *Peasant Wars of the 20th Century*. New York: Harper, 1973.

Womack, John. *Zapata and the Mexican Revolution*. New York: Vintage, 1968.

Wood, Elisabeth Jean. *Insurgent Collective Action and Civil War in El Salvador*. Cambridge, UK: Cambridge University Press, 2003.

Wright, Angus. *The Death of Ramón González: The Modern Agricultural Dilemma*. Austin: University of Texas Press, 1990.

Wright, Thomas. *Latin America in the Era of the Cuban Revolution*. Westport, CT: Praeger, 1991.

Zaragoza, Alex. *The Monterrey Elite and the Mexican State, 1880–1940*. Austin: University of Texas Press, 1990.

Žižek, Slavoj. *Violence: Six Sideways Reflections*. New York: Picador, 2008.

Zolov, Eric. "¡Cuba sí, Yanquis no! The Sacking of the Instituto Cultural México- Norteamericano in Morelia, Michoacán, 1961." In *In from the Cold: Latin America's New Encounter with the*

Cold War, ed. Gilbert Joseph and Daniela Spenser, 214–252. Durham, NC: Duke University Press, 2010.

——. "Expanding our Conceptual Horizons: The Shift from an Old to a New Left in Latin America." *Acontracorriente* 5:2 (winter 2008): 47–73.

——. *Refried Elvis: The Rise of the Mexican Counterculture.* Berkeley: University of California Press, 1999.

INDEX

Page numbers in *italics* indicate maps and photographs.